HUL! HUL!

PETER STANLEY

HUL! HUL!

The Suppression of the Santal Rebellion in Bengal, 1855

HURST & COMPANY, LONDON

First published in the United Kingdom in 2022 by
C. Hurst & Co. (Publishers) Ltd.,
New Wing, Somerset House, Strand, London, WC2R 1LA
© Peter Stanley, 2022
All rights reserved.
Printed in Great Britain by Bell and Bain Ltd, Glasgow

Distributed in the United States, Canada and Latin America by
Oxford University Press, 198 Madison Avenue, New York, NY 10016,
United States of America.

A Cataloguing-in-Publication data record for this book
is available from the British Library.

ISBN: 9781787385429

This book is printed using paper from registered sustainable
and managed sources.

www.hurstpublishers.com

For all the Hul's unnamed victims; Santals, Bengalis and sepoys

Sidhu, why are you bathed in blood?
Kanhu, why do you cry Hul, Hul?
For our people we have bathed in blood
For the trader thieves
Have robbed our land.

Santal Rebellion Songs
collected by William Archer

CONTENTS

PART V
AFTER THE HUL

LIST OF MAPS AND ILLUSTRATIONS

List of Maps

List of Illustrations

1. Walter Sherwill's drawing of a surveyor at work; possibly Sherwill himself, from R.H. Phillimore's *Historical Records of the Survey of India*, Vol. III.

2. The Rajmahal Hills seen from the Ganges. Walter Sherwill observed that while all Europeans travelling on the Ganges saw the hills from their steamers, few knew anything about the region or its people: some assumed that the hills were uninhabited. (*Illustrated London News*, 6 October 1856)

3. A Santal village, based on a drawing by Walter Sherwill. Visitors commented on their neatness, and how they were invariably laid out in the same way, with a street of huts adjoining a sacred grove of sal trees and a platform at which the Thakur was worshipped. (*Illustrated London News*, 28 February 1856)

4. A moonlit Santal ceremony, based on an engraving by Walter Sherwill, whose affection for the Santals did not prevent him from

followers, coolies and hangers-on prepared to march. The Company's forces used hundreds of elephants. Had the Santals attacked the Field Force's supply columns they could have prolonged their resistance.

27. A 'sagger'—one of the ramshackle bullock carts that Santals impressed to carry food and plunder—from Capper's *Three Presidencies*. Company troops seized hundreds in 'drives' in the Hul's final months. The distinctive roofs of the houses in the background can still be seen in the Santal country.

28. An advertisement in the Calcutta *Citizen* in 1855 announcing the scheduled services on the East Indian railway between Howrah and Raneegunge, a reminder of the advantage that steam-powered transport gave to Company forces.

29. Sidhu Manji depicted by Walter Sherwill after his capture. Sherwill, or the engraver who prepared the image for publication, gave Sidhu a curiously penitent expression, though his assertive demeanour when interrogated was anything but submissive. (*Illustrated London News*, 28 February 1856)

30. Singra, the alleged murderer of Miss Pell, depicted as a defiant prisoner. (*Illustrated London News*, 28 February 1856)

31. The 'martello tower' at Pakur, Jharkhand, today. It is located in a memorial park, now fallen into disrepair, named in honour of Sido and Kanhu. (Peter Stanley)

32. The major memorial to the Hul at Bhagnadihi, Jharkhand, the most extensive of dozens of village memorials to the heroes of the Hul located throughout the Rajmahal Hills. It is practically on the site of the 'Thackoor' which sustained the Hul, at the house of the four brothers of Bhugnadihee. (Peter Stanley)

NOTE ON THE TEXT

Several abbreviations are used in footnotes:

BL   British Library
NAM   National Army Museum
PP   Parliamentary Papers

All quotations are verbatim, and footnotes refer to full titles in the Bibliography. I have chosen to standardise common words and names rendered in a great variety of ways—manjee, perwannah, etc.—to give a flavour of the records, but Sidhu and Kanhu, rather than Seedoo and Kanoo because the names of Santal are usually rendered thus by Santals today. Place names are those used in contemporary sources rather than modern renderings.

Because the geography of the Santal rebellion, and especially the locations of many villages, will be unfamiliar to virtually all readers, a map folds out from the rear endpapers. Readers are advised to use it to accompany the text as they read.

ACKNOWLEDGEMENTS

My first thanks are to the Rector of UNSW Canberra, Prof. Michael Frater, and my Head of School, Prof. Shirley Scott, who approved Special Study Program leave in 2019, when much of this book was researched and written in Britain. As ever, I have relied upon the assistance of a great many librarians, archivists and others in institutions, mainly in Australia, India and Britain, and many individuals. I am grateful to: the Ames Library, University of Minnesota, Minneapolis; Dr Anshul Avijit, who kindly expanded upon his 2018 doctoral thesis on Santal material culture; Prof. Clare Anderson of Leicester University, for timely advice on transported Santals; the Asiatic Society Library, Kolkata; the Asiatic Society Library, Mumbai; the Australian National University and especially Dr Benjamin Jones, School of History, and participants at a seminar in October 2018; the British Library, India Office manuscripts: Dr Margaret Makepeace, Ms Karen Stapley and Ms Margaret White, and all the staff of its superb Asia and Africa Reading Room; the Connemara Library, Chennai; Durham University Special Collections: Mr Christopher Gilley; Bill and Pauline Edgar of Newport, Fife (in whose garden I wrote the book); Edinburgh University Special Collections: Ms Laura Cooijmans-Keizer; Ms Ngaire Gardner for her generous assistance over Walter Sherwill (her forebear); the Garrison Library, Gibraltar: Dr Jennifer Ballantine Perera and Christopher Tavares; Greenwich University and especially Dr Gavin Rand for making me a visitor in 2019 and Ms Charlotte Sowerby; Jadavpur University, Kolkata: Prof. Kaushik Roy and postgraduate candidates Arka Chowdhury and

ACKNOWLEDGEMENTS

Priyanjana Gupta, who undertook research in the West Bengal State Archives and elsewhere, Moumita Chowdhury, Sohini Mitra and especially Aryama Ghosh, who saved me from embarrassment by alerting me to Narahari Kaviraj's work; participants at the Jadavpur University 'Warfare in South Asia' conference, January 2020, and especially Dr Geetashree Singh, who suggested useful sources on elephants; Jonny McGinty at JP&L Travel, St Andrews; the National Army Museum, London, and especially Robert Fleming, who arranged for dozens of Hodson index cards to be digitised; the National Library of Australia: Dr Brendan White and Rhys Cardew, who provided maps; the National Library of India, Kolkata, and especially its newspaper reading room; the National Library of Scotland, Edinburgh: Mr Christopher Fleet and Ms Louise Speller; the Royal Scottish Geographical Society, Perth, and especially Margaret Wilkes, Andrew Cook (formerly the India Office collection's maps curator) and Michael Cairns; St Andrews University Special Collections, especially Ms Maia Sheridan and, for facilitating my becoming a Visitor at St Andrews, Professors Phillips O'Brien and Hew Strachan; the State Library of New South Wales; the State Library of Victoria; the Library of the United Service Institution of India, New Delhi, and especially Sqn Ldr Rana Chhina; the University of Bombay Library, Mumbai; the University of Madras Library, Chennai; the Academy Library at UNSW Canberra, and especially Michael Lemmer and UNSW travel staff, particularly Karen Monaghan and Luisa Caguicla; West Sussex Record Office: Clare Snoad and Abigail Hartley. I am also grateful to Dr Eileen Chanin, Bob Debus, Dr Ed Duyker, Dr Christopher Kenna and Prof. Soumyen Mukherjee, who generously shared their time and advice, and to Barbara Taylor for creating the maps.

At Hurst, I thank Daisy Leitch, Mei Jayne Yew, Ross Jamieson and Farhaana Arefin for commissioning Ahlawat Gunjan to design the cover, and my anonymous reviewer, whose comments and suggestions I greatly valued, even though I retained references to the controversial Sita Ram's supposed memoir. Above all, I am grateful to Michael Dwyer for again having confidence in my work.

PROLOGUE

'THE SKIRT OF THE HILLS'
THE SANTAL COUNTRY

In the cold weather of 1850–51 Santals living around Burhyte may have noticed a visitor in their valley, among the very few Europeans to reach their home in the Rajmahal Hills of Bhaugulpore district, in Bengal. Walter Sherwill, an officer of the East India Company's Bengal Army, had travelled by elephant through the hills and jungle of Lower Bengal. Leaving the cantonment of Berhampore a fortnight before Christmas, after more than a month of circuitous travelling around the jungle-clad Rajmahal Hills, he entered the broad valley to reach the substantial village, the heart of the Damin-i-koh; in Persian, the 'skirt of the hills'. Surrounded by neat villages, newly-cleared fields and swathes of virgin jungle, what he called 'the capital town of the hills' had grown to perhaps several thousand inhabitants, mostly Santals, but with about fifty families of Bengali merchants (or *maha-jans*). From Burhyte several passes led through the hills—north-west to the district headquarters of Bhaugulpore, north-east to the Ganges port of Rajmahal; south-east towards Pakaur.

Burhyte greatly impressed Sherwill. Standing on one of the low hills surrounding the wide valley, he condescendingly reflected on 'what can be done with natives, when their natural industry and perseverance are guarded and encouraged by kindness'. In just fifteen years of settlement, Santal migrants, urged on by the Superintendent of the Damin, Mr James Pontet, had turned what had been 'heavy forest, in which wild elephants and tigers were numerous', into a region of 'several hundred substantial Sonthal villages with an abundance of cattle and surrounded by luxuriant crops'. Santals watched Pontet show Sherwill the town's market, held, at Pontet's instigation, each Friday. They bought and sold rice, of course, which was newly harvested and threshed when he visited, along with tobacco, sugar, chillies, tamarinds and spice; as well as potatoes, the last being one of James Pontet's gifts to the Santals. In fact, on the map of the Damin which Sherwill later prepared, Pontet's bungalow, the bazaar and his potato plot appear beside the place-name of 'Burhyte'.[1] The goods on offer included mustard seeds, carried away on one of the Damin's few usable tracks eastward to the river, to be taken to Calcutta, then processed and exported to Britain, where it would add relish to the Englishman's roast beef.

A few days later, Walter Sherwill climbed up onto a howdah on the back of an elephant, and continued his tour of Bhaugulpore district.[2] Though a soldier, Walter Sherwill had no military purpose, but served on 'special duty', as the *Bengal Directory* made clear, investigating the region's geological character. He wore the comfortable 'mufti' of a civilian—he had not commanded a file of sepoys for over a decade. The son of a King's officer, with a 'classical' education at Christ's Hospital School in London, Sherwill had been commissioned into the Bengal Army in 1832 aged sixteen. After fewer than six years of uneventful service in the 66th Native Infantry, Sherwill found his calling as a revenue surveyor. His family had scientific and technical leanings: his grandfather had been a ship's surgeon with the East India Company, a Fellow of the Royal Academy and had accompanied Joseph Banks on an expedition to Iceland. Sherwill, a first-class surveyor and draughtsman, had spent the next thirteen years travelling about rural Bengal, particularly the districts of Beerbhoom and Bhaugulpore, on which he published detailed 'Geographical and Statistical Reports' just before the outbreak of the 1855 rebellion. Besides mapping their mineral wealth, especially coal, he also described their inhabitants' culture, and particularly that of the Santals, whom he knew well and evidently liked—he called them 'that interesting race', and published a long article on them in the transactions of the Asiatic Society of Calcutta.[3] Much of what Bengal's Europeans knew about the Santals and their country in 1855 derived from Sherwill's work, if they bothered to find out. The tragedy of his career was that the knowledge he gained and the maps he created became crucial to the campaign to suppress the costly rebellion, or 'Hul', upon which the Santals embarked in the monsoon of 1855.

In the Santal country the south-west monsoon usually set in between the middle and the end of June when the temperature fell from a maximum of about 98°, to about 89° in July. While less than an inch of rain fell in each month in the cold weather, in June 10 inches of rain fell, in July about 14, in August over 13 and in September 10.[4] Physically, the Rajmahal Hills dominated the region, a range no more than 2000 feet high, stretching about 70 miles south-westwards from the great bend of the Ganges as it turned from flowing east to south. From other hills several rivers flowed generally north-west to south-east between the valleys of the Ganges in the north and the Damodar in the south: the Bansloi, Brahmini, Mor and Adye rivers, flooding in the monsoon, trickles in summer. Jungle covered much of the land, but increasingly rice paddies were found in clearings around hundreds of tiny villages; by 1855 many of them inhabited by Santals. The heart of the Santal country was the Damin-i-koh, delimited not just on the Company's revenue maps, but also by a long chain of masonry boundary pillars marking the Damin as a government reserve where Santals had been encouraged to settle—and generate revenue rent on—what had been regarded as waste land.

From the 1810s the Damin had been earmarked as a suitable site for the settlement of migrants from Orissa and Chota Nagpore, mostly Santals. During the 1820s thousands arrived, encouraged by Company officials, notably Pontet, the son of a Calcutta schoolmaster, appointed as superintendent in the mid-1830s, responsible primarily for ensuring that Santal villages met revenue demands. More Santals farmed as tenants of mainly Bengali, mainly Hindu, landlords known as zamindars. Walter Sherwill documented the Santals and the land they occupied and tilled, noting the mahajans' presence, though none could have realised how within a few years their antagonism would not only bring death and suffering to the Santals, but also create a new relationship between the Santals and their British rulers.

PROLOGUE

We who were not born Santal can never hope to understand their culture as they do: even Santals today may have difficulty comprehending the lives of their forebears, so different were they from those of the 21st century. Equally, we may be deceived into assuming that because we can read the words of the Hul's British protagonists, we necessarily or easily understand the Santals. This problem confronts everyone who attempts to fathom the human past or the varieties of culture. Like Walter Sherwill, one of the few contemporary links between India's rulers and the people who in 1855 rebelled against them, we must make the attempt.

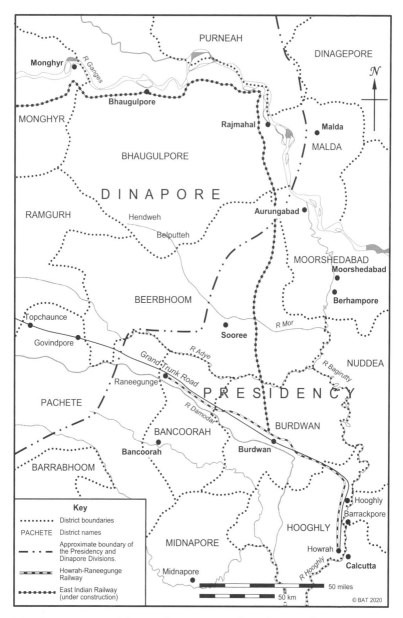

Map 1: Lower Bengal from Calcutta to Monghyr, showing the extent of the Rajmahal Hills, contemporary district boundaries, the approximate boundaries of the Presidency and Dinapore Divisions and the 'disturbed districts' proximity to Calcutta.

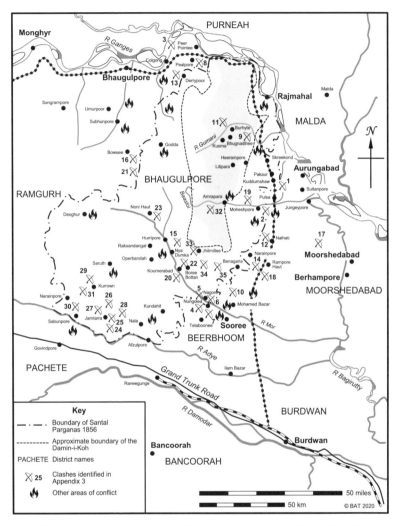

Map 2: Approximate location of clashes during the Hul, identified in Appendix 3; illustrating how conflict essentially moved from north-eastern Bhaugulpore into central Beerbhoom and then to western Beerbhoom before ending in the purgunnahs of Hendweh and Belputteh in southern Bhaugulpore. Other areas in which conflict occurred are shown by un-numbered 'flame' symbols.

INTRODUCTION

'IT WAS NOT WAR ...'

The Santal rebellion has been explained virtually from the moment it began in July 1855. An anonymous article in the *Calcutta Review* published early in 1856 set the essential narrative of the insurrection within months of its declared end, a narrative which this book seeks to elaborate and challenge. The essential chronicle of the rebellion has been that it erupted as an inchoate response to the exactions of Bengali merchants and saw savage reprisals against the money-lenders and landlords who oppressed the Santals. 'British' troops—their identity, numbers or strategy never presented clearly—moved against the Santals, and by unspecified but evidently murderous military operations, suppressed the rebellion amid the imprisonment, punishment and impoverishment of the Santals. At least 10,000 Santals died. In the wake of the rebellion, however, a more responsive system of governance at least moderated the worst of the abuses which had provoked resistance. This book investigates and interrogates that generally accepted narrative. It focuses on the Company's response militarily to the rebellion, an aspect which previous authors, more expert or interested in the Santal experience, had largely neglected, not least because they did not consult military records.

Memories of the insurrection remained fresh when Sir William Hunter's 1868 *The Annals of Rural Bengal* included a chapter on the rising. This, along with the article in the *Calcutta Review* set the interpretation for decades, reinforced by sections of the *Imperial Gazetteer of India*, which Hunter edited from 1881.[1] A Bengal civil servant seeking to understand and interpret Indian history, ethnography and society, Hunter began with an 'ethnical' survey of Santal life and culture, an approach followed by virtually all later chroniclers of the rising which Santal people called the 'Hul'; the rising. Just two substantive histories of the Hul exist: Kali Kinkar Datta's 1940 *The Santal Insurrection* and Narahari Kaviraj's *Santal Village Community and the Santal Rebellion of 1855*, published in 2001. As will become clear, both books were partial, in both being incomplete and in presenting interpretations unjustified by the evidence.

Ethnographic or anthropological understanding is fundamental to comprehending Santal motives, actions and memories. The Santals, with their complex relationship to nature, intricate cosmology, and vivid poetic oral culture, naturally attracted generations of ethnographers, amateur and professional, including missionaries, British officials, academics and later officers of Indian government agencies. They included officials such as Francis Bradley-Birt, author of *The Story of an Indian Upland*, and William Archer, author of *The Hill of Flutes*, one of the most evocative of the anthropological accounts of Santal culture, and missionaries such as the Norwegian, Paul Olaf Bodding and the Scot James Macphail. The work of both officials and missionaries demanded an intimacy with Santal language and culture, and all recorded it, affectionately, even lovingly, impelled by fears for the Santals' welfare amid a largely Hindu population or hopeful of their conversion to Christianity. The events of 1855 often figure in their interpretations of Santal life and belief. Especially popular has been the creation of fictionalised biographies of individuals and families who lived through and were affected by the Hul. It is notable that besides the imaginative reconstructions such as by Macphail, who in 1922 used the fictional characters of Manka and his family to dramatise *The Story of the Santal*, at least four novels set in the uprising have appeared: in English Robert Carstairs's *Harma's Village* (1937) and Sanjay Bahadur's 2013 *Hul—Cry Rebel!*.[2]

The attention devoted to the Santals by anthropologists of various kinds inevitably created not only a rich body of scholarship on Santal culture, but also produced insights into the place of the Hul in that culture as it changed in response to economic, social and official pressures in the century and more following the uprising. In 1945, for example, the journal *Man in India* published a long article on the uprising, interpreting it using Santal sources—songs, stories and community memories.[3] While offering insights into Santal experience and memory of 1855, however, anthropological works often drew on a conventional and simplistic version of the uprising. Many accounts, for example, quote the familiar words of Major Vincent Jervis of the 56th Bengal Native Infantry—'it was not war ... it was execution'—emphasising the brutality of the rebellion's suppression, but none give the anecdote any source or context.[4] Moreover, a popular revolt which occurred 170-odd years ago understandably does not figure coherently in studies of contemporary Santal society. Pradip Chattopadhyay's *Redefining Tribal Identity*, a comprehensive and revealing study of Santals in, among other districts, Birbhum, for example, makes just four references to the Hul, though to Chattopadhyay the Hul marked 'a new dimension of identity assertion'.[5] A visitor to the Santal country, and especially to the impressive memorial at Bhugnadihee, would understand the Hul's significance, and be led to see it in heroic, but also simplistic terms. This history provides unprecedented detail, though it also confirms the heroism of the Santals' doomed rebellion.

What justifies this new history? Simply that although the Santal Hul has been the subject of intermittent interest over the years, from both historians and anthropologists, no one has used the immense documentation available in the military records of the East India Company's archives in the British Library to attempt to produce a complete account of the rising, its suppression and its effects. This interpretation draws upon the work of earlier scholars but it essentially contributes what none of them have attempted: to understand the events of 1855 from the perspective of the vast and hitherto unexamined military records. It explains, for the first time, what happened when Santals armed with bows and arrows confronted Bengal sepoys armed with muskets and supported by artillery, rockets, river steamers, railway trains and the electric telegraph. This book constitutes the first explicitly cultural-military-political history of the Hul, and places it in a context that no other study has attempted: the history of insurgency and counter-insurgency.

At the outset it is necessary to discuss terminology and sources; crucial matters in seeking to understand the protagonists in this conflict. 'Nobody agrees in orthography of Indian names', Charles Dickens's *Household Words* cautioned in 1856.[6] The Revenue Survey used different spellings to the Great Trigonometrical Survey, while officials (and their often careless copyists) used different spellings to each other, and newspapers used different spellings for the same places even within the same article. Almost every place name exists in more than one spelling in contemporary documents, and the 1855 spelling often differs from places' names today; indeed, many villages that existed in 1855 cannot now be found on the most detailed maps of modern India. In 1855 newspaper correspondents complained on reading 'a list of barbarous [place] names and incomprehensible military movements'.[7] Nowhere is this ambiguity more apparent than in the very rendering, in English, of the word for the people at the heart of the events which this book deals with. Should they be called 'Sonthal' (the term favoured in official correspondence); Santhal (the name most often used in newspapers); or the variations, Santal and Sontal, or other renderings—'Southals', 'Sautals', 'Sonthurs', 'Surtals' or 'Sounthal' and (as the *Hindoo Patriot* preferred) 'Shanthals'? India's people today use 'Santal', but it was the least favoured option in English records in 1855. 'Santals' apparently called themselves 'Saontars'.[8] To make the difficult almost impossible, Santals often gave villages different names to those used by their Bengali neighbours.[9] I use 'Santal', except in direct quotations and citations.

The neglect the Santal rebellion has suffered is not because the events in Bengal in the second half of 1855 went undocumented. The English language sources alone are overwhelming. The East India Company, the archetypal colonial bureaucracy, generated massive quantities of paper. A cynical officer, for example, doubtful that the Bengal Army would actually increase its regiments' establishment of officers by two, thought that it would take 'half a century to discuss, and several tons of paper to record'.[10] Having worked through dozens of volumes of military and judicial papers his jibe seems justified.

Newspaper reports provide the diversity of opinion and candour of expression often lacking in official records capturing the reports and views of civil officials and military officers. The robust culture of the public press of British India, which published extracts of official documents (and commentary on them) snippets of private letters, gossip, hearsay, speculation, criticism, calumny and outright abuse, seemingly without heed of copyright or the laws of libel, make newspapers an especially valuable source. Still, they need to be treated with caution. In August 1855 Meredith Townsend, the editor of the *Friend of India*, one of Calcutta's more bellicose newspapers, observed, while attempting to summarise the situation in the what became known as the 'disturbed districts', that the letters arriving in the *Friend*'s office seemed 'so contradictory as to baffle every attempt to weave anything like a trustworthy narrative'.[11] A week later, he admitted that 'the details of this extraordinary movement'—already the Santal rebellion had become the most serious challenge yet to Company rule in India— were 'becoming confused'. Townsend found it impossible to 'even trace the daily progress of the revolt' between 'imperfect information, frightened newspaper correspondents, and the wide extent of territory occupied by the insurgents'.[12] Distance, time, and a wider range of sources has eased that confusion, and this is the most detailed account of the Hul so far produced, including a listing, again for the first time, of armed encounters in it (see Appendix 2). A new history of the Santal rebellion, then, based on these hitherto neglected military sources—sources which bear upon the conduct of the combatants on both sides—is capable of producing a new interpretation of the events of 1855 in the Santal country.

Late in 2017 in the British Library I began to identify, read and copy the Military Consultations, to capture the relevant published literature, ethnographic and historical, and to locate new sources. It soon became clear that contemporary British and British-Indian newspapers were both germane and unexploited. In 2018 I identified the many reports of the rebellion published in British newspapers, and more laboriously, found reports in mostly Calcutta newspapers which appeared through the rebellion and which documented events and British-Indian reactions to them. I completed my research in 2019–20. I twice visited the states of Bihar, West Bengal and Jharkhand in India to 'sniff the ground', travelling through the Santal country to gain an impression of much of the terrain (today massively changed) over which the rebellion occurred. These visits also revealed the enduring power of the iconography of Santal heroes in the statues erected in many villages in Jharkhand, though a study of the extent and nature of Santal commemoration is beyond the scope of this project, as is any real engagement with Santal community memory. Santal memory should be investigated by researchers better equipped in language and cultural sensitivity. My project essentially aimed to produce the first comprehensive history of the Santal uprising, drawing upon previously unused military sources, which has been enough of a challenge.

Beginning research on the rebellion soon raised a wide range of questions, about the events of 1855 and about the evidence upon which a new interpretation may be based. What caused or precipitated the uprising? At whom was it directed? Did the Santals act under direction, or with any purpose? How did they move about the country, sustain their operations and learn of their adversaries' locations and movements? How did they act toward the various opponents they encountered, for instance Bengali peasants and merchants, local rulers, British indigo planters and railway engineers, officials and military forces? How did the forces of the Company mobilise against the rebellion? What strategies and tactics did British-Indian forces adopt? What were the relations between civil and military authorities, and at various levels? What technological or organisational advantages did the two sides enjoy? What casualties did each inflict? What was the balance between sickness and wounds, on both sides? What did the forces of authority know or understand about the Santals and their cause? How, where and when was the uprising suppressed, and with what consequences? What were the longer-term effects of the Hul, and how is it remembered in India today? My engagement with the sources of course spawned further questions.

The greatest single flaw in the sources used for this book (and almost all interpretations hitherto), of course, is that they are all in English. Very few non-English sources exist or are available. They include a few paragraphs of Santal testimony gathered within memory of the Hul, by Chotrae Desmanjhi and Jugia Haram, translated and made available by W.J. Culshaw and William Archer in 1945.[13] More important is the narrative of Durga Tudu, based on an interview by Sagram Murmu.[14] Digambar Chakraborti's *History of the Santal Hool* comprises one of the few Bengali sources accessible in English. Ranajit Guha, who experienced the same frustration in surveying peasant insurgencies in nineteenth-century India, seemed downcast by the predominance of what he called 'elite' evidence; 'rebel conscious-ness', he felt, was 'meagre to the point of being insignificant'. But Guha encouraged scholars to find 'a rebel consciousness as a necessary and pervasive element within that body of evidence'; to explore the languages of peasant insurgency.[15] I have persisted in this endeavor: what alternative do we have—to ignore British evidence? I have tried to straddle the line between acknowledging the essential oppression of British rule and exploiting its exponents and products for the insights they provide into its history.

It is now inconceivable to attempt to interpret the Santal rebellion without what might be called the Santal voice. This is difficult; almost all the surviving evidence came from European officials, officers and civilians, even if quoting or paraphrasing Santal witnesses. It is often hard to avoid producing what Kim Wagner described in his study of the 'great fear' of 1857 as 'more than just an account of what one British officer wrote to another'.[16] Santal folk evidence is scanty, and seeking modern Santal views is falsely reassuring, because it cannot possibly get us closer to the views or voices of Santals from 1855. And yet the effort has to be made. I have striven to capture the words, actions, experiences, feelings, beliefs and decisions of otherwise voiceless Santals, such as Chotrae Desmanjhi and Jugia Haram and, for that matter, of equally otherwise voiceless Bengali peasants or sepoys. That the vast bulk of the contemporary sources stem from a small number of British men, almost all military officers or civil offi-cials, does not negate the value and utility of the evidence they cre-ated. The nature of that evidence of course tends to skew the story—we know much more about the attitudes and actions of Company protagonists than of any Indian—but the effort is worth making, and seeking out the voices of those who could not or did not record their own experience will still help us to recapture their experiences, cer-tainly much more than if we failed to try. Narahari Kaviraj, though using virtually only Company judicial records, also tried to present the Santal perspective, though not always successfully; but his exam-ple gave me encouragement to at least make the attempt.[17]

HUL! HUL!

The Santals are the first of three essential protagonists of this book, along with the civil officials of British Bengal and the officers and men of the Bengal Army. It is their community, culture and country we must first examine in seeking to understand the events of 1855.

PART I

BEFORE THE HUL

1

PROTAGONISTS AND CONTEXTS

In the sixty-odd years after Robert Clive's victory over Siraj ud Daula at Plassey in 1757, the East India Company had extended and confirmed its rule over Bengal. The Company's conquest of India astonished, impressed and enriched British contemporaries. But that conquest brought profound change to the people of Bengal, impoverishing what had been one of India's wealthiest provinces and leaving the governance of Bengal and most of India besides the 'princely states' in the hands of the directors of the East India Company and their civil officials. Company rule brought changes to all. One of the least noticed changes was the migration of entire peoples. From the 1820s officials encouraged landless indigenous Santals to migrate from the jungle plateau of what they called Chota Nagpore into the uplands of 'Lower Bengal'—the core of which was the Damin-i-koh and the Rajmahal Hills. In order to fully understand the brief but traumatic Hul on which these migrants embarked in 1855, it is necessary to comprehend the story's three main protagonists, and the context of rebellion in British India, before introducing events in the Santal country on the eve of the rising.

'Born in the soil': Santal culture

Though described as an indigenous people—one of the 'Scheduled Tribes' in the Indian government's inelegant bureaucratic

11

terminology—the Santals were migrants to the country in which they lived and for which they fought in 1855. Scholars have long argued over the Santals' origins: whether they straddled India's pre-Aryan and pre-Dravidian culture, or linguistically constituted 'the western most peripheral representatives of … the Hawaiian type family'. Others asked whether the Santals hailed from Persia, Afghanistan or Chinese Tartary; whether they shared a mythology with Greeks, German, or even Maoris and the islanders of 'Feejee'.[1] At least, this is what officials, missionaries, curious military officers, amateur ethnographers and later, professional anthropologists, variously contended; the Santals themselves had little idea of their origins, and for a long time no one actually asked them. It is known that by the eighteenth century they lived by shifting cultivation in the forests largely on the Chota Nagpore plateau within a few hundred miles south-west of what became by 1855 the Santal country in which the Hul broke out.

'The wonderful part of the story', thought Robert Carstairs, one of a succession of British district officers who fell in love with the Santals, was that in 1793, the time of the Permanent Settlement 'there was not a single Sonthal' in the whole of what became the Santal country. The first had arrived around 1810, gradually moving north-westward 'reclaiming waste land, and ousting no man', reaching the Rajmahal and other hills by the 1830s—barely twenty years before the rebellion.[2] In the decades of unrest that accompanied the gradual dissolution of Mughal rule in Bengal, the effects of the great famine of 1769–70 and the depredations of the Rohillas and Pindarries, the country north-west of Calcutta suffered desolation and decline. Vast stretches of country became depopulated; cultivated fields turned to waste lands and the jungle encroached on deserted villages: British officials encouraged migration to make the country productive.

Walter Sherwill's reports on his surveying tours provide insights into the Santals' way of life in the decade before the rebellion. He encountered a 'jolly, cheerful people', happy to eat virtually anything, in contrast to their rule-bound Hindu neighbours; glad to drink rice beer and enjoying a casual attitude to pre-marital sex. Women lived less constrained lives than their Bengali neighbours, but they remained essentially chattels—adultery was defined as 'theft' of a man's property and the belief in witches left women subject to inexplicable accusation, persecution and even execution.[3]

As Narahari Kaviraj showed in his book, *Santal Village Community and the Santal Rebellion*, the nature of Santal culture was central to their motivation in rising. In the absence of detailed anthropological studies dating from the time of the Hul, besides Walter Sherwill's observations all we have to go on are the writings of a few other travellers, missionaries and officials, with professional anthropologists contributing from the beginning of the twentieth century. Did Santal culture remain static in the half-century in between? It did not; for instance, penalties and prices cited in anthropological texts in the 1940s could not possibly have obtained a century before; while later commentators discuss the growing influence of Hinduism and Christianity upon Santal belief. We must infer much and should not regard Santal culture as fixed.

Santals were animists—spirits inhabited the trees, streams, animals and features of the country, an association created even as they settled a new land. They shared a complex awareness of the power of magic and sorcery, with a cosmology revolving around *bongas* (spirits) and Thakur, the creator or supreme being. Permeated by a belief in the existence and pervasive influence of spirits of the natural world, influenced by auguries (for instance, the sight of three quails was bad; a tiger's footprints, paradoxically, good), Santals lived with an intense and intimate identification with the land. As a Santal song expressed: 'I was born/ In the soil/ I was born/ In the splash of rain'; even if the relationship with the land in question was that of a migrant people.[4] Under the creator, bongas inhabited the country and everything in it—rocks, springs, trees, houses, Santal dead—governing family and sexual relations, hunting, the infliction and cure of sickness, determining fate and fortune: 'always mingling with Santals and interfering in their lives'.[5] Some bongas could be actively malevolent, demanding to be placated, while others acted benevolently, and all Santals remained wary of how sorcery impinged upon life.

Though illiterate, Santals revelled in a language highly allusive, rich in verbal complexity with a love of stories, songs, riddles, poems, proverbs and similes. Santal kinship and marriage customs included liberal courtship rules and ceremonies and festivals marking births, marriages and deaths punctuated their year. Their economy was tied intimately to the land and the climate that governed fertility and growth, their existence dependent upon what they could harvest, hunt or gather from it. Their weapons were the tools of hunting and clearing the jungle: bamboo bows, firing arrows made of sar grass long distances, and axes or knives, sometimes described as 'swords', but actually *baluas*, machetes for clearing undergrowth. Their skill in archery was noted, both in rapidity, supposedly being able to fire the tenth arrow before the first struck; and in accuracy, able to hit running hares and birds on the wing. They were not, however, a warlike people. While many Santals joined the Hul, and often fought with reckless bravery, none of them were what other societies and cultures called 'warriors'.

They lived in small, neat villages, all surrounded by jungle, invariably comprising a single wide, long street of mud-covered thatched bamboo huts, lined by sohaju trees, each village with its sacred grove of sal trees, the focus of the community's spiritual connection to their land. The village was the centre of Santal communal life, each regulated by traditional leaders known as 'manjees', who in turn owed loose allegiance to older men, the 'purgannaits', exercising a limited authority over groups of villages. While culturally homogenous, politically Santals exercised virtually no expression greater than a village of half a dozen or so families. By the late 1840s more than 100,000 Santals lived within the boundaries of the Damin-i-koh, and perhaps twice as many outside it.[6] James Pontet, its superintendent, found the Santals 'eager cultivators', clearing jungle to plant rice, maize and oil-seed, though still revering the forest and its abundant plant and animal life. Pontet tried to introduce new crops and induce the Santals to build roads and water tanks, mostly ineffectually on all counts.[7] Still, the revenue increased: from Santal occupiers alone in the Damin from Rs 6682 in 1838 to Rs 58,033 in 1855. What the Santals actually paid was, however, always inflated by 'illegal cesses' (charges) imposed by Pontet's functionaries, an oppression he seemed unable to curb, or possibly did not know of.[8]

Unlike what are today the densely settled and intensively farmed districts of Bihar, Jharkhand and West Bengal, what was then called 'the Sonthal country' was largely still covered with jungle. In clearings around their neat villages they grew pulses, vegetables and corn beside their huts, millet on upland slopes and rice in paddies flooded by rain and watered by irrigation bunds. At James Pontet's urging, Santal immigrants cleared the jungle, with effects described by Walter Sherwill, who in the 1840s observed that in less than two decades in the valley of Burhyte, a wilderness full of wild elephants and tigers had been supplanted by Santal villagers tending cattle and 'luxuriant crops'.[9] As Sherwill added, opening the Damin to Santal migrants had also attracted merchants and dealers—mahajans. Their exploitative relations with the Santals lay at the heart of the Hul. 'It is no matter of surprise,' a Company investigation later found, that mahajans soon enforced a regime of 'unmitigated dishonesty and extortion'.[10] 'No surprise' in hindsight: at the time neither Pontet nor other Company officials bothered to report or prevent this oppression. Government meant collecting revenue and maintaining order, both easy given the Santals' compliance. As they did over much of rural India, merchants acted as money-lenders and enforced, upon both Santals and their Bengali neighbours, extortionate interest rates—Santals accepted 25 per cent interest as reasonable, but mahajans often demanded 500 per cent, taking as their interest a huge proportion of the Santals' cash crops and trapping families in hereditary debt bondage.[11] To those who knew the region and its people, the mahajans' practices were common knowledge: 'if they borrow two rupees from a mahajuns, they pay five rupees, and still have the two rupees hanging over them … fleeced and cheated in every way', as the Calcutta *Citizen* explained, though only after the Hul had begun.[12]

No matter how industrious they were as cultivators, the Santals were hampered by being unequal to what a magistrate called the 'wily and unscrupulous set of Bengalis' in the mahajans.[13] Santal accounting used strings, in which knots and spaces represented amounts and durations of loans. In disputes, money-lenders deployed the documentation of ledgers, deeds and other records: naturally the Company's courts preferred the money-lenders' testimony, though few cases got that far—mahajans used chicanery and intimidation (including violence) to exercise and retain economic and legal power.

Unsurprisingly mahajans were hated; a Santal euphemism for excretion was 'going to pay a moneylender'.[14] Disputes, however, rarely reached court, not just because they were far from the Damin, in the district headquarter stations of Bhaugulpore, Sooree or Moorshedabad, but also because access to justice often depended upon bribing amlahs (lower court officials), so poor Santals were ordinarily cheated and oppressed. The majority of the Santals lived as tenants of zamindars (landlords) and had to pay heavy rents, without any recourse to review or appeal. *Darogahs* (or police constables) offered no protection and routinely colluded with zamindars and mahajans on whom they depended for the bribes in place of pay, not least in sexually abusing Santal women, who 'had to bear the indignity silently', as an historian of the Santals observed.[15]

Bengal's seasons absolutely governed the Santals' lives. In oppressive June heat great monsoon thunderclouds piled up over a hot, parched land, unleashing rain passing slowly across the country from the south-east and fields turned bright green with shoots. The corn crop, already planted, sprouted, to be harvested around June and July: exactly when the Hul erupted. As fields became sodden the monsoon rice crop grew, with plots ploughed by men by the end of June and seedlings transplanted by women and girls in July and August, men minding the earth bunds holding the water in the fields. In September and October, the rice might be ready for harvest, and in November, the millet crop was ready for scything. In December both would be threshed. With rebellion breaking out at the beginning of July and with many people abandoning their villages, the insurrection would cut across the most productive part of the annual cycle. Santals had often been described as 'improvident'; in the timing of the Hul, they certainly fulfilled that criticism, one made by the European officials who ultimately governed them, but who had little contact with them.[16] Who were these men?

'Honest and enlightened English gentlemen': the Company's government

The direction of Company policy and strategy fell to a small group of Europeans in Calcutta: the Supreme Council, the lieutenant-governor of Bengal, and, extraordinarily, a lieutenant grandly but awkwardly called the officiating secretary to the Government of India, Military Department.

The Supreme Council advised, and when necessary acted, in the governor-general's place, meeting every Friday in the governor-general's council chamber in Government House in Fort William, in Calcutta, and exchanging and commenting on verbose papers in between. With the governor-general absent in the second half of 1855, it comprised four senior officials, most wise in the ways of British India and all too aware of the complex responsibilities they carried. The Council's nominal head was Joseph Dorin, aged 53, an accountant who had joined the Council only in 1853 but was its most senior 'ordinary member'. Remarkably, after arriving in Calcutta in 1822 Dorin had never travelled further than Barrackpore. Neither he nor probably any other member had ever seen a Santal. Second was Major-General John Low, a 67-year-old Madras soldier who had mainly served in 'political' positions as a 'Military Civilian', and John Peter Grant, 48, son of a renowned Calcutta judge who had served as an official in the secretariat and was known for his stubborn advocacy of his own views. The Council's legal member was Sir Barnes Peacock, 45, a London QC with no Indian experience before his arrival in Calcutta in 1852.

The lieutenant-governor, Sir Frederick Halliday, 49, headed the Government of Bengal, assisted by its secretary, William Grey, a rising civil official, only 35 and destined for higher positions. Halliday had held judicial and revenue posts and had become Bengal's first lieutenant-governor in 1854. The Company created the new government, recognising that the affairs of a province of forty million people and a quarter of a million square miles, stretching from the borderlands of Assam and Arracan to the hills of Orissa and the Ganges valley, including the populous lowlands of Bengal, demanded its own government. So recently a separate government of Bengal been created, however, the relationship between it and the Government of India was still being worked out, and the Santal Hul would bring the two into contention. Halliday's frustration stemmed, as John Kaye had written, from his government having 'no military or political authority, and no financial control except in subordination to the supreme Government'. Indeed, the system was one of 'extreme centralisation', in that the lieutenant-governor 'cannot lawfully entertain [employ] an additional Cooley, on a salary of seven shillings a month', without the 'recorded assent' of the governor-general in Council.[17]

The most important individual in the military conduct of the rebellion was Lieutenant George Francklin Atkinson, a Bengal Engineer officiating (acting) as secretary to the Government of India's Military Department in the absence of his superior, the wily military bureaucrat Richard Birch, who had accompanied Dalhousie on sick leave to Madras. The 33-year-old Atkinson sat third-from-the-top of the Engineers' seniority list of lieutenants and had been refused promotion to captain in January, but he remained the key link between the Bengal government's officials and army headquarters in Simla, in the foothills of the Himalayas. He corresponded with the various departments of the army, and not just in co-ordinating the correspondence and orders necessary for operations against the Santals, but in the continuing routine administration of the army. The sheer quantity of correspondence over his signature in the Military Consultations confirms his extraordinary responsibility and the workload it entailed. Virtually every report from officers in the field passed through his office, as did every request or direction necessary to move troops or obtain the equipment and services they required. He corresponded with the Medical Board, the Commissary General, and the Bengal Army's powerful and pedantic Military Auditor-General; even with the Surveyor-General's Office to procure the maps units needed. Crucially for the evidence on which the analysis of Company operations is based, dozens of reports from officers in the field reached his desk. A gifted illustrator and writer, Atkinson was also at the time editing the *Delhi Sketchbook or Indian Punch* magazine, and completing the written and lithographed sketches published in his *Curry and Rice*, which gently satirised the inhabitants of 'our station', a small cantonment in the mofussil ('up-country' districts), like Berhampore, Sooree or Bhaugulpore, stations at the heart of the Hul.[18]

Atkinson dealt most often with William Grey, who liaised with both the lieutenant-governor and with civil officials in the districts. His correspondence forms a good proportion of the Judicial Consultations, and of course much of their correspondence can be found both in Judicial and Military volumes, complicating the business of research. Both the Government of Bengal's secretariat and the

Military Department worked in Fort William, but apparently in different buildings: their correspondence bears no indication that they resolved matters face-to-face, but always, in detail, on paper.

It is striking that the two figures absent from the higher direction of the suppression of the Hul were the Governor-General, Lord Dalhousie, and the Commander-in-Chief in India, General Sir William Gomm. Both were away from Calcutta, the seat of government, for the entire duration of the rising. Dalhousie, recently bereaved and exhausted from years of labour, was recuperating in the Nilgiri Hills of Madras while Gomm was spending the summer at Simla, both places over a thousand miles from Calcutta. Nearing the end of his term as governor-general, Dalhousie had become debilitated by the crushing work of the centralised Indian administrative system. Manifesting a forbidding inflexibility (the *Friend of India* quipped of a portrait of him that he had 'not the sort of expression that would encourage one to ask a favour'), he was a sick man.[19] Dalhousie, only 43, suffering from the degenerative bone disease that would kill him within five years, described himself as a 'poor, miserable, broken-down, dying man'.[20] As Commander-in-Chief, Gomm served as an 'extraordinary member' of the Supreme Council and, though he did not attend for most of 1855, as John Kaye waspishly pointed out, 'he has always drawn the salary'.[21] Gomm, 'a quiet, inoffensive, gentlemanly man' was 'for all active purposes ... almost non-existent' during the Santal rebellion.[22] Both received detailed reports but neither intervened significantly, not least because receiving and dispatching a response took a minimum of two weeks, by which time events had of course moved on.

It was then—and remains—astonishing that so few Company officials attempted to govern such vast areas and huge populations. Realistically, even if they embarked on tours of their districts in the cold weather, European officials remained practically invisible to the vast majority of those for whom they were responsible. Their duties were many, but they principally entailed ensuring that the 'Settlement'—the revenue fixed by a survey conducted decades earlier—was collected from the local zamindars, who were the people Company officials mainly dealt with. Few Company officials besides Pontet dealt with Santals directly.

The archetypal Company's civil servant could be expected to be, as John Kaye wrote, 'an honest and enlightened English [but often Scottish and Irish] gentleman, who performed a fixed duty for a fixed salary'.[23] Corruption and self-interest, the mainspring of Mughal administration, was rare: their informal schooling as gentlemen and their formal education at the Company's Haileybury College (in Hertfordshire) imparted a moral sheen. But corruption was not, perhaps, the worst possible sin. Civil officials were in the main dutiful and diligent, and many grew to love the people over whom they ruled, however patronisingly. They exercised seemingly absolute power over their charges, and, attended by crowds of servants and functionaries, seemed to enjoy lives of ease. Most worked hard in a climate which exhausted and aged those it did not kill. The obligation to accept the crushing load of precedent and rigid procedure, and above all, a stultifying atmosphere of reporting and scrutiny, all conspired to sap civil officials of initiative, imagination and flexibility. The contemporary compilation recording the *Regulations of the Government of Fort William* comprised 813 closely-set pages; rules defining 'the smallest possible limits' of official procedures.[24] Promotion came to those able to bear the physical and emotional burden, to hold out between infrequent furloughs, the first of which came only after ten years, and a willingness to accept that only seniority brought wisdom. As in the Bengal Army, in which their cousins and brothers served, every decision was reported and every action examined to be either approved or disapproved; every expense was audited and either endorsed or disallowed. For some, the Hul came as a release from routine, an opportunity to shine and impress; alternatively, it was a challenge or shock to men to whom routine and referred responsibility had come to govern their lives.

While appointments by competitive examination were about to be introduced, all of the civil officials who faced the Santal rebellion had been appointed essentially by the workings of patronage. Every candidate seeking an appointment to Haileybury and then Bengal had to demonstrate not just a suitable classical and mathematical schooling, but some connection to one of the East India Company's directors or some other association to it. Most were sons of British officials based in India or officers or royal officers in more modest circumstances, and all needed to obtain the support of a current or past director. Accordingly, both civil and military officers had much in common. Civil officials tended to be slightly better educated, but all were in some way 'friends of the ... magnates of Leadenhall street' (the Company's head office in London).[25] Despite committing their lives to India, they shared the assumptions about and prejudices against it and its people. Frederick Shore noticed in the 1830s how common it was for a young man new to India to profess that he 'hates the natives', without knowing, or troubling to know, much of them, their language or customs.[26]

The Company's administrative machinery that affected Santals in the districts, comprised a hierarchy of officials, with commissioners exercising both judicial and administrative authority; essentially rising from assistant to magistrate, collector and judge, with the assistants 'the pivot of the administration, combining revenue, magisterial and general administrative duties'.[27] Overworked and inadequately paid junior officials often had insufficient experience to meet their many and often unfamiliar responsibilities. This was frequently the case because senior men hung on to lucrative positions, while junior officials changed jobs on average once a year, so often, in fact, that the *East India Register* was often months out of date. Relatively few civil officers played leading roles in the three districts directly affected by the Hul. They included experienced men such as George Brown, commissioner of Bhaugulpore, who had served in the district for decades, ambitious senior men such as Alfred Bidwell, William Elliott or George Loch. Younger men eager to make their name, who were active in those districts, included Octavius Toogood, Robert Richardson or Ashley Eden. Interestingly, Eden, the 24-year-old, nephew of a former Governor-General, Lord Auckland, educated at Rugby but last in his term at Haileybury, would do better out of the Hul than anyone else.[28]

These men conducted all official business in writing though officials also wrote 'privately', mainly so that critical comments would not find their way either up the hierarchy or into the press. Even Dalhousie, who insisted on all business being transacted on paper, lamented the minute-writing 'to which there is no end'; but the end result is a massive abundance of documentation.[29] However, these men wrote about 'natives'; they did not correspond with them. Edward Braddon, an indigo planter who worked with civil officers in 1855, observed that 'the Government officials who directly ruled over the Santals were benightedly ignorant as to the character of these people', an alienation most significant in the administration of justice.[30]

British India's machinery of justice was elaborate and expensive, intended to impose British notions of jurisprudence onto an alien world. The hierarchy culminated in the High Court in Calcutta, sitting atop a judicial pyramid of judges, magistrates and 'moonsiffs' (the lowest functionary). Santal individuals and communities invariably encountered this system through the local darogah. These, the 'superior native police-officers' of the Mofussil Police, from their *thannahs* or stations, were charged with administering justice locally. Even apologists such as John Kaye conceded that the police 'demanded the most vigilant superintendence of the European officer to restrain it from becoming an engine of injustice and oppression'.[31] Given the size of the districts administered by a handful of civil officers, the darogah was the only functionary that Santal villagers were ever likely to meet, and those contacts were invariably oppressive. Largely unpaid, darogahs lived by charging both complainants and criminals a fee to proceed or desist, as seemed most profitable. Of Moorshedabad district's 21 thannahs, only five received payments beyond those they could exact from villagers, and then only Rs 3 a month. The others routinely extorted bribes and gifts.[32] A critic claimed that it was to the darogahs' 'unheard of extortions and villainies this miserable servile war was due'.[33] That war was to be conducted principally by the Bengal Army.

'They will endure so much in our service': the Bengal Army

If the Company's hold on India was 'the most extraordinary political phenomenon that ever existed', it owed its existence and survival to the remarkable army that it had created over the previous century.[34] The commander-in-chief, always a member of the Queen's (that is, the British) army, presided over a force mainly composed of 'native' troops, supported, and, it was believed, strengthened, by a small force of the Company's Europeans, mainly artillery and three regiments of infantry, and a force of Queen's cavalry and infantry. Britain's—or rather the Company's—dominion over India relied on a native army of over 250,000 men, comprising several regiments of artillery, 28 regiments of Light and Irregular cavalry, 74 regiments of Native Infantry, and a number of local corps. It was distributed across Bengal, from the newly-conquered province of Burmah a thousand miles north-west to the newly-conquered Punjab, up to the very borders of British India. The Bengal Army's command structure was paradoxically both geographically dispersed and organisationally highly centralised, located in nominal, geographically-based divisions, each commanded by a major-general. Few troops were stationed in Lower Bengal, conquered and supposedly pacified for a century.

The Bengal Army's units moved about the country in an elaborate programme known as 'The General Relief', in which most shifted stations during the cold weather every couple of years, making heroic journeys by road and river to reach their next cantonment. Regiments mainly from the Presidency Division commanded from Barrackpore, 15 miles north of Calcutta, and from the Dinapore Division, in Behar, would together suppress the Hul. Several regiments had just arrived in these divisions—the 31st and 56th had marched from Jullunder and Umballah in the Punjab, respectively, while the 42nd had come from Burmah; the 63rd from Cawnpore.[35]

The Company's force mainly comprised 'sepoys', who were, as Dr Samuel Maunder explained in a 'new and popular encyclopædia' in 1845, 'the name given to the Hindoo or native troops in the service of the East India Company'. They were 'disciplined after the European manner', he wrote (though he meant 'drilled'), describing them as 'hardy, temperate, and subordinate'.[36] The regiments of Bengal Native Infantry constituted the single largest military force in Asia, the foundation and guarantor of the Company's hold on India. The iconoclastic Frederick Shore pointed to the inconsistency that for all their condemnation of 'the natives', Britons in India extolled the sepoys' 'sense of honour, gratitude and devotion', pointing out that their praise was 'indirectly, flattery to ourselves. They are so faithful to us; they will endure so much in our service …'[37] And all for Rs 7 a month; about 2 per cent of their company commander's pay.

Each native infantry regiment nominally comprised about eight hundred sepoys, organised into eight companies of a hundred men each. Most were high-caste Hindus from the mid-Ganges valley, but every regiment included Muslims and, since 1849, Sikhs. Each was commanded by a lieutenant-colonel, though of the ten regiments that were to form the Sonthal Field Force, four were commanded by majors or even captains. The dozen or so officers serving with the regiment generally comprised lieutenants (with under a decade's service) or newly-commissioned ensigns. Twice as many 'native officers'—jemadars and subedars—supported the European officers, promoted by seniority and therefore often relatively old, but all subordinate in authority regardless of age or experience. Native officers are practically invisible in the records of the Hul, but they emerge occasionally to suggest their role in leading sepoys. Each regiment also had a European sergeant-major and a quartermaster-sergeant-major, ambitious men transferring from the Company's European corps (going 'for the blackies', as they said), vital to the regiment's routine administrative function but not its performance in action, and the records of their part in the Hul are obscure.[38]

The way this ethnically diverse military organisation functioned was specified in successive editions of the *Standing Orders* issued by the Adjutant-General and printed in English, Urdu and Hindi script, and the *General Orders*, issued weekly and read out on successive parades. The Bengal Army's notorious devotion to regulation stemmed partly from the Company's need to control a huge, multi-ethnic force spread over a vast sub-continent, and partly to ensure that its members served the Company in return for their due rewards—in pay, promotion and pensions—rights important to both its European and 'native' members, and rigorously managed.

The ten regiments ordered to join the Sonthal Field Force in 1855 represented a range of the Bengal Native Infantry's quality. Some regiments had shown their value in recent conflicts. In Afghanistan, the 37th had been 'one of the best in the service', Vincent Eyre thought.[39] (Eyre survived Afghanistan, though few of the 37th's sepoys did.)[40] The 31st had fought well at Chillianwallah, where the 56th had also displayed 'great gallantry', George Malleson judged.[41] The 42nd Light Infantry was acknowledged as one of the army's smartest regiments. Other regiments took a more casual approach to drill, discipline and bearing, crucially dependent upon the dedication of both their European and native officers and their willingness to work together to maintain standards: not all succeeded, or indeed, tried. Some officers, for example, allowed their sepoys 'when marching' to 'wrap … themselves up in cotton clothes … a practice … obviously unmilitary'.[42] It has long been contended that the arrival in the 1840s and 1850s of younger officers, some evangelical Christians, others less inclined to bother to get to know their men, impaired the relationship between sepoys and their European officers. Admonitions in the *Standing Orders* discouraging officers from using 'passionate or abusive terms' to their men and to work to gain their 'attachment and respect' suggest that lack of sympathy became a problem in some regiments: obviously a factor in their men's actions in the mutiny-rebellion in 1857.[43]

A Bengal regiment did not just comprise its fighting men. Every company included what Major John Liptrap, commanding the 42nd, called 'a proportion of public and private followers'—that is, the many servants who saw to the needs of sepoys or their officers.[44] A number of followers—*bhisties*, sweepers and *dhoolie* bearers—served the regiment. Bhisties carried water, sweepers disposed of waste and dhoolie-bearers carried the heavy covered litters for what sepoys called their 'sickmen'. British officers also engaged 'private' servants, up to a dozen for each subaltern, even on campaign, perhaps 25 for senior officers. But sepoys were often men of substantial families—land-holders, often Brahmins; respected figures—and they might employ servants too. Adding the coolies who put up tents and cut firewood, the *mahouts* responsible for its elephants or the *syces* who looked after the officers' horses, a company of a hundred sepoys with one or two European officers could be accompanied by half as many followers—and that was without counting the hangers-on who flocked behind every Company column—Liptrap reported 500 behind his detachments.

Each regiment notionally included some 23 European officers. In practice, ordinarily only about half were ever on duty with it, the rest on sick leave or furlough, or detached to staff or civil positions. In fact, the average number of officers in each of the ten regiments ordered into the field in 1855 was just under 14. Across the Bengal Native Infantry as a whole on the eve of the rebellion, 831 officers were absent; almost exactly the same number, 830, not counting 50 'unposted ensigns' who were present.[45] Officers generally welcomed active service, because it opened up the possibilities of promotion and distinction, and officers at Dinapore, Berhampore and Barrackpore, all 'half-batta' stations, gained extra *batta* (allowances) once in the field. The Bengal Army's system seemed to be calculated to weaken its efficiency. The Company's reluctance to appoint enough civil officials in the Salt, Opium, Customs, Survey, Public Works or other agencies, made the army's European officers a vital source, and as officers detached from their regiments commanded higher salaries and allowances, regiments generally lost out. Extra-regimental service attracted both the ambitious and the avaricious, leaving regiments with apathetic men uninterested in, or incapable of, exertion. Or so it was and has been believed; a new account of the Hul calls that assumption into question.

Many of these men knew or knew of each other—the Hul involved fewer than 200 European military and civil officers—if not actually related. The *East India Register* listed all civil and military officials, and the official gazettes and especially some half-dozen Calcutta newspapers provided a conduit for news and gossip. The position and salary of practically everyone who mattered could easily be discovered. Everyone's business was known to anyone who cared to know. Often names and families would be known on sight, by reputation or by turning a few pages of the *Register*; civil officials, military officers, surgeons or clergymen and their families, could quickly and securely be placed in the complex hierarchy of British Bengal. The names of the Company officers involved in suppressing the Hul constitute a directory of notable British-Indian families: Battye, Couper, Halliday, Loch, Low, Money, Raikes, Tucker, with no less than thirteen Birches listed in the *Bengal Directory*. As the planter and later civil official Edward Braddon put it, British India before 1857 was in the hands of 'a happy family of relations by blood or marriage'; though not so happy, perhaps.[46]

'One of those sudden risings': rebellion in British India

Bengal's garrison occupied a few stations: the Bengal Army, the Calcutta *Citizen* reminded its readers, had been 'pushed on towards the frontier' over the past thirty years.[47] While Lower Bengal had been governed by the Company for ninety years, it remained subject to periodic insurrections. From 'the first formidable peasant uprising' at Dinagepore in 1783, the Company faced resistance to its rule.[48] Though Augustus Cleveland had been praised by the Directors for his pacification of Bhaugulpore in the 1780s, he had been killed by a Paharia or 'hill man' protesting the imposition of the Company's rule. It had faced three insurrections in Orissa since it assumed the rule of that province in 1803, and had conducted two campaigns against hill tribes, as well as what Edward Samuells called 'numerous petty disturbances' between rajahs and the tribal people they ruled, 'which have only been prevented from spreading by threats of military intervention'.[49] Still, Company officials regarded Bengalis as peaceable— indeed, unwarlike if not actually cowardly. They seemed a 'feeble, languid race', the chronicler of the mutiny-rebellion wrote, 'easily intimidated, easily subjected'.[50] But historians of peasant labour and resistance in Bengal identify over a hundred insurgencies in India between the establishment of the Company's rule and the end of the nineteenth century.[51] In Bengal, the precursors of the Santal Hul included rebellion in Midnapore between 1799 and 1832, in Chota Nagpore in 1801 and 1817, in Bareilly in 1816, in Mymemsingh 1825–27 and 1832–33, insurrections in Assam between 1828 and 1830, in the Lushai Hills in 1831–32, Titu Mir's revolt around Baraset in 1830–31, the Kols 1829–32, revolts in Faidpur 1837–48, insurrection in Bundelkhund in the early 1840s and 'discontent' in Behar in 1845–46.[52]

Of these movements the Kol (or 'Cole') rebellion of 1831–32 was to be most influential as a model for Company officials, and the parallels between it and the Santal Hul are striking. This rebellion, among the Mundas, Oraons and other tribal people on the Chota Nagpore plateau, also arose from the 'evil consequences of introducing into an undeveloped tribal area a complex, legalistic administrative system', as its principal (and perhaps only) historian, Jagdish Jha wrote in 1964.[53] The rising, by tribal groups alarmed at the loss of control over their land, caught between alien landlords and unsympathetic Company administrators, broke out late in 1831. With four native infantry regiments deployed against the rebels (including two that were to face the Santals), Company officials secured the Kols' surrender within three months, using a combination of conciliation and aggressive *dours* (patrols or drives).

In 1855 the *Hindoo Patriot* at first dismissed what was at first called the Rajmahal revolt as 'one of those sudden risings … on the frontiers of the Bengal provinces' and nothing that Bengal's British rulers needed to become unduly concerned about.[54] In fact, it was to become the largest, if not the longest, popular armed resistance movement that the Company was to face, with the exception of the great mutiny-rebellion beginning in 1857 which was to spell the end of Company rule. How did it begin?

'To whom could we cry?': the Santal country 1854–55

With the exception of experts like Walter Sherwill and officials such as James Pontet, very few Europeans had much idea of Santal life or culture. Indigo planters knew their Santal labourers, and magistrates heard occasional cases, but Santals hardly impinged upon or were noticed by British Indian society. In 1854, in his report on Bhaugulpore district, Sherwill wrote that virtually every European traveller proceeding up the Ganges passed Rajmahal, but none saw more than the river-side station—many thought that the hills south-west of the town were uninhabited.[55]

The relationship between Santals and those who owned or controlled the land and its people is central to the question of whom the Santals rebelled against and why. In Bengal under Charles Cornwallis's Permanent Settlement and surviving traditional arrangements, a complex range of land tenure and tenancy systems co-existed. Much of the country was under landlords variously called zamindars or rajahs, depending on the size of their holdings and their pretensions; they were mainly high-caste Hindus and by 1855 they numbered about 1800 across the Santal country. Landlords of many kinds held or owned land under various arrangements; tenants paid rent under various customary or legal terms (in money, kind and labour), and the Company collected revenue under a series of arrangements.[56] Some Santal tenants paid the Company directly, through James Pontet, for instance, but most worked holdings under zamindars. The nuances demand a separate study. Crucially, however, even the civil records documenting the insurrection refer to 'zamindars' or 'rajahs' without qualification. In recent decades new zamindars had moved in to Beerbhoom especially, men whom a magistrate wrote had 'by means unknown suddenly risen to great wealth', and gained power over their Santal tenants.[57] The missionary Paul Bodding revealed in his collection of Santal folk tales that 'any landlord is called a raj' often translated as 'king'.[58] Many zamindars had pretensions to being regarded as rajahs, but just a few petty rulers held larger territories, notably the Hindu rajahs or ranees of Hetampore, Beerbhoom, Moheshpore, Luckinpore, Pakaur, and the Muslim Nawab of Moorshedabad, whose lands extended across much of the country west of the Bagirutty River, a distributary of the Ganges, flowing southwards toward Calcutta.

As the historian Ranajit Guha perceptively observed, in contrast to the mythology of insurrection, there was nothing 'spontaneous' about the outbreak of this insurgency.[59] The Santal country in 1854 saw a spate of the robberies and even murders that officials denounced as dacoities, the customary term for organised criminality. Only twelve such incidents occurred, but the surprise was that Santals, regarded as a notably law-abiding people, should commit robberies and assaults by gangs, including manjees and directed at mahajans or zamindars—men known to have oppressed tenants. These were not conventional criminals, but respected leaders, their names known—Doman, Bir Singh, Kaoleh Paramanik. Guha rightly judged that magistrates in Beerbhoom 'mistook rebellion for robbery'.[60] Some were seized and beaten by the zamindars' goons, which, Kali Kinkar Datta wrote, 'goaded them on to more extreme ... reprisals against the money lenders'.[61] One of the innocent men beaten by Mohesh Dutt, the darogah of Dighee, was Gocho, a relatively wealthy Santal who was determined to avenge the injustice. In court, some of those accused of dacoity confessed their guilt, explaining that the 'Bengalee maha-juns' had 'reduced them to beggary'.[62] A Bhaugulpore magistrate realised that such a 'spirit of angry discontent' was out of character for 'the peaceable Sonthals', and judged that the dacoities were 'not the unaided work of a mere gang, but were committed with the coun-sel, consent or connivance of the Sonthal population generally'. His recommendations were ignored.[63] A year later, it became clear, as Frederick Halliday acknowledged, that the dacoities of 1854 'were in fact the commencement of the present insurrection'.[64] While the idea of social banditry lay a century in the future of social history, the example of Robin Hood might even then have suggested itself to Europeans who cared to wonder why the peaceable Santal country had witnessed unprecedented criminality.

Jugia Haram ('Haram' signifying 'old man') recalled about 1871 that 'The money lenders give us little and take a great deal … to whom could we cry?'[65] Santal leaders—their village manjees and the *purgunnaits* representing groups of villages—strove to bring their plight to the attention of Company officials. In August 1854 two man-jees presented George Brown, the Commissioner of Bhaugulpore, with a petition, praying that 'the Mahajuns [be] removed from the Damin, and that we be saved from their claws'. They had presented their memorial (probably paying a Bengali scribe to write it) to an official ten months before the outbreak of the rebellion. 'If we get no protection from Government', they asked, 'what recourse is left to us?' Brown did not act on the petition. In the judgment of a later official investigation, he allowed it to 'lie altogether neglected'. He belatedly sent it to the collector at Bhaugulpore, who sent it on to the magistrate. The magistrate was supposedly 'making preparations' to enquire into it when he learned that the Santals had risen. A marginal notation in red ink on the Board's copy of the investigation refers to Brown's 'extraordinary neglect of duty'.[66] It is hard to disagree: Brown, who had been a prize-winning student at Haileybury, had let 34 years of service sap his initiative.

The end of the hot weather—the month of *Asar* in Santali—was traditionally when men would spend long hours in the fields planting in expectation of the coming monsoon, what Santals called the 'heavy-rain days'. But in the hamlets of the Damin, Santal villagers were in turmoil. The stresses of the oppression of mahajans and zamindars had already generated messianic tendencies, notably near Godda in 1854, when a relatively wealthy Santal, Bir Singh, declared that Chando Bonga, the Santals' principal deity, had appeared to him. Imbued with messianic fervor, Bir Singh took part in the dacoities that preceded the Hul, anticipating the union of religion and rebellion that would so powerfully combine the following year. As the days warmed, fantastic rumours arose—of snakes that swallowed men, and talk of portents swept the villages, so much so that amulets and symbols including a worn out winnowing fan, an old broom; a cow-bell; a bullock hide; a flute, were widely displayed to protect the village from unspecified harm. Durga Tudu, living on the southern fringe of the Damin, heard unsettling talk of a man with heads at each end of his trunk.[67] Women were denounced as witches and leaf cups of oil and vermilion passed from village to village; no one could say why, but villagers believed if the signs were not observed 'something dreadful would happen'.[68] In this maelstrom of supernatural signs, word from Bhugnadihee that a 'Thakur'—a deity—had appeared among them, accompanied by signs, makes explicable the Santals' turmoil. But the unrest in the Santal country, apparent to all but the Company officials responsible for it, led to no sudden outbreak. Even by the end of June 1855 manjees and pergunnaits had been wrangling about their oppression for months, sitting on verandahs and debating their response. Finally, by the last full moon in June talk ended and action began.

PART II

JAPUT (THE MONSOON)

2

SAN (JULY)

The end of the hot weather had seen cities, cantonments and towns somnolent beneath the beating sun, with many sepoys in their home villages on furlough. Now the month was 'attended with much rain … the weather frequently gloomy'.[1] Calcutta's European community pursued a sweaty round of entertainment in the damp heat, listening to Madame Frery's violin soirées in the Town Hall, the New York Serenaders at Dowley's Family Hotel, Garden Reach or, for those with a taste for the grotesque, entertained by the famed 'Indian Dwarf'. Seemingly minor events heralded further change: the Military Consultations sent from Calcutta to London recorded a 'Report on greased cartridges for new rifled muskets', but without comment, unaware of how rumours of the composition of the grease would in time lead to the Bengal Army's trauma, while in Calcutta the Hindu College had just been renamed Presidency College, heralding even greater change. Newspaper subscribers read of Dalhousie's intentions to annexe the kingdom of Oudh for India. And all the while, the rain poured down. 'The rains continue heavy', the *Citizen* reported, with 'copious showers' night and morning.[2]

'This is my authority': the murder of Mohesh Dutta

Four brothers living near Burhyte, at the heart of the Damin, became the instigators and leaders of the rebellion. Landless labourers—their

35

father, a manjee, had lost its land—perhaps they had seen Walter Sherwill when he visited in 1851, or at least heard of him—they lived at Bhugnadihee, just half-a-mile south of Burhyte. The two elder brothers, Sidhu and Kanhu, took the lead in broadcasting the visions they experienced in the hot weather of 1855. Their claim that Thakur Bonga, the great spirit, had repeatedly appeared to them struck a receptive chord among Santals seeking a solution to their plight. Sidhu and Kanhu's speaking for the Thakur qualifies the Santal rebellion to be regarded as what Stephen Fuchs called a 'messianic movement', representing them as 'rebellious prophets'. Indeed, the Santals in 1855 met most—and certainly the most significant—of Fuchs's criteria for identifying 'messianic movements'. They were intensely dissatisfied with their social and economic situation, responded to that situation with 'certain hysterical symptoms', produced charismatic leaders who demanded implicit obedience in pursuit of radical change through violent rebellion, punishing both opponents and traitors.[3]

Kanhu and Sidhu called for Santals to assemble in the valley of Burhyte, a summons that thousands obeyed. A Santal 'spy' (the first of many supposed spies arrested in the rebellion) told Ashley Eden that on the night of the last full moon—Friday 29 June—some 9000 Santals were said to have gathered near Moheshpore, a village which would soon become significant.[4] They had complied with a command from Kanhu, who though not a senior man himself, had addressed manjees authoritatively, even threatening 'if you do not attend, your head will be cut off. Heed these words …'[5] Of the four brothers, Kanhu emerged as the most dominant, closely followed by Sidhu, and they soon achieved a legendary stature among European newspaper writers. (And at least retrospectively among Santals as well—Durga Tudu recalled that 'the two brothers' names … surpassed the names of the others').[6] Their younger brothers, Chand and Bhairab, acted as lieutenants. Ostensibly, they gathered to protest against the punishments inflicted on the 'dacoits' who, it was well known, had acted on behalf of the Santal community and not out of individual greed. None of this, however, was apparent to the Superintendent of the Damin, James Pontet who customarily spent the hot weather and the monsoon in Bhaugulpore, 45 miles away. His bungalow in the Damin was less than a mile from the four brothers' home village, but he had no idea of the Santals' grievances or intentions. The Santal crowds shouted '*Hul! Hul!*' ('Rebel! Rebel!'), but for the moment it was not clear what they rebelled against, or for, and how.[7]

About 1 July at Panchkathia, a bazaar two miles north of Burheyte, a group of Santals murdered no fewer than five mahajans, a crime even the lazy Mohesh Dutta could not ignore. Dutta had been darogah in the Damin for about twenty years—as long as James Pontet had served—and was regarded as 'notoriously corrupt'.[8] He had acted severely and often unjustly against those accused or suspected of dacoity in 1854, and seemed determined to suppress further unrest. With a party of *burkendazes* (village watchmen armed at best with matchlock muskets), he arrived in Panchkathia on the afternoon of Saturday 7 July. There he met a crowd of Santals, at the head of which were several of the brothers who had travelled from Bhugnadihee apparently to worship at a shrine, placing them almost by accident in Dutta's path. They received Dutta civilly at first, but then taunted him and dared him to arrest them. Digambar Chakraborti recorded that Dutta beat the Santals with a dog whip, 'treating them most cruelly and abusing them indiscriminately'.[9] Dutta, surrounded and outnumbered, realized that he had provoked the crowd, sought to pacify them and, seeing that had failed, tried to leave. Jugia Haram said Dutta blustered, demanding to know how the Santals could detain him. 'Where is your permission?' he said, 'Show me your authority'. Sidhu replied, 'This is my authority', and he raised his sword and killed the darogah.[10] Kanhu cut off Dutta's head and the brothers incited the crowd to fall upon the burkendazes. Dutta and up to nine of his men were killed and decapitated.[11]

News of Mohesh Dutta's murder at first travelled on foot and by word of mouth. Two of his men, beaten and bloodied, escaped. They made their way to Bhaugulpore, arriving three days later. They told the Commissioner, George Brown or his functionaries about Sidhu and his brothers, a matter confirmed by reports soon collected by other magistrates.[12] Brown could not at first credit the news, nor the claim that the Santals had 'expressed the determination to seize the country'.[13] George Brown's dilatory response cost the authorities several days, and became another black mark against him during the rebellion. But other officials were also reluctant to believe, let alone act upon, the reports they began to hear from their darogahs. Robert Richardson and James Pontet travelled towards Rajmahal, seemingly the Santals' initial object, on 6 July, but for several days, when other officials began to discuss the news, rumour and hearsay distorted the picture.[14]

'Shall we go or shall we stay?': joining the Hul

Reading the correspondence of officials and military officers responding to the reports of unrest in the Rajmahal Hills, Halliday remained confident: 'I do not see any reason to believe that the rising is anything but a local one.'[15] By the accounts gathered by Digambar Chakraborti, the events of the following week showed that the Hul was, in fact, anything but a local rebellion. The Santals gathered around Burhyte 'became greatly excited', as Chakraborti wrote with a degree of understatement. They first went to nearby Kusma and looted the village, then flocked south to Litipara. Here they killed more of their oppressors. The village's two mahajans (who were brothers) escaped, leaving behind their *gomasta* (agent), who was notorious for 'exercising inhuman cruelties' on the brothers' debtors.[16] The Santals killed him, and moved on Heerampore, on the track to Pakaur. There the brothers met a manjee named Tribhuban, who joined the rising. To the sound of drums, the leaders debated their next move, the Thakur inspiring the brothers and their growing band of followers. They looted Heerampore: 'this news soon spread everywhere', as a Bengali source put it.[17]

Just ten miles to the east of Bhugnadihee was the railway being built running due north-south between Calcutta and Rajmahal. Within days of the outbreak, Santals were threatening its Bengali and Santal labourers, and plundering and burning the bungalows of its European engineers and supervisors. A 'Rajmahal Railway correspondent' wrote to the *Citizen* to report that 'they threaten to behead any man who will lift a stone for us', and reportedly had carried out their threat.[18] Santals joined the rebellion, whether willingly or, as one source had it, 'come out, a man from each house, and go and fight'— in other words, had been virtually conscripted.[19] Chotrae Desmanjhi described how once Sidhu and Kanhu led a force to loot Moheshpore, the manjees Mani and Ram also 'raised an army and went to loot Narainpore', near Rampore Haut. Desmanjhi, from Benagaria, about ten miles west of Rampore Haut seems to have become a part of this force. Conversations between civil officials and 'natives' threw out hints that not all Santals joined the Hul by choice. When Octavius Toogood addressed a group of men near Burhyte, he warned them of their 'folly' in joining in rebellion. One man explained that 'they were obliged to obey'; they had no choice but to accept a decision made by their communities, as theirs was a culture strongly bound by tradition and unaccustomed to individual decisions.[20]

Increasingly, Santals across the Damin and soon beyond faced a fateful choice. A Santal song captured this moment of decision, so ominous for the Santals, individually, for their communities and as a people:

Sahib rule is trouble full,
Shall we go or shall we stay?
Eating, drinking, clothing,
For everything we are troubled;
Shall we go or shall we stay?[21]

Most apparently decided to join the Hul, possibly to march to Calcutta to seek an audience with 'the great *Firingee Sahib*'— Dalhousie—asking why he allowed money-lenders to rob and harass the Santals, or to seek more immediate redress.[22] The next day the throng moved on to Mahadebpur, just twenty miles from Burhyte. Here they debated their actions again, while thousands more Santals joined them, through word of mouth of the brothers' defiance of Dutta. At Mahadebpur they invoked the spirit of the Thakur and Chando Bonga, the inspired ones declaring that any enemies' musket-balls would turn to water. Strengthened by this reassurance, they hailed Sidhu and Kanhu as their leaders, contributed a mass of pice (small coins) to fund the rebellion, and again set out southwards and eastwards, toward Pakaur, where the story Chakraborti told came from sources within his extended family.

As the Santals neared Pakaur, the Rajbati, the house of the Ranee, Khema Sundaree Debi, became a refuge. A large green-shuttered edifice, it resembled in a minor way the huge mock-Georgian palace of the Nawab of Moorshedabad, complete with classical pediment.

Crowds of dependents swarmed into it seeking shelter. Servants piled stones on the roof to deter attack, and the mahout, Roshan, was sent off to buy gunpowder for the few firearms they could muster. That night, the frightened retainers gave way to despair, especially after Roshan returned with the powder which had turned to pulp in the rain and told them that he could do little to resist. Chakraborti conveyed the flavour of the stories he remembered hearing within his family:

> Then there arose loud wailings of the females, children shrieked and screamed, men talked non-sense, and rushed hither and thither ... no one cared for the old, infirm and the sickly. There was tying and untying of bundles, everything turned up side down and mixed up helterskelter ...[23]

As he had been a child of six and among the ranee's dependents, it is likely that Chakraborti was describing a scene he had been a part of. Meanwhile, the inhabitants of Pakaur unable to claim the ranee's protection became the first of hundreds of thousands of Bengali villagers forced by the Santals' imminent arrival to flee, crossing the flooded countryside to the east.

The insurgent Santals hesitated before entering Pakaur, the first real town they had encountered; perhaps the first pukka (solid) buildings some had ever seen besides Mr Pontet's bungalow in Burhyte, which they had burned and looted. The Rajbati, two storeys high and defended by desperate retainers, especially deterred them. At last, Sidhu and Kanhu led their followers toward it, by which time its terrified occupants had fled. Santals looted what they could find, hacking to pieces an abandoned bed-ridden invalid reportedly, a sign of the ferocity into which Santal crowds could fall, freed from the restraint under which they customarily lived. Chakraborti recorded other accounts of brutality—a blacksmith shot out of a tamarind tree with arrows and then beheaded; a Hindu mendicant dragged from his hiding place and killed; two Muslim fakirs caught while cooking their dinner and killed by arrows. The insurgents took to plundering and then burning every village they came to, their paths marked by pillars of smoke arising from the dozens of villages that lay in every direction on the fertile river flats below the hills. A rare Bengali source, a ballad written in 1855, describes the Santal descent on Nagore, when they 'with cheerful hearts ... cut off the heads of about 40 or 50 men'.[24] But amid this terror, inexplicably, the Santals also gave rice and some coins to two old women whom they found abandoned.[25] Narahari Kaviraj added that Santals had been joined by 'large bodies of Mals, Dhenooks and other low castes', though how many and what contribution they made is unknown.[26]

At this point an incident occurred that suggested the complex nature of the rising and how it unleashed individual and collective forces unconnected to the Santals' cause. Once the Santals appeared to have left, Dindayal Roy, the diwan, essentially the Pakaur ranee's chancellor, described as 'a corpulent old man', returned to the town, proclaiming that as his master had fled he was now the Zamindar of Ambar (or Umbar, as Pakaur was also confusingly called). Roy brought with him his enforcers, 'four demons in human shape', who resumed their abuse of Pakaur's resident Santals. Roy, looking forward to enjoying the life of a zamindar, took his brother, Nanda Kumar and his sister, Bimala Debee, to bathe one morning in one of the tanks still to be seen east of Pakaur. There Nanda Kumar saw cattle running at a distance, and wondered if they had been startled, perhaps by a tiger. 'Let me finish my bath', Dindayal said. Then Nanda realized that a party of Santals had disturbed the cattle, perhaps a group returning from attacking a nearby indigo factory. Bimala and Nanda were able to escape, but Dindayal was too fat. The Santals caught him: his protective 'demons' were nowhere to be found. Chakraborti described how Santals tortured and killed Dindayal Roy in the Pakaur Kali temple where he had sought refuge, setting dogs on him, cutting off the fingers with which he had counted money, before burning him to death.

The murder of Dindayal Roy became one of the emblematic episodes of the Hul, retold in essence even by those who had never heard of Roy and his part in the oppression of the ranee's Santal tenants. The story exists in numerous versions, but all included the element that the Santals, taking revenge for the mahajan's exactions, turned his death into a grotesque parody of the repayment of a debt, with the victim representing all the mahajans the Santals killed. Having hacked off his arms, they cried out '*Sike eUsul*': a quarter of the debt had been paid. Then they chopped off one of his legs: '*Adha Usul*'—a half; and

41

so on until they beheaded him: '*Farkhat*', all debts paid. Then they placed Roy's head in a niche in a temple—Chakraborti claimed to have seen the dried blood forty years later. All of this Bimala Debee saw, hiding in a nearby ditch. The ordeal seems to have unhinged her—Chakraborti recalled seeing her slash about with a stick, crying '*Farkhat, Farkhat*'.[27] The manner of Roy's death, shocking as it was, became generalised. Lewis O'Malley, the author of the gazetteer of the Santal Parganas, wrote that 'when a *mahajan* fell into their hands, they first cut off his feet …', adding that vengeful Santals betrayed a 'savage sense of humour' by cutting up a zamindar into 22 parts, 'one for each of his ancestors'.[28] Whether such brutal executions were usual is uncertain: no one documented these deaths, but their savagery struck all those who knew the Santal as utterly incongruous. Reflecting on the Hul later, the *Calcutta Review*'s anonymous author could only invoke the idea that Santals went 'mad with long-suppressed passions and the thirst of the blood they had tasted'; and nearly 170-odd years later, no more satisfactory explanation emerges from the evidence.[29]

Here, with the Santal host going in different directions, the narrative must also divide. Gocho Santal, who had led Santal dacoits in avenging the mahajans' imposts in 1854, and Tribhuban who had urged the brothers to rebel, led parties westward and southward, toward Beerbhoom and the southern purgunnahs of Bhaugulpore, where the Hul was to end six months later. The brothers led the largest force southwards toward Moheshpore, the residence of another of the region's larger landowners. Santal movements and actions can only be traced through the official and unofficial reports, published and unpublished, recorded by Europeans. According to reports collated by the third week of July, the Hul seemed 'much more formidable than it appeared at the beginning'. According to magistrates and newspaper reports, Santal forces threatened all of the major stations in the region: Rajmahal facing a force of 20,000, Pakaur 10,000; isolated indigo factories besieged; Jungeypore encircled; Aurungabad and Moorshedabad in danger of being sacked; a force within eighteen miles of Sooree.[30] The Calcutta newspapers' 'Mofussil News' columns printed the first notices of what the *Morning Chronicle* called 'terrific doings' near 'the beautiful Station of

Rajmahal', where several thousand 'insurgents' had 'made the place perfectly desolate', killing indiscriminately.[31] In fact, Rajmahal had not been sacked, but the report was the first of hundreds to appear documenting the rebellion over the next six months.

'Read the savages a lesson': European civilian volunteers

The Santal country over-lapped Bengal's indigo growing areas, so indigo planters were among the Europeans directly affected. For twenty years, since the Company had opened land in Bengal to British-born purchasers, it had produced the dye-stuff indigo, and growing and processing it had become 'a most troublesome and hazardous speculation'.[32] European planters stood accused of coercing peasants into unfavourable contracts and setting cripplingly low prices, allegations which would precipitate conflict in a 'Blue Mutiny' in a few years.[33] Expressing their detestation of foreign landlords, Santal bands attacked and destroyed indigo factories in the rebellion's opening weeks. The outbreak, as Edward Braddon later recalled, came 'as a complete surprise' to him and his fellow planters who though living in Bengal disdained 'to study the native races or differentiate them'. News that Santals approached came 'as something wholly unintelligible ... We might just as well have been told that a Jabberwok was around.'[34]

As Pakaur burned, a small force seems to have broken off the Santal main body to venture towards Charles Maseyk's indigo factory at Kuddamshaw, about five miles south-east of Pakaur. As they moved eastwards from the outbreak's origin in the Rajmahal Hills, Santal bands either made for, or found themselves close to, indigo factories. Most of their owners, if present (many spent as much time as they could in Calcutta) had fled to the river towns; but several owners remained, strengthening their bungalows and outbuildings. Some accepted the mutual aid of railway engineers whom they had come to know during the line's construction, and armed their own workers, unless they too had not hastily left. John Mudge, an engineer, had been at Pakaur when on 8 July he heard from one of his assistants of turmoil at Burhyte. He was one of the first Europeans to learn of the outbreak. At first, he disregarded rumours that Santals were planning to murder all Europeans, because he thought them 'the most cowardly race of beings', but when he learned of the killing of Mohesh Dutta, he mustered his Bengali labourers, numbering nearly a thousand, and asked them to stand with him. Then came word that a railway bungalow had been burned, and his labourers, probably armed only with their tools, deserted him, leaving just fifteen Europeans, who hastily shifted to the Maseyks' 'Indigo Concern' at nearby Kuddamshaw.[35] Mudge was among the 'Railway chaps' who had considered fortifying one of Maseyk's go-downs (warehouses) but thought the better of it and fled. They made their way along the line to Pulsa, packing their belongings but no boats could be had: 'so here we were in a fix …'. Mudge and his companions swam across a flooded river, losing everything, then walking 20-odd miles in nothing but a flannel jacket and a pair of jack-boots. Helped by indigo planters and villagers, they eventually met troops marching from Aurungabad and went with them back to Pulsa, where Mudge found his bungalow and all his possessions looted and burned. He lost his papers, several hundred books, all his instruments, a thousand cigars and all the stores which had just been delivered. He gratefully joined Walter Birch's column, demonstrating the solidarity Europeans manifest in the crisis. It brought together civil officials and indigo planters socially as never before. Formerly officials had tended to disdain planters. One of them once complained that in a Bengal civil station, officials mixed only with 'a knot of three or four individuals of the Civil service, who form the little self-laudatory coterie'.[36]

The Maseyk brothers, whose forebears had come from the Netherlands a century before, adventurously reaching India overland from Aleppo, owned several indigo factories. Undeterred by the railwaymen's departure, Charles Maseyk 'displayed great strength and presence of mind', an admirer reported from Berhampore, providing boats to help refugees from Pakaur cross the flooded flats that now mark the border between Jharkhand and West Bengal. He had kept a boat ready for himself on a creek leading to Jungeypore, about eight miles distant. When he saw perhaps 500 rebels approaching his bungalow, he realised that defending it would be impossible. He boarded the boat and with a few 'companions' (his servants had fled) fired at the Santals from midstream, killing four or five and somehow even capturing one, driving the attackers off and saving his factory. Soon, on 13 July, a party of the 7th Native Infantry arrived to protect the factory. Admiring word of Maseyk's stand of 'a few Englishmen armed with fowling pieces' soon spread among the European residents up and down the Bagirutty.[37]

Indigo planters and 'Railway chaps' bolstered European military prowess, especially in eastern Bhaugulpore around Skreekond and Rajmahal, and along the railway line under construction. Thacker's *Bengal Directory* listed 27 engineers in the disturbed districts in 1855, and that number did not include surveyors, accountants, clerks or various managers. While some planters and engineers, especially those with families, decamped hurriedly, those who remained made an important contribution. The planters, often employing Santal labourers or farmers, were able to pass to magistrates hints about the Santals' frame of mind, while the railway gentlemen were able to act as scouts. One of them was William Taylor 'a young railway engineer', the son of a Bengal Engineer, whom Octavius Toogood praised in the rebellion's first month.[38]

A 'force of European Gentlemen' remained in and defended the Rajmahal.[39] Led by Robert Richardson, the magistrate, with James Pontet, several 'Railway gents' and the planter Edward Braddon, a dozen British civilians patrolled the approaches to the town armed with revolvers, rifles and hogspears, later praised for having 'kept Rajmahal clear of these vermin'.[40] The energy of a young engineer, fittingly named Tom Vigors, who fortified his bungalow (an old Mughal palace) and by the sheer visibility of his resistance was regarded as having deterred Santals from approaching the town.[41] Civilians attracted plaudits for their plucky conduct: one defended a bungalow for 'weeks', another 'protected an entire station', a third 'raised a force of fifty men … and read the savages a lesson'.[42]

Indigo planters like Charles Barnes became especially useful. Unlike railwaymen, they knew the country and spoke its languages, including Santali, because they employed many Santals, and they had a stake in suppressing disorder. Barnes, whose factory near Pealpore was among the first destroyed by the Santals, became 'of the utmost service', providing the troops with supplies and carriage and, most of all, with information.[43] Barnes was such an asset that Alfred Bidwell wanted to appoint him as an assistant starting with two months' salary although as an uncovenanted servant at only two-thirds of the covenanted rate. Barnes, however, preferred his freedom and declined to become a servant of the Company.[44] The non-official European community displayed a hostility to well-paid officials, as the *Citizen*'s criticism of 'Commissioners, Amlahs, Mofussil court pimps and every other procrastinating abomination' suggests.[45] However, Edward Braddon found working with civil officers more congenial, and he became a district official during and after the rebellion. He later recorded that he found fighting Santals 'a splendid substitute for … tiger shooting'.[46]

Familiar with the country and its people, planters and long-standing unofficial residents, who often already abused and beat their servants without restraint or sanction, had little compunction in mistreating Santals. 'We have great fun when a Santal falls into our hands', one of them admitted to a man from Raneegunge who subsequently wrote to a newspaper. The former had captured three Santals that morning 'and the hauling and mauling they got, they will never forget'.[47] Were these men actually rebels—very few rebels got close to Raneegunge—or did they suffer merely because they were Santals?

Living in exposed and isolated stations, a few European civilians fell victim to Santal attacks. Lawrence Braddon, a railwayman, was caught by a Santal band while crossing a swamp with three others near Peer Pointee, just south of the Ganges. As his elephant became mired, 'fanatical Savages' swarmed onto the animal and decapitated not only him but also, with more difficulty, the elephant, or so it was said by the survivors, who reached the river and crossed to safety.[48] Other victims included, near Aurungabad, an indigo planter named Henshawe and his two sons, attacked while travelling on elephants to villages in which their labourers lived, to reassure them. They ran into a party of 2000 Santals when, deserted by their armed followers, they were 'suddenly surrounded', their elephants either alarmed at the tumult or possibly bogged in soft ground. The Santals killed the father and one son and the two were 'pierced from head to shoulder' by arrows.[49] When the other son turned back to help, he too was killed. They may also have been decapitated and the victorious Santals were said to have drunk their blood or smeared it over their bodies. In that all three Henshawes died, the accounts of their deaths can only have come from Bengali witnesses. 'This is very revolting if true', the writer concluded. Santals 'deserve no mercy'.[50]

Within weeks it was reported that two European women had been murdered and possibly abducted by Santals, again in western Moorshedabad. A letter from Purneah, which is far from the scene, claimed that a Mrs Thomas had been 'shot and cut in pieces' in an attack which left her husband severely wounded, and her sister-in-law, a Miss Pell, abducted; perhaps murdered.[51] Gruesome rumours circulated: that their hands had been cut off while they lived; that they had been roasted alive.[52] The report of murder seemed correct and the perpetrator was reportedly arrested, but the abduction was never verified.

The ordeals of the rebellion's European victims excited remarkably little interest or sympathy at the time, even among Calcutta's relatively small European community. When 'A Citizen' proposed a fund for [European] sufferers, 'H.M.' riposted 'who in the name of goodness is interested in the poor sufferers by the Santhal insurrection?'[53] This indifference was all the more marked because Bengal's European community had donated a huge amount for the relief of families of British troops killed or incapacitated in the Crimea. Given the reaction, in India, Britain and across the empire, to the massacre and supposed outrage of European women in 1857, the lack of response to the report that 'A Mrs Thomas and her sister have been butchered' is perplexing.[54] Though the report was 'no rumour', the press reaction to the death and possible abduction of the two women was muted. Indeed, once the story reached Britain, *Punch* published a purportedly humorous item, discussing the supposedly abducted Miss Pell as 'Mabel the Mildewed' and claiming that she existed only in 'the misty imagination of some foggy paragraph-monger for the Indian Newspapers'.[55] The absence of evidence is puzzling.

'No cause for this rise': why did the Santals rebel?

The rebellion began in the Rajmahal Hills 'like a sudden thunderstorm', an apposite metaphor as monsoon rains swept across the country practically every day for the first few months.[56] Within three weeks, in one of the fortnightly 'special narratives' which formed the basis of the official advice forwarded to the Supreme Council and to the Company's directors in London, William Grey described the Santals' 'ferocious barbarity', the 'frightful devastation' they had inflicted and the 'immense plunder' they had gathered, explaining that their aim seemed to be 'to set up a Rajah' and to that end 'immediately to exterminate the Europeans and the Bengalees' to become 'rulers of the country'.[57]

What did the Santals seek to achieve by rising? The 'spy' Ashley Eden questioned told him that 'at the order of a God' they intended to kill all Europeans and native rulers and install a king. Eden's reliability, however, maybe open to question. While an official appointed to a district in Lower Bengal in 1849 might be expected to have some knowledge of Bengali, Eden had yet to pass his Hindoostanee examination, and may not have understood even basic Santali.[58] Living among Hindus as they did, however, many Santals spoke or could understand Hindoostanee or Bengali. Within days George Brown at Bhaugulpore had heard that the Santals were 'revenging the punishment inflicted on their Comrades concerned in last year's Dacoities'.[59] But no one understood that the uprising represented an intensification of what social historians following Eric Hobsbawm would later call 'social banditry'.[60] The *Hindoo Patriot* discounted any suggestion that they could have any political agenda beyond freedom from 'revenue officials, landlords and European blackguards'—the latter referring to indigo planters and railway contractors.[61]

James Pontet, who as superintendent of the Damin lived for some of the year in Burhyte and could be expected to understand them, was spectacularly wrong a month after the Hul's outbreak in declaring that there was 'no cause for this rise but a mistaken religious one'.[62] Pontet was an 'uncovenanted' officer; that is, he was paid much less than the well-connected, Haileybury-trained covenanted officials superior to him. He had served in the Damin-i-koh for twenty-odd years but was not noted for energy or initiative. Revenue from rents certainly had increased, though not from his efforts but by the huge increase in the Santal population, by both births and by the arrival of further migrants most from Chota Nagpore. A damning return in the Judicial Consultations revealed that in his legal capacity as the grand-sounding Moonsiff of the Damin, he had dealt with just two cases since his appointment in March 1855.[63] A Judicial Department investigation in 1856 judged that Pontet had 'wilfully neglected' his duties.[64] He certainly did not cultivate sympathy with the Santals' predicament: when a deputation had asked him to intercede because of the money-lenders' exactions, he told them, harshly and unhelpfully that they had 'eaten the mahajuns' advances'. 'What could he do?' he asked helplessly.[65]

Some officials, claiming a familiarity with Santals dismissed the Hul as 'the impulse of the moment', as Edward Samuells put it.[66] Did they know of the disquiet in the Santal country before the outbreak? Vasudha Dhagamwar, in her study of Santals and the law, suggests that officials' swift responses implies that they had known of Santal grievances but had dismissed them.[67] Before the end of July, though, Santal leaders near Rajmahal had sent to Robert Richardson a 'perwunnah'—a message or manifesto—which revealed more clearly the motivations behind the insurrection. 'An old woman' came to Richardson's *cutcherry* (magistrate's office) bearing a document written in Hindoostanee, revealing that Santal leaders had literate supporters. Probably dictated by Kanhu or Sidhu, it ordered Europeans to 'quit this part of the Country at once or take the consequences'. They condemned the mahajans' exactions and oppression, called for rents to be based on a family's capacity to pay and the productivity of their plot, and asserted the Santals' dream of freedom: 'the land does not belong to the sahebs', it stated. Achieving that end would involve conflict—'it will rain fire', they warned—but the Santals were fortified by sorcery: 'when you fight with guns and bullets, they will not strike the Sonthals'.[68]

Richardson decried this 'free and easy Document'—that is, one not couched in the respectful terms usual in communicating with Company officials. But it confirmed that neither the impositions and insults of railway workers nor the 'extra screw' demanded by James Pontet's rents were at the heart of the Santal cause. However imperfect was Richardson's translation, as one of the few authentic Santal documents it deserves to be noted. Other reports flowed in to magistrates' cutcherries and newspaper editors' offices, always at least several or more days late, often tinged with alarm, speculation, wishful thinking or rumour, and never in such detail as to enable comprehensive analysis. Officials paying attention both to what they picked up from questioning villagers and prisoners began to realise that the Hul was not just a product of religious fervor.

One of the most frequent explanations at first was that some men from the railway had abused Santals, and especially women. It was said that 'Mr Thomas, [the husband of the murdered Mrs Thomas] had 'misbehaved' with Santal women: Narahari Kaviraj's prudish terminology might explain Mrs Thomas's death.[69] 'The principal cause', asserted a correspondent from Sooree in mid-July, 'is oppressive treatment by the … contractors' assistant[s] … and the debauchment of their women'.[70] James Pontet endorsed this explanation which conveniently deflected the blame from his own regime in the Damin. A newspaper letter dismissed this explanation as 'absurd', asking how 'isolated cases of ill-usage'—accepting that they occurred—could possibly 'drive a large tribe into rebellion'.[71] Indeed, abuse by railway employees proved not to be a cause of the outbreak, though the allegation remained popular among those seeking a pretext. Itinerant workers, both native and European, had indeed harassed Santal women, but not sufficiently to explain rebellion on such a scale.

The 'Santhal war' became 'the topic of the day', in the Calcutta papers joining columns of news from the more distant theatre of war in the Crimea.[72] (Though the *Friend of India* thought that its readers knew more about the siege of Sebastopol than 'the revolt raging at our own doors').[73] From the earliest reports of rebellion in the Rajmahal Hills, newspaper reports speculated about the rebels' motives. The Santals had been described by those who knew them as truthful, uxorious, faithful, hospitable and above all peaceful. What had happened to induce them to rise so bloodily? Newspaper reports fostered intense speculation.

From the first days of the Hul, believing Santals to be, as Ashley Eden put it, 'a very simple people', Europeans suspected that they must 'have been put up to this'.[74] Many letters to newspapers continued to speculate that the outbreak had been engineered by external agents. *The Times* even imagined 'a suspicion of Nepaulese gold', a speculation supposedly corroborated by reports of a 'flat-nosed man' seen among a group of Santals.[75] The rumour acquired 'the shape of a confirmed report' but, a correspondent warned, it 'must be received with great caution'.[76] Others saw 'the Nagpore Ranees' behind the Hul—minor Hindu rulers had supposedly pawned their jewels to pay the rebels, though why no one could say.[77] It was rumoured—on no better evidence than that horse tracks had been found—that Armenians were advising the Santals: but why would they? Or were they Russian, taking revenge for Crimean defeats, as Sergeant Joseph Cheers had heard in far-off Sealkote, though, as even the *Friend of India* conceded, who among the Santals was sufficiently influential to be worth bribing?[78]

The most persistent rumour concerned the former Emir of Scinde, Meer Abass Khan, who had been exiled after resisting the Company's conquest of his domains during the previous decade and now lived in a modest palace in Hazaribagh, in Behar. The hapless George Brown dutifully passed on to William Grey that he had heard that Santal leaders were in communication with the emir, and included the text of a message ostensibly from Sidhu to the emir dated two days before the initial outbreak.[79] It was of course a mischievous forgery, but Brown knew that each year the emir employed hundreds of Santals as beaters in his hunting expeditions, and guessed that he would be motivated by an understandable desire to avenge his humiliation by fomenting rebellion. This was plausible, but absolutely groundless. The rumour recurred throughout the next six months, sometimes bolstered by spurious supposed facts and claims to infallible sources. That George Brown had passed it on in the first place probably buttressed his reputation for mis-judgment in Fort William. After being repeatedly investigated the allegation was eventually proved to be 'totally without foundation'.[80] But if the Santals were not rebelling because they were put up to it, why had they risen?

'And rule ourselves': the Santals' cause

Of the thousands of words published in debating the causes of the uprising, virtually all were written in English and overwhelmingly by Europeans. One of three surviving Santal memoirs was recorded by Chotrae Desmanjhi, who was about fifteen in 1855:

> Sido and Kanhu spread it abroad that we should give 8 annas per buffalo plough and 4 annas per bullock plough ... and if the Government

51

did not accept these terms we should begin to fight; we should kill the unspeakable Deko [Dikkus: foreigners] and rule ourselves.[81]

This, a succinct statement of the Santals' political program, remained obscure to Europeans at the time, for want of evidence, lack of reliable informants and prejudiced assumptions. None of these distorted perceptions remain relevant. It is now clear that as a community across several districts, Santals felt the weight of economic oppression and, mobilised by religious rhetoric, sought redress. Exactly how and from whom remained for the time being uncertain, both for Europeans and for Santals themselves. Whether the Santal desire for justice extended beyond the idea of proposing more equitable rents is debatable. Narahari Kaviraj claimed that the Santals 'did their best to run a regular government', but the evidence does not support the claim.[82]

The Santals' resentment of zamindars and rajahs meant that their first victims were the landlords who farmed the peasants to meet Company officials' demands for revenue, the foundation of Bengal's value under the Permanent Settlement over the previous sixty years. In his later statements, when interrogated by officials, Kanhu made plain against whom the Hul was primarily directed:

> the Zemindars and Mahajuns oppressed the Santhals so much which made them rebel and kill all the Zemindars.[83]

While most of the 'rajahs' in the Santal country were little more than wealthy landowners with more pretension to their titles than longevity in holding them—like the Santals they too were mostly immigrants—the disturbed districts included the western domains of the Nawab of Moorshedabad, the much diminished successor to the rulers of Bengal under the Mughals and who had been ousted and neutered by Clive's conquest. The nawab, sustained by extensive estates, lived in a vast European palace, the 'Hazaduari', so-called for its supposed thousand doors. The 25-year-old nawab, Mansur Ali Khan, heard news of the Hul with increasing concern: a Moorshedabad correspondent recorded that the nawab was 'very much frightened' at the prospect of Santals storming his palace.[84] The Company agent who 'advised' the nawab pressed him to provide 200 of his sepoys and 40 elephants to support the Company's forces. With reports of

13,000 Santals massing on the plain across the Bagirutty river which his palace overlooked, his highness was happy to comply.[85] The nawab's relations with the Company were delicate: the two were engaged in a protracted and complex wrangle—he pressed 'numerous grievances' in a dispute over money, honours and illegalities going back forty years—and the nawab saw both short and long term advantages in supporting the Company.[86] The smaller rajahs and zamindars living on their estates across the Santal country also had much to fear, and through July stories emerged of zamindars' houses looted and burned and their occupants killed. The Hul upset accepted notions and sanctions, symbolised perhaps by the incident when rebellious Santals killed and ate tigers in the ruler of Moheshpore's hunting reserves, a prospect a European witness described as 'most repulsive': tigers provided trophies, not meals.[87]

The other major target of Santal resentment were the mahajans, the merchants, mostly Bengalis, who had lived among them and exploited them. While Company officers found evidence of indiscriminate Santal violence toward Bengali villagers, Santals seeking retribution looked for particular victims, burning and looting the houses of mahajans but also leaving peasants, even Bengali Hindus toward whom they were antagonistic, unscathed.[88] The historian Sugata Bose saw 'the deliberate decision not to attack the non-tribal poor' as an expression of the Santals' class solidarity with fellow exploited peasants.[89] Many villagers, of course, did not wait to see if they would be spared and fled.

'Panic': the wider European response

Early estimates—actually guesses—of the numbers of Santals advancing from the Rajmahal Hills to the north, north-west, east, south-east and south were at first huge—estimated at over 20,000 and even 40,000. These immense columns could at first be opposed by fewer than a thousand armed men—perhaps 300 of the Bhaugulpore Hill Rangers, 300 regulars of the 7th Native Infantry, 168 of Ashley Eden's collected burkundazes and 200 sepoys provided by the Nawab of Moorshedabad. Eden asked his colleague 'what could 168 burkendazes avail?' They would be 'utterly useless': 'the affair is more serious than I at first supposed'.[90] But obtaining any reports from the disturbed districts was complicated by the dawks (posts) being stopped: as a Monghyr correspondent complained,the insurrection had 'played the devil with the dawks'.[91] As late as September officials complained of disruption to the posts, because the Santals 'ill used the runners'.[92] Though largely ignorant of Santal movements and certainly of their intentions, while awaiting the arrival of troops, magistrates summoned the darogahs and their few burkendazes, and asked zamindars to arm retainers in expectation of attack. Edward Man, one of the first chroniclers of the rebellion, averred that by promptly requisitioning armed men from the zamindars on the right bank of the Bagirutty, Ashley Eden had turned back Santal masses and had saved western Moorshedabad district from devastation.[93] If so, the deliverance was both fortuitous and temporary, and the claim a product of Man's admiration for Eden.

Newspapers implied that officials knew of the planned outbreak but had 'made no preparations'. It was said that Robert Richardson failed to take seriously the first accounts of unrest in the Rajmahal Hills, because 'reports had not reached him officially'.[94] Though at first reluctant to act upon what they called 'demi-official' advice— chits or notes from indigo planters and railway officials—once their police officers made clear to the magistrates closest to the reported outbreaks what had happened near Burhyte, they acted with commendable celerity. On 9 July Robert Richardson called out the Bhaugulpore Hill Rangers and Ashley Eden at Auraungabad summoned troops from Berhampore, and sent off 'expresses'—letters carried by mounted sowars or riders—to officials in neighbouring districts, and of course to William Grey, the Secretary to the Government of Bengal, in Fort William. In the criss-crossing network of belt-and-braces correspondence usual in Bengal, Grey immediately wrote to Colonel Henry Templer, the commandant at Berhampore, asking him to 'place any troops which may be deemed necessary at the disposal of the Magistrates' to 'act in aid of the Civil Authorities ... as circumstance will dictate'.[95] These formal exchanges hint at the delicacy of the administrative relationship upon which Company rule depended, especially in a crisis. Civil officers were to direct responses, but armed force remained under military officers. The balance between the two was to dominate the Company response to the growing insurrection.

As the Collector responsible for Bhaugulpore, the district in which the outbreak occurred, George Brown's decisions became crucial. He firstly asked Major Frederick Burroughs, the new commander of the Bhaugulpore Hill Rangers, to send a force to Rajmahal, but soon after demanded that they defend only the station of Bhaugulpore. 'Mr Brown's stoppage of troops' was only one of his mistakes. 'The Bhaugulpore folks' were described as exhibiting 'a state of great alarm', an anxiety Brown surely communicated and exacerbated.[96] In August William Grey called Brown to account for his ill-considered actions, in withholding troops to protect a station not actually in danger. Challenged to explain why he had claimed he needed 'a whole regiment' to defend a station never threatened let alone attacked, he could only reply lamely that he was 'not conscious of having despatched such a message'. He now realised that the lieutenant-governor considered that he had 'spread an exaggerated idea of the power of the Sonthals'. Brown was right to entertain fears of Halliday's 'unfavourable opinion of my conduct'.[97]

Unusually, Brown acted on his own initiative, possibly because of the difficulty of communicating with Calcutta. He sent some of his despatches 100 miles up the Ganges, then going the long way by land and taking a week to arrive. He issued a proclamation on 18 July, translated into Bengali (but not Santali, because its written form post-dated the rebellion). He condemned the 'great insurrection' which, he admitted 'increases daily' and mentioned the deaths of Mohesh Dutta and 'several European gentlemen and ladies, besides innumerable Natives'. He professed that the government was ready to redress Santal grievances but deplored the crimes of 'a race so ferocious and savage who do not understand the difference between right and wrong and care not for the orders of established authority'. Brown then transgressed one of the cardinal rules of the Company's financial administration by offering rewards of Rs 10,000 for 'whoever shall seize the leader of the Rebellion' and smaller sums for the apprehension of Santal 'counsellors' and 'pretended rajahs', but without authorisation from the Company. He then committed a further grave error of judgment by proclaiming that Bengali villagers were free to 'as a matter of self defence, kill them [Santals] as they would a Tiger or a Bear'. Though warning that 'the Government does not wage war with women and children', George Brown had nevertheless sanctioned the slaughter of Santals regardless of whether they were actually in rebellion or not.[98] This extraordinary lapse would end his career.

The proclamation, the Supreme Council decided, had been 'substantially unlawful'. John Peter Grant explained that 'it officially told the people that Govt was prepared to exterminate a race (i.e. the whole tribe of Santals)'. As many Santals had not joined the Hul it condemned innocent people to the prospect of being killed by alarmed Bengali neighbours; such an incitement to communal discontent was to be avoided. Grant was certain that Brown, 'a worthy and benevolent gentleman' had not intended such an outcome, but 'a competent Commissioner could not have issued such a proclamation'.[99]

Though Joseph Dorin had been Brown's exact contemporary at Haileybury, the relationship did not help. Brown naturally contested the charges but Halliday reiterated his censure, that Brown had displayed a 'distracted and unbalanced state of mind … absence of self-possession and calm judgment'.[100] After ten days deliberating—dismissing a Commissioner was no light matter—Dorin and the other members came to an agreement and suggested to Halliday that Brown be dismissed. Typically, Halliday prevaricated before finally sacking Brown, who had refused to make the matter easier for the government by simply resigning. Brown pursued his dismissal into 1856, without result: Dalhousie's successor, George Canning, confirmed his fate.[101]

But George Brown's alarm was only the more extreme manifestation of an anxiety many officials shared. Within a week the Supreme Council decided that it would be prudent to reinforce the military force in the disturbed districts, despite the monsoon authorising the despatch of artillery and cavalry. Since Dalhousie was in Madras, the Governor-General's Bodyguard had no reason to remain in Calcutta, and it was becoming clear that more troops would be needed for fear of the rising spreading.

From the outset, Company officials expressed concern not just at the outbreak in the Rajmahal Hills and the surrounding districts, but for the possibility that a tribal rising might herald a wider insurrection. One of Frederick Halliday's first acts had been to write to William Allen, the commissioner of the newly created Chota Nagpore Agency on British Bengal's 'south-west frontier', warning him to beware of insurrection.[102] Allen's charge included a large Santal population and for months officials wrongly believed that the impetus for rebellion had come from outside Bengal proper and that rebellious Santals were communicating with their fellows in Pachete, Manbhoom and Singbhoom districts. The prospect of the Hul spreading 'to the districts which are the original site of the Sonthal tribe' would be 'most serious'.[103] The desire to quarantine the districts south-west of the Grand Trunk Road became an increasingly important aim of Company strategy. Halliday, responsible for the tranquility of the whole of Bengal, returned repeatedly to the 'contagious character of insurrection', fearing the responses of 'the semi savage inhabitants of our South western frontier … exaggerating the successes of the insurgents, and gloating over real and imaginary disasters'.[104] William Allen kept a wary eye on the borders of his province. He counselled a Bengal colleague, surely needlessly, that 'nothing is more hurtful to the prestige of the Government and nothing is more likely to ripen disaffection into revolt … than the present unsatisfactory state of affairs in the disturbed disticts'.[105] Observed at a distance, more pragmatic observers were unconvinced of the rebellion's potential threat—The Times later argued that there was 'no more fear of the insurrection spreading … than there ever was of the Rebecca rioters marching to London' from Wales fifteen years before.[106] But even as newspapers were reporting the final movements in 1855, local commentators warned darkly that the Santal Hul was only the first they would face, and that it presaged 'a rising of all the jungle tribes … half-a-million athletic savages … a formidable affair'.[107] The doomsayers were correct in anticipating a vast rising, though the threat in 1857 did not come from the Kols or the Santals.

The rebellion profoundly discomfited the assumption that even Lower Bengal been pacified. The Bengal Hurkaru's editor, Sydney Blanchard, even called for 'dotting the country with small but strong forts', each holding a company of sepoys and a couple of field howitzers, a symptom of extreme alarm.[108] Realising that finding troops to suppress the Santals disturbed the entire system of the 'General Relief', Halliday pressed for a re-distribution of military force south and east of Dinapore, and later in 1855 succeeded in gaining an increase in infantry, artillery and cavalry with remarkable ease, news of which was swiftly released to the newspapers to allay European foreboding.

Reports, and even more, rumours, of Santal moves generated waves of fear among British communities far from the Hul's origin in the Rajmahal Hills. At Jungeypore 'much frightened' wealthy inhabitants, both European and native, engaged boats ready to take them to safety to Berhampore, the nearest cantonment.[109] At Berhampore, where Europeans 'all in a tremendous fright … do nothing but rush about to each other's homes', the station commander Henry Templer, did little to ease the panic, rushing about himself with a large telescope under his arm, 'half wild with excitement, giving orders one minute and counter-ordering them the next'.[110] As the Europeans at Sooree, the main station of Beerbhoom, encountered fleeing railway refugees they felt 'great alarm', the Collector removing his Treasury to the jail and fortifying it as a 'citadel'.[111] From Bhaugulpore, Europeans fled up-river to Monghyr, and George Brown held a government steamer at the ghat 'for the purpose of putting the ladies on board the moment the insurgents make their appearance'.[112] These fears seemed understandable.

Even communities far from the outbreak expressed alarm. At Purneah, 25 miles north of the Ganges, the judge fortified a house 'in regular war fashion', surrounding it with trenches 8-feet deep and ramparts 4-feet high all around.[113] The magistrate at Bancoorah asked for troops to protect his cutchery from 'very turbulent and dangerous tribes', though no Santals actually appeared anywhere near.[114] Likewise, planters in Midnapore, even further south than Calcutta, conceded that the district was 'at present quite quiet' but feared that any factory manager 'might be murdered and his place burned before any aid could be obtained'.[115]

In the Santal country the threat seemed real enough. Europeans living in smaller stations faced a dilemma, whether and when to leave. At Narainpore, 5000 Santals surrounded the zamindar's house, threatening to 'cut up' the police party defending it. The engineer's bungalow became 'a regular hospital' for Bengali refugees, and engineers and contractors hung on, until deciding that troops were too dilatory and prudence dictated a withdrawal down the unfinished railway to Rampore Haut.[116] A week later patrols returning to Narainpore found it burnt to the ground and many of its 10,000 native inhabitants dead. 'I saw a number of dead bodies', a witness wrote, 'and might have seen many more but had quite enough'.[117] Railwaymen who visited to see whether their bungalows had survived found 'butchery'.[118]

But not all officials reacted fearfully. 'Our Magistrate' at Monghyr, one William Tucker, 'a sharp active man … intelligent and energetic', had the foresight to mobilise the 'ghatwals', traditional Paharia custodians of the passes leading to the settled plains near the Ganges, paying them to watch for Santal intruders.[119] A long-standing European resident of Raneegunge refused to quit his bungalow, remaining with his servants, mostly Santals.[120] Major Arthur Saunders, a staff officer, told Major-General George Lloyd who was commanding the Dinapore Division and sending detachments down-river at civil officers' requests, that he was 'inclined to believe that the disturbance is exaggerated' and that the troops he had arranged at such effort would return unused.[121] Before long, Lloyd would be responsible for commanding the force charged with suppressing the Hul.

'They can be crushed': the Company's military response

Though the Company's rule depended ultimately upon military force, only two military units were stationed across the districts of Bhaugulpore and Moorshedabad, and there were no troops at all in Beerbhoom. Bhaugulpore was the headquarters of the six companies of the Bhaugulpore Hill Rangers, and at Berhampore, a cantonment a few miles south of Moorshedabad, lay the 7th Bengal Native Infantry. Any other troops had to be summoned from the cantonments of Dinapore and Barrackpore, the headquarters of the Dinapore and Presidency Divisions respectively. To anyone accustomed to the portrayal of the Bengal Army's habitual torpor ('a tendency to laxity … a good natured gentlemanly slovenliness', a correspondent to the *Friend of India* chided), one of the most surprising revelations of its records in July 1855 is how speedily it moved.[122] Orders were issued to and complied with swiftly by its component units and functionaries and at such an unpropitious time of the year, at the height of the monsoon. Bengal's climate and geography impeded rapid movement, however swiftly decisions might be taken. Steamers might be summoned by electric telegraph, but they took time to steam up-river; artillery marching from Fort William could take up to twelve days to reach Berhampore over rising rivers and muddy roads.

The nature of the governance of British India militated against vigorous responses. While the President in Council, Joseph Dorin professed that the suppression of the insurrection 'must be left to the commissioners, magistrates and officers in command of the troops', in practice the Supreme Council's members could not help intervening.[123] Every level of administration submitted lengthy reports to those above, which were in turn passed on to more senior officials, and senior officers saw no difficulty in commenting on or intervening in the decisions made by subordinates. Such a system eroded individual responsibility and initiative, making subordinates hesitant to trust their own judgment and wary of their superiors' likely responses. Dorin, for example, wrote on the very same day endorsing Robert Richardson's suggestion to move troops to Beerbhoom to 'cut off the rioters'—even though Richardson had a commissioner as his superior who reported to the lieutenant-governor, who in turn reported to the Supreme Council.[124]

The Hul increasingly drew in troops: before long ten of the army's 74 regiments of native infantry—more than 10 per cent of its strength. Regiments were called down-river—the 42nd Light Infantry, for example, which had been at Benares and had expected to go 700 miles to Hoosheyarpoor, and the 13th, which had expected to move 560 miles from Dinapore to Meerut, both going north-west. All now found themselves travelling south-east to a region where few sepoys had served before. Though the largest disciplined military force in Asia, the Bengal Army soon experienced difficulty finding troops to allocate to the rebellion. The regiments at Barrackpore were all below their nominal strength—the 2nd Grenadiers having only 209 sepoys fit for duty, the 37th had 227 and the 50th just 399; collectively little more than one full strength regiment.[125] Major-

General James Eckford, the Presidency Division's commander, reported that he was only able to meet requests for further contingents by reducing routine guards and putting half-trained recruits on duty. Soon sentries at public buildings in Calcutta had been reduced or withdrawn, at the General Hospital, the Clothing Agency's godowns, and even Government House which was in any case hardly used in Dalhousie's absence. As so few regular troops were available, the Supreme Council considered using 'local' units such as the Ramghur Battalion, 'weak and much scattered', and the newly raised Shekhawattee Battalion at Midnapore; in the end it employed neither.[126] But the Calcutta Native Militia, a ramshackle unit much inferior to regular sepoys, was sent to guard Raneegunge, with unfortunate effects. William Elliott dismissed it as 'worse than useless' and Frederick Shore had condemned it as 'a disgrace to any Government'.[127] How would the sepoys perform? The Queen's officer Frederick Middleton, joining the 7th Native Infantry at Pulsa, reported that officers 'had not much confidence in the pluck or endurance of the "faithful sepoy", as he was then termed', but the view was not universal.[128] From Raneegunge an observer, watching sepoys disembark from the trains, thought that they seemed 'in high spirits' exhibiting 'every hope that the rebels within a few days would smartly suffer at their hands'.[129]

Exactly how this suffering might be inflicted remained in doubt. The Bengal Army had no manual of operations, no procedures or doctrine; no notion of what we call counter-insurgency. Its regimental procedures, expressed in *Standing Orders* revised by successive *General Orders* specified what returns should be submitted, how Treasury Escorts were arranged and how routine matters such as pay, leave and religious requirements should be administered. Its highest practice of training involved stereotyped camps of exercise during the cold weather, with field days mainly demonstrating drill and evolutions practised for the purpose of the yearly inspection reports, dutifully and usually mechanically undertaken for visiting general officers. What experience, then, did civil and military officers draw upon in responding to the outbreak?

There seem to be three answers to that question. The first answer is that they drew upon the experience of officers in other similar situations. Officers must have been at least aware of what they called 'guerrilla warfare' or 'bush-fighting' in other colonies at other times. They all knew something of the defiance of Andreas Hofer in the Tyrol, perhaps of Russian patriots in 1812 and certainly of Spanish guerrillas in the Peninsular war, though whether and what they took from those examples is unknown. What passed for the professional military press at the time published a few articles that might have been relevant, but literally over a span of decades. *Colburn's United Service Magazine*, which took an interest in the Company's forces and was certainly read by Indian army officers, published articles on the Dutch subjection of their East Indies, items on the series of contemporary 'Kaffir' wars that British forces improvised in South Africa, and even historical examples such as the Maroon wars fought against runaway slaves in Jamaica in the 1790s.[130] All of these articles contained snippets and hints that officers in 1855 may have seen as relevant—if they had read or remembered them. A few years before, for example, an article on 'our little war' in South Africa included a passage which might have summarised the Bengal Army's policy toward the Santals:

> We keep our handful of troops hard at work—covering the towns, patrolling the open country, and driving the enemy before them wherever he appears.[131]

It is likely that some Indian army officers knew something of the intermittent war fought by a few British units against the Aborigines of Australia, perhaps from accounts in colonial papers, or because some Indian officers took leave in Perth, Sydney or Hobart. Calcutta newspapers also commented on comparable conflicts.

The second answer is that officers in Bengal in 1855 acted in accordance with the instinct to direct a military force to the site of a rising and to suppress it by the simple application of force. Not until August would the troops' orders reflect even a rudimentary plan of operations beyond the actions of regimental officers. For the Hul's first month isolated units and detachments acted against Santal bands at the direction of civil officers, as Joseph Dorin conceded, 'without any general direction'.[132]

The other answer, though, is that the Company had often faced resistance and outright rebellion—guarding against the possibility provided one of the reasons for the army's existence and distribution—so its officers could have been expected to ponder the problem, at least in the abstract, and some of them might actually have had experience or knowledge of previous campaigns. The expansion of Company rule in India after Plassey had not proceeded without resistance. In a succession of wars against Indian states—the Mughals, Marathas, Gurkhas, Sikhs and various native states—the Bengal Army had faced and mostly defeated a succession of enemies in open warfare, sometimes achieving narrow victory, as against the Sikhs, and once being humiliatingly beaten by the Afghans. The regiments drawn in to the Santal insurrection had served in many of those conflicts—the 2nd Grenadiers in Afghanistan and against the Sikhs; the 7th against the Marathas; the 13th against the Sikhs; the 31st against the Marathas, Afghans, the Sikhs, and against native rulers at Bhurtpore and Maharajpoor. The 40th had served twice in Java and in Burmah. While few officers had faced what might be called a guerrilla enemy, they shared a collective experience. One of the Bengal Army's main purposes was to deter or suppress rebellion and its senior officers' memories went back at least forty years. The officers soon to be appointed to command the Field Force had been commissioned in 1804 and 1807 respectively, and had decades of experience in formal and informal conflicts. Long-serving officers, both civil and military, certainly knew enough about the recent past to draw on lessons from another major insurrection that British Bengal had recently faced: what they called the 'Cole campaign'.

Civil officials especially, familiar with local records and advised by older colleagues, repeatedly drew lessons from the suppression of the rebellion of the Kols of Chota Nagpore in 1831–32. Ranajit Guha, surveying insurrection across the century, confirmed that policies adopted against the Kols 'figured in official thinking at the highest level on the occasion of the Santal *hool*'—and indeed not just at the highest level, but among the military officers and district officials who actually faced the rising.[133] William Elliott, officiating commissioner of Burdwan, a district with a large Santal minority but which was never actually threatened by rebellion, had served in Bengal from 1828. Drawing on his experience, he urged William Grey who was his administrative superior but actually a younger man, to be bold, emphasising that 'in the Cole campaign our grand mistake lay in opposing the Rebels with a force which they could drive before them'. He recommended that 'if they be *at once* shown that opposition is useless … they can be crushed.' That explains why Octavius Toogood and Walter Birch marched a wing of the 7th Native Infantry into the Rajmahal Hills as soon as Toogood summoned it from Berhampore. Elliott acknowledged that the military force available was small—he had three companies at his disposal—but advised that even 100 or 300 sepoys could surely defeat bodies of even 5000 Santals. The lesson of the earlier insurrection, Elliott argued, was that 'to act on the defensive is assuredly to embolden the Rebels.'[134] This insight alone explains the Company officers' initial response of aggressive if uncoordinated forays, even if that reaction could not be called a 'strategy' as such.

Two Bengal Native Infantry regiments used against the Santals, the 2nd and the 50th, had served against the Kols, therefore some of their older non-commissioned ranks and native officers had experience of bush fighting in the jungle of Chota Nagpore and the brutality it entailed.[135] Senior officers who had fought the Kols included Captain Thomas Birch of the 31st, Colonel Louis Bird of the 13th, Major William Cooke of the 2nd Grenadiers, Lieutenant-Colonel Joseph Hampton of the 50th, and Captain William Hampton, Major William Legard and Lieutenant-Colonel Stephen Wheeler, all of the 31st. Major Henry Shuckburgh and many of the 40th Native Infantry had also fought in the Bundelkhand insurrection in 1842–43, as had Lieutenant-Colonel William Mitchell, who took command of the 56th later in the campaign. Memories and stories handed on at mess dinners, say, must surely have helped to shape the Bengal Army's collective understanding of how to respond to what they regarded and described as a tribal uprising. In October, while urging 'extreme measures' (but not actually asking the Supreme Council to declare martial law), Frederick Halliday discussed 'our former experience in cases of this kind' and reminded his senior colleagues that in 1832 rebellion had only been snuffed out by 'destroying the villages and granaries of the insurgents'.[136] Through the energy of a well-matched military officer and his civil counterpart, the Company's first formal advance against the rebels extraordinarily reached the focus of the insurgency.

'We killed an immense number': the fight at Moheshpore

Walter Birch had seen his wing of the 7th Native Infantry comprising four companies with about 400 men aboard a steamer which happened to be at the ghat at Berhampore on the afternoon of 11 July. By tiffin (lunch) next day they had disembarked at Aurungabad, 44 miles upstream and, at the direction of Octavius Toogood, energetically marched for the nearby indigo factory at Kuddamshaw, which, Toogood wrote to a newspaper, 'I am sorry to say the insurgents had left'. Toogood, receiving 'information' asked Birch to march towards Moheshpore, 25 miles south-south-west. They made a 'most difficult and fatiguing march' through inundated fields until reaching the track made for the railway contractors' carts, passing deserted villages. Struggling through muddy rice fields and tracks, they saw 'dead bodies … all in the same mutilated state', along with vultures, what the *Citizen* called 'a frightful spectacle of the atrocities committed by these murderers'.[137] After briefly halting at Pulsa, where they found the railway bungalows looted and burned, Toogood asked Birch to march through the night for Moheshpore eight miles away in response to a plea for help from its rajah. They left in pouring rain in the dark, but were at least spared having to march as 33 of the Nawab of Moorshedabad's elephants carried 200 sepoys. They arrived at dawn on 15 July, finding about 5000 Santals on the banks of a large tank, evidently awaiting them.[138] The tank, an earthen reservoir, remains, one of two near the Amrapara-Murarai road, a few hundred metres south of the Bansloi river. Tracing the topography today, the Santals gathered around what is today the location of Ma Sumitra Saloon, a pharmacy called Beauty Medical, a State Bank of India auto-teller and Jamal Poultry Farm; the sepoys probably emerged from a grove of mango trees around what is now Kamal Auto Centre.

Dismounting, the troops formed ranks, though, according to the sceptical Frederick Middleton, 'Jack Sepoy did not seem to be very enthusiastic' and marched toward the Santals getting within 30 or 40 yards before opening fire at Toogood's request.[139] The Santals, facing regular troops for the first time but perhaps emboldened by the promise that the sepoys' bullets would turn to water, rushed towards them, shooting arrows.[140] Here, Santal leaders showed their willingness to be seen at the forefront of combat when two of the Bhugnadihee brothers, Kanhu and Bhairab, 'danced' with their swords before their followers. While no European participant seems to have noticed or at least recorded them, Toogood already knew of the brothers' leadership.[141] Sidhu, the third brother, later explained that he had intended to 'make my salaam to the sepoys, and tell them I was not fighting with the Government, but with the zamindars'. Naturally, the sepoys would not let him approach and, he later explained simply, 'they shot me'.[142] The troops, a European eyewitness noticed, seemed 'half inclined to run away' when facing several thousand Santals, and some fired in the air, as frightened sepoys had in the Anglo-Sikh wars. Their officers 'knocked several of them down for doing so', but most men retained their dressing and remembered their drill.[143] As they fired, Santals, understandably 'much frightened', cried out to Sidhu to save them using the magical powers he had invoked. He stretched out his arms, chanted verses and ordered the sepoys' guns to stop working.[144]

John Mudge watched the fight and soon after described it in a letter to his father. As the Santals saw the troops, he said, they 'set up a yell' and began beating their drums, he thought there were about 300 of them, and 'charged down on us'. When they came within 40 yards of the sepoys' line, they loosed their arrows, withdrawing when the sepoys opened fire. Others came at the sepoys from another direction, and again withdrew after the sepoys' volleys. They came on a third time and again retreated, with the sepoys charging after them.

After two-and-a-half-to-three hours of skirmishing around the burning village, littered with villagers killed by the Santals and Santals killed by the sepoys, they crossed the Bansloi river and disappeared into the jungle. Here 'we killed an immense number', Mudge recalled, some while they were crossing the river chest-deep.[145] Toogood described the Santals' 'determined opposition', counting over a hundred Santal dead; Middleton estimated 120 killed and wounded (Mudge thought it was nearer 200). At least as many must have been dragged away wounded, many of whom must surely have died. Some Santal wounded were swept away by the fast-flowing river, but Mudge saw many 'frightfully wounded' Santals who, left untreated, gradually died over the following night.

The wounded Santals included three of the four leading brothers: Sidhu shot in the wrist, Kanhu in the back and Bhairab in the abdomen. The Santal leadership was arguably crippled in the Hul's first major action involving regular troops. The wounded leaders were carried off on charpoys, their wounds surely beyond the skill of the Santals' *ojha guru*, accustomed to treating illness by divination and sorcery. Five sepoys had been wounded but, to the troops' relief, not with poisoned arrows—the sepoy Sita Ram remembered that because of this, the Santals were initially 'much feared' by sepoys.[146] The troops recovered much loot, some of it from the villages the troops had passed. The local rajah, spared the destruction of his house and the murder of his family, gratefully contributed elephants to the Company, used presumably to carry off the recovered plunder under the guard of the Nawab's sepoys. Mudge went with them to Jungeypore and on to Berhampore after a week of being continuously wet and hungry; he was poorer by Rs 6000, but at least alive.

'The Head Quarters of the Insurgents': at Bhugnadihee

By this time Toogood knew that the insurrection had begun near Burhyte in the Rajmahal Hills, about 30 miles north of Moheshpore, and Birch agreed to lead his weary sepoys on, marching 'without food, shelter or change of clothes', having been on the road already for a week. But he only had fifteen 'sickmen', even though 'a great part of the country' was actually under water and mountain streams swollen by rain cut the track into the hills.[147] Characteristically of the Bengal Army, Birch made sure to write to Captain Andrew Ross, the Assistant Adjutant-General of the Army in Simla and a fellow member of the 7th; it always paid to ensure that someone in headquarters knew of your successes. Two Queen's army captains, Frederick Middleton of the 70th Foot and Christopher Garstin of the 96th, accompanied the column; strictly speaking, they were the only two 'British' soldiers to serve in the campaign.[148] Both had served together in New Zealand with the 58th Foot, reunited in Calcutta.

On 24 July Birch's sepoys 'skirmished' over a saddle and saw before them the broad, largely jungle-clad valley of Burhyte, the same view that had so captivated Walter Sherwill five years before. At

Raghunathpore, on the track to Burhyte, Santals defending the home of their Thakur resisted fiercely, rushing at the sepoys with 'naked swords and bows and arrows', but the leading company pushed on and the intimidated defenders withdrew into the surrounding hills. By early afternoon sepoys reached the burned out ruin of James Pontet's bungalow. It was beside a tank, probably the one still the town's most notable feature. Toogood learned that the Thakur could be found in Bhugnadihee, a small village on a low spur south of Burhyte, and with a party of the Nawab's troops he, Captain Middleton and a civilian, went to investigate. (Middleton commanded the Nawab's mounted sowars but found them disinclined to close with the Santals. Mounted troops later in the Hul had greater success.)

Bhugnadihee was deserted, but Toogood discovered 'The Thackoor' in what he learned was the compound outside Kanhu's house—some Santal or Bengali neighbours must have remained. This represented the spiritual focus of the rebellion, a small, low circle of dried mud, like a miniature version of the solid bullock cart wheels used on hackeries all over Bengal. It bore signs of animal sacrifices— milk, segments of goat and even buffaloes. Standing nearby were four elephants, taken from the Rajah of Pakaur or from the murdered Henshawes: they made a welcome addition to the force's baggage. Inside the house was an even more useful discovery: a tin box containing documents said to have been written by or rather for the brothers—by now Toogood believed Sidhu to be the Santals' main leader. The troops confiscated the box and led the elephants away, setting fire to the village as they left. That night, Toogood began examining the documents, translating what he could and writing a report. Having questioned villagers, he confirmed that 'this rebellion has been instigated by four brothers … Kanu, Sedu, Chand and Bhyrub, all manjhees'. Ironically, he had no sowars or dawk runners so had to rely on a Santal willing to venture the 40-mile walk to Aurungabad.[149] Meanwhile, Birch seems to have appropriated for his own use a female elephant, named Bachawabe. She was later recognised as having been taken from Pakaur earlier in July, and at the end of the rebellion he restored her to her owner.

Resting in the valley 'lately the Head Quarter of the Sonthals', Birch's men faced attacks by small parties of Santals aggrieved that the

site of the shrine had been occupied—some, Birch thought, intoxicated on bhang (liquid marijuana). Frederick Middleton was attacked
by an intoxicated man, but killed his assailant—he had faced Maori
warriors and seemed unmoved by the encounter. Birch's sepoys
'speedily repulsed' them, but were unable to move on, not least
because the rain poured down.[150] When they did move, leaving a
company of the 7th to garrison the valley, they were able to make
only about seven miles a day, marching from six in the morning until
late in the evening, through paddies, sinking up to their knees in
mud.[151] Sepoys, though obliged to wear the uncomfortable and
unsuitable red woolen coatee, usually wore dhotis rather than pantaloons, and were able to cross streams bare-legged.

On the way back to the river, Birch's wing encountered another
large Santal force on 28 July. They attacked as the sepoys were making camp, 'coming on in two dense masses, shouting and yelling'.
They advanced to 'long rifle range'—about 500 yards—but two
officers firing, possibly with hunting rifles, 'sent the whole [mass]
flying into the jungles'. The Santals were already wary of the sepoys'
firepower. Thereafter, even if the troops moved with 'secrecy and
quietness', Santals eluded them, though the troops did force them to
jettison some of their plunder, including chamber pots looted from
railway families' bungalows.[152]

About the same time, a sepoy performed one of the deeds that
brought the award of the Indian Order of Merit to two members of
the Sonthal Field Force. While searching a Santal village, men of the
7th Native Infantry under Lieutenant Gilbert Pasley came upon a
solitary Santal, armed with a sword apparently in pursuit of game.
They surrounded the man in an attempt to seize him. Pasley, armed
only with a walking stick, tried to persuade him to relinquish the
sword, realising that he was intoxicated, probably on bhang. The man
lunged at Pasley, first missing him, but then knocking his hat over his
eyes. Before the Santal could strike again Sepoy Nehal Sing bayonetted him, in doing so gashing his own hand and wrist. For saving
Pasley's life Sing was later awarded the Indian Order of Merit 3rd
Class, entitling him to a silver medal and a pension. Did Sing remain
loyal to the Company when the 7th mutinied in 1857?[153]

Birch and Toogood's expedition saw the wing of the 7th Native
Infantry march about 150 miles in just over two weeks at the height of

the monsoon in 'a most difficult and harassing country … intersected by mountain torrents and surrounded on all sides by jungle'. Its men had often been surrounded by hostile forces and had fought several actions against much larger forces, but returned with fewer than twenty sickmen, some wounded, in the column's dhoolies. Toogood, who had accompanied them, praised the sepoys' 'zeal and energy', as well as the military officers and civil officials who had co-operated harmoniously and effectively. In that Toogood had reached the 'Head Quarters of the Insurgents' within a fortnight of the outbreak and had obtained vital intelligence of Santal intentions, it arguably struck a significant and perhaps fatal blow against the insurgency.[154]

Octavius Toogood and Walter Birch's expedition to Burhyte was to provide the first sign of the effectiveness of European military force against the Santals, and indeed produced not just a cheering success for the Company but also intelligence vital to both the outcome of the Hul and its interpretation centuries later. Toogood and Birch had displayed notable energy and initiative in the opening weeks of the uprising, setting an example of active leadership and effective partnership between civil and military officers, standards which others failed to meet. While praising Toogood as 'just the man to quell a disturbance', the *Morning Chronicle* criticised George Brown, the collector at Bhaugulpore who 'seems to be doing nothing'.[155] In fact, the Company's force in Bhaugulpore was doing worse than nothing: its advance resulted in disaster.

'Encouraged them more than anything': the fight at Peer Pointee

George Brown's fears had not eased—he incautiously confessed to a colleague that he thought he could 'barely hold his ground'.[156] The Military Consultations record a confused sequence of troop movements in which detachments of regular regiments and the Bhaugulpore Hill Rangers were shifted along the Ganges, to little purpose. Even Brown, whose caution not to say timidity prompted the indecisive use of troops, had to admit that 'little has been done' in the rebellion's first ten days.[157] Captain Walter Sherwill, the authority on the region and its people, who had immediately offered his services to Brown, was frustrated when he took a small detachment of forty sepoys of the

40th Native Infantry (all that Brown thought he could spare) from Bhaugulpore. They went to Rajmahal and then back to Colgong, in several places finding detachments kicking their heels. The only result of Sherwill's journey, Brown reported, was to confirm that 'the Sonthals are now in force along the [old Mughal] high road from Bhaugulpore to Rajmehal', a 60-odd-mile stretch of the Ganges.

With misgivings, Brown then consented to Frederick Burroughs leading the Bhaugulpore Hill Rangers in what Burroughs grandly described as 'sweeping down from the ... river ... to clear the dawk road', leading east towards the Bagirutty. On 16 July a steamer took the Rangers from Bhaugulpore down the Ganges to the little station of Colgong, where Burroughs found that a detachment of the 40th Native Infantry had just landed. Instead of waiting for it to join his column, Burroughs marched his men eastwards on the muddy track towards Peer Pointee, named for a Mohammedan saint buried there, about 12 miles away. His plan, so he later disclosed, was simply to 'descry' the rebels and attack them. The Santals knew exactly where the troops were, whether from scouts hiding in the jungle or from what Burroughs claimed were 'low cast Hindoo' informers, while his own intelligence was, he confessed, 'most deficient'.[158] The Rangers marched across the swampy Ganges flood plain, a stretch cut by many deep nullahs, now full of water, over spurs clad in jungle. About ten miles from Colgong they reached a deserted village but saw perhaps 2000 Santals in the jungle behind it, with a marshy nullah between the two forces. Burroughs, outnumbered by ten to one, halted, hoping that the Santals would attack and allow him to use his greatest asset, his sepoys' firepower.

Burroughs had hoped to catch the Santals between his companies and those commanded by his adjutant, Lieutenant William Gordon, but the plan fell apart when Gordon was late, and Burroughs found his men facing a large Santal force. He formed them into two lines, Burroughs with the front rank and his sergeant-major, Walter Lennox, watching the rear. The sepoys at last raised their muskets, but to Burroughs's astonishment and rage, many misfired, and many fired into the air; were they frightened, or was it a show of sympathy for Santals? Soon, men began to run away. Burroughs called to Lennox to stop them, but Lennox (extraordinarily) 'could not speak a word of Hindoostanee'. Then Lennox, a Somerset mill-worker who had served in the Company's European force for eighteen years, slipped in the mud and as Santals fell on him, was 'literally hacked to pieces' trying to rally his men.[159] In the panic that seized them—'nothing would bring them to order'—27 sepoys died.

Burroughs later explained that 'this was the first time the Rangers were ever under fire,' but that they knew how accurate and deadly Santal hunting bows could be in skilled hands. As hill men themselves, probably Paharias rather than Santals, they were susceptible to the stories of sorcery, that their musket balls would turn to water. When many found that their muskets would not fire, as only one in five appeared to work, many assumed that their weapons had, in fact, been cursed and, Burroughs admitted, they were 'seized with a panic'. In his defence, Burroughs optimistically argued that 'regiments that have experienced this misfortune have subsequently fought bravely' but no one accepted that excuse.[160] The Rangers, Bengal's European civilians believed, were 'a dastardly corps'.[161] They had been poorly trained and were wretchedly equipped—they kept their cartridges in brown leather pouches hanging from waist-belts, not in waterproof cartridge boxes like regular sepoys. They had no coats, capes or hats to keep the rain off (though nor did many regulars)—and all day the rain poured down. Although Walter Sherwill had praised the Rangers in 1851 as 'as fine a body of soldiers as any in the regular army', they proved a disappointment.[162]

The civilians at Peer Pointee behaved variably. Charles Barnes, the indigo planter who had lived near Colgong for fifteen years virtually as a zamindar, rode on his elephant towards a party of Santals and demanded to know what they wanted by rising up. They responded by loosing arrows at him. Barnes shouldered his rifle and 'knocked over two of the fellows'.[163] But the assistant magistrate accompanying the corps, Charles Chapman, apparently led the rout. He had allegedly boarded a boat and refused to leave it. When a couple of planters taunted him 'he promptly burst into tears', or so the Calcutta newspapers published and repeated.[164]

Back at Colgong, Burroughs now refused to move against the insurgents even though 'hourly notices are brought in of villages being looted and people murdered' and the sepoys of the 40th expressed themselves 'most anxious to march off against the insurgents', distancing themselves from the inept Rangers.[165] Brown realised that his earlier caution exposed him to censure, and he attempted to blame Burroughs now that the insurgents, he admitted, were 'gaining hourly courage as no one checks them' because of the troops' inaction, and claimed that 'it has not been owing to want of urging on my part'.[166]

Informal reports soon circulated—that 'the hill troops have refused to do their duty', that one of their officers had been killed; that their ammunition had become 'caked'; the last claim at least true. 'No confidence can be placed in them' wrote an alarmed Purneah correspondent.[167] Within days the Rangers, though, had joined the 40th in beating off a Santal attack at Pealpore and were now said to have 'quite redeemed their character'; but it was too late for them and their unfortunate commander.[168] Though his force had now been more than doubled, Burroughs still declined to move even though George Atkinson heard that the Santals had fired villages within sight of his sentries. For the time being, while further troops arrived by steamer, operations in Bhaugulpore remained in abeyance. 'Strange to say', George Lloyd, the divisional commander, wrote wryly a week afterwards, 'no report has yet been received'; typically, he already knew of the disaster from British India's inescapable gossip network.[169] Soon, Lloyd heard the sorry story from Brown for himself: Burroughs had prudently decamped to Bowsee, but he must have known that the Bengal Army would catch up with him. Eventually a report of the Rangers' failure did indeed reach Joseph Dorin, who made it clear that he considered it a 'disgraceful flight' and Burroughs learned, as he must have anticipated, that he would face a court of inquiry.[170]

The leader writer of *Allen's Indian Mail*, reading Calcutta newspapers as they arrived in London six weeks later, summed up the actions of the Hul's opening weeks as 'a few little affairs, in the majority of which we have succeeded'.[171] His confidence was ill-founded: a less bellicose correspondent in the same paper warned that 'a guerrilla war will cost much and may be carried on for years'. Even two months later, civil officials met Santals a hundred miles from the scene of Burroughs's disaster, who affirmed that his 'misfortune … fanned the insurrection into a flame' that 'encouraged them more than anything'.[172] At exactly the same time some 120 miles away to the south-west, detachments in Beerbhoom also experienced defeat.

'A terrible tale': Company setbacks in Beerbhoom

The 56th Native Infantry, summoned from Barrackpore, reached the terminus at Raneegunge by rail. It was the first time many sepoys had even seen a locomotive. Sita Ram, who probably served with the 56th, described his first sight of the 'iron road and the steam monster'. When he asked bystanders how it worked, they told him that 'the English had put some powerful demon into each iron box', but then he noticed the water, the coal and the steam and he realised it was a machine, like the familiar paddle-steamer. Sita Ram travelled several times on the railway to and from Calcutta. 'It went so fast', he told the officer who transcribed and enhanced his memories, 'it nearly took away my senses'.[173] The *Citizen* told its readers that trains travelled at 70 miles per hour, but in fact they made the 110 mile journey in about six hours. Even so, the *Citizen* rightly speculated on 'how surprised the Sepoys must have been at being whirled along at such a pace'.[174]

The 56th then marched for Sooree, through the night and the rain. Vincent Jervis, the commander of the first detachment, recorded that they found 'panic in every village' and at Sooree 'things, if possible, worse', with civil officers keeping horses saddled and trying to hide coins in a wall.[175] From Sooree, the 56th soon sent parties out in mostly company-sized detachments in south-east Beerbhoom and up the unfinished railway line towards Rampore Haut. Its officers encountered varying success, but also provoked the only clash in which a Company officer was to be killed.

In these early weeks of the rebellion, Company officers learned by making mistakes: marching their detachments out in various directions, sometimes informed by reports, sometimes at random. Sometimes they were accompanied by a civil official, but there were always more detachments than even junior officials able to guide them, and inexperienced as they were, made errors, as events at Nagore demonstrated.[176] On the morning of 21 July a company, about 80 sepoys under Lieutenant Henry Raikes approached Nagore, about 12 miles north-west of Sooree. As they reached the village, they realised that they were 'nearly surrounded' by several bands of about 1500 Santals—the first either officers or sepoys had encountered. Raikes was about to attack when he received a rooboocary (or despatch) from one of his ensigns, who reported that his even smaller detachment faced a large Santal force and he felt it prudent to withdraw. Robert Richardson, who was accompanying these inexperienced subalterns, decided that he needed to ride back to Sooree for support. By the time he returned next day with a few reinforcements—just twenty sepoys under Lieutenant Tom Toulmin—they encountered stray sepoys who told 'a terrible tale'. They said that Raikes's company had been forced back and that the Santals were looting Nagore. Raikes, 'with more courage than discretion', had attacked the Santals and pursued them recklessly. The Santals had then rushed in behind him, and the sepoys had to barricade themselves in the house of the local rajah, leaving the town to be burned and looted. The sepoys fell out among themselves, berating a man who had 'showed the white feather at Chillianwallah' (a major battle in the second Anglo-Sikh war) but who had somehow been promoted. Other men, as Toulmin found, straggled back to Sooree. The young officers told Richardson that they had given the Santals 'a splendid beating', but actually the sepoys had been holed up without ammunition while the town they had tried to save burned around them.

Henry Raikes, exhausted and separated from his men, failed to mount the elephant on which he tried to escape, and lay in the jungle fearing that the Santals would find him. A servant, though wounded by an arrow, brought villagers to him and they helped him back to Sooree. The servant later died of his wound. Would the defeat, an officer from Burhyte wondered, encourage the Santals to 'adopt a more plucky system'?[177]

Toulmin, a 24-year-old who had been born in Agra, the only son of a Bengal officer, reacted impulsively to the disaster. He galloped back to Sooree to plead for Major John Nembhard to release more men, and returned with 90 sepoys to relieve Raikes. His impetuosity would soon bring disaster. Nembhard, who was to be condemned before the year's end as 'unfit for command … and of indifferent private character', felt overwhelmed by requests for troops by military and civil officers over a wide arc of country north of Sooree and he responded by detaching small groups of sepoys willy-nilly.[178] For example, learning that 'thousands of Sonthals' approached Lieutenant

John Delamain's detachment at Nungolea, only six miles north-east of Sooree, he again sent just 20 sepoys. Nor did officials co-operate fully with each other: Richardson complained that William Elliott had 200 troops at Rampore Haut, unthreatened by Santals (for now), so were 'no earthly use' there; and Elliott had an undue share of the scarce elephants 'which makes mine a very hard game to play'. Elliott, however, professed he was unable to move for want of elephants.

The Santals facing troops around Sooree appeared to be among the most aggressive of the entire insurrection, presumably under influential leaders. They faced some of the most ineffectual Company commanders in Major Nembhard and later Colonel George Burney of the 56th, who seemed incapable of directing their regiment's detachments. Their timidity, contrasting with the initiative of several civil officials, provided the most effective refutation of the demand that officials 'better stop in their cutcharies [sic] ... and leave fighting and councils of war to the military'.[179] Burney had only just taken command of the 56th; he had transferred from the 32nd because of the Bengal Army's seniority rules, not because he particularly sought active service.

Inevitably, rumour magnified the actual Santal threat. A letter from Raneegunge on 4 August while decrying the 'Santhal panic' at Sooree, also passed on reports that on the northern bank of the Mor near Sooree, the Santals were improbably building 'stockades with a full determination to hold their ground'.[180] No wonder, perhaps, that the nervous Nembhard, though commanding his own regiment and with part of another, the 50th, nearby, reported that he 'fears his inability to maintain his position at the numerous outposts he is required to defend' and—of course—asked for reinforcements.[181] Nembhard's unease may seem exaggerated, but the fighting in Beerbhoom saw the most serious defeat the Santals inflicted on regular troops. A week after Henry Raikes's setback at Nagore, the impetuous Thomas Toulmin, suffered the rebellion's single most serious defeat that the Santals inflicted on regular troops.

On 27 July, Raikes and Toulmin again marched out from Sooree looking for Santal bands to attack. Near Banskole, which happened to be a place named only once in the records and unrecorded on maps, Raikes's detachment stumbled across a band, suffering four casualties. Toulmin, nearby, marched to Raikes's aid, but on the way came upon about a hundred Santals cooking breakfast. He reacted immediately and attacked the surprised group, who perhaps had not thought to set a watch, killing four without loss to his own men. Toulmin learned that more Santals were to be found nearby and set out, reporting that 'he hopes to fall upon' them.[182] A fellow officer drawing on surviving sepoys' accounts, described how Toulmin's men met a huge body of Santals—perhaps 10,000—on the opposite bank of a nullah. Toulmin's 'daring spirit could not be restrained', and he led his men across the nullah, his horse sinking in mud to its knees. Seeing this, a group of Santals rushed toward him and in the hand-to-hand fight that followed Toulmin and many of his men were overwhelmed and killed.[183]

Toulmin's service record described his death: 'stooping down [from his horse] to make a cut at a Santhal, when an arrow wounded him in the neck, while twenty Santhals rushed on him with their axes'.[184] Newspaper reports based on Raikes's account described Toulmin as having been shot with an arrow in the neck and cut down while stupefied. A letter from Sooree from a man who knew him, offered an epitaph: 'Young blood when up overcomes discretion'; true, but Toulmin had also taken twenty of his men to their deaths.[185]

The survivors fell back, reportedly disputing every yard and fighting 'nobly', but as the writer recorded that 'each man became separated from his comrade', it seems the retreat turned into a rout. Of Toulmin and Raikes's detachment of a hundred, as well as Toulmin, a havildar (or sergeant) and two sepoys had been seen to be killed, but a further 17 sepoys were missing, presumed killed: 21 deaths. The officers of the 56th gathered a purse of Rs 20,000 as a reward if Toulmin could be brought in alive, but the Bengali villager who rescued Raikes found Toulmin's decapitated body, allowing him to be buried in Sooree's cemetery.[186] However, forty years later when inscriptions of 'tombs or monuments in Bengal possessing historical or archaeological interest' were recorded, Toulmin's grave seems to have been lost.[187]

In the way of the Bengal Army, in which promotion went by seniority, Toulmin's death gave Ensign Charles Goad his lieutenancy, which was dated to the day of Toulmin's death. When a party of the 56th returned to the scene of Toulmin's defeat, they found the mutilated corpses of eight sepoys, whom their comrades naturally wished to cremate; they were supposedly surrounded by about 200 Santal dead.

'Rank and experience': George Lloyd's appointment

In accordance with Joseph Dorin's preference, while the Supreme Council declined to declare martial law, its members did agree to place the rebellion's suppression 'in the hands of a Military Officer of rank and experience' who could be trusted to act with 'vigour and speed', and they agreed that such an officer was Major-General George Lloyd, presently commanding the Dinapore Division.[188] The Tipperary-born, 66-year-old Lloyd had served in the Bengal Army for exactly fifty years and had gained fame as the founder of the hill station of Darjeeling in the late 1830s, while adjudicating a boundary dispute between Nepal and Sikkim. He had experience of fighting in Macao and Java in the Napoleonic wars, and against the Nepalese, Marathas and Burmese. Accordingly, next day George Atkinson telegraphed Lloyd to advise him that 'you are requested to proceed immediately to Rajmahal to assume command of the Troops and to conduct operations in the field against the Santal insurgents'.[189] But Lloyd was not to be a Santal insurrection supremo: in a later message, Atkinson reminded him that he was still to 'consider yourself ... under the orders of the Government of India'.[190]

The area of the disturbed districts actually mostly lay within the Presidency Division, commanded temporarily by James Eckford.[191] The boundary between it and Lloyd's Dinapore Division placed Beerbhoom and Moorshedabad under the Presidency and Bhaugulpore in Dinapore's area. In the event, of the ten regiments detailed to the suppression of the Hul, six came from the Presidency Division (the 2nd, 7th, 31st, 37th, 50th and 56th), three from Dinapore (the 13th, 40th and 42nd) and one (the 63rd) from the Cawnpore Division. Command of the Sonthal Field Force was to be given to George Lloyd, though he was to retain administrative command of his division throughout. Eckford seems not to have been put out even when Berhampore, the base for operations on the eastern front of the Hul, was temporarily removed from his divisional area and given to Lloyd. Eckford's willingness to denude his own formation to serve under Lloyd, demonstrated that Bengal officers could exhibit gentlemanly qualities. The allocation of regiments to the campaign, however, was made with an eye to the financial advantages accrued from field service in the payment of bonus to men and sepoys, called batta, the roster for the allocation for which was accorded a special page in the *Bengal Directory*. As more troops were required in August, the Adjutant-General worried that ordering the 8th Native Infantry into the field would give it an unfair financial advantage. As it turned out, the 8th only relieved the 50th at Barrackpore and so remained in a 'half-batta' station. The Adjutant-General's office noted in relief that 'the Presidency and Dinapore Divisions will be equally attained': financial equity was preserved.[192]

Lloyd left Dinapore by steamer for Bhaugulpore as soon as he received his orders, and wrote to Atkinson on the way down-river discussing his plans and making requests. He wanted to appoint two further brigadiers, and named his choices, but there seemed no willingness to pay more than one brigadier and the idea lapsed. He also asked for maps of the disturbed districts. Atkinson applied to the Trigonometrical Survey for lithographs mounted in linen books against the mould and damp of the country, some based on Walter Sherwill's revenue surveys.

Accepting that he could only have one brigadier and realising that he could not effectively control forces in both Beerbhoom and Bhaugulpore simultaneously, Lloyd proposed appointing a subordinate brigadier to command a subsidiary southern force, to be called the Beerbhoom and Bancoorah Field Force. Soon after, Colonel Louis Bird was urgently summoned to Raneegunge to take command. Eckford warmly commended Bird as 'an able and distinguished officer possessing great experience', demonstrating that perhaps merit as well as patronage counted in the Bengal Army.[193] The 63-year-old Bird was experienced, with an eventful career. He had been suspended as a cadet soon after arriving in Calcutta but joined a King's regiment and having served in the capture of Mauritius was reinstated in the Company's army and went on to fight the Nepalese, Marathas and Sikhs and in several other conflicts, crucially including the suppression of the Kol insurrection. Thanks to the Bengal Army's peculiar seniority rules, he had also been a member of several of the regiments serving in the Sonthal Field Force, the 13th, 40th, 50th and 56th.

Bird spent a couple of days sizing up his command and cautiously decided that the infantry reinforcements he was expecting would be insufficient and that he needed light artillery and more cavalry to meet 'the critical state of affairs'.[194] Indeed, Bird's first orders were to withdraw the detachments dispersed across the district to the headquarters stations of Raneegunge and Sooree. This, John Peter Grant immediately saw, meant the abandonment of 'extensive tracts of rich and populous country to as bloody and barbarous an invasion as can be conceived'. It was an unpropitious beginning.

By the time Lloyd and Bird had been appointed, communications with the main stations on the northern and southern flanks of the disturbed areas had been improved—the telegraph reached Berhampore and Raneegunge, while frequent steamer services connected Lloyd in Bhaugulpore with Calcutta. Lloyd and Bird could not communicate directly, but the Bengal Army's practice of centralising control meant that everything was copied to and transmitted by George Atkinson and often William Grey in Fort William.[195] A month after the Hul's outbreak, the Bengal Army was finally organised to meet the challenge of suppressing it.

3

BHADER (AUGUST)

Early in August the *Friend of India*'s editor, Meredith Townsend, attempted to 'trace the daily progress of the revolt', a task as difficult to those who lived through those weeks as it remains now. He was hampered by 'imperfect information, frightened newspaper correspondents ... the wide extent of territory occupied by the insurgents' and, he implied, the complete absence of evidence from the Santal side of the hill, including 'the almost unknown names of Sonthal villages'.[1] Already, though, the broad outlines of an explanation for the Hul were visible. The Santals had been 'exceedingly irritated' by grievances against mahajans and by the impossibility of gaining justice. The two elder brothers from Bhugnadihee were known, as was their theological appeal, their attempted sorcery, and the savagery and destruction which the Hul had brought to thousands. What Townsend could not suggest was exactly how the rebellion might be suppressed. 'This guerrilla war' being fought across the rice fields and jungle of Lower Bengal 'cannot last', he affirmed, but how could it be ended? Ultimately, Townsend concluded, 'whether martial law be declared or not, the jungles must be entered at all hazards'.

'Unable to protect our own subjects': impasse

The Hul had hardly begun, but it was going badly for the Company. A week before Meredith Townsend had mused gloomily that rebellion had broken out 'here, in the heart of the province we have held for a hundred years ... where the smoke of an enemy's camp has never been seen since the battle of Plassey'. Now the Company had been exposed as 'unable to protect our own subjects ... from spoilation and massacre'.[2] The lack of co-ordination among Company forces was about to change. George Lloyd commanded a considerable and growing military force even if, he thought, one still too small for the task. George Atkinson asked Lloyd to advise on 'the nature of the operations necessary and the extent of the force ... required,' allowing Lloyd to request more troops.[3] It was now disposed in the three main theatres in which the Company conducted operations against the rebellion. In the east, in Moorshedabad district, based on the cantonment of Berhampore, was the 7th Native Infantry, one half of which was resting after its epic march to Moheshpore and Burhyte, with detachments of the 31st Native Infantry arriving at Jungeypore. As fighting in Moorshedabad district was about to end, that was sufficient. In the north, in Bhaugulpore, the 40th Native Infantry was based on Bhaugulpore, with the 37th arriving from Dinapore and the 42nd Light Infantry about to join it from Benares, along with the 13th. (The Bhaugulpore Hill Rangers, which Atkinson did not even mention, remained in disgrace in the district headquarters.) In the south, with its base at the railway terminus at Raneegunge, actually just inside Bancoorah district but operating in Beerbhoom, was the 56th Native Infantry with detachments posted up the unfinished railway as far as Rampore Haut, and a wing of the 50th, which was holding Sooree, the district's head station and what was to be the focus of operations over the rest of the monsoon. Other parts of the disturbed districts—notably western Beerbhoom and southern Bhaugulpore—as yet attracted almost no military presence; nor was the Grand Trunk Road actively patrolled: those changes would follow as the rebellion developed.

Few guns had yet arrived, just a couple of 9-pounders and three 3-pounders at Berhampore, but more were on the way. Also on the move was the Governor-General's Bodyguard marching up from Calcutta, and the 11th Irregular Cavalry, mainly Muslims and described by the Military Auditor General as 'a rough and ready body', marching down the Grand Trunk Road from Segowlie.[4]

Raneegunge, their destination, was becoming a major, if improvised base, with a temporary hospital being set up, after protracted correspondence with the Medical Board; while commissariat officers, warrant officers and gomastas were gathering, storing and distributing supplies, especially food. Upwards of a thousand troops and their numerous followers, including water-carriers, sweepers, coolies and mahouts, all of whom had to find accommodation, crowded into a station which usually hosted no military force at all.

In response to military and civil officers' entreaties, in August more troops would be ordered toward the disturbed districts. This entailed a complex scheduling of reliefs and transport—stations were not to be left vacant—which all took time. The 63rd Native Infantry was called from Cawnpore, though marching would be too slow: George Atkinson sent a telegraph message to Allahabad asking its men to be 'put on any steamer that may be available'.[5] The 8th was likewise summoned from Futteghur by steamer, to release the 50th from Barrackpore, but not until early October. Despite this force, no one yet seemed to have much idea of how it would be used. 'No definite plan of operations has been laid down', a Raneegunge correspondent noticed in a letter published as Lloyd was appointed.[6]

Editors, military officers, civil officials and civilians such as planters and railwaymen were arguing about what had been learned and achieved. 'A whole month has now elapsed since this tribe openly declared war against us', John Peter Grant minuted on 31 July. Inclined to be pedantic, in this minute at least he wrote plainly: the security of a huge area of Bengal 'has never been worse than it is now … we have a regular campaign … before us'.[7] Even Grant, Halliday's friend at court and constitutionally inclined to dissect and often object to his colleagues' proposals, argued that 'defensive operations' hitherto had been 'conducted in an unconnected manner', though he thought 'this must always be the case in the very commencement of an insurrection'.[8] His colleagues grudgingly agreed; at some length. General John Low summed up his colleagues' position: 'we have given him [Halliday] good troops under a good commander' and would allot more troops if they were needed—if they could be summoned from up-country in time.[9] For now, the suppression of the insurrection was in the hands of George Lloyd and the civil officials obliged to work with him and his officers.

Perhaps the most significant sign of how seriously officials took the Hul was marked by William Grey writing to George Atkinson to pass on Halliday's suggestion that 'it seems very desirable that the rules of the Commissariat Department should not be rigidly adhered to'.[10] This suggestion, amounting to heresy, was pointless without the endorsement of the Military Auditor-General, the arch-fusspot Colonel Andrew Goldie, but it suggests how the rebellion had become a crisis.

Throughout the month, George Atkinson had been sending reports to army headquarters in distant Simla, and individual officers had corresponded with members of its staff. Though the Commander-in-Chief, Sir William Gomm, was never less than ten days behind the news, he followed events in Bengal, his army's only active campaign. Gomm did nothing to intervene in the conduct of operations, merely signalling his 'satisfaction' at its conduct.[11] Newspapers published letters and articles criticising Gomm as enjoying '*otium cum dig*' (unemployment with leisure) on his monthly salary of Rs 17,000 though 'all India may burn'. Gomm should have placed himself at Allahabad, one critic wrote, to be able to direct operations against the Santals and against Oudh if necessary.[12] The *Delhi Gazette* sarcastically reported his travels as 'the movements of a nonentity'.[13] But command of the Company's force would not long remain Lloyd's responsibility alone.

'All the measures necessary': Alfred Bidwell's appointment

In late July, after many icily polite minutes and possibly heated but undocumented arguments in the council room of Fort William, the Supreme Council at last seemingly prevailed in inducing Frederick Halliday to accept that if the rebellion were to be suppressed, military operations needed to be directed and coordinated by a senior military officer, George Lloyd. The tenaciously argumentative Halliday accepted this decision, but only for about two days. On 2 August, he again submitted a long and densely argued minute, this time not contesting the general's right to direct military operations, but proposing that the military commander should be assisted by a senior 'Civil Commissioner', a man 'able to undertake ... all the measures necessary to coerce the insurgents and restore tranquility to the country'.

Halliday's plan involved the appointment of subordinate assistant commissioners, including their salaries and allowances, an essential item in the cost-and-status-conscious Bengal government. Capping his argument was the appeal to precedent: it was modelled on what had succeeded twenty-odd years before during the Cole insurrection. So confident was Halliday of his case—suggesting that he had put it in person in the intervening days—that he merely asked that 'the needful instructions' be issued.[14] In discussing the proposal, George Atkinson pointed out that 'when the Military have once been called into the field a large discretion must necessarily rest with the officer in command ... and he alone should be left to judge' the support his troops needed from the civil authorities. But Atkinson's objection seemed to have been a formality—he was still only a lieutenant—and the Supreme Council swiftly accepted Halliday's plan. Atkinson advised Lloyd to communicate freely with the commissioner and act in concert with him.

The special commissioner Halliday proposed was Alfred Bidwell, commissioner at Nuddea, who had already been active in operations in Moorshedabad. George Brown's failure in Bhaugulpore had persuaded Halliday that 'a younger and more energetic man' was required: Bidwell was a decade younger, though still, at 44, an experienced official.[15] A bachelor, and the son of a Norfolk brewer, Bidwell had served in India for over twenty five years, as controller of Salt Chowkies and was already paid Rs 28,000 annually as a rising official.[16] He had survived allegations of 'laxity' in his management of the salt agency and in 1855 gained a position that seemed to promise to make his career.

Bidwell considered the names of some younger civil officials who had already distinguished themselves in the suppression of the Hul to be appointed as his assistants. They included Ashley Eden, who had first reported the outbreak, albeit belatedly, and Charles Chapman, whose publicly exposed breakdown at Peer Pointee probably harmed his career; as well as William Money, 'most usefully and zealously engaged' with military detachments. The ambitious Octavius Toogood and Robert Richardson were not, it seemed, considered, on paper, and Charles Barnes, the indigo planter Bidwell sought, excused himself. Halliday decided that Bidwell's assistants would be Ashley Eden and, perhaps surprisingly, James Pontet. Pontet's supposed knowledge of the Santals probably trumped the lassitude he had displayed as an uncovenanted officer in a backwater of Bhaugulpore district.

Bidwell relished the privileges of his appointment. He always signed his reports and letters as coming from 'The Special Commissioner for the Suppression of the Sonthal Insurrection' and, accustomed to the perquisites of high civil office in the Bengal administration, commandeered one of the few steamers available in which to travel around his area of operations. George Lloyd received news of Bidwell's appointment with regret, but accepted that he needed to work with—or at least not against—the new civil commissioner. The appointment of the two most senior military and civil officers raises the question of the relationship between the two generally.

Bidwell immediately intervened in planning operations. As George Lloyd travelled down the Ganges and into the Bagirutty, interviewing and conferring with subordinates on the way, he tried to work out what had been happening in the disturbed districts over the past month, pondering how he could respond to the task the Supreme Council had given him. Lloyd's was not merely a military problem. He also had to deal with a civil bureaucracy sensitive about its prerogatives and authority. He had been in command for less than ten days when he 'had occasion to complain ... of his plans being deranged by ... the suggestions of the Civil functionaries' accompanying his columns, as Alfred Bidwell explained to his own superior, William Grey.[17]

As an experienced bureaucrat, Frederick Halliday had professed to accept the Supreme Council dismissing his request to declare martial law. As an experienced Bengal civil official, however, he also knew that he was able to continue to press his case, and he did, and on characteristically casuistic grounds. Replying almost immediately to the Supreme Council's ruling, he submitted a further minute, disingenuously protesting that 'it did not occur to me that troops could be directed to act independently of the civil power'—something he had actually argued against. He warned, adopting a disinterested tone, that he was merely concerned that not declaring martial law would be 'productive of some embarrassing consequences' and professing that he was now unsure how to instruct his district officers.

Halliday claimed that because Lloyd had command of troops operating in his province, he had somehow usurped civil authority, a seemingly deliberate misreading of the Council's decision. He even wondered whether he should advise his commissioners, collectors and magistrates to 'abstain from all exercise of their functions', even though the Supreme Council clearly wanted civil officers to work with military officers to find and fight the rebels.[18] Halliday's dog-in-the-manger tone would today be regarded as passive aggressive. It suggests that he was more interested in maintaining his authority than in actually defeating the rebels devastating his province. His attitude would exacerbate relations between civil and military officers.[19]

George Atkinson, writing on behalf of the Supreme Council, patiently explained to William Grey, though it was actually intended for Halliday, that its members 'did not intend that the Military should act independently of the civil power' except that in the direction of military operations General Lloyd's orders would prevail over those of civil officials.[20] Further sterile minutes passed over the question in the following week, rehearsing familiar arguments, all couched politely but revealing that despite their formality senior members of the governments of Bengal and India held fundamentally different views.

Though affirming that the Supreme Council's orders would be 'zealously obeyed', Halliday continued to sulk, writing long, pedantic minutes in which he complained that 'my authority is entirely set aside'.[21] The 'embarrassing consequences' that he foresaw were not long in appearing, and characteristically for British India they involved a matter of no intrinsic importance. In an unusual slip, George Atkinson, who had a mountain of correspondence to get through every day, failed to ensure that Halliday's official on the spot, George Loch, knew of Louis Bird's appointment before Bird actually arrived. Worse, Loch had ordered that the Calcutta Native Militia should be directed to mount guards around Raneegunge, a purely decorative matter—the Bengal Army posted guards on every public building to little purpose but to keep sepoys occupied.[22] This order was now countermanded, supposedly on the order of the Supreme Council and they were sent elsewhere. (That the President-in-Council might be bothered to intervene in the guard duty of a rag-tag local unit is not at all incredible.) Loch then learned that his order had been changed and telegraphed his superior, William Grey, complaining frostily and pointedly that 'the orders I received from the Government of Bengal' had been countermanded.[23] It was this minor administrative confusion that Halliday condemned in another long minute as the inevitable consequence of the Supreme Council's decision as soon as he heard of it, which he did, immediately, from the affronted Loch.[24] The next day, Bird arrived to find that he had inadvertently got off on the wrong foot with the senior civil official on whom he depended for the efficient working of everything from his supply to his intelligence system, and the accommodation of his troops. The Calcutta Native Militia, which had been more trouble than it was worth, eventually returned home by a special train early in August.

Beyond the Council Chamber in Fort William, critics questioned the new special commissioner's qualification to direct the rebellion's suppression. 'General Bidwell', an anonymous critic wrote, 'knows everything military because he once spent a week at a house where the bugles of the body guard could be heard'. Brigadier Bird ('who has more experience in his little finger than Messrs. Loch, Bidwell and Taylor have in their whole bodies') was treated 'as a constable'.[25] In truth, some district officials presumed to take what we would call operational decisions. William Grey had occasion to reprimand Robert Richardson, for example, for 'going beyond the strict line of your duty' by 'requisitioning' rather than requesting military aid.[26] But, to the soldiers' chagrin, civil officials, who knew their districts better than them, were hard to restrain. Bidwell, and other senior officials such as Loch, Elliott and Ward, became 'Civilian Generals' directing Company forces in the rebellion.[27] James Ward, a Raneegunge critic complained, was 'totally misplaced' planning military operations, who 'stultified' Lloyd and Bird.[28] These were the sort of 'Military Civilians' who, aping military fashions such as moustaches, were derided as 'Cutcherry Hussars'.[29]

'Cleared of the rebels': operations in Bhaugulpore

As in other districts, in northern Bhaugulpore in August more detachments began seeking out Santal bands, trying to 'disperse' them: the usual verb used. General Lloyd's policy was to intimidate the Santals by 'the movements of strong detachments'.[30] Officers adopted the tactic familiar from the Kol rebellion of 23 years before: the *dour* (patrol). Directed largely by military officers, nota bly Major Henry Shuckburgh, and advised by Captain Walter Sherwill, dours largely occurred without any clear direction, but their effect, as was occurring in Beerbhoom and Moorshedabad, was to impel large Santal bands south and westward. 'From all accounts', George Lloyd learned early in August, 'it seems that the Insurgents have for the most part left the northern and Central parts of the Hill Country' for the south.[31] Alfred Bidwell, learning how to get on with the older and more experienced general, agreed both with Lloyd's analysis and his plan. The dours in Bhaugulpore, he reported to Grey, 'have the effect of driving the insurgents ... towards the South of the District ... where they will again be attacked by the forces advancing against them'.[32] The reality was not quite as neat nor as soon as Lloyd's optimistic subordinates foresaw, but it heralded the decisive shift of the centre of gravity of the insurgency, once the monsoon began to ease.

Having received repeated requests from George Brown to send troops to Bhaugulpore, while still at Dinapore, George Lloyd had already concluded that 'the Commissioner seems to entertain fear' for the safety of Bhaugulpore, and criticised his appeals for cavalry, because the monsoon made horses useless. He agreed, however, to send two 24-pounder guns, the largest field ordnance the Bengal Artillery possessed, but plainly remained sceptical.[33] Lloyd's criticism, circulated to senior civil officials, corroborated the poor impression Brown had made in Fort William.

More active commanders ventured further. Charles Barnes reported that the river flats between Bhaugulpore and Rajmahal were 'perfectly quiet' by 10 August, whereupon the axis of operations in Bhaugulpore district moved further south, largely at the instigation of regimental commanders such as Majors Henry Shuckburgh and John Liptrap.[34] Lloyd's arrival reinvigorated Company operations in Bhaugulpore. Already, the arrival of more troops, with the 13th and 42nd joining the 40th, under officers eager to close with the Santals, had seen detachments sent out on dours. As ever, particularly enterprising officers set an example. Shuckburgh led parties of the 40th southwards from the Ganges. These long dours depended upon the advice not so much of civil officers, who following the example of the supine George Brown were much less active than in other districts, but upon the experience of Captain Walter Sherwill, the acknowledged expert on the Santal country.

Lloyd probably already knew of Sherwill's work and his reputation—his revenue survey area largely coincided with the Dinapore Division and they shared a Darjeeling connection. He wanted Sherwill to join his staff ('… of the greatest importance to enable me to conduct effectively the operations against the Sonthal insurgents') rather than Captain Dean Shute, who had no particular expertise.[35] Lloyd persuaded the Quarter-Master General, Lieutenant-Colonel Arthur Becher, the officer responsible for postings, that even if Shute were given to him, Lloyd would still need an intelligence 'department', and begged the Commander-in-Chief 'not deprive me of [an officer] intimately acquainted with the Sonthal population'.[36] Becher allowed Lloyd to have both.

Under Sherwill's guidance, parties of the 40th and later the 13th went out on patrols, sometimes for up to a week, essentially to find and attack parties of Santals. Shuckburgh marched eastwards, determined to seek out the Santals who had 'depopulated' the country through which they marched, though 'half the country we passed through was under water' and he had mistakenly loaded supplies in hackeries,presumably because he was short of elephants. He marched 'straight into the Damin-i-koh'. As his men entered the jungle at the edge of a valley, Shuckburgh heard the Santals' 'peculiar sounding drum … in all directions'. The Santals did not attack, but they kept drumming as the sepoys advanced. Frustrated, Shuckburgh ordered a village burned and withdrew.[37]

A typical example of this active policy, one seemingly unprompted by civil officials, unlike in Beerbhoom, was a dour undertaken by another detachment of the 40th under Lieutenant William Cahill just before Lloyd's arrival. Cahill described how he set off from near Colgong before dawn on 29 July with a strong force of 160 sepoys, three other European officers and no fewer than twenty native officers. They marched for five miles before reaching an indigo factory, still smouldering after a Santal raid. Pressing on, they saw and shot two Santals, perhaps scouts for a Santal band. Reaching Derrypoor, Cahill's men fought a group of Santals who resisted, 'flourishing their swords, bows and arrows', the sepoys retaliated firing a couple of volleys, and then burned another village—possibly their adversaries'—and seized 500 cattle. A little way on Cahill's force discovered a village 'full of English goods'—the haul of Santal attacks on railway and indigo bungalows a few weeks before, a collection of cloth, rugs, glass, even furniture, which they destroyed, unable to carry it all back, and confiscated another 400 cattle. On the way back to their camp, the sepoys burned more villages—'in all Eleven'—returning early in the afternoon having marched 19 miles, most of them through wet rice fields. Cahill attributed his success to 'the able assistance I received from Captain Sherwill and Mr Barnes', the latter was the planter who declined Halliday's invitation to become one of Bidwell's assistant commissioners.[38]

A week later the 40th made contact with the 7th and 31st Native Infantry to the east of the Damin, as far as 'the Valley of Burhete which is one of the chief strongholds of the Rebels'.[39] There, on 1 August near a village named Bissohuwa, the 40th's adjutant, Lieutenant James Burn, encountered a group of Santals blocking his march. 'We advanced cautiously', one of Burn's subalterns wrote. Soon, about 500 Santals 'arose as if by magic from the ground'. They advanced on the sepoys in a semi-circle and 'jumped about flourishing their swords ... and yelling in a most diabolical manner'. With arrows falling about his men, though 'not poisoned' ones, Burn ordered his sepoys to shoot. They fired 'as if the men had been on parade'. The Santals stood several volleys before retiring—the subaltern did not write 'fled'—Burn ordered a feigned retreat. His ploy worked: the Santals followed. Just as the sepoys were about to fire again, Shuckburgh hurried up with his detachment, and seeing this the Santals did flee, outpacing the pursuing sepoys.[40]

By these bold forays into the plains around the Damin, local commanders ensured that, as the subaltern heard his superiors claim, 'a very considerable distance from Bhaugulpore to Rajmahal is cleared of the rebels'.[41] When he assumed command, Lloyd learned that the actions of this group of enterprising officers had succeeded in re-establishing Company control over a band of country perhaps twenty miles deep, and extending to the edge of the Damin, though it seems not to have persuaded him to allow active dours to continue.

Elsewhere in Bhaugulpore, patrols of Shuckburgh's 40th Native Infantry and Liptrap's 42nd Light Infantry pushed towards the town of Bowsee, thirty miles south of the Ganges on the Bhaugulpore plain near the sacred Mandal Hill. Shuckburgh and Liptrap seemingly planned to maintain the pressure on Santal bands still in the Damin by marching north-eastwards from Bowsee toward the Soondhur River, where they understood there to be large concentrations of Santals, perhaps as many as 25–30,000.[42] Shuckburgh devised a plan in which his detachment of the 40th would march on the Santals from the north, while Captain Robert Francis's of the 13th would approach from the west and south, catching them between their converging columns. Two days before, on 13 August, Lloyd had sent both an order directing 'a Simultaneous attack' but it failed to reach either officer.[43] Shuckburgh's unduly ambitious plan failed, because the two officers had no way of knowing where the other was or of communicating; the Santals disobligingly vanished. The failure demonstrated the constraints operating on Company forces in such country against such an enemy. It persuaded Shuckburgh that 'making "dours" to catch the rebels is perfectly useless' because 'they are light footed … and dodge about in various directions'.[44] He surely told Lloyd this when they met soon after.

The Santals in Bhaugulpore seemed disinclined to be simply herded about by the movements of sepoy columns, a fact that Robert Francis learned soon after leading his detachment south. In the first days of August Francis had marched from Bowsee intending to make 'an excursion' to attack a Santal village. Sending his scarce supply elephants back to Bowsee, he marched on, when a sowar arrived with an 'express' from his subedar, Rhoddy Misser, who reported that he feared a Santal attack. On the afternoon of 3 August, three Santal bands, about 3000 men, made simultaneous attacks on the Bowsee depot from three directions. Subedar Misser and his forty sepoys placed the elephants in a compound and opened volley fire at the unusually long range of 300 yards, presumably seeking to demoralise the attackers before they reached arrow-range or closed with their axes. A chance shot killed the Santals' leader, Lall Soobah, and the attack swiftly collapsed—'the whole party instantly fled'.[45] Misser showed Francis the ground and his officer warmly endorsed the subedar's account and actions. Lloyd, learning of the Santal attack hailed Misser as 'deserving of much praise'.[46] He is one of a handful of Indian troops whose name is associated with any incident in the entire rebellion, and in due course Colonel Henry Tucker, the Adjutant-General commended 'all concerned' but Misser did not receive a decoration.[47]

Despite such seemingly positive reports, Lloyd seems to have realised as he read his subordinates' reports in August, that the Santals were more elusive and demanding adversaries than he and others had assumed. An episode related by Walter Birch, still operating with the 7th Native Infantry in the south-eastern purgunnah of Bhaugulpore around Moheshpore, also made sobering reading. Based on intelligence apparently obtained by Robert Richardson, Birch had marched his troops westwards from Moheshpore seemingly 'driving the Sonthals before him the whole way'. Richardson, like Elliott in Beerbhoom, had made contact with Santal manjees and they had persuaded him that they could deliver up Kanhu and Sidhu, who were rapidly becoming fabled Santal leaders, especially Sidhu, the elder, who 'appears to be the most active and to be supreme'.[48] As Birch reached Amrapara, on the Bansloi River, he learned that a Santal party had returned to attack the garrison he had left at Burhyte. It seemed to Lloyd that 'Mr Richardson has been deceived by false overtures into leading troops away ... on a useless errand.'[49]

If Lloyd had believed that a series of energetic thrusts in Bhaugulpore could simply push the Santals southwards he may now have realised that the Hul could not be defeated so easily. He later admitted that 'I had endeavoured to carry out [this plan—to defeat the Santals] with the Infantry alone in August and September, but it was defeated by unforeseen and unavoidable delays'.[50] He now realised that these 'fruitless and ill advised' operations in eastern Bhaugulpore confirmed 'the utter inutility of our present operations'.[51] He had already decried 'these (in my opinion) premature advances into the Hills', and now he saw that they were not only not actually 'punishing the rebels and ending the rebellion', but feared that further dours would merely induce them to shift. He thought that the pressure which they had been subjected to in Bhaugulpore would result in them being 'scattered Southward', an impression which only strengthened as Lloyd read further reports through August.[52] That the forces in the district to the south, Beerbhoom, now appeared to be coming under stress, might seem to bear out Lloyd's apprehensions.

Lloyd advised Alfred Bidwell of his plan to curtail active operations and order the withdrawal of detachments and the reduction in active sweeps, with the northern force's regimental headquarters at Bowsee (42nd), Colgong (40th), Godda (13th) and the 7th still split between Rajmahal and Berhampore.[53] The Company's campaign in Bhaugulpore for the moment halted.

'Inglorious work': the Company's use of military force

Company officers in the field soon concluded that they could not defeat the Santals by pursuing them, a situation they realised that Santal leaders also grasped. Alfred Bidwell, after speaking to junior officials, wrote that they 'shew by their demeanour that they are perfectly aware that Infantry Troops have no chance of coming up with them'.[54] William Money had just told him that they had soon noticed how slowly sepoy units moved. 'So callous have [Santals] become', he wrote, 'that they have in some cases continued their revels until the arrival of the parties within 300 yards of them'—that is, more than twice the effective range of the sepoys' muskets.[55] The inundated country precluded the obvious alternative, cavalry, so the task would be left to slow-moving infantry, untrained in what would later be called counter-insurgency warfare.

Thoughtful officials accepted that the bold but haphazard dours of the rebellion's first month could not continue. William Money, one of the more reflective Company officials, ventured that the 'attacks made by the Magistrate of Moorshedabad [Toogood] will never again be repeated'. But Money also predicted that the Santals would learn from the rebellion's opening clashes. The Santals' rank and file, as it were, had surely realised from the losses inflicted by the sepoys' muskets at Moheshpore that 'the statements of their leaders are false ... something besides water proceeds from our Muskets'. In fact, as Santal leaders became accustomed to musketry, they adapted a range of responses to their adversaries' military advantages. But if Santals were easily able to elude Company troops in the jungle, tactically, they were nevertheless subject to the strategic pressure which Company columns were able to exert. Money was among the first to consider the protagonists' respective situations and prospects. Already, in mid-August, he foresaw that however clumsy the troops were, their very presence limited the Santals' freedom of movement. Money believed—more by inspired guesswork than by informed analysis—that 'their only recourse' would be 'to take refuge in the South', in the remote purgunnahs of Belputteh and Hendweh, in the south of Bhaugulpore district.[56] Money was correct, though the full detail of his prediction would be revealed only in the last month of the rebellion.

The first refugees of the conflict had been the families of zamindars and rajahs when Santals advanced out of the Rajmahal Hills and made for Pakaur, and then the families of European railway engineers and European civilians living in mofussil towns. But much suffering was inflicted upon Bengalis and, indeed, Santals otherwise uninvolved with the Hul. With such a huge area subject to despoliation, conflict forced tens of thousands of villagers, mostly Bengali, from their homes—at one point an estimated 80,000 people, all moving 'anywhere out of reach of the Sonthals'.[57] Some fled temporarily, though wealthier farmers and merchants, with more to lose and greater resources to fund flight, went further. Soon stations were surrounded by temporary camps of refugees unwilling to risk returning lest Santal marauders return, soon suffering from dysentery, cholera, malnutrition and exposure. A witness described 'in a depressed state of mind' the sight of thousands of refugees 'with loud cries bemoaning the loss of their nearest and dearest whom the Santals had butchered in cold blood'.[58] Others, though living in areas protected by Company troops, feared that if the troops left they would be exposed to despoliation. A petition addressed by Gungaram, a villager in eastern Beerbhoom, to James Ward made the point:

> We have been residing in British Territories for a long time in perfect happiness and without any fear … [now] we have been subjected to hardship … [the Santals] have plundered our property and murdered several people.[59]

Gungaram wrote that 'we are passing our days in great trouble during the rainy season … suffering great hardship for want of food'. Now that the sepoy detachment was leaving his village, near Moheshpore, the Santals could return, and they feared further murders and looting. The Bengalis protested that officials had told them 'you yourselves should protect your houses', but having been denied arms by Company administrators they had 'no means of protecting our life and property'. No wonder the Supreme Council was concerned: Gungaram had effectively asked, what use was Company rule if it could not even guarantee the lives of the people of Bengal?

Digambar Chakraborti, having been a refugee as a child, devoted a paragraph of his 'History' to their plight, recalling:

> the great hardship and want suffered by the unfortunate fugitives, and especially women who had never before had to leave their villages wandering in the inclement weather in the streets of distant villages, with children in their arms thoroughly wet and shivering with cold and crying for food.

Chakraborti felt that he could 'never do full justice' to these victims of the uprising, of whom 'many fell down to rise no more'.[60] The only way to end this suffering was by force. 'Hunting savages out of their dens' was, the *Hurkaru* lamented, 'inglorious work' for regular troops, but no other force was available.[61]

All this Governor-General, Lord Dalhousie, observed while on sick-leave in Ootacamund. The inevitable 'private letters' directed to Madras from friends in Calcutta provided a chorus expanding on the official accounts he received. Though Dalhousie was embroiled in dealing with the consequences of his application of his 'doctrine of lapse' (by which native states without a natural heir were forbidden from adopting heirs and were annexed by the Company), he was said to be 'mad with the Santhal insurrection', an impression not confirmed by the occasional entries in his diary. News of the outbreak brought on a worsening of Dalhousie's precarious health—one evening at the end of August he was found unconscious. When he rallied, it was rumoured that he had 'given a wigging to some of your big men for allowing the outbreak to continue so long', and had even affirmed that he wanted the rebellion suppressed even if it cost 'the sacrifice of 1,000 sepoys!'[62] It was in fact the possibility of high casualties among his troops that inclined Lloyd to defer any precipitate action.

'Object of care': the sepoys' health and Lloyd's strategy

The Company's suppression of the Hul depended upon the sepoys of the ten native infantry regiments committed to the campaign. The *Friend of India*'s account of a clash between a detachment of the 56th Native Infantry and a body of Santals near Sooree late in July offers a reminder of how the Bengal Native Infantry represented a distinct if not unique partnership between British officers and sepoys recruited from Oude and Bengal's North-West provinces. Two bodies of Santals, one of about 1000, the other slightly smaller, attacked a detachment of 80 sepoys under Lieutenant John Delamain. As they attacked 'from right and left', forcing the sepoys to divide their fire-power, Delamain was said to have 'quietly stepped forward and shot down eight, while a raw recruit at his side, a lad not yet admitted into the ranks, slew eleven more'. The sepoys' disciplined volleys seem to have been decisive: 'the mass of dark forms was seen to sway from side to side and in five minutes the scene was clear of the enemy'—except for the dead and wounded they left.[63] This was not the kind of warfare for which sepoys had been trained, though, after initial discomfiture, they adapted with surprising ease.

While their headquarters were at the major stations, most regiments had been broken into up to a dozen detachments, each commanded by a European officer, living for weeks at a time in often isolated tented camps, in the outbuildings of zamindars' compounds or in abandoned police thannahs, usually surrounded by dark, hostile jungle, an environment quite different to the villages from which their men hailed. Henry Norman, for instance, lived with his detachment, for months his only society his subaltern, seeing 'rough and unhealthy service' but becoming 'intimately acquainted with the character of the native soldiers'.[64] Their colonels faced many problems—how to supply distant detachments in the monsoon with too few elephants at their disposal, was a major one. Troops could rarely obtain food locally, partly because they ate wheat not rice, and the villagers had usually fled. How were the troops to be kept healthy in the sickly monsoon and how to ensure that the regiments had enough European officers?

Although Louis Bird praised his native troops as 'adopted to the jungle warfare we are engaged in', it is hard to see how they were especially fitted.[65] The *Hindoo Patriot*, with less investment in the Company's prestige and with recourse to 'native' sources up-country, judged that many native infantry units were in a 'state of happy forgetfulness of military tactics'—the tactics required of troops against the Santals were very different from those used against the Sikhs.[66] Did this hint at ruthlessness? Though their officers praised them publicly, sepoys did not necessarily cope well with the demands of campaigning in Bengal in the monsoon. *The Patriot* (significantly, as its name suggested, edited by a Bengali, Hurrish Chandra Mukherjee), claimed that sepoys had 'not conducted themselves well' and argued that 'a few scanty, ill-appointed, ill-supplied and ill-disciplined detachments' had been 'unable to hold their ground', even though facing 'savages'.[67]

Sepoys displayed no particular desire to capture rather than kill the Santals they encountered. An exchange reported in the *Citizen* suggests a cavalier attitude to taking prisoners. 'There is a report amongst the sepoys', a Rajmahal correspondent offered:

> that the General *saheb* [their commanding officer] must not shoot the men taken as the *Jungly Lat* [civil officers] would be *burragoosa* [very angry] but that he would be quite pleased if the jacks [sepoys] made no prisoners.[68]

Sepoys, he frankly admitted 'prefer shooting them to taking them alive', but as Vincent Jervis recalled of one encounter that 'the prisoners were for the most part wounded men', sepoys must have refrained from executing wounded Santals or at least took some wounded prisoner.[69] One of Walter Sherwill's drawings, in fact, showed a captured, wounded Santal on a litter. A correspondent writing to the *Citizen* was less discreet. He quoted a Santal describe their treatment by sepoys, his gloss: 'our sepoys have a short way of dealing [with Santals]: they bring their muskets a little below the level of their own shoulders, with the barrel's mouth inclined towards the navel of their antagonists'. It was 'dreadful to see the results ... those who escape Jack's musket get his bayonet'. A missionary later described Santal communal memories of an officer whose 'one command' was '*Katl Kare*'—'execute him!'[70]

But sepoys represented a valuable resource, and concerns for their health came to dictate that the Company's campaign would need to be curtailed for the time being. One officer after another voiced concern that campaigning in Lower Bengal in the monsoon would be dangerous for the sepoys' health and regimental surgeons reported outbreaks of dysentery and fever. The dangers seemed considerable. The *Hindoo Patriot* warned that 'the virulence of the miasma' arising from inundated country could spread 'a fever more deadly than the weapons of the enemy'.[71] In six weeks on service at the height of the monsoon, however, the regimental returns reported remarkably few sickmen. Though Edward Braddon described the country as 'a hotbed of disease', sepoys remained healthy.[72] In Sooree they were in 'excellent' health, 'notwithstanding the fatigue and exposure' they had undergone. The 56th had 'very few men in hospital from actual sickness', with a few being treated for arrow wounds, though more from jungle thorn pricks which had turned septic.[73]

Crucially, Walter Sherwill warned George Lloyd about sickness endemic to the Santal country. Sherwill had published articles and reports, including *Geographical and Statistical Reports* on Bhaugulpore in 1854 and on Beerbhoom earlier in 1855. Lloyd heeded Sherwill's expertise and, as the monsoon continued, medical officers confirmed his warnings, reporting growing sick lists. In late August a fifth of the men of one detachment of the 13th were suffering from cholera.[74] Illnesses were not necessarily caused directly by rain and damp, but rather from troops living for weeks in temporary camps with poor sanitation, often fouling rivers and tanks. Sepoys' lines were ordinarily 'quite infamous', a sanitary inquiry soon after found.[75] At Berhampore, the Civil Surgeon found dysentery and cholera among the sepoys of the 31st, alimentary conditions attributable to poor hygiene.[76] At Sooree sepoys lived in the jail hospital, 'one of the best in Bengal', George Loch thought.[77] At Rajmahal, though, for months they lived in tents and in open thatched sheds, in cramped and damp quarters with hardly room for a man's bedding, kit and belongings.

The difficulties of moving and camping in the field during the monsoon should certainly not be underestimated, but it is possible that George Lloyd used his troops' health as a pretext for not taking the initiative. 'The health of troops engaged in active warfare', the *Hindoo Patriot* warned, 'ought certainly be an object of care; but it ought to be a consideration of secondary importance'.[78] Lloyd was happy to wait for the country to dry out before launching his grand advance, which everyone agreed could not begin until November. Did he suspect or hope that in the interval the Hul would begin to collapse from within?

'With all possible speed': administrative confusion

The force's routine correspondence reveals that while the regiments' mobilisation had proceeded with unusual celerity, that speed came at the price of not having all that they needed. In everything—clothing, ammunition, maps, the provision of dhoolies in which to carry sick sepoys and even in ensuring that enough 'native doctors' were available to treat the sick—unit after unit found itself in protracted correspondence over administrative deficiencies. Commissariat staff arrived at Raneegunge without the scales to enable them to dole out the right portions of flour, ghee and lentils, the sepoys' staple foods. On the other side of the disturbed districts, the 13th had the miserable experience of going on dours in the monsoon without camp equipage, and the 31st had no medical officers at all, European or native. Commanding officers and their staff waited a month for the maps ordered for them to arrive, and then not all sets were complete, nor were there enough for all officers sent out on dours. This was partly the embuggerances inherent in large, complex organisations— the waterproof caps and capes promised in July naturally arrived once 'all signs of rain have disappeared'—but it was also a product of the Bengal Army's notorious devotion to procedure over proficiency.[79]

The saga of the 63rd Native Infantry's dhoolies exemplifies the failure of the Bengal Army's supply agencies. The regiment had been hustled on from Barrackpore in July so quickly that it had been unable to bring its full establishment of equipment, including its dhoolies. They had later been forwarded by rail to Raneegunge, but an officious chuprassie sent them back, claiming the brigade-major had told him to return them as unneeded. It took several weeks, inexplicably

1. Walter Sherwill's drawing of a surveyor at work; possibly Sherwill himself, from R.H. Phillimore's *Historical Records of the Survey of India*, Vol. III.

2. The Rajmahal Hills seen from the Ganges. Walter Sherwill observed that while all Europeans travelling on the Ganges saw the hills from their steamers, few knew anything about the region or its people: some assumed that the hills were uninhabited. (*Illustrated London News*, 6 October 1856)

3. A Santal village, based on a drawing by Walter Sherwill. Visitors commented on their neatness, and how they were invariably laid out in the same way, with a street of huts adjoining a sacred grove of sal trees and a platform at which the Thakur was worshipped. (*Illustrated London News*, 28 February 1856)

4. A moonlit Santal ceremony, based on an engraving by Walter Sherwill, whose affection for the Santals did not prevent him from describing their dancing as 'lewd' and 'absurd'. (*Illustrated London News*, 7 June 1851)

5. The tank at Moheshpore (now Mahespur, Jharkhand) in 2020, where elephant-borne sepoys of the 7th Bengal Native Infantry routed a Santal force under the Bhugnadihee brothers, three of whom were wounded in the fight. The tank is one of the few sites of the Hul which can be firmly identified. (Peter Stanley)

6. The 7th Bengal Native Infantry (wearing coatees and dhotis) escorting Santal prisoners to Jungeypore after the march to Burhyte and Moheshpore. The portly officer on the pony may be Walter Birch, drawn by Walter Sherwill. (*Illustrated London News*, 28 February 1856)

7. The country around Burhyte (now Berhet, Jharkhand) in 2020, with the Rajmahal Hills in the distance: the heart of the Hul in 1855 and now the location of a large memorial to the brothers who led it. (Peter Stanley)

8. George Atkinson's depiction of 'Our Sporting Sub', from his *Curry and Rice*, conveys the self-assurance (not to say arrogance) of young officers of the Bengal Army, suggestive of officers like Lieutenant Tom Toulmin, the only Company officer killed in the Hul.

9. An engraving based on a drawing by Walter Sherwill showing sepoys of the 40th Bengal Native Infantry on a 'dour' in Bhaugulpore, with bullock hackeries carrying off Santal loot, elephants bearing the sepoys' baggage and villages burning in the distance. The engraver gave the surrounding landscape a strangely Scottish look. (*Illustrated London News*, 28 February 1856)

10. Railway surveyors crossing a flooded nullah in the monsoon, an engraving based on a drawing by Walter Sherwill that suggests the difficulties of travelling during Bengal's rainy season. (*Illustrated London News*, 28 February 1856)

11. An indigo factory, from Colesworthy Grant's *Rural Life in Bengal*. Especially in the Hul's first month, factories like this became both the targets of Santal attacks and bastions of European resistance.

12. The plains between Godda and Bowsee (now Bausi, Bihar), photographed during the 'cold weather' of 2019–20. For months in the second half of 1855 large Santal bands and several sepoy regiments skirmished in this country. (Peter Stanley)

13. George Brown's substantial cutcherry at Bhaugulpore, an imposing classical edifice beside the Ganges, in which he made decisions which for him were disastrous in the monsoon of 1855. It is now the chancelry of Tilka Manji University. (Peter Stanley)

14. 'Our Magistrate', from George Atkinson's *Curry and Rice*, conveying the commanding demeanour of the Company's civil officials responsible for the suppression of the Hul. This official is directing labourers building roads of the kind the Company used to impose order on the Santal country in the aftermath of the Hul.

15. Some of the Directors of the East India Company, who ultimately both wielded and benefited from British power in India. These men held and exercised the patronage that appointed all of the civil officials and military officers involved in the suppression of the Hul. (*Illustrated London News*, 18 February 1843)

16. East India House, in Leadenhall Street in the City of London, the British head-quarters of the East India Company. The Company's Directors and senior staff were not pleased at the reports of events in Bengal which reached them there from the autumn of 1855. (*Illustrated London News*, 18 February 1843)

drawing in William Grey's clerks, the Barrackpore divisional staff, the superintending engineer, the Public Works Department and the 'servants' of the East India Railway for the dhoolies to finally reach the 63rd's headquarters. By that time most of the regiment was in the field. The episode took pages of the Military Consultations, faithfully copied and transmitted to Fort William and Leadenhall Street in all the embarrassing detail of requests for missing receipts, pedantic 'corrections' of supposed 'aspersions', claims and counter-claims. Eventually the entire sorry mix-up was blamed on an ordnance corporal who had since either died or been posted out of harm's way, but in any case, could not be located.[80]

Lloyd himself discovered a shocking example in the Bengal Army's ramshackle supply system when visiting Calcutta to consult officials at the end of August. He saw that artillery and musket ammunition and barrels of gun powder destined for Bhaugulpore had been loaded on his steamer, the *Jumna*, but 'in a most unsafe position'. Barrels of powder had been stacked on the steamer, and not on the vessel's towed 'flat', open to crew, passengers and servants, any of whom might smoke beside it, and separated from the engine only by an iron bulkhead, itself heated by the boiler to 120 degrees Fahrenheit. Lloyd found that the canvas awning protecting the barrels from the rain bore scorch marks from sparks and smuts from the funnel. Lloyd swiftly convened a committee of enquiry and on its recommendation ordered the cargo unloaded and re-stored. Extraordinarily, Lloyd's report of his action, which may have saved the *Jumna* from exploding, concludes 'I therefore trust I may not have incurred blame for the measures I have adopted'.[81] Lloyd's diffidence speaks volumes about the Bengal Army's habitual lack of initiative and its devotion to form and process rather than rewarding action and results.

At the same time, the Company's administration could at times pull off impressive feats. When the Hul began no telegraph line linked Calcutta with Berhampore, one of the main bases for the Company's campaign. The Supreme Council in July had authorised the construction of a telegraph line, against some of its members' wishes as they did not think the rebellion would last long enough to justify the expense. The Telegraph Department included some of British India's most energetic young technocrats, inspired by the brilliance of its head, the Irish polymath Dr William O'Shaughnessy. Parties of engineers and coolies erected the 108-mile line 'with all possible speed' in under a month. The superintending engineer warned that it was 'not constructed for permanence'—it used lighter wire strung on bamboo posts and suffered short circuits from the wires touching sodden foliage and even wet-plastered buildings—but on 9 August the first messages passed along the line. The telegraph, and the permanent line connecting Calcutta with Raneegunge, gave Company commanders a further advantage in communication and control.[82]

'A chain of posts': Moorshedabad and Rajmahal

Having begun in the north-west of Bhaugulpore district, with large numbers of Santals threatening the river stations, within a month Santal attacks diminished. Whether because troops arrived in greater force, because the villages had all been looted or because Santal bands were impelled, ordered or called southwards, disorder ended. Alfred Bidwell, the new special commissioner, energetically assumed the role of effective military commander in the area, directing military officers to place detachments and issuing directions to them to 'disperse' bands of Santals. Bidwell's initiative, a contrast to the inactivity of his counterpart in Bhaugulpore, attracted the notice of Grey and through him Halliday.[83]

Rajmahal had been the initial focus of the Hul, but within a month conflict in the area had virtually ended. James Pontet, the superintendent of the Damin, complained by the end of July that 'we sit here idle … doing nothing'. A hill man (probably a Paharia) had warned him that the Santals would attack the next day ('I wish they would') but the heat had gone out of the rebellion in Rajmahal and the nearby hills.[84] In the last week of July the 31st Native Infantry arrived by steamer at Jungeypore and Aurungabad and marched west, passing through deserted Santal villages. Few large Santal bands remained—some had already moved south—but the troops were unnerved to see 'parties of insurgents hover around, keeping aloof'.[85]

On the border of Moorshedabad and Beerbhoom districts, other detachments ranged about the country, sometimes meeting Santal bands and sometimes pursuing them into the jungle, burning villages when they found them. Officers' reports tended to the optimistic—Ensign Francis Sitwell of the 31st claimed to have 'completely dispersed' a 'large body of rebels' that disappeared into the jungle after they exchanged musket balls and arrows on 3 August. A few days later about 1200 Santals 'in 3 divisions' attacked Lieutenant Hunter Smalpage's detachment of the 31st near Moheshpore, the scene of Birch's first success and where few Santals had been seen since. Smalpage repulsed the assault, possibly a surprise attack, without loss, and another a few hours later. He urged his sepoys to pursue the Santals, but the Santals 'took to the heavy Jungles' and the sepoys lost them. Like almost all Company columns, Smalpage's could not find the enemy, could not bring any serious firepower to bear against them, and could not catch them if they chose to disengage.[86]

While Lloyd's force as a whole was finding the Santals a surprisingly difficult enemy to defeat, the officers actually conducting operations and their sepoys, were grappling effectively with the challenge of meeting an elusive and ingenious enemy in the field. A detailed account of a dour undertaken by a detachment of 250 sepoys under Ensign Sitwell of the 31st, offers a picture of how native infantry units responded to the campaign's trials. Sitwell, garrisoning Pakaur, heard that a large force of Santals had been seen about eight miles south of the town. Apparently acting on his own initiative (he had had 'spirited encounters' before), the 24-year-old Sitwell set out at 4 a.m. 'for the purpose of dispersing them'. Reaching a village, he encountered bodies of Santal parties converging, possibly at the direction of drums. Undeterred by the sight of his sepoys' red coats, they retired slowly as he advanced toward them, except for one party, bolder than the rest. Wishing to guard his flank, Sitwell sent a section off to his left and continued to advance, though as usual the soaked ground prevented his men from catching up with the Santals.

Just when Sitwell had decided to recall his detached section, the Santals on his left began to shoot arrows at it. The havildar in command of it, Bucktour Doobey, ordered his men to fire back and to charge the Santals, four of whom fell to their fire. Sitwell, alarmed that Doobey could be cut off, ordered his own drummer (probably a Eurasian) to beat the recall but without effect. Perhaps because Doobey's blood was up, but Sitwell thought that Santal drumming drowned out the puny sound made by one drummer. Sitwell, who like all British officers was mounted, cantered off to recall Doobey himself, but then came under what he called 'fire' from bushes 200 yards distant. This is much greater than arrow range, and even suggests that the Santals had matchlocks captured from burkundazes; alternatively, perhaps Sitwell's judgment was faulty. He called for his sepoys to follow him and galloped as fast as the boggy ground would allow to attract Doobey's attention. Doobey's men advanced, and as Sitwell reached the bushes, he saw four of them 'shewing a bold front to about 15 Sonthals'. They shot arrows at the sepoys, wounding two, while an arrow bounced off Sitwell's wicker 'Solah hat', but the Santals ran off as he fired his pistol after them. Havildar Doobey returned with his section, with Bengali villagers driving a hundred cattle the Santals had tried to take, which they handed over to officials of the Ranee of Pakaur, reinstated under British protection. Sitwell asked for a native doctor to treat his two wounded and reported his encounter in which, he rightly judged, 'the sepoys behaved very steady and well'.[87] The episode suggests not only the enterprising leadership of British and 'native' leaders: Havildar Doobey is one of a handful of non-commissioned sepoys named in official accounts, but also how their men acted in accordance with their discipline and training.

Though the Nawab of Moorshedabad remained apprehensive—as late as August he was ordering that gongs should summon his troops if the Santals should attack his palace, though safely located on the eastern bank of the Bagirutty—it was clear that the emergency in that district was over.[88] By early August the 31st and 7th Native Infantry held 'a chain of posts' stretching from Nalhati to Skreekond, about 15 miles up the unfinished railway from Pakaur. Walter Birch reported that two weeks after his expedition his men had 'seen nothing more of the Sonthals'.[89] This did not prevent a short-lived 'panic' in a district untouched by Santal bands for almost a month, but it meant that the right or western bank of the Bagirutty River had 'nearly been cleared' of rebels, as the *Hindoo Patriot* reported with satisfaction. But the south of Bhaugulpore district remained 'infested'.[90]

'First catch your Santhal': debating insurrection

Calcutta's newspapers argued about the causes of rebellion, how it should be suppressed and how the Santals might be punished. As usual, in the quarrelsome world of British Indian-journalism, editors or writers could not agree on any of these subjects. But all agreed that insurrection needed to be ended. Newspaper correspondents called for severe collective punishments: 'hang a lot in each village, and it would be a long time before there would be an outbreak again', wrote a man from Raneegunge.[91] Newspapers published letters advocating the most brutal and bloodthirsty methods. The *Friend of India* reproduced with approval two letters to the *Bengal Hurkaru* which advocated burning the Santals into submission. The second noted that the elusive Santals could not be found in the jungle. But, the writer added ominously, 'brushwood will burn'.[92] In August Meredith Townsend, the *Friend of India*'s editor, had proposed that the entire Santal people be deported to Pegu (Burmah), which would both punish rebellion and, incidentally, create a huge colony of transported labour able to feed Madras. The liberal *Morning Chronicle* hinted that this plan originated with Halliday himself, flying a kite for newspaper editors to propagate. The *Citizen*'s editor objected that this would amount to 'wholesale massacre', reminiscent of the United States' government's forcible transplantation of Native American peoples a few decades before, denouncing Townsend as 'monomanical'.[93] Soon, Frederick Halliday noticed that 'natives'—that is, Bengali merchants apprehensive for the security of their commercial interests— were asking 'Is no punishment to be inflicted on the great body of the insurgent Sonthals?' Were they to evade retribution by 'simple submission'? Halliday pondered whether 'to inflict some general punishment' on the Santal people.[94] The *Friend of India*, widely read by evangelicals, proposed the most extreme collective punishments, including, as its contemporary, the *Hindoo Patriot*, wrote, the deportation of the 'entire race', amercement (fining the entire Santal people), and the summary execution of all men taken in arms.[95] 'The most popular' plan, *The Times*'s Calcutta correspondent reported, was to condemn leniency 'as an encouragement to rebellion' and force the entire Santal population to build roads through their country in irons.[96] Pragmatically and ironically, the liberal *Morning Chronicle* reminded readers that 'you must first catch your Santhal'.[97]

The extreme reaction of the Calcutta press is explained by the reports emanating from the Santal country. From the first, European accounts made much of Santal brutality. Often second-hand, they are littered with details of atrocities committed by Santal bands. Sometimes referred to elliptically—'murdering indiscriminately', 'mad and blood thirsty'—but often explicitly: 'they burnt a woman alive', William Elliott recorded.[98] Newspaper correspondents retailed survivors' stories: 'they tear the children from their mothers' arms and dash their brains out'.[99] A Berhampore correspondent wrote of 'decapitated bodies … found with the hands tied behind the back and even infants cut in pieces'.[100] Near Sooree officers passed on accounts of, for example, Santals roasting a woman alive, but first killing her child and forcing her to drink its blood—presumably to coerce her to reveal her hidden valuables.[101] Stories spread beyond Bengal, both true and false. From distant Sealkote, in the Punjab, Sergeant Joseph Cheers wrote home to Cheshire retailing a story he had read in a Delhi paper describing how three (not two) ladies had been 'butchered', adding gory and untrue details that, published in the *Cheshire Observer*, appalled and fascinated folk at home.[102] Narahari Kaviraj decried these references as 'highly exaggerated', but then acknowledged that Santals 'took pleasure to torture them [Bengalis] to death'.[103]

The Bihar archivist-historian Pranab Chandra Roy Choudhury claimed that Santal atrocities had been 'overdrawn'; that 'a few instances' had been wrongly taken to be representative.[104] But one of the few, partly translated, Santal sources, Chotrae Desmanjhi's memoir, acknowledged that 'during the rebellion the Santals did many cruel things', including indiscriminate killing, describing young women 'snatched from the protection of their husbands' and killed as witches. 'Who would not weep at this cruelty?' Jugia Haram asked.[105]

The most repeated story described how Santals exacted retribution against the mahajans and zamindars they caught. A Rajmahal correspondent described what he had heard:

> Their cruelties are frightful, and the way they kill people, horrible. They commence by cutting off the hands and feet, then the limbs, and lastly the head.[106]

Before the outbreak of rebellion Santals had been portrayed as mild and inoffensive, if anything timid. Soon Europeans accepted that Santals were capable of the most appalling cruelty: William Money had heard (incredibly) that 'a Sonthal finding his child somewhat impeded his flight cut its throat and left it on the ground'.[107] As the balance of conflict now moved to Beerbhoom district, barbarity seemed to be given full rein.

'The vultures hover': fighting around Sooree

'Private sources'—the letters from friends and colleagues often published anonymously in newspapers—constituted effectively an informal intelligence network. But, as is clear from comparing private and official sources, it was by no means reliable. Louis Bird, who had been reading newspapers in Dinapore, initially accepted George Loch's pessimistic accounts of how large bands of Santals threatened Sooree. On reaching Beerbhoom he immediately 'deemed it advisable to call in the detachments', a decision he later found to be precipitate.[108] As a forest people it is unsurprising that the Santals remained reluctant to approach any habitation larger than villages. Despite this wariness, officials and residents in virtually every station at one time or another feared Santal attack. Reports repeatedly anticipated raids on headquarters stations—the false report that the Santals had sacked Rajmahal became widely accepted—but despite civil and military forebodings, not once did the Santals attack Sooree, Bhaugulpore, Rajmahal or other major stations.

Bird's caution seems unjustified. He had at least 700 sepoys at Sooree and as many more 30 miles away at his headquarters at Raneegunge. Even so, he professed himself 'hard pressed' and like his predecessors called for reinforcements.[109] It seems that numerous accounts of the Santal bands at large in eastern Beerbhoom, at least some of which appear to have been multiple reports of the same bodies, and the shock of the disaster that had overcome Toulmin and his detachment, for a time dented even Bird's confidence.

As more troops joined the campaign, impinging upon the bands' freedom of movement, and the fruits of plunder diminished, those Santals able to see beyond the limits of the jungle clearings in which they lived, surely wondered how the rebellion could continue, if not yet how it might end. William Elliott, who questioned Santal prisoners and spoke to villagers who did not join the Hul, told Louis Bird that 'shrewd natives … finding themselves pressed by troops' had 'sent their women and children far into the jungles, and are preparing for a desperate struggle'.[110] That desperate struggle developed on the plains of Beerbhoom in August.

Santal bands, some moving south from Bhaugulpore, had threatened Sooree from the middle of July—the magistrate Henry Rose, had reported that he 'along with the Railway gentlemen' were 'expecting an hourly attack', requesting troops directly from Barrackpore.[111] By the month's end a Public Works Department engineer at Rampore Haut wrote describing how he could see the smoke of burning villages rising over the surrounding plain. He had heard that 5000 Santals were encamped to the north, 10,000 on the west and 8,000 to the south, naturally fearing attack. The streets were crowded with refugees, mainly terrified Bengali villagers, 'wounded and hacked, especially old men and women'. He sent coolies to fortify Rampore Haut, 'and we have scouts out in every direction'.[112] A newspaper having claimed that Santals were planning to attack 'swearing to cut the throats of all the sahibs', the arrival of a detachment of the 56th brought 'great joy'.[113] They heartened Henry Rose, who decided that 'instead of bolting … we … intend to remain', with a force of 15 sahibs 'well armed', 62 sepoys, 2 officers and 100 chuprassies, even if only fifteen of the latter had guns.[114] Though William Elliott at Sooree could spare no more troops for Rampore Haut's defence, no actual attack came. In the coming month, however, Sooree and eastern Beerbhoom became the focus of the rebellion.

Military and civil officers repeatedly expressed concern at a Santal threat to Sooree, but paid less attention to the large Santal bands devastating villages to its north largely with impunity. The effect of Santal raiding was usually expressed in abstract numbers of villages burned or looted. An account by Koosham, a Bengali, of their raids on Narainpore offers a compelling example of the effects of their attacks. The first Santal descent on this large and prosperous village, wealthy on trade in rice, rum and sugar, and the home of many mahajans, occurred in mid-July, when Santals looted the zamindar's house. Then Santals killed ('or rather butchered') three Brahmins and 48 labourers, burned the cutcherry and nine stalls and carried off Rs 10,000 in goods. Another correspondent said that on 19 July they returned and 'slaughtered hundreds'. On 25 July they came back again, this time pulling down and burning houses, plundering barns of rice and killing more villagers. Four days later they returned, this time, it seems, merely destroying the place, but leaving a white flag on a bamboo pole proclaiming—how it is not known—that Manick Manjee, the Santals' leader, would 'henceforth be the King of this and the surrounding villages'. Narainpore's people fled these 'scenes of horror and devastation', asking for help from the civil authorities.[115]

Once Louis Bird gained a clearer idea of the rebellion, he deprecated alarmist reports of civil officials such as William Elliott and military officers such as Joseph Hampton and George Burney. Elliott's first report to Bird admitted his 'alarm'. He described how large Santal forces had 'committed great atrocities along many miles of railway without opposition', a sly dig at his military counterparts. Octavius Toogood, his reputation high from the march to Burhyte, had met the rebels 'and killed some of them', but even he could not 'stop their atrocities'. They had threatened and raided across a 50-mile swathe of country, from Afzulpore on the Adye north-eastwards to Rampore Haut, with Sooree more-or-less the pivot of the arc, approximately following the present border between Jharkhand and West Bengal. This line, and the country ten miles on either side of it, became the main theatre of war between Santal bands and Company detachments from late July through August.

The pattern of fighting across Beerbhoom in this period involved a confusing range of clashes, some occasioned by Santal attacks, raids and movements, some by dours and patrols by detachments of troops. William Grey expressed a widespread belief in optimistically stating that the 'rough treatment' troops inflicted on Santals 'will probably have prepared them for submission'.[116] While military officers were wary of being charged by officious civilians for actions which in civil life would merit prosecution, they believed that rigorous measures were necessary and like many civil officials wanted martial law: 'let us have Martial law', wrote George Loch from Raneegunge, 'and

Liberty to burn and destroy'.[117] Indeed, until the declaration of martial law in the final month of hostilities decided the matter, Company officers and officials discussed the degree of force they should apply to the suppression of the insurgency. They had long debated what acts they could or could not, or should or should not commit or condone, their speculation not helped by a lack of clarity by senior officials. Frederick Halliday, even if not reading descriptions of explicit acts of killing or the destruction of property in officials' reports, must have heard of them informally. In a minute in which he canvassed the seeming lack of progress in suppressing the Hul, he recognised that already troops had committed 'acts of which no lawyer could … approve', and suspected that if martial law were to be proclaimed 'there will doubtless be an amount of what is called "Military punishment"'—in other words, summary execution.[118] In the meantime, a familiar and limiting legalism prevailed: absurdly, it was said that on his epic march to Bhugnadihee Octavius Toogood had been unable to arrest Santals for having weapons if they had for the moment laid them on the ground, evading the stipulation inherent in the idea of 'arms in their hands'.[119]

Both civil and military officers agreed with Frederick Halliday that 'a severe example should be made of these savages with as little delay as possible': but how was that to happen?[120] Company parties took different views of the limits on their conduct: were they empowered to destroy the property of Santals who were not present? Octavius Toogood on the way to Burhyte passed deserted Santal villages seemingly full of plunder but decided not to destroy them, partly because it would impede his progress, but also because he decided that taking the rebellion's ring-leaders, whom he believed were close, would be the most effective way to stop it. Alfred Bidwell at first believed that it would be illegal for him to destroy Santal villages even if he could see plundered goods, but as he travelled with sepoy columns toward the Damin he changed his mind, and on the march came to think that 'the Insurrection will be effectively suppressed in no other way'.[121]

Increasingly, military officers especially argued that the only way rebellion would be 'perfectly quelled' was by employing what contemporaries called 'severity'.[122] In practice, this meant deciding whether troops should be allowed or ordered to burn Santal villages—that many villages were also inhabited by Bengalis who had fled seemed not to register even with the civil officials responsible for them. Some, such as the unusually reflective William Money argued that destroying villages would alienate Santals loyal to the government as well as those indifferent to the rebellion, and that leaving villages intact would make conciliation easier.[123] Most, however, disagreed, but the policy applied or permitted differed in the field, far from scrutiny. In north-eastern Bhaugulpore, officers of the 31st received 'a severe wig' for burning Santal huts. At the same time, the admonition was given tongue in cheek—it ended 'it had served them right': that is, the 'savages' whose villages had been burned.[124] As the uprising continued, either a policy or at least the practice of 'severity' became accepted. Henry Norman, also of the 31st, told his biographer that he felt that 'firing volleys into villages and the slaughter of ill-armed Santals' was 'unworthy of his profession'.[125] In the end, severity seemed the only effective course. Even when, as Robert Richardson wrote hopefully to Bidwell, 'more may be done by conciliatory measures than by coercion', officers and officials did not see how else they could appease or pacify a people who remained in active rebellion.[126]

The fighting in north-eastern Beerbhoom has become the best known, insofar as any actual incident in the Hul is known, because of a reminiscence by Major Vincent Jervis which came to be quoted in virtually every account of the insurrection. Jervis, a long-serving officer of the 56th who had been badly wounded at Chillianwallah, evidently spoke to William Hunter in the 1860s. Hunter did not name Jervis, but from the description of the siege of a mud-brick house the words must be his. In the passage, Jervis seemed to describe the suppression of the Hul as a whole; certainly, it has been presented thus in books, articles and websites.[127] Jervis led his men on dours in northern Beerbhoom, often from Rampore Haut. He appears briefly in the Company's official records, once describing how his men trapped a party of about thirty Santals in a house in a village near Narainpore. They besieged it until every Santal had been killed, an incident briefly described by Jervis himself in a report to John Delamain, the 56th's adjutant. The event bears discussing in detail.

On 26 July, on Elliott's orders Jervis took 30 sepoys and 10 constables, all mounted on elephants, from Rampore Haut to Nalhati, nine miles up the railway track. There they found a hundred Santals burning the village. As the sepoys advanced most Santals ran off, but up to forty of them sought refuge; in the account Jervis gave to Hunter, it was a 'mud house'—that is, made of brick. The accompanying magistrate, possibly William Elliott, called upon the men to surrender. The Santals replied with a shower of arrows. The sepoys cut a hole in the house's wall and again Jervis called upon the occupants to surrender. The Santals opened the door and again loosed a shower of arrows, and again. By this time several sepoys had been wounded, and the village was burning around them. In his official report, Jervis recorded that for the next three and-a-half hours sepoys and Santals exchanged arrows and shots, and the sepoys succeeded in killing or wounding about thirty of the hut's defenders. 'At every volley we offered quarter', Jervis recalled, and when the arrows slackened at last, hoping to 'save some of them alive', he ordered his men to storm the house. Inside, they found an old man, 'dabbled with blood', standing among the corpses. A sepoy called upon him to surrender, but he hewed the soldier down with his axe. It seems that ten wounded Santals became prisoners.

Jervis did not report whether his men reached Rampore Haut that night with or without the captives. Four sepoys had been wounded in the fight, and Jervis reported that they had 'behaved most splendidly'. As he described them as acting 'in good discipline', they probably did not massacre the Santals who surrendered. Even so, the fight, one of the most sustained in the Hul, must have been a bloody, dangerous and unpleasant experience for all involved.[128] Jervis's summary of it came to stand for the suppression of the rebellion as a whole: 'it was not war … it was execution'.[129]

From the mass of military and civil reports submitted during August in Beerbhoom, a pattern emerges: one that might suggest a Santal strategy, or at least a reaction. Countered on the plains of eastern Beerbhoom, Santal bands now sought refuge in the jungle and hills in the purgunnahs of Belputteah and Hendweh. Thus, while some Santal bands continued their 'depredations', as a whole, whether by intention or merely reaction, Santals effectively went over to the strategic defensive, responding to the movements and initiatives of their adversaries. Lacking strong central leadership or any way to impose it, the Santals could devise no way to positively prosecute the rebellion. Narahari Kaviraj wrote the Santals lost 'because they did not know how to win'.[130] But even if they had known, they could not make victory possible. In retrospect, the fighting in eastern Beerbhoom can be said to mark the beginning of the end for them.

Of this period, Jugia Haram recalled, 'we suffered much ... for three months we were in the forest ... it poured with rain'.[131] Confidence and commitment to the Santal cause drained away with the downpours. Within the dripping jungle camps, feuds and back-biting grew. In Chotrae Desmanjhi's camp, men suddenly turned on a group of women, blaming their misfortunes on witchcraft and kill-ing 'five or six'. Then there was a frenzy of forced marriages, includ-ing two of Desmanjhi's sisters. 'What could you do?' he asked, 'If you did not listen and obey the people ... killed you'.[132] Durga Tudu also described Santal leaders taking women they desired and threatening or killing their male protectors, later condemning Sidhu and Kanhu as 'defiled and unclean'.[133] From this refuge, some swept through and despoiled villages before disappearing back into country into which no Company troops could yet go. Sometimes they met detachments on dours or at outposts, often accidentally, but troops still wasted much energy chasing bands they could never catch. Instead, Bird and his regimental commanders now placed their faith in a 'line of posts'—which they hoped and expected would at least shield undis-turbed districts from further plunder. These posts were not 'a cordon of block houses' as some civilians expected, but merely villages held by a company or fewer.[134] It was around them that further fights developed in August.

'To hear from their own lips': intelligence and negotiation

The Santals' ability to move swiftly dismayed their opponents: it was said a band had been 'known' to march 35 miles in a night, though not every night.[135] William Elliott, who accompanied troops trying to protect the railway line running through Rampore Haut, com-plained that he had seen parties of up to 3000 Santals disperse as soon as sepoys marched toward them. Pursuing them 'without positive information of their next intended place of gathering' proved 'worse than useless', because 'it would dishearten the troops'.[136] This demonstrated, as Elliott admitted, that 'one of the worst of our difficulties is our ignorance of their movements'.[137] How did the Company force gather and use intelligence of their enemies' dispositions, movements and intentions?

The East India Company's empire was founded not on spices, silks, tea or opium, but on paper. Officials reported to their superiors frequently, and invariably copied correspondence to anyone in the chain of authority who might need to know: hence the frustrating duplication in much of the Company's records. Letters and reports reached their recipients by post office dawk—only the most urgent requests and responses went by electric telegraph. The dawks, sometimes literally carried by runners, more usually by fast horse-drawn gharries (or carriages), were liable to delay by muddy roads and swollen rivers, and by alarms of Santal bands. Steamers were more reliable, but limited to riverside stations. Officials who knew their way around the system could expedite matters—Alfred Bidwell, frustrated at the delay in getting reports by post, eased matters at the Bhaugulpore dawk office by arranging for its staff to receive housing and rations.[138] This system enabled officials to communicate with each other and, almost as importantly, to read of matters in other areas. Official correspondence was virtually public, imposing expectations of formality and politeness in official letters, leaving to 'private letters' gossip, rumour and malice; newspapers were 'chiefly dependent for news from the interior on voluntary contributions'.[139] All this contributed to the intelligence—'*khubber*' in Hindoostanee—available to civil officials and, to a lesser extent, military officers.

Their knowledge of the country and ability to communicate with its people gave civil officials their greatest value, if military officers were prepared to accept their advice. Active collectors and magistrates already controlled a network of police darogahs, and enterprising officials developed networks of informers and men they called 'spies'. George Atkinson also allowed military officers to draw on 'Secret Service Money', and Walter Sherwill, who could speak local languages and knew the country intimately, certainly did so, even if the details of informants remained undocumented.[140] Charles Chapman reported that Kanhu had threatened a 'Brahmin' who had told Chapman of Santal bands' whereabouts, warning that he would 'take vengeance on him for giving us information'.[141] But we should not imagine that district officials were necessarily on intimate terms with those they ruled. Frederick Shore revealed that 'few Englishmen can ever have ridden into a village without seeing many of the people run and hide'—and that in times of peace.[142] And could officials even believe what they were told? A planter, decrying the officials' habitual arrogance, bluntly observed that 'no one ever dares to tell him the truth'.[143]

Civil officials were expected to furnish 'information and assistance' to their military counterparts, something contemporaries called 'news'.[144] Their efforts were not always appreciated. A critic damned intelligence gathering as being run by 'a pimping amlah … with a large bag of rupees': in India, it was well known that evidence could be bought—why would anyone trust 'news' obtained from paid agents? But commanders had little choice. He claimed that 'a poor decrepid' peasant was 'made to confess to seeing 20,000 or 30,000 Santals within 20 miles of Raneegunge, supposedly justifying a sweep under Brigadier Bird swearing like any of the troopers of the Ramghur Light Horse', only to realise that they had been 'chasing a bag of wind'.[145] At least some of the fruitless dours recorded in the Military Consultations must have been prompted by such flawed intelligence. Later Company officers tried to conceal the objectives to ensure what would later be called operational security. In October officers of the 50th planned movements 'with the greatest secrecy', the name of the 'doomed village' not spoken but spelled out in the presence of servants who could not speak English. Still, they found that 'the movement was known' and that by the time they got within an hour of their objective they faced Santals who had sallied out to face them, even if they 'bolted' after a few volleys. But the loot in the 'doomed village' had been removed—the Santals must have had 'timely notice' of the troops' objective. Repeatedly, troops returned to camp 'tired and disappointed'.[146]

Civil officials were also charged with finding 'efficient and trustworthy guides' for military detachments operating in unfamiliar and often jungle-clad country, usually without maps.[147] But procuring guides was not always easy or even possible, especially when Bengali villagers had fled and Santals feared retribution. On a dour south of Bowsee, Captain Robert Francis found that his guide took him on such a circuitous route that he was sure that the Santal band he sought had been forewarned. When Francis at last found them the Santals 'advanced boldly to the attack' and though his sepoys drove them off, killing fifteen, they had to camp out in the jungle overnight.[148] John Delamain advised Captain William Gott to keep his guides between two sepoys, and to bind their wrists and rope them to his orderly to 'prevent any treachery'.[149]

Military officers, who had never served in the Santal country, operated under severe disadvantages; disoriented and ignorant, dependent on either civil officials or native subordinates, neither of whom they could necessarily trust.[150] Frederick Shore had noticed that it was the fashion 'chiefly among military men' to ridicule those who exhibited 'pretensions to a better knowledge of Hindoostanee', let alone languages like Bengali; still less Santal.[151] Beleaguered in an isolated post in Belputteh, in successive rooboocaries George Fooks lamented that he was 'unable to ascertain the truth' of anything 'the natives' told him, 'impossible to know friend from foe' and complaining that he had 'no man with me on whose information I can depend'.[152] Military officers were ordinarily ignorant of vernacular languages. Later, as officers became familiar with the country and the people, even if they were not fluent in local tongues, some developed their own intelligence sources, and so became able to evaluate their civilian colleagues' advice rather than simply accepting it—Hugh Pester wrote of 'my own spy', and of using a zamindar's retainers to check and confirm what he was being told.[153]

Civil officials' growing intelligence networks not only enabled them to advise on or propose military operations; they also used local knowledge to contact local landholders and even Santal leaders. William Elliott, eager 'to hear from their own lips the causes of complaint', arranged through the intercession of a darogah and a zamindar near Afzulpore to actually meet five Santal manjees who claimed, not entirely convincingly, not to have joined the rebellion. From them he heard not just the explanations becoming familiar in the newspapers for the rebellion, but about the adversary he faced. Elliott was cautious: he was not empowered to negotiate, but he learned more in this one meeting than had any other official since Toogood destroyed the shrine at Bhugnadihee a month before. Elliott confirmed that the Santals had fallen under the 'extraordinary spell' of the brothers of Bhugnadihee, and especially of Kanhu Manjee, who had given the Santals a vision of 'becoming a great people' free of oppression of either Bengali or British.[154] One of the manjees hailed from Bhaugulpore, and had obeyed Kanhu's summons to the gathering in late June. They had believed the sorcery that the sepoys' bullets would turn to water and that their dead would be resurrected, though after a month many had doubts. 'Numbers of Sonthals have been killed and wounded', they admitted, and 'the rest see the uselessness of fighting against the Government', or so Elliott reported.[155] One Santal leader, Lulkin Manjee, was said to be a purgannait—in charge of 45 villages totalling 23,000 people, a number probably exaggerated but still a powerful figure. He admitted having been present at Nagore when Tom Toulmin and his detachment had been defeated. Elliott did not try to detain him, but allowed them to go, though warning that those persisting in rebellion could expect no mercy.[156]

Village leaders—darogahs and purgannaits or manjees—who had to deal both with Company officials and troops and with Santal visitations, often found themselves caught between competing demands and expectations and therefore became compromised. In mid-September, for example, a chowkidar (or watchman) entered the camp of Captain William Gott of the 56th to tell him that Santals were plundering his village, in Belputteh. Gott had his detachment march to assist, but on the way the chowkidar ran off: 'I have no doubt to acquaint the Sonthals of my approach', he speculated, adding 'all the village chowkidars beyond the [River] More have fraternized with the Sonthals'.[157] Bengali villagers, if they had not already fled, were easily intimidated by the appearance of Santals, and were induced or coerced into selling grain and other supplies to the Santals, grateful that they did not simply take what they wanted. Frederick Burroughs, though his own troops had displayed no great valour, was scathing of the timidity of Bengali villages: 'the moment a Sonthal drum was heard … its inhabitants (if they even waited so long) fled in the opposite direction'. And who could blame them?[158]

'A great fight': Koomerabad

The fourth of the theatres in which Company forces confronted Santal bands was the uplands of central-west Beerbhoom stretching into Belputteh purgunnah in Bhaugulpore. From Sooree, Company officials could often hear Santals even if they could not see them. In mid-August, George Loch became so concerned at the sound of drumming carrying across the Mor River that he 'sent out a man to ascertain the cause'—the man presumably was a Santal. Loch assumed that the drumming was a signal inciting the Santals to attack Mohamed Bazar but the spy returned, telling Loch that the drumming was to tell Santals to move in a westward direction. Armed bands had already left to plunder fresh areas, and their families were to follow in 'a day or two'.[159] Loch's intelligence, whether reliable or not, heralded the shift occurring around the end of August which saw the focus of the fighting move again, from eastern to western Beerbhoom, a 'thinly-inhabited, hilly, and elevated jungle territory', as Walter Sherwill described it in 1855, and into southern Bhaugulpore, specifically at first around the otherwise insignificant village of Koomerabad, located on a low ridge above the River Mor, where a line of great boulders lay across the river bed.[160]

While Santal bands clashed with troops, or more usually avoided them, at many places between the Adye and the Mor rivers, some became scenes of repeated contention, perhaps because they commanded river crossings or were situated on hills. The Santals around Koomerabad were led by a particularly resolute manjee—a planter who spoke to Santals described them as 'likely to stand'.[161] It seems probable that while some Santal bands travelled across country—Sidhu's force in July certainly included men from neighbouring districts—other Santals remained close to country which they knew and were willing to fight for. This seems to have been the case around Koomerabad.

In mid-August, George Loch had reported that Santal bands had 'once again come down', this time plundering villages around Afzulpore, at the southern end of the arc on which the two sides clashed throughout August.[162] For much of the month the Koomerabad garrison was commanded by Lieutenant George Fooks, adjutant of the 50th Native Infantry. It was a sign of the scarcity of European officers that regiments' adjutants commanded outposts, but also possibly a sign of the importance of this one. Fooks faced perhaps 4000 Santals who approached his post 'as active and bold as ever' and at times cut him off from other detachments.[163] Loch, emboldened by Elliott's disclosures of wavering Santal morale, confidently proposed an operational policy; he urged Bird to send a strong force to confront a likely Santal incursion. Bird was reluctant to denude the garrison of Afzulpore, the anchor of his line of posts. Loch persisted, suggesting various combinations of detachments, arguing that an aggressive stance would 'certainly break the strength of the Sonthals in the Country North of Sooree'.[164]

Bird recognised the need to maintain the initiative at Koomerabad, though the troops found the post uncomfortable—they had no proper huts and the monsoon continued. By mid-August Fooks, still a lieutenant, commanded 500 troops of three regiments there, 'thus restoring confidence in that part of the country', Bird affirmed, and he planned to relieve Fooks with the headquarters of John Liptrap's 42nd Light Infantry.[165] In the meantime, Bird attempted the most ambitious military operation of the rebellion thus far. Believing Fooks's reconnaissance reports—he evidently sent patrols out from his post—indicated that a Santal force was gathering, Bird issued orders to send several detachments out in a complex co-ordinated plan.

On 16 August, Fooks forwarded to Bird a report by Lieutenant Frederick Dunbar, who had seen large Santal bands in the neighbourhood. Dunbar sent a company of the 37th to 'disperse' them, which the sepoys did, killing a dozen Santals at the cost of a couple of sepoys wounded. But later in the day, the Santals returned, undeterred, close to Dunbar's post on three sides. Other parties found that 'the Plains and Hills are filled with Sonthals', and Fooks realised that sending out small detachments would leave them in danger of being cut off. He felt the pressure of his command, a large one for a lieutenant, though he was 31. 'I am surrounded by spies', he wrote—he did not trust the villagers he defended—and confessing that 'at times I am at a loss to know what to do'.[166] At night, the troops could hear the war drums all around. Although plainly tested by his singular command, Fooks remained resolute. He was one of the most impressive junior officers in the force, substantiating the inspection report earlier in 1855 that had praised his 'zeal and ability', and he deserved his promotion to brevet captain that was confirmed while he commanded at Koomerabad.[167]

Next day, about 4000 Santals surrounded Fooks's post, seemingly in minutes. He posted a company on each face of his compound and the sepoys blazed away at long range for about three-and-a-half hours. Fooks reported that a few of the Santals had firearms—probably matchlocks taken from burkendazes, but also perhaps muskets taken from Toulmin's sepoys. Late in the afternoon the Santals just as swiftly dispersed, but Fooks expected them to return—again the drums sounded through the night. Fooks found himself practically besieged—he was only able to get reports back because 'messengers', again, probably Santals, were 'obliged to creep through the jungle'. He had only two days' supplies left and no salt, and sending a slow-moving party to a neighbouring post was impossible—and anyway, the Santals had burned the nearest post at Shadeepore, nine miles south.

It seems that the drummer Durga Tudu took part in this fighting. His account of a clash seems to chime in with Company accounts of the fighting around Koomerabad:

> …Then suddenly the British soldiers met us. We started to fight. We did not win. Many Santals were shot and killed, some were hacked down and killed, some were carried away by the Mor River and died, and some of us were saved by running away. I carried the kettledrum on my head and ran away along the river bank … countless numbers of people were killed in that place.[168]

Fooks's messages did reach Bird who, recognising his predicament, swiftly organised a relief column under Henry Raikes, who with a company of the 56th and sixty irregulars under the dependable Sergeant (or Mr) Gillen, reoccupied Shadeepore and soon Fooks was re-supplied. He was to hold Koomerabad for a further ten days. From this advanced post, Fooks again sent out patrols, harassing Santal parties as they moved south-westwards. Just before the post was withdrawn, for example, he sent out parties of fifty sepoys under two ensigns after he had heard that a thousand Sontals were approaching the Mor river. The sepoys caught the Santals as they forded the river, killing perhaps twenty, their bodies swept downstream.[169]

Withdrawing the outposts surely bolstered Santal morale. As soon as Fooks's troops marched out of Koomerabad 'large bodies of Sonthals' entered the village and it was soon in flames.[170] Holding the post had, it seemed, done little to either suppress the Hul or impede the Santals' movement towards the Grand Trunk Road. Lloyd later acknowledged that abandoning Koomerabad, though 'a measure of absolute necessity' because the locality was unhealthy, 'may have been misjudged by the insurgents' who felt 'emboldened to further acts of outrages'.[171]

Abandoning Koomerabad had been a set-back for Company forces, and a clear sign that the Hul was not being suppressed as the Supreme Council wished. Bird not surprisingly exuded confidence. 'With our detachments thus placed', he wrote, 'I dare say the Sonthals will disappear from that part of the country', and even considered sending out more columns in hopes of 'overtaking the Rebels as they proceed from Post to Post'.[172] Bird claimed to have received 'private' letters giving a more positive account of matters on the Mor river ('fled to the Hills and afraid to come out'), but such optimism is hard to reconcile with Fooks's rooboocaries written from Koomerabad.[173] Perhaps in re-reading Fooks's reports Bird realised that he had narrowly avoided being overwhelmed, that in the circumstances, protecting Beerbhoom was the best he could do, along with a positive gloss on his accounts to his superiors. As Raikes's column marched out, though, the drums did fall silent, and Bird may have been justified in concluding that the entire line from Koomerabad to Rampore Haut, a further slice of the district, actually had been cleared of Santals. But if the Santals had not been destroyed—and they probably lost fewer than fifty men in battle, though their casualties included two manjees—where had they gone? Bird knew the answer to that question: the Grand Trunk Road and the South-West Frontier beyond it.

'The water has risen in the river': moving in the monsoon

Few roads pierced the Damin, and movement by any vehicle during the monsoon was almost impossible. In Bhaugulpore tracks reached southwards from the Ganges, connecting the rich plain with the river trade, at least in dry weather. In Beerbhoom, however, Walter

Sherwill reported, for a third of the year 'all communication is cut off … there are no boats, no bridges in the whole country'.[174] While the Grand Trunk Road crossed the southern boundary of the disturbed districts, Charles Joseph's *New and Improved Map of the Grand Trunk Road*, published in 1855, showed how narrow was the corridor the road and the railway cut across the country.[175] A muddy track went north from Kaksa, twenty miles west of Burdwan, towards Ilam Bazar and thence forty miles north-west to Sooree, but no usable road connected Raneegunge, the terminus of the line and the head station of the district of Beerbhoom. Indeed, only four tracks traversed the district's 80-mile boundary, all crossing the Adye and Barraker rivers by ford or ferry, but most of the Santal country was effectively roadless, impassable in the monsoon.

Company officers' accounts repeatedly document the difficulty the monsoon imposed on their troops' movements on water and on land. Santals knew well the annual cycle of rain and flood—a Santal song began 'the water has risen in the river'.[176] At Bhaugulpore the Ganges was half-a-mile wide in the hot weather, but in the monsoon its course was up to eight miles across, with inundations reaching ten or more miles over the northern bank, giving it 'the appearance of an extensive sea', Walter Sherwill reported.[177] The river Mor near Koomerabad was over 500 yards wide in the monsoon.[178] The rain falling every day made travelling down- and especially up-river tedious if not hazardous. Steamers could make eleven miles-per-hour going down-river, but barely four going up, and the flow during the monsoon often imperilled even that speed.[179] The superintendent of Marine had to write to explain to Halliday (to whom Bidwell had complained) that a 12-knot current acting on even a 60-horsepower steamer severely strained both boat and crew. He described how the captain of the *Horungatta* simply could not turn against the current no matter how vigorously Alfred Bidwell had signalled the steamer as it struggled up-stream at the end of August. A few days before, the *Jumna*, the vessel Lloyd often used, had taken six hours to push up a bend in the Ganges near Rajmahal.[180] Crossing rivers was also difficult. Walter Birch's sepoys and their coolies took most of a day—from 4 in the morning to 2 in the afternoon, floating rafts of ammunition and camp equipage across a flooded nullah on the way from

Burhyte. Other detachments had to camp beside raging rivers hundreds of yards wide, sometimes for days at a time, waiting for water to subside. Louis Bird's orders to recall the detachments to Sooree could not immediately be acted upon—he learned that troops could not cross the flooded nullahs because 'the very heavy fall of rain ... has continued incessantly for the past Four and Twenty hours'.[181]

Santal bands disliked having to cross deep, swiftly-flowing nullahs but they were able to move much more easily in their own country. Soon after his appointment Alfred Bidwell complained that repeatedly 'no Sonthals were to be seen in the places where it was expected'.[182] While Santals also had trouble crossing flooding rivers, they were much more agile in the hills and jungle they knew so well.[183] As late as October, in lamenting Company forces' lack of success, Frederick Halliday admitted that the Santals had 'evaded all attempts at pursuit by their active and jungly habits'.[184] These habits would make the Santals hard to defeat, but equally by themselves they would not ensure Santal victory. Given the Company's latent military power and the absence of a co-ordinated Santal command, a Santal victory was never likely or even possible.

With only foot tracks connecting much of the Santal country, able to bear bullock carts called *saggers* only in the dry season, Company commanders soon saw that if they were to suppress the Hul they had to be able to move through the Santals' country. Eventually roads were to become one of the means of extending control over the region, and in the meantime necessary military roads were begun. Alexander Moncrieff, a native infantry lieutenant seconded to the Public Works Department, reported on what would be required to create a road of 25 miles between Raneegunge and Doobrajpoor, that is, from the railhead to close to the district's headquarters near Sooree. He found the existing foot route passed over rice fields and streams, 'very winding and ... much under the level of the surrounding land' and therefore knee deep in mud. A new route would involve much negotiation with land-holders but he began the necessary work. In the meantime, the arrival of pontoons from Calcutta would at least make crossing the Adye easier.[185] This muddy track connected the two most important stations in the campaign's southern theatre.

Administrative deficiencies often prevented troops moving. Getting supplies and baggage to the railway station from Barrackpore often failed because station staff could find neither boats to cross the Hooghly nor carts to carry goods from the ferry ghat to the railway station. The railway continued to operate despite the monsoon, though more slowly because of debris washed onto the line. Newly opened, its 'railway servants' had little experience in operating troop trains, and sometimes left detachments sitting in the open, soaked or broiled, delayed for hours waiting for carriages to be gathered. Officials must surely have rued the decision taken in May 1855 not to buy an entire train for troop transport.[186] Nor could the Commissariat and the railway deliver enough rations for the troops—as Louis Bird took command in Raneegunge the gomastahs held 21 days' stock of lentils—the sepoys' chief source of protein—but only three days' worth of flour to make the essential chupatties.[187] It is important to recall that Raneegunge was the railhead: the problems of keeping remote detachments supplied by elephant columns became the subject of much correspondence. Bird asked for 'as many Elephants as can be made available' soon after assuming command there, not for the last time.[188]

If what was called 'ordinary carriage'—hackeries drawn by slow-moving bullocks—was useless, experienced India hands knew that elephants were the only draught animals able to move across the monsoon-sodden country. Civil officials and railway volunteers began gathering both official and privately owned beasts from across the districts surrounding the Santal country, while George Atkinson began requesting the Commissary General to provide and procure elephants to sustain the increasing number of troops committed to suppressing the rebellion.[189] A single regiment of native infantry needed at least thirty elephants, with more to transport extra equipment, such as headquarters records, tents (necessary in the monsoon) and officers' mess tents, mess furniture, baggage and equipage. Others carried additional food supplies or equipment such as the sets of pontoon rafts sent to both Berhampore and Raneegunge to enable troops to cross monsoon-swollen rivers.[190] Early in August George Atkinson assured George Lloyd that 'elephants are being collected on all sides', but just a week later William Grey warned that the supply of animals in the disturbed districts was already exhausted and that agents needed to look further afield.[191] Soon Holden Ravenshaw, the magistrate at Dinagepore, over 130 miles from Bhaugulpore, was sending 34 animals, some bought, others leased, though mahouts seemed to be harder to find.[192]

Getting the animals to where they could assist the troops proved to be hazardous. By early September, civil officials in Malda district alone had gathered 46 elephants, but transporting them across the swollen Ganges almost ended disastrously. They loaded the animals into unwieldy rafts and attempted to cross on a windy day. Some got across, but one boat disintegrated, hurling men and animals into the wide and swiftly flowing river. The elephants swam to shore down-river, but the men were swept along for some miles before they could be rescued. The rest of the elephants were later swum across.[193] Monsoon flooding made even land travel difficult—George Lloyd had the commissariat staff at Dinapore send 30 elephants overland to Bhaugulpore, but they did not arrive until late August.

Perhaps 500 and more elephants were gathered to support the campaign, each costing between Rs 24 and Rs 30 a day to feed and maintain. To put that figure in context, less than a decade before watchmen counting traffic on the Grand Trunk Road at the Paudu River bridge, just west of the Santal country, recorded only 287 elephants passing in the course of an entire year.[194] The beasts were worked hard. William Elliott complained that his finest elephant had been reduced to 'a bag of bones'.[195] He objected to an inexplicable ruling by the Commissary General's Department which reduced their forage allowance drastically: animals hired from zamindars in Beerbhoom were fed 16 seers of forage a day, but the Commissariat elephants working beside them were given only 7 (the latter less than 20 pounds).

Elephants were sufficiently valuable to demand their own nominal rolls—making up such a list was one of Robert Richardson's many tasks. A return of elephants supplying detachments around Sooree listed them by name—Emperor, Maharanee, Rajender and Dick. Elephants, like locomotives, were powerful and valuable, meriting names rather than numbers. While Emperor had been given 12 seers of forage, he was now getting only 9, and poor Dick only got 6. Reading these figures and knowing how the entire military effort against the Santals depended upon hundreds of beasts staying healthy,

George Atkinson urgently asked the Deputy Commissary General in Bengal to distribute 'immediate orders for the issue to the whole of the Government Elephants employed in the field' an increased allowance sufficient for their needs, regardless of regulation. The Deputy Commissary General, who might have been expected to have resisted the disruption of his budget, indicated his immediate compliance, a further sign of how seriously the Bengal establishment saw the rebellion.[196] A month later, however, commissariat officers remained recalcitrant. Atkinson took his complaint to army headquarters in Simla, but distance, time and the Bengal Army's habitual inertia defeated him. Like the Bengal Army, elephants moved slowly—at little more than human walking pace, and they too could not be rushed—but they were invaluable both for carrying supplies and even troops. They remained the Company's most scarce and valuable resource throughout the suppression of the Hul.

'Fruitless and laborious marches': Lloyd bides his time

As his steamer chugged up and down the Ganges from Bhugulpore to Rajmahal through monsoon rainstorms, George Lloyd read and heard the reports of his subordinate officers in Bhaugulpore and Beerbhoom with growing frustration. On 18 August he issued a general order, admitting that it was 'impossible with Infantry alone to overtake the various parties of the Insurgents' and signalling a change in strategy. He thought it best to 'avoid harassing the troops by fruitless and laborious marches' and decided that the best policy as long as the country remained inundated and the weather sickly was to 'hold … the Rebels in check, confine them to the hills and jungles of the "Damunikoh"' and to order the detachments to occupy larger, healthier posts, with just a few outposts.[197] In the Bhaugulpore district this meant stationing the 7th and the 31st Native Infantry at Rajmahal and Aurungabad, on the Bagirutty, the 42nd at Bowsee and the 13th near Godda, both on the southern edge of the Bhaugulpore plain, and the 40th at Colgong on the Ganges; the Hill Rangers, still not considered trustworthy, were to be stationed at Bhaugulpore under Lloyd's own eye, with a company of the 40th for safety. Each unit had a company or two at outposts, with detachments of the 42nd as far south as Deoghur (actually in the neighbouring district of Ramghur) and the 31st at small posts around Pakaur. At their furthest extent, the Bhaugulpore troops were scarcely twenty miles from Bird's advanced posts on the Sooree-Rajmahal railway line, seemingly closing the ring around the Santals' heartland of the Damin-i-koh. But Lloyd remained doubtful of his troops' ability to operate in the jungle and the season. Even before taking command of the force, he had recommended that because of the monsoon and the inundated state of the country, it would be possible only to protect towns in open country and 'deprecated any expeditions in pursuit ... until after the rains'.[198]

An account of another of Walter Birch's operations explains Lloyd's decision to cease fruitless dours. Birch, hearing at Burhyte that a party of rebels under three named manjees was at Heerampore, about 15 miles south, he led out a column of the 7th Native Infantry. After two forced marches 'at times up to our hips in mud' they reached Heerampore, only to find them gone. Learning the direction they had taken, Birch pushed on, but after a day's march missed them again, and again after a fourth day's 'long and fatiguing march'. Again, 'the enemy was too quick for us'. Birch nevertheless believed that manjees and their followers were losing heart—he took prisoners, but 'only a few of them showed fight', but unless the Company's forces could find and defeat the rebels, the insurrection would continue.[199] Lloyd had a response to that challenge, but it would take months to mature.

Just as Lloyd had ordered his regiments into quarters until the wet weather eased, so Bird followed the same procedure for the southern force. To the west, the 63rd Native Infantry was to be distributed between Bird's headquarters at Raneegunge and posts on the Grand Trunk Road, as was the 2nd Grenadiers. To the east, the 50th held Sooree, the 56th Rampore Haut, with the 37th distributed in smaller posts, though some, exposed to Santals or sickness or both, were to be withdrawn, including Koomerabad, which George Fooks had held for so long. A 'Moveable column' under Joseph Hampton, composed of mounted troops and the Grenadiers, patrolled the Grand Trunk Road as far west as Parasnath, the great mountain sacred to the Jains that rears out of the plain north of the road, just over the border of Ramghur district.

Plotted on a map, however, two conclusions become apparent. First, it is clear that the Bhaugulpore force was actually split into two parts divided by the Rajmahal Hills and the Damin itself, and secondly that a wide gap remained on the force's western flank: precisely where Walter Sherwill had warned that the Santals were going. The Santals, of course, were not subject to George Lloyd's orders, and they continued to move in accordance with imperatives which can at best be inferred.

One of the greatest difficulties which Company forces faced was that they were fighting a campaign on what students of Napoleon's campaigns called 'exterior lines': that is, the Santals held the interior of the districts of Bhaugulpore and Beerbhoom, and the Company's forces occupied and worked from peripheral lines to the north, east and south. Even if the Santals lacked any means of transportation or communication besides bullock saggers, and human voices, their opponents also had great difficulty communicating, even with steamers, the railway and the electric telegraph.[200] Accordingly, in late August Lloyd and Bidwell agreed that it would be useful to travel to Calcutta to confer with 'Govt'—Halliday and even the Supreme Council. Securing approval, and inviting other key figures—Brigadier Bird and Mr Loch—because they met in person, the Military Consultations include no record of their discussions, but it is clear from later papers that they agreed with and approved of the strategy that Lloyd proposed.

But who actually devised the plan that Lloyd propounded to his civilian colleagues and superiors? Did the orders really express what newspapers described as 'General Lloyd's plans'?[201] It is possible that Lloyd thought of the plan himself: a reasonable presumption. Naturally, because he was the senior officer in command, he took the credit, but in the light of his appalling incompetence in 1857, the question has to be asked: did he devise the strategy himself or did he merely adopt a plan proposed by others? Four other authors are possible. One was the regimental commanders under him, especially John Liptrap, who seems to have been unusually active in pressing the 42nd Light Infantry to attack Santal bands in western Bhaugulpore. While Lloyd essentially seems to have agreed with Liptrap, there is no evidence that Liptrap proposed any wider plans to him. Second, civil officials with whom he worked, notably Alfred Bidwell, might have suggested a plan, though Bidwell's official correspondence either with Lloyd or through Grey shows no evidence that he made such suggestions. Given the military officers' sensitivity toward civilian interference, and that William Grey discouraged officials from imposing on military plans, it seems unlikely. A third possibility is that the officers on Lloyd's staff, in the time-honoured manner, suggested ideas or plans which all then attributed to Lloyd; the loyal anonymity which remains the basis of military staff work. It is possible that Dean Shute or Walter Sherwill thought of it. Shute joined Lloyd only in mid-August, but Sherwill had been advising Lloyd since his arrival at the end of July, and while Lloyd later talked of devising the plan in August, it was only approved in early October; that gave Shute or Sherwill or both time to realise that a better plan was needed and to persuade Lloyd of it. As is the case in other conflicts, no trace of this remains in the Military Consultations, because the only documents emanate from Lloyd—'internal' headquarters papers were not included in the documents forwarded to higher authorities.

Finally, it is possible that one or other of the Queen's officers who accompanied Walter Birch suggested the idea of a 'drive' or coordinated advance to Lloyd. Christopher Garstin and Frederick Middleton had served together in New Zealand and both had accompanied Birch and Toogood to Burhyte. Garstin had served in the 96th Foot, in Van Diemen's Land (as Tasmania was called until 1856) as well as New Zealand, between 1839 and 1849. The 96th had not been involved in the extensive operations against Tasmanian Aborigines in the notorious 'Black Line' of 1830, when a huge force of soldiers and settlers advanced in a line across the island in an attempt, futile as it transpired, to corral Aborigines into a portion of the colony's southern coast. The operation occurred a decade before the 96th arrived in Van Diemen's Land, but it was far the most notorious event in the colonists' forty-year war against Aboriginal resistance, and it is feasible to suppose that military officers learned of it from settlers or their military predecessors. Perhaps they speculated on why the 'Black Line' had failed—partly because there was no military force against which the line acted, a major difference from Lloyd's plan in 1855.[202] It is possible that Garstin told or reminded

Toogood or even Lloyd about it (Lloyd visited Rajmahal in August, where he could have met Garstin)—perhaps they knew about the Black Line, which was mentioned in British-Indian newspapers, and officers took leave from India in Hobart. The connection is tenuous, perhaps, but tantalising.

Of these possibilities, perhaps the least persuasive is that Lloyd devised 'his' plan independently, but it was as Lloyd's plan that the Company's strategy became known, and no one, least of all Lloyd, said or wrote anything to the contrary. In due course the newspapers would judge that 'the Major General has shewn his wisdom' in devising a strategy that would, they thought, deliver victory; though, as will be apparent, that assumption seems unjustified.[203]

'Ill-judged leniency': Bidwell's proclamations

George Lloyd's orders halting the uncoordinated and unavailing pursuit of Santal bands in monsoon weather and often rough country coincided with a decision taken by Alfred Bidwell to attempt conciliation in place of aggression. Military force having failed in six weeks to end the Hul, the civil commissioner tried persuasion. Early in August, he issued a proclamation, in 'Hindee and Bengallee'—but not, of course, Santali—offering 'that the Government will freely pardon all who may tender a speedy submission'.[204] In this, like the archetypal Bengal civil official, Bidwell followed precedent. The Kol insurrection had apparently been swiftly ended by a combination of aggressive military force and conciliatory proclamations, and Bidwell employed a seemingly tried formula.[205]

Bidwell had hoped that his initiative would lead to 'a disposition to submission', but the Santals proved to be less amenable.[206] A report from one civil official working with the foremost detachments explained why the proclamation achieved nothing. William Money first heard of Bidwell's proclamation a week after its issue—copies chased him around the district as he moved about between detachments. He then had no opportunity to distribute proclamations until ten days after its release—he posted ten copies at one village and another ten at Noni Haut, in Hendweh pergunnah, presumably nailed to trees. Not surprisingly, Money reported, 'no one … has yet come in to surrender'. Not only were Santals almost universally illiterate, in English, Bengali or Hindi, but Money had seen none within 30 miles of Bowsee. But rebellious Santals were on the move. The dours mounted by the 40th and 42nd Native Infantry had driven them further south.[207]

Money, whose outspokenness was to gravely impair his career, had the temerity to put to Bidwell the uncongenial view that while Europeans might 'place implicit confidence in the faith of Govt if pardon were offered ... with the insurgent Sonthals it is different ... they do not believe in such Magnanimity' and were unwilling to risk their lives responding to what they feared must be a trap. In any case, Money pointed out, their leaders, and particularly the charismatic Kanhu Manjee 'is aware of the proclamation and kills everybody who offers us assistance or even hints at surrendering'.[208] An apparent pause in fighting later in August may have suggested that conciliation had succeeded, but it did not last. No one, besides Bidwell, seems to have believed that conciliation would work, and it did not.

An electric telegraph message from Raneegunge on 24 August, however, seemed to show the value of Bidwell's new policy. James Mangles reported from Palgunge, north of Parasnath, that he had made contact with a huge column of Santals, including women and children—perhaps 7,000 people. Mangles sent the remarkable word that this was no war party, but one wishing to give up the fight. Mangles, the magistrate at Govindpore, had come across them while travelling by elephant accompanied by a couple of Road Police sowars and four burkendazes (seemingly a rash act in the very country to which the Santals were heading) in thick jungle north of the road. Though at first 'alarmed at my approach', the Santals, reassured that Mangles was not accompanied by troops, began to talk, encouraged by word of Bidwell's proclamation. Soon, Mangles had persuaded them that giving up and following him to Topchaunce, 20 miles west of Govindpore, would be preferable to risking crossing the heavily patrolled Grand Trunk Road. Mangles evidently allowed the manjees to believe that they could still cross the road—they may have understood that he was offering them protection.[209] Newspapers in Britain later hailed Mangles ('the son of the director and a rising man') but his coup came to naught—in the end only a few hundred surrendered, mostly old or infirm, unable to bear the nomadic life.[210] The able-bodied and combatant members of the band decided to abandon the old and sick and to fight on. Atkinson and Grey both admonished both Major Hampton and Mangles for trying to bend the policy forbidding Santals passage of the road.[211]

Embarrassed reports from civil officials soon demonstrated the failure of Bidwell's plan (a misjudgment he surprisingly survived) but not why it had failed. An account picked up by a correspondent from a Rajmahal darogah offered an explanation. The policeman had spoken amicably to a group of Santals on the road, asking whether they were inclined to testify their loyalty, a further sign that not all Santals joined the Hul. They replied that they thought that the invitation was 'a trap' and declined to surrender their weapons, which they needed to hunt. Indeed, they said that they had heard of Santals who had been given their parole and had then been attacked in their villages by sepoys; the sepoys, meanwhile, were acting on the orders of officers who thought it their duty to 'vex, harass and annoy the rebels', even if the 'rebels' had professed their loyalty. The writer pointed out that such a contradictory approach would do nothing to induce Santals to submit. The Santals warned the darogah both that 'they will beat us and drive all the Europeans and Bengalees away' but also that a nearby leader was planning to attack Rajmahal, resurrecting a widespread fear.[212]

Bidwell's first proclamation was a failure also in that it attracted criticism among the newspaper-reading community that constituted British India's articulate and outspoken public opinion. Press commentary from Bengal and beyond condemned Bidwell's failed proclamation extending clemency to rebels. The Calcutta *Morning Chronicle* quoted with approval the *Madras Spectator*'s strictures on Bidwell's 'ill-judged leniency'. Decrying the rebels' 'butcherly proceedings', the Madras journalist argued that Bidwell's 'ill-timed exhibitions of humanity' could 'leave a deep impression on the Native mind and most likely produce evil fruit hereafter'. The *Spectator*'s concern was hardly disinterested: Madras had seen insurrection in the resistance of the intractable Muslim Moplahs of the Malabar coast. 'Asiatics do not comprehend the policy that suspends the sword', the *Chronicle* fulminated, 'severity to the few is mercy to the many.'[213]

While Bidwell's proclamation failed, some observers detected a change in Santal morale. The editor of the *Citizen* claimed that near Sooree 'thousands ... are coming ... to lay down their arms', their destitution 'pity-exciting'.[214] He later decided that 'the rebellion is dying' because looting had made rebels 'rich', and that Santals were 'secreting their battle-axes'.[215] In August, the *Friend of India* observed, 'the rebellion may be said to languish': but if the Santals were not visibly winning, they were also not being defeated—'languishing' did not bring either side closer to victory.[216] Many Santals, it was said, had made enough to pay handsome dowries and were going home to make use of their haul. But if some Santals made good from the insurrection, it was also clear that the Hul was not dying, though many more Santals would die before it did.

Despite the failure of his August proclamation, Bidwell again tried to persuade Santals to give up by issuing another proclamation, on 18 September, again offering amnesty to all but the 'Instigators of the Rebellion' and 'principals in the Commission of Murder'.[217] This, derided as an attempt 'to come the artful dodger over the Santhals' also failed. It neither reached Santals nor convinced them that the government's offer of amnesty, for all but those who could be proved to have engaged in murder and plunder, was genuine.[218] Darogahs in the disputed area, who had the task of distributing proclamations, presumably by actually proclaiming it to non-literate people, reported that the inducement had been 'treated in the most contemptuous manner by the rebels'.[219]

The failure of a second proclamation led the Supreme Council's members to again consider martial law and while Edward Peacock now became persuaded, Dorin remained obdurate. He could not see, considering that troops had already 'attacked and dispersed them with considerable slaughter', how martial law could make a difference. Typically, he pedantically affirmed that if Frederick Halliday were to ask for it, he would consent—but that Halliday had to ask; Low sycophantically agreed.[220] The Supreme Council was now evenly divided on the question of proclaiming martial law.

Not that military officers had a very strong idea of their authority even if martial law were not declared. The delay in deciding whether to impose martial law, widely known through newspapers, itself fostered confusion. Members of the Supreme Council had noticed instances where officers plainly did not understand their powers. One officer, for example, even after being called out on active service, mistakenly believed that his men were 'not at liberty to fire upon armed Bodies', unless Santals fired first, a misapprehension leading to his sepoys watching Santals pass them by, allowing the rebels to get into a stronger position and attack his men. Above all, many officers feared that they could face prosecution for warlike acts. General Low wanted to assure such an officer that 'he is not punishable for any amount of activity that he may display in putting down this lamentable Insurrection'.[221]

Bidwell's failures to 'come the artful dodger'—doomed though they were for want of any effective means of communication between the Company authorities and the Santals—meant that the Hul could only be ended by armed force. Understanding how to apply that force, however, seemed as elusive as ever.

PART III

NIRON (AUTUMN)

4

DESAE (SEPTEMBER)

In September the rains began to ease, though the inclement weather could still deliver unpleasant surprises—the rivers remained high and storms at the end of September blew down the building at Raneegunge used as a mess room by officers of the 63rd, killing two syces sheltering from the downpour and wind. The same storms caused John Liptrap, one of the more vigorous regimental commanders, to call off a large dour he had planned, leading 250 troops east from Bowsee 'to give confidence to the [Bengali] villages' around Godda.[1] As the rain eased, the sun returned as a scourge: Walter Sherwill warned that in Bhaugulpore in September the sun retained 'the power of blistering the skin as if an actual cautery had been applied', though Sherwill saw little of it—he was granted sick leave, exhausted and practically blind from his exertions.[2] Meanwhile, news of the outbreak had at last reached Britain.

'Military Letter from Bengal': news arrives in Britain

The Supreme Council dithered in informing the Court of Directors: its first report on the Hul, dated 7 August, arrived only on 24 September.[3] Clerks at East India House the next day began transcribing and indexing the 'Military Letter from Bengal' and it was circulated to the Company's London officials and to members of the relevant committees and more widely among the Directors. The detailed Military Consultations and periodic 'Special Narratives' allowed determined readers in London to work out what had transpired in Bengal seven weeks earlier. In fairness, it is also apparent that unrest among one tribe represented only one minor item in a torrent of letters, reports, orders, despatches, accounts, returns and all manner of written documents dealing with a host of significant subjects. These included the all-important 'Revenue' (including the salt tax, customs and excise), Public Works (irrigation, canals, roads), the judicial, medical, educational and ecclesiastical establishments, including appointments, promotions, pensions, furloughs, memorials and appeals, the management of the post office and the new electric telegraph department, the building of railways, relations with neighbouring states such as Nepal and Burmah and with native states (including Oudh, then in turmoil under Dalhousie's policy of the Doctrine of Lapse), not to mention the routine administration of an army a quarter-of-a-million strong. Reports of events in the Santal country occupied a few folios in ledgers a foot thick.

Word of the rebellion had already reached the press. British newspapers reported on the Hul as editors across Britain filleted Calcutta newspapers sent through the 'overland mail'. Reports were at first dismissive, even jocular: Halliday, the *Glasgow Herald* quoted the *Englishman*, 'has got up a little war of his own', before repeating snippets from various Calcutta newspapers.[4] Soon, editors and leader-writers were observing that the news from Bengal was 'alarming' and 'shocking', while old India hands published letters explaining what was 'not likely to be thoroughly understood by the majority of your readers' about matters in such an exotic place.[5] A retired 'Hill Ranger' assured *Daily News* subscribers that the reports had surely been 'grossly exaggerated'.[6] Many middle-class readers had an interest in Indian affairs, whether because they owned East India stock, depended upon British-Indian commerce or had a family connection with those living, serving or working in Bengal.

Among the first intimations of the uprising reached London not in reports issued by (or leaking from) Leadenhall Street, but in letters from relatives of those affected, such as the letter passed on by John Mudge's father. In this way readers of the *Sherborne Mercury* read of

Sidhu's wounded wrist at Moheshpore, and of the books found in his house wrapped in a white cloth and bound with gold string—but only in that little Somerset town.[7] While about 75 items appeared in British newspapers between August and the year's end, the rebellion could easily be missed in the mountain of newsprint created by metropolitan and provincial newspapers. In August and September just a dozen items appeared outside London: only one in Ireland, none at all in Yorkshire, Devon, Dorset, Sussex, or Kent, and as the months passed, fewer appeared. The single mention in Edinburgh in November comprised one line: 'The Santhal insurrection not completely put down'.[8] To most Britons, the rising remained practically unknown. Indifference or ignorance was hardly surprising. When John Wolley (possibly the egg-collecting naturalist) returned to Britain from abroad in 1855 he found that even the war in the Crimea, Britain's greatest conflict since Waterloo, 'sits upon us so lightly'.[9] If the drama of Sebastopol, Balaclava and Inkerman could create so little impression on people in Britain, why would a tribal rebellion in Bengal be of any wide interest?

Britons with an interest in India, however, were able to keep up through *Allen's Indian Mail*, published from an office in Leadenhall Street as soon as the Indian mails could be digested. Dalhousie also seemed to be dissatisfied that the insurrection persisted—he read the Indian newspapers daily as well as his officials' correspondence. Halliday had sent him a lengthy and distinctly critical minute in which he admitted that operations had not secured 'anything but a very partial and inadequate submission'; operations, he had made clear, over which he had little authority and therefore no responsibility for the lack of success.[10] Company officials noted that Dalhousie could have overruled the Supreme Council, but chose not to.

'Santhal Dazzlers': the Company's auxiliaries

The Santal emergency provoked criticism by both newspaper writers and officials that Lower Bengal, for so long a Company possession, had been denuded of troops because of the drive to the north-west. At the end of August Halliday began asking his officials (though pointedly not military officers) for their views, and soon began lobbying the Supreme Council. It was the Council, and not the Commander-in-Chief, which controlled the distribution of military force. It decided to increase the force ordinarily stationed in Lower Bengal by several regiments by forming a 'Military Police Corps' in Bengal. This would solve the problem of the scandalously poor local police, whose oppressive behaviour had aggravated Santal grievances and whose tactless demeanour at Bhugnadihee had precipitated the first outbreak. Recruiting a new police force would at least obviate the need to 'turn out the Regular Troops on every occasion of internal riot'.[11] Though often denigrated, some darogahs and their burkendazes remained at their posts in areas threatened by Santal bands, and had even brought in Santal prisoners; the appointment of 'a young man of action and bolder disposition', for instance, transformed the security of one thannah.[12] Others, either actually threatened or frightened of retribution, left their posts and joined the crowds of refugees fleeing the Santals' appearance. A Rajmahal correspondent derided 'trembling burkendazes', but their trepidation was understandable.[13] Joseph Dorin was unhappy that weak and poorly armed police parties understandably allowed troops to take the burden of tackling Santal bodies, and until they could be strengthened in leadership, arms, numbers and capacity, this 'erroneous and mischievous' behaviour could not be expected to change.[14]

By August military officers and civil officials, realising the limitations of relying on sepoys, began to urge the recruitment of the auxiliaries they called 'bildars'. From Koomerabad, virtually besieged, George Fooks urged that 'country burkendazes' be recruited, a suggestion George Loch took seriously and urged on Frederick Halliday.[15] Some zamindars and rajahs already had armed retainers while indigo planters recruited (or conscripted) their workers to defend their factories and even follow their employers in seeking out Santal bands. At Monghyr, William Tucker raised companies of sepoy pensioners regarded as 'more effectual as a force than the [Bhaugulpore Hill] Rangers', and was said to have encouraged a thousand natives to volunteer to serve.[16] In the messy fighting for villages around Rampore Haut, 150 tenants defended the house of zamindar Fukeer Innundal until a detachment of the 31st Native Infantry arrived, driving off the attackers. Halliday learned that in

July a planter near Burdwan had raised a force of fifty and led them to 'the scene of the disturbance', acting as unofficial freebooters, perhaps picking up loot from deserted villages, perhaps regarding Santals, whether in rebellion or not, as legitimate prey.[17] 'My men', the planter proudly told Halliday, 'march up as bold as brass to from 1000 to 1500 [Santals] who on every occasion fled'. He urged more rigorous methods to force the Santals out of their villages: 'how are we to do that without burning them down?' he demanded. Having seen 'the horrors ... in villages taken by the Sonthals', he wanted them extirpated.[18] Another indigo planter offered to raise a force of 4000 if the government would arm and pay them, promising to 'not leave a Santhal alive in the jungles'.[19]

One of the most successful expedients is also one of the poorest documented. In August Company officials appear to have agreed to allow a man variously referred to as Gillen, Gillan, Gillow or Gillon to raise a company of bildars, who swiftly became one of the Company's most valuable military assets. Unusually for an organisation so careful in documenting its transactions, no record seems to exist of his appointment, and he remains a mysterious figure. Referred to in some documents as 'Serjeant' he may have been a serving or former European soldier of the Company, but an extensive search of the Registers of European Soldiers for the previous three decades disclose not a single man with any of those names alive in 1855. From a reference to 'Mr' Gillen, it seems that he was a civilian, perhaps a railway contractor (which would explain his speaking some Bengali) with some military experience (hence 'Sjt') who became effectively a mercenary for the duration. Whatever his name, he was described by William Elliott as 'an excellent working man if he will keep sober', but Ward judged him on his martial skill and reassured Elliott that 'I doubt not that all that lies in his power will be done'; as indeed it was.[20]

Gillon (as he called himself in one of his reports) rapidly trained a company of some sixty 'Irregulars', possibly Bengalis and Paharias, armed with an assortment of weapons (but at first including only twelve muskets) and soon showed that they could achieve results impossible for slow-moving sepoys. His value was shown when in September he was sent from Sooree to prevent Santals looting

Mohamed Bazar, or rather to punish them for their temerity in trying. Summoned overnight, Gillon marched his men out in the small hours and reached Mohamed Bazar, across the Mor and ten miles away, by sunrise. He tracked the Santals to a further river crossing and on reaching more open country ordered his men into 'Echelon of sections'. The Santals, who comprised about 300 men and 30 women, gave them 'a salute from their arrows' and Gillon, by now very close, ordered his men to open fire. Though armed with just a few muskets they killed ten, wounded 'a great number' and put the rest to flight. Among the prisoners was the Santal leader, Sona Manjee, whom Gillon took to Sooree for questioning. Gillon's exploits ensured that energetic civil officers such as James Ward and Robert Richardson asked for his services, and Bird thought that a hundred more such irregulars under European supervision 'would be most useful'.[21]

Mr or Serjeant Gillon having proved the worth of his irregulars—John Peter Grant praised them as 'most useful'—civil officials naturally wanted to raise more of them.[22] Robert Richardson, having served in Behar, thought that he could easily raise up to 400 irregulars in Oudh, in Ghazipore on the Ganges and Chhapra, near Saran in Behar and have them in the field by November. Ward promised a further company of a hundred burkundazes, commanded by a man named Long, possibly also a civilian, who joined Gillon and his irregulars in western Beerbhoom by the end of September, and later at least three others, possibly seconded from the 'Town Major's List', but with the unhelpfully common names of Jackson, Gordon and Smith. The most likely possibilities were working-class English or Irishmen who had served the Company for twenty years, mostly with 'native' units, who volunteered to transfer temporarily to a more active posting.[23]

Bird proposed raising several companies of bildars, each 100-men strong under a European sergeant in five sections; the sections commanded by a duffadar (a native cavalry sergeant), and all armed with muskets. He secured approval within days of making his request.[24] They would be coordinated by Bird's commissariat staff; this was unusual, but the Bengal Army often lived with inexplicable arrangements, and as proponents recommended that auxiliaries needed to be paid regularly and promptly, perhaps the commissariat had recourse to ready cash.[25] Lloyd went further—he hoped to see 800 bildars in the field, and wanted to attach parties of 30 to each regiment to act as scouts.[26] 'Every [military] officer who has served in the jungle,' assured Robert Richardson of 'the necessity of having such men as these attached to each company'.[27] It seems that in the fighting in western Beerbhoom that was exactly what occurred. Charles Chapman, who watched Lieutenant Robert Aitken of the 13th miss capturing three 'chiefs' near Umurpoor in October, regretted that 'those fine irregulars ... had not been with us' at Peer Pointee.[28]

A day's march from Bird's line—seven to ten miles at most— 'little can be done except by our irregulars', Ward reported.[29] Lightly equipped and unburdened by elephant-borne tents or supplies of food, irregulars could move faster and further. 'These Guerrillas', an appreciative civilian observed, 'require no Commissariat nor any hackeries to carry their baggage'.[30] Officers on the spot praised the bildars' contribution. At Jamtarra, First Lieutenant Hungerford Boddam, who happened to be there with his improvised rocket troop, reported that Sergeant Long's company had 'behaved extremely well' when he led them out against the Santals on the bank of the Adye around 11 October, 'although they had just come off a long march' they 'vied with the Regulars whenever there appeared the slightest chance of a brush with the Sonthals'.[31]

The irregulars' main difficulty was that they possessed too few effective weapons. Appreciating what an asset they had become, officials did all they could to obtain weapons, frustrated to find that muskets given to railway contractors' employees were left out in the rain, and managed to get the arsenal at Fort William to consign hundreds for distribution to the companies of bildars being formed. Officials must have emphasised that the irregulars needed arms that worked, not cast-offs. The Inspector General of Ordnance took the trouble to explain to George Atkinson that these were not 'old' muskets but new weapons, along with accoutrements and ammunition. A correspondent to the *Englishman* wrote that the irregulars had been nick-named 'Sonthal Dazzlers'.[32] They probably contributed more to the suppression of the Hul than any single unit of the Company's forces.

'Disturbing these hornet's nests': September

The monsoon of 1855, old Bengal hands averred, had been unusually wet. While downpours eased in September, the ground remained saturated and the rivers continued to flood—in mid-September troops at Sooree were unable to cross the Mor river even on elephants. The 42nd, in its march from outstations back through Noni Haut to Bowsee, sometimes managed only 2 miles a day, had to halt three days in one week from flooded tracks and because of a stream rising 11 feet and had to retrace its steps to find higher if not drier ground.[33]

Canny officers ensured that their doings were known where it mattered. Liptrap wrote demi-official letters to Captain Andrew Ross, an officer of Liptrap's regiment serving as Officiating Deputy Adjutant-General of the Army at Gomm's headquarters. Liptrap was one of the most charismatic of the force's regimental commanders. Devoted to the 42nd, he had served in the regiment for 37 years (at 59 relatively old for a major, but promotion proceeded by seniority). Sensibly discarding his tight uniform trousers, woolen coatee and leather shako, in the field he affected a cool, short 'Grecian tunic' and a 'Sola Topee', as described by one of his admiring subalterns. Despite Lloyd's orders he continued to lead the 42nd southwards from Bowsee, in search of Santal bands identified by William Money.[34]

'The whole country', The Englishman wrote, 'is ringing to know who these people are who have defied the Majesty of the Government of India'. The rebellion had continued for two months. The Hindoo Patriot, which had at first deprecated the Hul's importance, now thought it had become 'less a rebellion than a revolutionary movement'.[35] If the Santals' example were to be followed by other peoples in India, The Englishman warned, 'the army of one hundred thousand men may not be sufficient to keep internal order'.[36] With the failure of Bidwell's August proclamation and Lloyd's decision to call off active operations, officials in Calcutta considered how the Hul was to be defeated. When Lloyd had issued his orders, it seemed to Halliday that 'the Sonthals seemed to retire sullenly from active outrage', though still 'without any signs of general submission'. By mid-September, though, officials had reported further outbreaks of plundering and burning, and Halliday now feared a 'renewed outbreak'. Alfred Bidwell conceded that 'the Sonthals appear to be extending the sphere of operations', his language implicitly granting them the status of formal combatants.[37] From Rajmahal, which had seemingly been free of Santal incursion since late July, a railway engineer expressed his fear that Santal bands had reappeared nearby: 'I expect some of us to be murdered in our beds'.[38] But where were the Santals?

Gillon's irregulars, able to travel faster than sepoys and to traverse inundated country more reliably than cavalry, brought in the first synoptic intelligence available to Company officers in the Beerbhoom theatre. Robert Richardson, learning about intelligence work more-or-less from scratch, turned Gillon's reports into a map, one of the surprisingly few that were copied into the Military Consultations, which gave a picture of Santal dispositions at the end of September.

Gillon's sketch map showed that despite Burney's timidity, officials, especially Robert Richardson, had pushed Company forces out to a series of villages north and north-west of Sooree, most held by small mixed forces of sepoys and irregulars.[39] A force of 200 sepoys at Sooree supported native infantry posts at Gurjore, the furthest out, Nungolea, Doobrajpore, Mohamed Bazar and Afzulpore, with irregulars at Digoolee and Nagore who were ranging over the country, while Doobrajpore also held 300 'well armed villagers', with more armed civilians at Digoolee. James Ward, who must have seen the map, while satisfied that eastern Beerbhoom had been secured by a 'line of posts' between the Adye and the Mor rivers, yet acknowledged that 'to the north west of this line I fear little can be done except by our irregulars'.[40] Indeed, Gillon's men had seen large numbers of Santals north of the Mor: 3000 around Raneebehal and 5000 around Boree Bottan, with another 4000 near Dautiapore. Most worrying for Company forces, however, was Gillon's notation in the area between Kundahit and Operbandah: 'the whole of this part of the district is in [the] hands of the Sonthals'. Richardson's spies told him that the raiders had marked each burned village with leather symbols 'denoting that the Sonthals have obtained possession of the land' and suggesting that some Santal leaders persisted with the dream of self-rule.[41]

One of Halliday's particular concerns was the East India Railway, the main line of which was being constructed through Sooree and Rampore Haut to Rajmahal and then on toward Bhaugulpore: exactly bounding the region in which the Hul had been fought most fiercely so far. The insurrection had completely disrupted the railway's progress—a Parliamentary committee later heard that it caused a year's delay.[42] Its European employees mostly fled, ultimately to Calcutta, while its Bengali and Santal workforce moved away, as refugees or as economic migrants. The main construction contractor in Beerbhoom, whose line became one of the arteries of the Hul because its lineside cart track permitted movement, reported that 26 of his surveyors and engineers' bungalows had been destroyed, though Santals had not damaged the line itself. The principal contractor, J.B. Nelson, led a delegation to 'wait on' Halliday, as the phrase went, making clear that as long as the Hul continued work on the railway could not. Halliday agreed to supply weapons to defend railway parties, while Nelson agreed to tender to build roads and bridges to make the disturbed country more accessible to troops and wheeled transport.[43] Nelson was cannily keeping men at work even if they could not for the moment finish the railway. Nor was this confidential: Halliday's minute appeared in full in the press within days.

Lloyd, more than Bird, sought to restrain the bolder spirits among his officers. He and Bird directed the operations of their respective forces, but in the way of British India everyone felt free to criticise their decisions. Members of the Supreme Council wondered at the tendency to 'break up the military into far too many and too weak detachments', but officers on the spot could see their initiatives succeeding.[44] Civil officers joined in: James Ward disagreed with both Lloyd and the Supreme Council, arguing that 'our only way of stopping these outrages is by scattering parties in different directions'.[45]

Lloyd had variable success in limiting his force's operations. Officers often acted on their own initiative, like civil officials eager for individual distinction, but also seizing opportunities invisible from headquarters at Bhaugulpore or Raneegunge. To give just one instance, Lloyd had left the advanced post of the 42nd Light Infantry at Deoghur, 25 miles south of John Liptrap's headquarters at Bowsee. The Deoghur detachment's commander was Major David Gaussen, an Irishman who served as Lloyd's sometime brigade-major. He responded to the presence of Santal bands rather than following Lloyd's direction to remain quiescent, and early in September led a strong force 35 miles eastward towards the village of Noni Haut on the Dumka Upland in search of a body of 4000 Santals. On the way

Gaussen's men passed through looted and largely deserted villages whose Santal inhabitants, he was told, had 'gone off south'. Lloyd did not openly admonish Gaussen or Liptrap, but he did counsel against 'the utility of disturbing these hornets' nests until … troops can be concentrated … and they can be attacked on all sides'.[46] The dour, even if it contravened Lloyd's policy, confirmed what all Company officers suspected, and showed that Lloyd had a clear idea of what he planned to do once large scale troop movements became possible.

In all this planning, neither Lloyd nor Bidwell had a clear idea of their enemies' motivations for rebelling. But Santal leaders had attempted to convey their desires and demands from the outset. Early in the Hul Sidhu and Kanhu had issued a *perwunnah* (proclamation) to those living around Rajmahal who were prepared to stay to hear it. Exactly how it was distributed and who might have heard it—it could only have been spoken—is uncertain. At the very least, though, it reveals the pronouncements of one or both of the Hul's most notable Santal leaders. Bidwell had the document translated, supposedly by Ashley Eden, but as he had not yet passed his examinations in the vernacular, he probably had it translated with the assistance of the munshi, a linguist and translator in the cutchery at Bhaugulpore, and sent Grey the text.[47]

Sidhu and Kanhu spoke as the interpreters of the will of the Thakur who had descended to them in their house. The Thakur spoke to them in person, assuring them that he would support them in their fight against 'the sahib and the white soldiers'. The Thakur would fight, and aided by Mother Ganges, 'fire will rain from Heaven'. Turning abruptly from inspiration to administrative detail, the Thakur laid out what was effectively the revenue programme Company officials had known about since Octavius Toogood captured documents at Bugnadihee, in which Santals would be taxed based on the number of ploughs and buffaloes they possessed. Essentially the taxation regime proposed was one anna for each ox plough, two for each buffalo, with an annual limit of the amount payable as interest of one rupee.[48] The Thakur then returned to rhetoric, declaring that the mahajans who oppressed them had committed 'a great sin', one which the sahibs and their amlahs had aggravated. 'On this account', the Thakur affirmed, 'the country is not for the Sahibs'. The Thakur then offered the Company's regime a bargain:

> If you Sahibs agree, then you must remain on the other side of the
> Ganges. And if you don't agree ... it will rain fire and all of the Sahibs
> will be killed by the hand of God in person.

'On seeing this purwannah', the Thakur said, 'you will understand
all'. By the time it had been translated and reached Company authorities in September, it was too late. The Santal people had risen in
rebellion and, harried by military parties, were now living in jungle
often far from home and without hope of gaining what they desired:
freedom from oppression.

'European soldiers and a gun or two': troops and technology

While it seemed that calls made by virtually all military and civil
officers for more sepoys could not be met, one military resource in
Lower Bengal there remained unused: European troops. The Bengal
Army in 1855 included ten regiments of British infantry and three of
the Company's European troops, and correspondents and officials
often raised the possibility of deploying one or more of these regiments. European troops were regarded, as John Peter Grant wrote,
as a 'resource of infinite utility'.[49] In Burmah, officers of the 2nd
European Bengal Fusiliers heard rumours that they would be called
back to Bengal to join in the rebellion's suppression. Lieutenant
Kendal Coghill wrote to his sister from Moulmein to affirm that his
corps was to 'put an end to a rabble of some 60,000 Southals ... great
cowards ... any number of them have been licked by a handful of
native troops'.[50] His assumption, one widely shared, was that the
appearance of European troops would terrify the Santals and lead to
the Hul's swift collapse. Would sepoy units be enough? 'This insurrection', a railway gentleman predicted after escaping across the
Ganges, would surely need 'European soldiers and a gun or two'.[51]

The 2nd Fusiliers was not brought back from Burmah, but the 3rd
Bengal European Regiment, formed only in 1853, was available at
Chinsurah, the European recruit depot near Calcutta. It was repeatedly warned to be ready to send several companies to join the field
force. In the event, only its light infantry and grenadier companies
went to Berhampore late in July, 'for service in the field during the
Southal Insurrection', as its regimental digest recorded, but not a

single man of the regiment actually saw action.[52] Despite calls for them, it became clear that sending inexperienced Europeans to serve in the jungle during a 'sickly' season would be foolhardy. The Military Consultations record orders issued to two companies of the 3rd to go to Raneegunge—along with tents carefully ordered to keep them dry, and coolies to erect them. But in the event, they did not actually leave, once Louis Bird realised that 'Soory is not so hard pressed as represented'.[53] In any case, the 3rd was 'very denuded' of officers—no fewer than seven of its captains had been allowed to be absent on staff and civil employment, leaving just two on duty; European corps notoriously needed more officers than native units, mostly because their men, often the worse for drink, required closer supervision than did sepoys.[54] George Atkinson countermanded the order that they be sent on active service.[55] Although previous writers have often referred loosely to the presence of 'British troops', in fact the only 'British' soldiers to serve in the rebellion were the sepoys' European officers.[56]

The Hul's first months had exposed the Bengal Army's undue reliance on European officers, but also their scarcity in the Sonthal Field Force. 'Native officers'—jemadars and subedars—were not generally required or indeed trusted to command troops on operations, and yet there were too few European officers to command detachments. Accordingly, the Adjutant-General's office directed detached officers of regiments serving in the Santal country to return to duty. A sign of the urgency of the case was that they were empowered to travel at government expense. Naturally, officers on sick leave, absent 'on private affairs' and those enjoying lucrative staff or civil situations complied reluctantly or appealed, but most reached their regimental headquarters in time to join in the second half of the campaign, travelling, as one described his journey from the Hills, by jampan (sedan chair), palki (palanquin), horse dawk (carriage) and steamer. One officer who, 'sighing for active service' actually applied to rejoin his regiment—the 31st—from a dull staff job in Ambala was the ambitious Lieutenant Henry Norman, who quickly arranged an exchange to command an outpost 'to get closer to the rebels'.[57]

Military officers themselves were resigned to the hardships of this campaign, having lived for months in the field. In cantonments they lived in large bungalows attended by troupes of servants and, though plagued by money worries (often of their own making) and the chances of dying before qualifying for their pension, they managed as well as any European of their rank in India. On service, officers had to adjust to more Spartan conditions. They shared improvised chummeries, in a school house, for example, in Raneegunge, or lived in tents. Eight officers of the 7th Native Infantry had seven tents between them, naturally making the sole ensign share with the junior lieutenant. Edward Braddon's memoir, *Thirty Years of Shikar*, reveals that on a dour officers lived frugally, often 'tentless and benighted in a swamp', eating 'rice, fowl and pigeon', with 'one brandy per diem'; privation indeed for both officers and gentlemen volunteers.[58] Their baggage would be carried on an elephant though they invariably rode horses while their servants plodded along with the company's other followers. While servants may have been as devoted to their employers as Anglo-Indian legend imputed, the example of Lieutenant Charles Hawtrey of the 50th offers a salutary corrective. He did not accompany his regiment on service because he was being prosecuted for killing his bearer at Barrackpore a few months before. Hawtrey had kicked the man, later claiming he thought he struck a bundle of clothes, but was sentenced to six months imprisonment in Calcutta's jail.[59]

Lloyd's decision to order his troops to quarters while waiting for Bengal's weather to improve, soon inspired some officers to try to get away from the discomfort and danger of active service. Applying for leave even on active service was accepted in the Bengal Army, and few had much compunction in asking. Lieutenant John Briggs of the 40th wrote to George Atkinson (not to his commanding officer or even Lloyd) pointing out that 'as the "Sonthal Insurrection" would appear to be nearly over', he was 'taking the liberty' to ask to be allowed to return to his civil situation in Tenasserim, which, he did not have to emphasise, was much better paid and more comfortable. Atkinson, possibly deciding for himself, one of the few perquisites of the job, refused curtly: 'your services with your Corps cannot be dispensed with'.[60]

The campaign was to cost the life of only one Company officer, Tom Toulmin, but they all endured the range of illnesses endemic to service in Bengal—Brigadier Bird himself suffered a bout of dysentery in mid-September, and went off to Barrackpore for a 'change of air', while Lloyd later returned sick to Dinapore to rest. Lieutenant George Kempland and Major John Nembhard both fell seriously ill during the campaign, and William Gott almost died, though most Company officers remained well and on duty.[61] The only officer wounded seems to have been Bernard Cracroft, the junior ensign of the 50th, who was wounded in 'the seat of honour' by an arrow.[62] Ensign Cracroft's wound seemed symbolic—the Santals were, it seemed, successfully defying the Government of India and its army.

The new technology permitted the exercise of traditional patronage. The only definite intervention Sir William Gomm made in the entire campaign was the suggestion—it was not an order—that rockets might be used against the Santals.[63] Newspaper correspondents agreed—Sydney Blanchard thought that they would be 'very efficacious in the jungles … calculated to inspire the demi savage Sonthals with terror'.[64] Senior officers thought that 'the impenetrable nature of the country' made rockets feasible, though it would also make moving them a nightmare, and began canvassing possible officers to command a rocket detachment. Typically, the need also became an opportunity for the preferment the Bengal Army practised routinely. Henry Tucker, the Adjutant-General, suggested a lieutenant he favoured; Gomm proposed Halliday's ADC, but they agreed to allow James Eckford the choice, since the artillery units in his division would have to provide the officer, and few candidates were on offer—Eckford was already complaining about the difficulty of holding courts martial in Barrackpore. The officer commanding the artillery depot at Dum Dum ended all jockeying by pointing out that Hungerford Boddam was the only artillery officer available, and he had to be recalled from Arracan. Boddam took an interest in rockets, asking about 'the best mode of using them' against the Santals.[65] The rocket tubes were brought out of the ordnance stores and sent off by rail to Raneegunge and, after a three-week delay, by steamer to Berhampore. Boddam had great difficulty finding crews and artificers for them, and the mechanics detailed to Berhampore demanded a month's pay in advance.[66] But how could rockets be used? James Ward hurried a rocket detachment to join the fight in western

Beerbhoom early in October, sending it to James Phillips, one of the most able detachment commanders, but there is little evidence that they proved decisive.

Officials and newspaper writers placed a great faith in the efficacy of artillery. In Ootacamund, Dalhousie mused in his diary 'if they only could get them within reach of artillery they would certainly be dispersed'.[67] Few appreciated the difficulties of moving even light pieces over inundated country. The difficulty of getting guns to the field forces' bases, however, let alone using them, suggests that they were far from useful, much less decisive. Native gunners had to be poached from batteries, some half a dozen artificers were found, including smiths and carpenters from the ordnance workshops, and tools and 'Greese and Materials' consigned to Raneegunge and Berhampore. All this, the Inspector of Ordnance explained, took time.[68] When First Lieutenant Burnett Ashburner tried to find horses at Berhampore, a station said to be healthy for horses, four of his gun horses died; and while awaiting more to come from Calcutta he investigated using bullocks or elephants, though the latter were too valuable to allot on the off-chance the guns might be useful.[69] Atkinson warned batteries at Dum Dum and Dinapore to be ready to move but the only guns actually committed were seven 3-pounder mountain guns, four of which were sent to Raneegunge and three to Berhampore, and they were to prove an encumbrance.[70] It seems that two mountain guns fired three shots at Santals in the distance near Telaboonee, but fruitlessly. They had been taken out on a dour possibly from the enthusiasm of young civil and military officers, but everyone regretted the decision: 'they are heavy and not easily moved … three shots … had no effect'.[71]

At best, guns had a limited psychological value. Bird and Elliott agreed that firing a morning and afternoon gun in Sooree would 'make a good impression on the Sonthals in our parts': a tacit admission that large numbers of hostile Santals remained encamped within earshot of Beerbhoom's head station.[72] But even light guns were too cumbersome to make any difference on dours. Major John Nembhard, for example, led out a force including a mountain gun, searching for a band of 3000 Santals reported to be near Mohamed Bazar in October. He called out 150 men of the 56th and marched toward the spot. After an arduous night journey, including crossing the Mor river, Nembhard saw a party preparing breakfast and opened fire at long range. The Santals naturally fled, encouraged by a shot from the mountain gun, though it inflicted no casualties.[73] Several other officers reported turning out after the reappearance of Santal bands in an area where a month before it had been reported that they had disappeared. It was a further sign that blocking any chance of movement to the south-west had impelled Santals to move toward western Beerbhoom.

'The Sonthals must be somewhere': Operbandah

It had become clear, as Walter Sherwill had foreseen in August, that Santal bands, and many of their dependents, were indeed moving south-westwards toward a region in which Company forces had not yet established posts or even patrols. From his beleaguered outpost at Koomerabad, George Fooks had seen thousands of Santals, men, women and children, moving south-west, very slowly, at just a koss (about two miles) each day, but he feared that these people were 'only an advance guard'.[74] A Raneegunge correspondent passed on news that up to 200,000 Santals were believed to be moving west-ward, driving 50,000 cattle, confirming that they were moving very slowly.[75] Exactly where they were coming from, where they were going and where they were at any time remained opaque. The effort of finding them and attempting to stop them brought a further shift in the focus of the campaign: further westward to the vicinity of Operbandah, which Sherwill had described as a 'mean-looking village', of little value except as a focus for the actions of both Santals and Company forces.[76]

Officials found this ignorance frustrating. James Ward was reading roobocarries from the darogah of Operbandah, who reported that he was watching Santal bands approaching 'by slow marches'; but Ward received the reports days later, and had no means to get troops to the area—the nearest were around Govindpore, 50 miles distant to the south-west, and their focus was the immediate defence of the Grand Trunk Road.[77] 'The Sonthals must be somewhere', Ward wrote in vexation: but where? Ward had already begun urging that troops be sent to protect villages around Saruth and Operbandah, urging that Gillon's bildars be moved from Sooree, where they were not needed, to western Beerbhoom, which he argued was becoming the crucial theatre of the campaign. As with other phases of the campaign, military officers were not in sole charge of what might seem to be military operations. Civil officials remained the primary instigators of troop movements, and James Ward was among the most energetic. Robert Richardson, reading similar signs, also urged Bird to move troops westward toward Saruth, and Bird agreed to raise the matter with Lloyd, who commanded the campaign overall, though he remained wary of 'exposing troops at this season in the deadly jungle'. The Santals 'are no doubt masters of the jungles', Bird acknowledged, and they may have been devastating the upper Adye valley, he conceded, but emphasised that 'it would be bad policy to harass and destroy our troops in vain pursuit of them'.[78]

Richardson persisted. Indeed, he had already written another report, describing 'looting, burning and murdering in all the villages' and urging Bird to dispatch Lieutenant William Gordon and 200 men of the 63rd to Saruth. Gordon, now free of the opprobrium attaching to the Rangers, was under Bird's orders, Richardson reminded him, adding that there was good accommodation and food there: Gordon could stay in the moonsiff's cutchery and Saruth was much healthier than Deoghur.[79] Henry Rose wrote to William Elliott boldly proclaiming that renewed Santal aggression was the inevitable result of the abandonment of Koomerabad, and that in the following fortnight over thirty villages had been burned in the borderlands between Bhaugulpore and Beerbhoom.[80]

Rose reported that his scouts had identified two large bodies of Santals, one about 5000 strong near Raksandangal, a few miles north of Operbandah, and the other, perhaps three times larger, near Afzulpore. The second, especially, seemed to pose a greater threat in that it appeared to have penetrated the chain of posts that Elliott, Ward and the military officers had been trying to create. Another 5000 Santals lay near Operbandah, which they burned on 16 September. Confounding the criticisms of the local police, the darogah and his burkendazes remained at their posts until the last minute, escaping back to Afzulpore with only their clothes. The darogah reported that he thought that Afzulpore would be the Santals' next objective.[81]

Increasingly, the country west of the lines of posts became the focus of military and civil officers concerned at Santal pressure on the Grand Trunk Road. But should they meet the Santal movement on the road itself or in the country north of it? No one had a clear picture of Santal dispositions or intentions, despite the confidence of their reports. Some admitted their ignorance. Joseph Hampton, commanding the posts and patrols on the road, complained that 'the want of information here is dreadful'.[82] Atkinson duly raised with Bird the need to extend his operations and Bird reacted cautiously. 'By looking at the map', he replied dryly, 'you will observe what an extent of country, mostly dense jungle, is to be provided for'. And he warned that the task of intercepting Santal parties could not detract from the need to hold the Grand Trunk Road, from which 'not a man should be withdrawn'.[83] While officials and officers had trouble establishing what was happening under the great jungle canopy that stretched north of the road, some had a clear enough idea of the broader picture later in September. James Ward reported to Grey that 'things are looking bad' on the frontier opening up to the west of Beerbhoom. Moreover, civil officials criticised some military officers' failure to act as decisively as they thought necessary. Ward decried George Burney's timidity when with Santal bands within two miles of Afzulpore he would 'not move a man'.[84]

Burney protested that he had 'only ... 200 Bayonets' in Sooree and could not provide 'even a naik and his sepoy'. He declined to send Gillon and his irregulars forward, and when eventually Robert Richardson ordered them to scout into the disputed country, Burney countermanded the order.[85] Other civil officials also complained of Burney's caution, and William Elliott claimed that he had actually hoarded 500 troops who were needed elsewhere. Richardson unwittingly fuelled Burney's caution by telling him that 'the Sonthals are assembling in large numbers' and were waiting only for 'leaders and reinforcements' from the Rajmahal Hills before launching a renewed movement.[86] In fairness to Burney, he was reading reports from officials which included suggestions that Santal bands could not only reappear before Sooree, but 'might even go to Elam Bazar'. Ilam

Bazar was on the Adye, south of Sooree, and had never seen hostile Santals. Burney's response to this contradictory intelligence was to do nothing, not even answer rooboocaries—Ward found it impossible to get him to answer a letter within 36 hours, and the two were only 35 miles apart.[87]

Worried officials, exasperated at hesitant senior military officers, especially George Burney, Joseph Hampton and John Nembhard, warned that 'the rebels have been embolden[ed] of ... troops which they think retreat from the jungles', and that 'the rebellion may now spread'.[88] While older military officers seemed to not have learned much about their adversary, their generally younger civil counterparts judged the reports reaching them with growing assurance. Increasingly, civil officials with contacts and scouts in the disturbed country were identifying not just where Santal bands were located, but their leadership, a sign that Company intelligence improved during the rebellion. Henry Rose believed that the Raksandangal Santals were led by four manjees: Mochua, Konjole, Rama and Soondra. Richardson even claimed that a Santal leader, Babodor Manjee, had sent him a message directly, using the traditional branch of sal leaves.[89] By contrast, James Ward, two decades older than Richardson, found it 'useless to ask the name of the leader of their respective gangs or the plans made for future operations'.[90]

The new area of operations encompassed a rough quadrilateral, between the Adye and Mor rivers, with Jamtarra and Afzulpore on its southern base and Koomerabad and Taldanga on its northern side. Officers on the spot began to report on the extent of the fighting, with 'the whole country from Jamtarra to Deoghur' being plundered and destroyed—officials produced lists of burned villages, one list comprising sixty-five names.[91] Officials began receiving desperate appeals for aid from villages as far as 60 miles away, from darogahs, zamindars and rajahs. Few of these appeals could be met, and a list of murdered zamindars demonstrated that Santal resentment of oppressive landlords remained unsated.[92] Conflict between zamindars and their rebellious tenants was vicious—both had everything to lose. When a zamindar enticed a Santal 'chief' to come alone to see him to state his grievances, the zamindar's retainers, probably on his orders, waylaid the man and decapitated him.[93]

At the end of September Bird began to create a new chain of posts, trying to control this disputed area, while maintaining the posts and patrols on the Grand Trunk Road. It had been begun not on Bird's orders, but at the instigation of restless civil officials ordering troops to move regardless of senior regimental officers' caution and with the compliance and even complicity of more junior officers. Captains and lieutenants led detachments ranging out, with Gillon and his irregulars, who were at last released from Burney's inertia, patrolling the gaps between them. While they suffered from a dearth of supply elephants, together they pushed the Santals further west. Soon there was an intermittent line of posts from Sooree to Deoghur and Bird was confident that Santals would 'hardly return to that direction again'.[94] Indeed, so strong did the Company's troops' line appear that it seemed that Santals were returning northwards, back toward Bhaugulpore, where Lloyd's troops were establishing their own line. A month after directing the northern units to wait until the ground and clear weather allowed more aggressive operations, Lloyd even seemed to change his thinking, authorising Liptrap's 42nd to patrol southward, reaching toward Saruth, only ten or fifteen miles from Bird's most advanced posts.[95] Actually, that forward move was ordered by Bidwell while Lloyd returned to Dinapore for his health; the most aggressive commanders in this campaign often wore the alpaca jacket of a civilian rather than the scarlet shell jacket of a native infantry officer.[96]

Lieutenant William Gordon led the 42nd's forward parties, assisted by fifty sepoys of the Bhaugulpore Hill Rangers, on trial after their disgrace at Peer Pointee in July. Gordon tracked and surprised a body of a thousand or more Santals, attacking at dawn. Both sepoys and Santals were learning. The troops moved through the jungle in the dark and managed to get within musket shot without detection, and the Santals, rather than fleeing at the first shots, offered 'an unusually prolonged resistance'.[97] But they were still driven into the jungle, losing ten men killed, one of whom said to have been a leader, and many wounded. The Santals moved off, not to the south-west but to the north, a further sign that the cordon that Bird and Lloyd were creating was affecting Santal movement. By mid-October the 42nd's patrols had actually made contact with those of the 63rd moving northward from Operbandah. The meetings were symbolic rather than practical, but they suggested, perhaps to the Santals how their freedom of movement was increasingly becoming curtailed.

'Here comes the headman': Santal leadership[98]

The Indian historian Sugata Bose was not alone in presenting the rebellion as 'a fully fledged armed confrontation between the rebel fauj (or army) and the state's military forces'; but was the Santal force truly an army?[99] From their very first reports, based on interrogating Sonthal 'spies' or Bengali witnesses, magistrates suggested that they faced a 'Fouj'—the man whom Ashley Eden questioned talked of a Santal 'army', with 'officers' and 'sepoys', corroborating his suspicion that 'it is evidently a planned and concerted thing'.[100] Narahari Kaviraj consistently wrote about the Santal 'Fauj', as if it were an organised, disciplined force under command, formed in four 'divisions' of 5000 each, comprising a number of 'companies'.[101] A newspaper letter contested the idea: 'to look upon the Santhals as organized troops is simply absurd'.[102] The *Hindoo Patriot*, however, certainly thought that 'they appear to be under something like regular organization'.[103] Some observers did describe Santals moving as 'divisions', as if they had spontaneously devised a Napoleonic conception of Grand Tactics.[104] A correspondent writing to the *Morning Chronicle* elaborated on this apparent organisation:

> The Santhals are said to be in 3 divisions. One division is marching for Bhaugulpore, the other is at present below Rajmahal, and the third and largest division is between Colgong and Pointee. The police between these places have all been annihilated ... cut to pieces ...[105]

The *Friend of India* pointed out that in their annual hunts, Santals were 'accustomed to hunt in enormous bodies, collected with the rapidity of regular troops' and directed across large distances, presumably by the sound of drums.[106] Vennelakanti Raghavaiah, the authority on *Tribal Revolts*, recorded that Frederick Burroughs had noticed that Santals moved in small bands (presumably for ease in the jungle) which then converged at the sound of drums.[107]

If true, this reinforced the idea that Santal forces obeyed a higher direction. Though Company forces increasingly encountered large

Santal forces that displayed no signs of discipline or organisation higher than a loose band of men from a group of villages under a purgannait, the identification of leaders buttressed the idea that the Santals were a more formally organised adversary than they actually were. As late as October Charles Chapman, a junior official, could report on a 12-hour dour intended to capture Kanhu and his surviving brothers at the head of what he called 'their grand army', while Lloyd and Bird both referred to the Santals' 'main body'.[108] Given that the Santals had no martial tradition, did not go raiding or resolve disputes by force, had barely seen sepoys and had no idea of what a European-style army was, or what it could do before 1855, it would be surprising if they could have suddenly devised an army in anything more than a rudimentary form. Still, the idea persists, perhaps because those idealising peasant insurgency wished it so: Ranajit Guha, for instance, referred to 'the Santal high command'.[109]

European observers described Santal movements assuming co-ordinated or even centrally directed leadership. The rebels defeated at Moheshpore, for example, were described as 'coming down to effect a junction with the Beerbhoom rebels' gathering near Rampore Haut.[110] But were these motions deliberate or directed; by whom, and how; through what process of consultation or command? We do not know. Most European observers, even while writing of 'the Sonthals' as a single entity, usually dismissed the idea that they operated at the direction of a single individual.

Sidhu seemed as much of a spiritual figure than a general-in-command, or a political leader, the Santals having no concept of overall ruler. 'From first to last', the *Friend of India* concluded:

> they never had a leader or a vestige of a concerted plan of action. Each band moved where its own brute impulses led ... murdered, burnt and plundered, and retreated into the jungle.[111]

Evidence for a Santal 'high command' is not convincing. As a people, Santals manifested a strong egalitarian ethos, acknowledging no more authority than the village headman, a manjee, often a heredi-tary office and informed by a democratic or consultative tendency, at least among men. William Archer observed how village meetings sought unanimity, with manjees facilitating the general will; the anthropologist Nabendu Datta-Majumder described the Lo bir (or 'hunt council'), a small-scale men's parliament convened during the annual communal hunts.[112] A sympathetic correspondent who had toured the Santal country before the rebellion, unusually on foot, described gatherings in which 'the whole village seems one happy family'.[113] Chakraborti's account clearly showed that the Hul's initial leadership made collective decisions through discussion or consensus. Octavius Toogood's discovery of the leadership of Sidhu and his brothers in the Rajmahal Hills gratified the Company assumption that the Hul must have been instigated and directed by 'ringleaders', but it is unclear the degree to which Santal movements—and they can only be inferred from often unclear Company reports—were actually the result of a deliberate and conscious system of authority. Toogood seems to have under-estimated the Santal brothers' charisma or ability to lead. He described them as 'common sort of men much in debt' who defaulted on their debts. Indebted they were, but they were hardly common.[114]

Sidhu and Kanhu certainly appointed soubahs (or subordinate leaders), supposedly drawing on the model of the ranks of the Company's administration.[115] Narahira Kaviraj, in his chapter 'Rebel Hierarchy', represented the Santal leadership as having been as complex as the Company's, a claim that does not bear examination. It had seemed that Santal movements were subject to the direction of a few leaders, though to what degree is uncertain: Santal society was organised around small communities, at most groups of villages: to expect a general staff to emerge was inconceivable. However, hints in Company records suggest a degree of leadership greater than the village. As had become apparent around Sooree in September, the Hul had thrown up effective individual Santal leaders, even if they could not always be named by Europeans. Civil officers repeatedly anticipated, for example, that particular Santal bands were 'likely to stand', a sign that they had insights into their temper and perhaps even their leadership. Later in the rebellion their reports more often identified individual manjees. Lieutenant Robert Aitken of the 13th just missed a band of Santals who escaped from a dawn ambush just south of Godda ('alas! They were too quick for us'). As he pursued them on horseback ahead of his panting sepoys, he fired at three 'chiefs … conspicuous in red garments'.[116]

The Santal leaders that Company officials did know about continued to exercise their fascination. Alfred Bidwell conceded in September that the remote country on the borders of Bhaugulpore and Beerbhoom remained 'infested with Insurgent Sonthals'. He attributed their persistence to the influence of Kanhu, who had already acquired a near-legendary standing in European eyes—not least because he seemed to be everywhere. The influence of leaders like Kanhu, Bidwell believed, had prevented Santals accepting the amnesty he had offered with such poor results.[117] The legend of Kanhu Manjee grew as more stories and rumours filtered in from across the disturbed districts, his 'divine agency' mentioned by Santals whom William Money questioned. But they did not join Kanhu's cause merely from 'religious fanaticism'. 'They are all more or less impressed with the idea that the exactions of the mahajans caused the disturbance in the first instance', Money advised his superior, Bidwell.[118]

Company spies brought important news at the end of September. Robert Richardson made a tantalisingly brief reference in his diary claiming that a 'grand meeting of the Sonthal chiefs' had been held at Ranebeehal, near Taldanga. Richardson's 'spies' had tried to ascertain what had been decided, but to no avail.[119] Did the council debate what the Santals should do to contest the Company troops' gradual encroachment, or their blocking the route to the south-west? Did they agree to challenge the troops' operations in western Beerbhoom, or to hold out in Belputteh and Hendweh? Did the Company's forces' move to occupy Jamtarra 'take them by surprise', as James Ward claimed a day before?[120] What did they know or think about their enemy's strategy? Richardson's spies soon told him—on what basis is unclear—that the Santals would be concentrating on holding the country around Belputteh, and that they were 'well armed'.

Santal leaders remained strictly amateur commanders. If they identified one of the Company's troops' weaknesses, for instance that their outposts depended upon slow-moving and vulnerable elephant supply columns, they did not, it seems, attempt to strike them, though Santal bands 'hung upon the line of march', as Frederick Halliday's officials had told him, perhaps harassing columns from the jungle.[121] They may have picked off some of the crowds of unarmed Bengali villagers following every detachment rather than risking aggravating the sepoys, but if so the attacks went undocumented. The other weapon Santals seemed not to use was picking off sepoy sentries with their powerful bows—if they had, even if the arrows were not poisoned, they might have grievously impaired morale among unnerved native infantry parties in the unfamiliar jungle. But Santal leaders certainly understood the value of stopping the dawks: Halliday complained that as late as October that Santals had interrupted communications with his officials.

In the skirmishing that continued north of the Grand Trunk Road, William Gott heard of a Santal band which had reportedly built a stockade to defy the troops. It seems unlikely that a force without firearms whose main asset was mobility would entrench, but Gott took the story so seriously he asked that 500 men and a couple of guns be sent to attack the supposed stockade. The 'Soobar' leading the band, he heard, was 'a young man who was wounded on the leg at Koomerabad'.[122] Did this suggest that within the Santal forces, even in the course of a rising still not quite three months old, casualties and challenges were bringing to the fore dynamic younger leaders? Vague reports even suggested, in contrast to the subordination characteristic of Santal society, that a woman soubah had emerged, when the body of a supposed leader, found dead in a palki near Sangrampore, south-west of Bhaugulpore, was discovered to be a woman.[123] Certainly Santal women were more assertive than Hindu women, but this sounds rather unlikely; perhaps another of the fictions circulated during the rebellion.

That a degree of collaboration did occur between Santal leaders became likely when officials learned that they exchanged messages, signified by various combinations of the branch of a sal tree, in which configurations of branches and leaves conveyed messages both impenetrable to outsiders at the time and lost forever now. Santal leaders used the same method to try to communicate with Company officials. Robert Richardson in Sooree recorded that he had received the token of a sal branch, which arrived from Nagore via a complicated chain of police jamadar-to-chowkidar-to-zamindar-to-district cutcherry. It appeared to mean that Soobah Rabaan (or Raboo in other accounts) wanted to meet officials, but where, when and to what end remained unknown, and the meeting seems not to have occurred.[124]

The turmoil within Santal leadership is suggested by the unexpected incursion southwards toward Sooree by a Santal band presumably seeking food. It achieved little but at least perhaps enabled George Burney to feel vindicated in his refusal to detach troops to where they were more urgently required. Alarmed villagers reported to Robert Richardson the reappearance of Santals to the north of Sooree and Burney took out what he self-righteously called 'the whole of the troops at my disposal' to meet them. As his force comprised almost the entire 56th, 490 men, and four mountain guns, Burney was hardly short-handed. After a long march he faced the 1500 raiders but they fled before he could get within range. Burney had been told that the soubah he faced was resolved to 'give battle'—and had taken his guns because it was rumoured that the Santals would build a stockade—but was disappointed to find that the Santals were not planning to 'adapt a new mode of warfare'. In growing heat Burney marched his force back to Sooree, his sepoys like him regretting that the Santals had not been 'waiting for the attack'.[125]

'Why need you suffer?': Santal disillusionment

No one knows what sustained the Santal cause as it became clear that they had not achieved victory. William Money claimed that Kanhu ruled his army by coercion and intimidation. Santal 'sepahis' (sepoys) were, he claimed, 'scouring the country, killing all who refused to join'—he had interrogated five of these men and heard their own account.[126] At the end of September, Hugh Pester heard that 'almost every Sonthal village is furnishing its quota', implying compulsion—men from a country with a militia tradition easily accepted this claim.[127]

As the atrocities committed by Santal bands showed, a people who had previously been known for their lack of aggression seemed to be acting out of character. Europeans described Santals patronisingly as 'intelligent, obliging, but timid', or 'cowardly towards mankind but, brave when confronted with wild animals'.[128] Even if the pronouncements that the Santals had been misled by 'religious fanaticism' were wrong, it is certainly justifiable to regard the outbreak as imposing severe tension, even trauma, enough to induce a notably peaceable people to commit acts of savagery. But the powerful feelings of resentment that had driven Santals to leave their villages to attack, kill and rob zamindars and neighbours seemed insufficient to sustain a long insurrection. Ashley Eden told George Lloyd early in August, when Lloyd was interviewing civil and military officers on taking up his command, that he thought he saw signs that Santals he spoke to (admittedly mostly prisoners) were already 'waking from their delusions'.[129] They had believed that 'if any man's head of theirs was taken off, it would be fastened on by the … Chiefs'. This belief, like the conviction that 'our guns only poured forth water', was discredited. 'Now they see it is not true', a correspondent had written to the *Englishman*.[130]

Perceptions in July or August that the Hul was losing momentum had plainly been premature. But by September, signs of exhaustion became apparent. One manifestation of the disillusionment that Santals, and especially manjees, increasingly felt, was that Company officials received overtures not just to explain their predicament but to negotiate over the betrayal of their leaders. Their plans coincided with those of their adversaries: James Ward warned his juniors not to simply allow manjees to submit, but to use their desire to surrender as a way to find and capture Santal leaders, and especially Kanhu, who was becoming the symbolic or perhaps actual Santal commander.[131] As ever, Santal evidence is scarce, but an echo of it might be seen in the testimony of Jugia Haram, who fifteen years later remained embittered at what he saw as the false hopes Sidhu held out for Santal independence. 'We almost died of hunger', he said, 'all because of the false words of those Suba Thakur cheats'.[132] Durga Tudu, the most frank Santal witness, explicitly described how his manjee agreed to turn in Santal leaders when asked by 'the Saheb'—an unnamed civil official. When they had done so, the official told the followers 'Return to your own villages', threatening them with death if they were seen again.[133]

While Company operations in Beerbhoom had proved frustrating and even counter-productive, in the course of them, manjees had offered to deliver up Kanhu and Sidhu in return for immunity from retribution. Lloyd believed that Richardson and Birch had been duped by Santal leaders planning a descent on Burhyte, but the evidence is at best ambiguous. Richardson especially had tried to find the brothers, at least partly because success would do his career good. But Lloyd himself learned of instances in other areas where Santal manjees had offered to turn in their leaders or actually had seized them. Days after expressing his suspicion that Richardson and Birch had been fooled, Lloyd learned that actually Santals had brought in Ram Manjee, described as a 'Gossain or chief priest' and Moochea Manjee 'the Sonthal Soobadar'.[134] Overtures like these were a sign that 'the Sonthals' were not a monolithic or unified mass, but were subject to schisms, challenges to authority, shifts in loyalty and fluctuations in commitment.[135] Refracted by brief references in British records, visible only in their approaches to Company officers, the interior world of the Santal leaders is as opaque as are the lives of their followers. But such offers were to become more common as the insurgency continued.

Digambar Chakraborti claimed that disillusionment with the brothers' ability to lead set in early in the rebellion, perhaps soon after Moheshpore, leading to 'secret councils' in which some manjees plotted to hand the brothers to the Company. He named the manjees who both attempted to capture Sidhu and those who defended him, claiming that after an attempt to render Sidhu senseless with *handia* (rice liquor) Kanleh, one of Sidhu's supporters, shot down and decapitated the leading plotter, Doman. The victorious faction is supposed to have presented Doman's head to 'the Captain' at Bowsee, who, Chakraborti recorded, had Kanleh shot. Company records make no mention of this occurrence, not surprisingly, but it exposes that as well as contests between Santal and Company and Santal and zamindar, Santals also waged a struggle for influence, power and even survival among themselves, one largely unrecorded by British sources.[136] A hint exists in a fragment of song recorded by anthropologists that suggests that an egalitarian people who traditionally travelled everywhere on foot expressed unease when the brothers took to travelling by other means: 'Sido and Kanhu in palkis/ Chand and Bhaero on horses ...'[137]

Company reports, recording impressions picked up from interrogations of prisoners, encounters with Santal bystanders and negotiations with manjees considering turning on their erstwhile leaders, all suggest that the Santals' failure to quickly gain freedom provoked dissension and conflict within their senior ranks. Jugia Haram described how, once captured, 'the Englishman coaxed us … "Why need you suffer?" [they asked] "Tell us the leaders and we will let you go at once"'.[138] Robert Richardson, for example, reported that a group of manjees who had surrendered to him and had returned to bring in other chiefs, had not returned. Had they been killed, thought better of the offer or been persuaded of their loyalty? A Mr Wilson, a planter who seems to have maintained contact with his Santal employees, reported that a manjee who had surrendered had then been attacked by Santals resenting his defeatism, and that they had burned his village as they had many others. Other officials gathered grisly accounts of the consequences of defection. William Money learned that Kanhu Manjee had discovered that Bugna Manjee had been in contact with Company officials and had taken Bugna's son hostage as a guarantor of his loyalty. When Bugna Manjee came to claim his son, Kanhu seized him and one of Kanhu's confederates killed him by what Money was told was 'a slow process of crimping'—that is, by cutting slices from him, as a demonstration of the price of treachery. To Money's relief, Bugna Manjee's son escaped from bondage, taking with him the head of the man who had killed his father.[139]

'It is said', reported James Ward, that Santals around Dumka were 'peaceably inclined', but he 'can't tell with what truth' lay behind the rumours.[140] At the same time newspapers were claiming that Santals of Bhaugulpore had fallen out with those from Beerbhoom, the former wishing to fight on, the others to submit, though whether Santals identified with districts as such is doubtful.[141] But despite rumour and speculation, no European really knew what was happening around the fires of the many Santal bands at large in the great swathe of jungle stretching from the hills of the Damin, across the Deoghur uplands and down the valleys and ridges leading to the Grand Trunk Road and beyond. Some contended that a split had developed between 'Bhaugulpore' and 'Beerbhoom' Santals and that the dispute looked like 'a case of Kilkenny cats'.[142] Jugia Haram remembered how, having retreated into the deep jungle, 'then Santals killed Santals from hunger'.[143] By September, the Hul was breaking down.

'Vulgar petty jealousy': civil-military relations

If the insurgents were divided, the Company's leaders were scarcely more united. Though among the first actions of local officials was to call for military force, all understood that the civil authorities remained in charge. John Peter Grant's minute on the 'Rising of the Sonthals' made clear that Bengal's lieutenant-governor was 'responsible for the management of this business' and for 'every prompt, vigorous, and wise measure' that demanded.[144] In principle, while military force remained securely under civil direction, in practice, 'discord still reigned' between civil and military authorities. Vincent Jervis told William Hunter that matters were so vague that 'constant misunderstandings resulted, and every post carried an angry reference on the point'.[145]

An emergency such as an insurrection cut across the careful financial control which was at the heart of the Company administration. One explanation for the customarily notorious slowness of civil and military processes was the need to document, approve and audit minutely even minor expenditure, leaving officers at all levels dependent upon superiors for authorisation. The weaknesses of such a system of control soon became obvious. The decisive William Elliott warned that ignoring the Military Auditor-General's regulations could cost 'a few hundred or thousand of rupees', but that failing to approve enough troops could mean 'devastation of property and the destruction of life'.[146] Early in the rebellion ingrained habits of financial prudence deterred men from taking decisions and initiatives, in case making unauthorised expenditure might later be used against them. Institutionalised pusillanimity like this infuriated some contemporaries, including an observer familiar with the system of personal initiative prevailing in the recently-conquered Punjab. A correspondent signing himself 'Punjabee' was scathing about the Bengal government's conduct during the rebellion. It had not acted vigorously, had not proclaimed martial law, had not used enough troops but had shown deplorable leniency toward captured rebels. Above all, he affirmed, it had 'tolerated the vulgar petty jealousy between the Civil and Military Services'.[147] That relationship lay at the heart of the Hul's suppression.

At first the only civil officers available were those allocated to the districts affected, but soon others were called in from other districts. William Money came to Bhaugulpore from neighbouring Monghyr, Henry Rose from Pubna, 200 miles to the east, to help in Beerbhoom. Civil service in Bengal offered 'very few prizes for men in the regular line': the rebellion represented an opportunity for ambitious men to demonstrate their worth.[148] As ever, the crisis revealed leaders who responded to the challenge, as well as men who failed the test. In Beerbhoom, George Loch emerged as a civil officer of 'intelligence and activity' and William Elliott had himself attached to columns operating outside of his own, peaceful, district of Burdwan, just as Ashley Eden, Robert Richardson and Octavius Toogood gained merit for their willingness to take the initiative in the field. Despite his officials' individual efforts, Halliday soon argued that the suppression of the rebellion 'should no longer remain in the unskilled though very energetic hands of the District civil authorities': but neither he nor his senior officials were willing to surrender control to their military counterparts.[149] What was the solution to be?

One of the clearest signs of tension between military and civilian thinking about the best way to end the Hul was seen in their attitude toward the declaration of martial law. At Frederick Halliday's urging, the Supreme Council first considered introducing martial law late in July. Its members' discussion of the question revealed divisions between them, and one of the perennial weaknesses of the government of British India: its tendencies to timidity, equivocation and prevarication, and the absence of dynamic leadership when it was most needed. The Council's members were inclined to write long, pedantic, heavily qualified and ultimately irresolute minutes, which they circulated even when they met in the Council Chamber at Fort William. The minutes reveal the extent of their forebodings and concerns, but they also show them to have been unwilling to take decisive actions. Powerfully influenced by precedent, senior officials familiar with the suppression of the Kol rebellion knew that it had been ended—and in three months—without resort to what an officer called 'a commission to punish at discretion'.[150]

Joseph Dorin, the President-in-Council, its head but not the Governor-General's actual substitute, saw no advantage in proclaiming martial law: the troops would not act with any greater vigour and surely embarking on such a step would 'inspire a vague feeling of alarm in the minds of the public'. Who 'the public' were he did not specify: Bengalis? 'Respectable natives'? The British community? Typically, Dorin looked to established procedure, concluding that Halliday had 'not shown that the force already employed is insufficient', as if suppressing insurgency were a mathematical proof.[151] Dorin's fellow Council members offered equally tepid responses. Barnes Peacock, expert in law but largely ignorant of India, made a masterfully vague observation that he was 'not prepared to say that a sufficient case has been made out' for martial law. General Low (whose son Robert was about to take the field with the Governor-General's Bodyguard) was at best 'doubtful' about martial law, but supported the military officers in the field 'with the responsibility of putting down this insurrection'. Only John Peter Grant seemed to endorse Halliday's request, but in a rambling and contradictory minute ended up agreeing with his colleagues, expressing the desire for exemplary justice: 'capital punishment in cold blood [for] the leading men of the insurgents'. But the Council recognised that regular criminal courts could not deliver such a lesson. Many thousands of words of minutes, dutifully copied out by scribes, at last resulted in agreement on the appointment of a military commander but with carefully specified powers. Insultingly, perhaps, Halliday only learned that the Council had declined his first request to declare martial law the day after it decided to form what became the Sonthal Field Force.[152] Word of the protracted disagreement—'unseemly dissentions'— between Halliday and the Supreme Council leaked to the newspapers across the porous boundary between official and unofficial Calcutta.[153]

Frederick Halliday, who had always been restive at his reliance on military force, argued that the relationship between civil authority and military power was flawed: 'as if two persons were at the same time to use one pair of shears, one at each handle'.[154] This seems to express Halliday's resentment at having to share responsibility rather than any inherent flaw in the relationship between the Government of Bengal and the Bengal Army. How else should civil and military authorities work together but by each providing one blade of the shears? If the hinge of those scissors were rusty or sticky, was that not a reflection on Halliday himself?

But the insurgency continued regardless of minutes in Fort William. Its gravity was suggested by what appeared to be a routine communication between Alexander Russell (Grey's deputy) and James Ward. Russell passed all of Ward's travelling expenses, which were far higher than the usual, querying or contesting none of them; the senior Bengal civil official's customary attitude to financial expenditure. This crisis was too serious for quibbles over a few hundred rupees. In August even the auditors acknowledged the existence and gravity of the rebellion, directing civil officials to debit all expenses in their accounts under the catch-all heading 'Santal Insurrection'.[155]

Calcutta's newspapers continued to provide an outlet for stress between military and civil officers, though the divide did not simply reflect their allegiance by service. A sarcastic item in the *Citizen* derided Sir William Gomm, suggesting that he had better remain in the Hills and not interfere, but warned that if he did return to Calcutta 'General Too*good* C[ivil].S[ervice]. may prove too *much* for him'.[156] An officer of the 2nd Irregular Cavalry, one of only a handful from that regiment sent to Raneegunge, wrote while on the way lamenting that his unit had to serve against the Santals, but directly criticising those directing the Company's campaign. The rebellion could have been suppressed long before, he complained, 'had we proper men at the head of affairs'.[157] The Company's services had a long tradition of accommodating individual protest, even within a system often hobbled by deference and submission: it was one of the paradoxes of Bengal under the Company. Relations were ordinarily strained. Civil officials of eight years standing ranked as majors, whereas everyone knew that attaining a majority took at least 16 years, and probably 25 years. This meant that younger civilians out-ranked older military officers.[158] Civil officials could, however, earn military officers' respect. William Elliott at Sooree they regarded as 'decidedly of a Military turn'. He had been 'always ready to enter the jungle', 'much loved by the unfortunate residents here, as likewise by both officers and men'.[159] But generally, because civil officials were actually in charge of their detachments, military officers resented being 'ridden over rough shod by the civil functionaries', as an officer later complained to the *Citizen*.[160]

'Our principle and immediate care': on the Grand Trunk Road

Brigadier Bird's instructions on taking command in Beerbhoom in August explicitly directed him to keep open the Grand Trunk Road and prevent Santals from crossing it and making for the Chota Nagpore territory. From August this aim became one of the principal Company strategies, and its significance in influencing later operations and arguably in underpinning eventual Company success needs to be traced. The great highway originally built by the Mughals ran for 900 miles from Calcutta to Delhi and 500 beyond to Peshawar, India's best road, 'smooth as a bowling green'.[161] Maintained by the Public Works Department at a cost of Rs 50,000 each year and patrolled by Road Sowars, it enabled everyone from pilgrims to marching sepoys to the gharris operated by the North-West Dawk Company, to move quickly and safely. But the Grand Trunk Road was exceptional in every way. Even a few miles north of the highway, secondary roads simply disappeared.[162]

Holding the Grand Trunk Road involved the Hul's first extensive use of mounted troops, as well as large numbers of infantry. At first Bird had the hundred sowars of the Governor-General's Bodyguard, 60 of the Ramghur Horse (a local corps but useful for exactly that reason), and from mid-August a squadron of the 11th Irregular Cavalry. Road Sowars acted as messengers, enabling Bird to control operations from Raneegunge. The Ramghur Horse had arrived at the end of the first week of August, just as Bird left Raneegunge for Sooree, though the mounted troops were unable to follow him, being 'knocked up' (tired) after their journey of several weeks.[163]

By mid-August it became apparent that whether from pressure in Bhaugulpore or because Santal leaders intended to incite rebellion in the districts south-west of the road, as many officials believed and feared, large numbers of Santals were now moving towards the road. Having invested considerable effort to develop a line of outposts across southern Beerbhoom, Louis Bird decided that the security of the Grand Trunk Road 'must now be our principle and immediate care'[sic].[164] Bird's grasp of spelling was uncertain, but he understood that if the rebellion was to be suppressed it could not be allowed to spread. Allowing Santals to cross or cut the Grand Trunk

Road would have been an embarrassing military failure. Ordinarily the road was protected by guard houses placed every couple of miles and patrolled by constables, well-armed and wearing a 'becoming uniform'.[165] Now the road needed a regular garrison to safeguard the South-West Frontier.

Walter Sherwill, the resident expert at Lloyd's headquarters and evidently collating reports from his contacts all over the Santal country, substantiated the hunches of less expert officers. In August he had predicted that up to 200,000 Santals—nearly the entire population of the two districts—were on the move, a figure he claimed he had 'carefully calculated'. 'The mass will strike the Grand Trunk Road between Parasnath and the collieries at Raneegunge', he predicted, arguing that they were making for the districts of Singbhoom, Manbhoom, Hazaribagh and Ramghur, the region the Santals had migrated from decades before.[166] Sherwill's intelligence heralded a further major shift in military operations, even if his demographic calculations were awry.[167]

Bird gave the responsibility for this new command to Major Joseph Hampton, commanding the fresh 50th Native Infantry. His instructions were simple: 'your object will be to prevent the passage of the Sonthals ... and to recover so much of the plunder accompanying them as you can'.[168] Hampton's force would soon grow to include the newly-arrived 2nd Grenadiers and a substantial mounted force: the 11th Irregular Cavalry, the Ramghur Irregular Cavalry and the Governor-General's Bodyguard. Lieutenant Boddam's rocket detachment was also to be hurried on (as much as bullocks could be hurried) from Raneegunge up the Grand Trunk Road to Govindpore and on to Jamtarra. Soon some 400 infantry and 200 cavalry were posted along a 40-mile stretch of the Grand Trunk Road. Hampton may not have been the best candidate for the task—he had already written to the Adjutant-General protesting that his health was 'very indifferent', leaving him 'quite unable to do my duty', though he remained.[169] Although the road was British India's major highway, even a few miles off it seemed remote. When an ensign of the 2nd Grenadiers was ordered to Govindpore he wrote it was 'some place, God knows where!'[170]

Soon cavalry outposts began reporting signs of the movement Sherwill had predicted. Lieutenant Alfred Needham sent to

Hampton a breathless rooboocary on 19 August, reporting that one of his 'patroles' had detected Santals between Topchaunce and Parasnath. His sowars must have spoken to Santal villagers: he claimed that they said that they were trying to persuade uncommitted Santals to join them and, even more worryingly, that they were trying to get to Chota Nagpore where the Kols were ready to rise. 'I would most urgently beg you to support me', Needham wrote, 'I cannot hope to do more than keep the rebels in check with so small a force'.[171] In an unfortunate anti-climax, Needham later had to report that these Santal bands had not actually tried to cross the road. It was not, however, the last emergency the guardians of the Grand Trunk Road faced.

'This cannot be allowed to continue': Jamtarra

Santal movements—essentially further to the west and south as September advanced—occurred more swiftly than the Company's supply arrangements could cope with, and as military officers met calls to move towards the line Jamtarra, Taldanga, and Govindpore, the country north of the Grand Trunk Road, they faced a further shortage of elephants. Captain James Phillips had only five to support his 200-strong detachment, complaining that he could not recruit coolies as porters to make up the difference because the villages around him were deserted.[172] Nor did slow-moving commissariat warrant officers or civilian contractors help. Officers operating at this, the extreme end of Bird's line, complained that government wagons were reluctant to carry forage which was needed to allow irregular cavalry patrols to scout out into the country in which Santal bands seemed to be gathering. Joseph Hampton begged Bird to intervene to induce a recalcitrant 'Mr Jordan' to carry grain to his cavalry posts.[173]

Despite these difficulties, Phillips led his detachment toward Jamtarra, confronting a force of a thousand Santals in the jungle around the village, 'I am glad to say ... I killed and wounded a great many'. Around 50 or 60 Santals were killed, and the same number wounded.[174] He knew that he had saved the village from being plundered and burnt, though he also knew that his force was unable to press on further where Santals were burning and looting unhindered.

'Unfortunate villagers' were 'begging for assistance' from Phillips all around: Jamtarra had been fortunate.[175] Phillips reported 'proof of the increasing boldness of the Santals', who seemed untroubled by the size or proximity of his force. Bird, disinclined to accept reports of Santal initiative, was sceptical of Phillips's account, dismissing it as 'skirmishing'.[176] But soon Bird began to receive reports confirming Phillips's version, and he seems to have been persuaded that the latest encounters around Jamtarra represented a fresh and growing confrontation. The Santals attacked Phillips's men while they were out on a dour on 22 September, but were repulsed with eight dead, including a manjee; and again at Jamtarra on 24 September, another of the few instances in which they attacked a village held by regular troops. Phillips reported that his men had driven off the raiders and had inflicted a further 25 fatalities. Again, it seemed that the dead included two Santal 'chiefs'—Phillips commandeered the man's horse. The frequent claims that Santal dead included 'chiefs', 'manjees' or 'soubahs', confirmed that Santal leaders led their followers into battle.[177]

But Phillips's initiative seemed not to have actually deterred Santal movement. James Ward, studying the patchy reports coming to him, confessed his uncertainty over the directions the insurgents were taking after they struck the line of detachments and posts. Some now appeared to be moving north-westwards—exactly where no troops lay: were they trying to circumvent Bird's force? Phillips's intervention had 'split the gang', certainly, Ward conceded, but both of the fragments were still plundering.[178]

Despite Bird's scepticism and Lloyd's orders that his regiments were to refrain from engaging the Santals until the country dried out at the end of the autumn, a combination of Santal movements and initiatives by several energetic officers responding to local developments meant that the end of September saw sepoys and Santals still in contention, and on a relatively new front. Moreover, fresh fighting in western Beerbhoom did not seem to betoken victory for the Company. James Ward summarised the unpropitious British situation in the last week of the month:

Their depredations have not only not been checked, but continue, and on a more extreme scale than ever. The whole population has fled panic struck and here we are positively powerless. We can prevent them crossing the Grant Trunk Road but that's all ... surely this cannot be allowed to continue.[179]

In fact, it seemed that despite the number of troops posted along the road, they could not prevent Santal bands probing, looking for places to cross. Patrols reportedly caught 'four Santhal spies armed to the teeth' reconnoitering later in September, but who knew how many others slipped through?[180] The next month, a correspondent to the *Citizen* claimed that 'hundreds' crossed 'every night'.[181] Three months after its outbreak, the Hul dragged on.

5

KARTIK (OCTOBER)

George Lloyd had largely closed down active campaigning in August and in Bhaugulpore saw a great reduction in conflict, though perhaps not because of the decisions of Company officers, but from the orders and actions of Santal leaders. Alfred Bidwell, collating reports from across the district described the 'totally different character of the present outrages from what prevailed a month ago'. 'Outrages' still occurred—notably in Bhaugulpore district's southern purgunnahs of Belputteh and Hendweh, but the district's 'Abstract of Police Reports' seemed optimistic. While in some thannahs 'Santals were collected … ready to plunder', in more areas the reports read 'no accounts of Sonthals in this Thannah'. In one place 'the Sonthals are returned … and settling down in their own villages'; in another 'some are seen about but meddle with no one'; and 'a number of Sonthals came in to make submission'. This gave Lloyd a stable base from which to eventually launch his operation.[1] In the meantime, the focus of conflict moved again, to western Beerbhoom.

'Great execution': fighting in western Beerbhoom

While the balance of the campaign was shifting to western Beerbhoom, not all Company officers recognised how the campaign was changing. Lieutenant-Colonel George Burney still kept a strong garrison in

Sooree, now 50 miles behind the new front, to James Ward's frustra-tion: 'I really do not know what is to be done', he confessed to William Grey, and continued to complain about Burney's timidity and obstruction.[2] This was no mere spat over precedence: for a week in late September, Burney in fact commanded the Company's forces in Beerbhoom, while Bird was sick. Despite the quiet, Burney con-tinued to worry that he had too few men. Bird sought to soothe his fears: 'I do not think it likely that the Sonthals will attack Sooree', he wrote, but Burney would not be reassured.[3] James Ward, who argued with him about leaving outlying detachments unsupported, damned Burney in letters to Grey, deploring his 'panic' and reiterating that 'my request [to send troops to Afzulpore] was most urgent' and that not doing so, and in fact sending a company southwards to Doobrajpore, away from danger, had been 'positively useless'.[4] The wonder was that Burney was not removed to a less crucial post. Company authorities often inconsistently tolerated dysfunctional incompetence rather than take difficult decisions.

In the light of Burney's timidity, Bird's force's effectiveness depended upon its staff. Just as Lloyd's force depended upon Shute and Sherwill, a constant presence in the southern force's records is Captain Benjamin Parrott, chosen by Louis Bird to act as his brigade-major. Parrott had at first served with his company of the 37th—his last act before joining Bird's headquarters had been to lead his detach-ment in a patrol across the Adye river, as far as Afzulpore, a name with which he would become familiar when collating and recording the reports from Bird's force in coming months. He appears to have had a volatile temper—his Record of Service details only that he had become entangled in a feud with a fellow officer, Lieutenant Hans Leslie, a disagreement so protracted that it could be resolved neither by his fellow officers, his commanding officer, nor the intercession of a visiting general who, unusually, thought it so harmful to the har-mony and efficiency of their corps that he recorded it in his inspection report.[5] Parrott's value evidently transcended the irritation of the feud and he retained Bird's good opinion. Certainly, his conduct as brigade-major was exemplary.

Among other vigorous young officers was Hungerford Boddam, the artillery officer who had been sent with his rockets to the crucial post of Jamtarra, where Phillips's sepoys protected the local rajah and its residents from Santal bands that he knew were 'lurking in the jungle'. When early in October sepoys were ordered to vacate the post, he realised that as soon as the troops marched off the Santals would emerge to plunder and burn the place. Boddam enterprisingly suggested that infantry be joined by a troop of cavalry—the country around Jamtarra was open and now drying out. Bird, who regarded Boddam as 'an active and intelligent officer', ordered the detachment to 'stand fast'; but also had him replaced by an infantry officer who had become available.[6] But he also sent a troop of Alfred Needham's irregular cavalry to the area and two weeks later noted that Hugh Pester had found the sowars 'most useful'.[7]

Indeed, the post at Jamtarra became one of the most crucial, because it commanded what effectively became the hinge between the Grand Trunk Road line to the west and the country stretching north to Nya Dumka. Through October Phillips and Boddam operated a mixed force that enabled Company troops to hold the link between these two chains of posts. The garrison included Phillips's sepoys, Sergeant Long and his bildars, 25 sowars of the 11th Irregular Cavalry and Boddam's rocket troop. These troops did not just hold the post, but ranged out on day-long sweeps up to ten miles out. Boddam did not often get a chance to use his rockets, but when scouts reported the presence of a Santal group on the banks of the Adye, Boddam took out a small party of bildars, sowars and sepoys, and as the Santals fled into the jungle, he fired 'a few Rockets' at them, reportedly killing 13.[8] But rockets were not Jamtarra's most effective weapon. Boddam praised the rissaldar in charge of the sowars, who were 'admirably adapted for Raids of this nature' and suggested that 'a squadron [of cavalry] would clear the whole neighbourhood of the Rebels'.[9] Robert Richardson also believed that the government had erred in not committing enough cavalry to the field force: 'if we do have an engagement', he predicted, 'we shall feel the want of cavalry much'.[10]

Bird's willingness to develop two lines of posts left his command spread thinly. With only 99 sepoys at Raneegunge, finding routine guards became difficult, and he was at last obliged to withdraw troops from the Grand Trunk Road to bolster the parties covering the disputed area. The arrival of the other long-delayed wing of the

50th Native Infantry helped to alleviate that temporary problem.[11] By mid-October, Bird's troops held what Ward described as 'a line of posts' from Jamtarra north to Nagore which he thought would 'very effectively prevent further plundering' by the Santals.[12] Bird's force held two lines, one of 80 miles along the Grand Trunk Road and one of 60 'along the skirt of the jungle' from Jamtarra to the hills in Belputteh. Company forces were gradually curtailing the Santals' freedom of movement.

Staff officers prepared for the 'plan of operations' proposed by Lloyd, agreed to by Halliday and in mid-October endorsed by the Supreme Council—Lloyd again went to Calcutta and described his plan. Even the querulous John Peter Grant conceded that Lloyd's operations in advancing southwards in Bhaugulpore had been 'excellent' and that Bird's even more difficult operations in Beerbhoom had been 'perfect'.[13] All agreed that the grand advance Lloyd planned could not be opened earlier than November, so October became a matter of waiting before Company forces could take the offensive. Inevitably, Santal imperatives intervened.

Even as they waited for the country to dry out so they could implement Lloyd's plan, the force in contact with the Santals on the two lines of posts in Beerbhoom, did not remain idle. Junior officers continued to harry the Santal bands they could reach, ostensibly trying to 'disperse' them, but also seeking to unbalance and intimidate Santal leaders. Once secure posts had been established, at Afzulpore, Jamtarra and Gajore, bold younger officers led sorties to disrupt and overawe Santal bands. Among the officers who stood out in this period were Francis of the 13th, Dunbar of the 37th and Pester of the 63rd. Again, a detailed narrative of their dours would become tedious, but some examples show how Company officers were gaining in boldness and energy. If Santal parties had ever been subject to higher direction, they were now bereft of it; a correspondent writing from Beerbhoom described them as 'wandering about in large parties without any settled plan'.[14]

Reports from Hugh Pester demonstrate how this worked in practice. Early in October Pester, commanding a detachment of the 63rd at Nala, a few miles north of the Adye, took out another party, this time in search of a band of just 200–250 Santals, which he stalked.

As the Santals were in open ground on a hill they saw the sepoys while they were still 400 yards off and broke into small parties heading for the jungle. Pester's men 'gave chase' for two miles, eventually capturing 259 cattle and 42 buffaloes and burning three encampments and the grain stored in them. Though every Santal had got away, they lost all of their food.[15] Civil officials noticed 'a new feature': that as Santal supplies ran out, they began raiding fields to cut and carry off crops which were just ripening. This enforced privation may explain a resurgence of attacks on isolated indigo factories, such as one near Rajmahal in November.[16] Others found that they could track Santal bands by following the trail of discarded rice leaking from rotten or broken baskets or dropped by weak or unwilling carriers. Some Santal bands began kidnapping Bengali villagers to carry the grain on which their continuing ability to operate depended. These reports suggested that the scarcity of food sustaining the rebels was diminishing their ability to continue resistance, and that by November 'reports from various outposts state that the rebels are much pressed for food'.[17]

Like Pester, James Phillips also ranged out ahead of the sepoys' posts. On 8 October he reported arriving at Kurrown, one of the few unburned villages in the area. The residence of a substantial zamindar, whom Phillips called a rajah, Kurrown was one of the few places where sepoys could obtain food. The zamindar thought that 'three divisions' of Santals were planning to attack Kurrown, which Phillips was reluctant to allow.[18] He decided to hold the place, another example of how relatively junior officers shaped operational policy.

There were several detachments operating from these advanced posts. On 17 October, for example, Captain Henry Nicholl led a mixed force of 150 sepoys of the 50th Native Infantry, 28 sowars of the 11th Irregular Cavalry and Boddam's rocket troop. Nicholl had learned of Santals in 'great force' with much plunder near Sabunpore, north of the Adye. For the first time, the two sides fought a running battle. The sepoys advanced as usual, through thick jungle but keeping their alignment in itself a feat. The Santals did not simply run away: though they lost about 65 dead, they fell back about three miles, in good order. Hungerford Boddam and his rocket troop kept up with the sepoys, firing several rockets at groups of Santals he could see on hillsides through the trees, which may have caused them to at last withdraw. Rissaldar Futtehab Khan's sowars tried to cut off the Santals' retreat, and they succeeded in doing 'great execution in a hand to hand encounter cutting up 20 Santals', and but for thick jungle would have killed more. Nicholl's force obliged the Santals to abandon their supplies—he judged that the amount of grain could have fed the band for two years—and 500 cattle. A few of his men had been wounded but he estimated that up to 150 Santals had been killed and wounded.[19] Nicholl seems to have had a talent for this sort of fighting. Two days later he again attacked 'a large body' near the Adye, this time catching them so unawares that the sepoys came upon food still cooking on their camp fires.[20]

Reverses like this fed Santal disillusionment. Military officers in the field received further approaches from manjees anxious to end hostilities, though naturally wanting assurances that they would not be punished. What should officers do, they asked? The answer was to refer the manjees to civil officers, who were free to exercise discretion. Pragmatically, officials began issuing manjees with certificates testifying to their loyalty, an expedient Grey endorsed. However much their work depended upon close adherence to legal procedure, knowing the impossibility of securing convictions for rebellion, officials adopted a method they believed would at least turn Santal leaders from adversaries into relieved by-standers. These assertive moves signalled how the Company's forces were beginning to take the initiative. Santal forces now seemed to respond to their adversaries' moves, not to force British commanders to react.

'Dying like rotten sheep': Santal prisoners

Company dours increasingly collected Santal prisoners; not always willingly. The Moorshedabad correspondent of the Calcutta Bengali newspaper, *Sambad Pravakar*, watched Santal prisoners arriving there late in July:

> We have seen with our own eyes that their persons bore wounds of weapons and were covered with blood. Some women and boys and girls were among them …[21]

Military officers displayed little interest in Santal prisoners, handing them over to police and officials. Some were probably not even rebels: a letter published in several newspapers alleged that Mofussil Police had seized 'unfortunate villagers caught … to make a show of zeal'.[22] Civilians who saw the prisoners had little sympathy: they felt those taken 'with arms in their hands should … have been hanged on the spot'; and some probably were simply executed.[23] Without martial law in force, civil proceedings were supposed to prevail, but who knows what the jungle concealed.

By mid-August some 300 Santal prisoners were held in jail in Bhaugulpore alone, while another 300 lay at Sooree, and another thousand had been sent to Moorshedabad.[24] They remained placid, even apathetic, awaiting their fate 'quite indifferent to the bustle and hubbub around them'.[25] Identifying and registering them took time. Interrogating them needed command of Santali, which could not be assumed, even for officials who had served in districts where they lived. William Elliott confessed, astonishingly, 'I do not know what language is spoken in the Monghyr and Bhaugulpore thannas'. Like other officials, he needed to employ interpreters, probably Bengalis; some of them the very amlahs and peons who had abused the Santals, contributing to their oppression.[26]

Some of these prisoners included 'a leader called Moohea', taken by Birch's sepoys near Amrapara, on the boundary of the Damin, whom Robert Richardson described as 'a captive of some importance'.[27] Some saw that captured leaders could be turned, used to entice or trap other Santal leaders. Richardson promised Moohea his life if he helped Company officers to capture rebel leaders. This he achieved seemingly by persuasion. At Amrapara Richardson also held 'a Sonthal high priest' who had refused to speak 'but I dare say will tomorrow', Richardson thought. This might appear to be a dark hint of coercion or even torture. No official admitted to using force, and the evidence suggests that Santals spoke openly of their actions and had no deep loyalty to a wider cause or even to particular leaders. Santal prisoners increasingly disclosed that, as Robert Richardson felt confident in claiming, 'the Sonthals are much discontented with their leaders'.[28] In August his optimism seemed premature, but by October it seemed to reflect a justifiable tendency.

Many prisoners faced trial, and until the declaration of martial law in November, that meant their becoming involved in the complex

British-Indian legal system, which demanded that cases be tried by the full weight of procedural formality, especially including the need to produce and cross-examine witnesses. Many cases did not reach that point, however, because—bizarrely—officials thought that under civil law prisoners had apparently done nothing wrong, though the *Indian Penal Code* prescribed death as the punishment for 'offences against the state'.[29] The *Friend of India*, urging that martial law be adopted, reminded its mainly evangelical readers of the limitations of trials in Bengal:

> Who is to declare that this lotah [pot] is his, and that anklet the property of his wife? The original owners are dead. The jewels were hacked from corpses … even the omnipotent English law cannot serve a subpoena on a coffin.[30]

James Ward was able to try only 12 out of 43 prisoners in his cutcherry jail. He found that the only charge he could press was 'illegally and riotously assembling with offensive weapons for the purpose of plunder and committing a breach of the peace'. But once charged, where were the witnesses? Ward himself conceded that while they may have been taken with weapons in hand, 'there is no proof of any of these Sonthals having been concerned with murder or in any attack on a village'. Obedient to the tenets of procedural fairness which Company officials (and Bengali lawyers) had created as a fetish, Ward even had to release men who had been arrested as 'Sonthal spies'.[31] The term 'spy' was used often and loosely in Company reports—a woman who bought items such as tobacco, salt or spirits in a market for a Santal band in Beerbhoom was arrested as a 'spy'.[32]

Killing or 'dispersing' rebels left no administrative consequences, but as larger numbers fell into Company hands, civil officials grappled with the problems of how they were to deal with the cases that awaited them once they returned to their cutcherries. While Narahari Kaviraj rightly described many trials as 'nothing but a farce', it is also true that many of those charged did not face court.[33] Many Santals, especially women and children rounded up near the Grand Trunk Road, were simply released and told to go home. Provincial jails were already overcrowded. By late October the jail at Sooree, intended to house 375 prisoners, was holding 446.[34] Bhaugulpore jail, constructed for 200 prisoners, held 717 Santals alone, and would have held over

1200 but almost 500 were released as unable to be charged.[35] Ominously, at Bhaugulpore 87 prisoners had died in custody, some perhaps of wounds, but most of disease—at Sooree one man died on the day of his trial. Even before the crowding during the Hul, the lieutenant-governor had conceded that the prisons were 'highly insalubrious'.[36] Many Santhals had been described as 'sickly and feeble' when captured.[37] No wonder a Bhaugulpore correspondent frankly described Santals in the station's jail as 'dying like rotten sheep'.[38]

Many of the prisoners were women and children, rounded up and held for months; when they were finally arraigned, the charges were dismissed, but in the meantime they suffered from the insanitary conditions in the jails and pens in which they were held. The Weekly Sanitary Reports disclose that women and children (some born in jail or still at the breast) suffered from cholera, dysentery and dropsy, the latter being retention of fluid, probably caused by malnutrition. Virtually all were released—only three women are recorded as having been sentenced, and two were the wives of rebellious manjees— but in the meantime they sickened and died. The civil surgeon at Beerbhoom urged that 'it would be an act of great clemency to liberate the remainder of these poor creatures before they die'.[39]

Prisoners languished for months in prison—the Santals taken at Moheshpore in July, in their first clash with sepoys, were not seriously questioned until September and not tried until late October. In the meantime, confusion intensified. In September, the officiating magistrate at Berhampore, John Dodgson, asked what he should do with them: he had 'no information'. Octavius Toogood, who had taken them into custody, had the note he had sent with them to the officiating magistrate, Robert Abercrombie, hastily sent from Malda: 'Mr Abercrombie—Here are the prisoners—put them in jail'. No other details arrived. Toogood explained that 'the confusion was such as to prevent any official preparation of documents', and in August 'many prisoners escaped—many were released', though no one could say who, when or why. It seems that nine of the 28 escaped on the way to Berhampore. Bidwell exasperatedly summarised the debacle: 'they were taken and they escaped and there is an end'. Toogood, resenting the rebuke, wrote over Bidwell's head to complain to William Grey that the Special Commissioner's words had 'impugn[ed] not only my public conduct ... but my private character as a Gentleman'. Bidwell dismissed Toogood's 'ignorance, folly, dishonesty and falsehood'. Toogood, who had gained renown by his bold conduct early in the Hul, did not prosper, probably because he publicly crossed Bidwell.[40] While he officiated when Abercrombie left on leave in August, Toogood was damned, criticised as 'not straightforward'.[41]

James Ward, having been asked by Halliday to discern the causes of the outbreak, reminded the lieutenant-governor of these legal complications. Given the awkward charges they were obliged to prefer ('Illegally and riotous assembling' and similar), and the difficulty of gathering legally admissible evidence, Ward anticipated that 80 per cent of cases would be acquitted. In his own court he had been able to secure convictions on ten out of 22 prisoners before him. He instanced the man responsible for the ambush of James Phillips's detachment at Bewa on 21 September. The man had been sitting on the steps of a house smoking a hookah, projecting an impression of normality. The sepoys asked him where Santals were and he reassured them that they were nowhere about. The next minute 30 or 40 armed Santals burst out of a nearby house and attacked the sepoys, wounding one. They repulsed the attack, killing eight rebels, and arrested the man who it seemed had tried to trick them. 'If ever a man deserved hanging it is this scoundrel', Ward fulminated, 'but how am I to deal with him?' he asked. To charge him with complicity he had to prove 'guilty knowledge', which was clearly impossible.[42] The man was probably released, as were other cases Ward found frustrating—a man caught carrying an enigmatic (written) message; one of Mr Wilson's Santal employees, arrested in disguise in the bazaar at Raneegunge, far from his home in Belputteh. Ward was helpless.

The solution, Ward urged, was to at last declare martial law, allowing 'justice unfettered by law'. Had courts martial 'tried a few of these wretches ... and sentenced them to death, the probability is [that] the Santals would long ago have seen their folly'. He conceded that 'the remedy is indeed severe but I can see no alternative ... the Govt has been defied'.

'Always at feud with the Santhals': the rebellion as civil war

Indian historians especially have represented the Hul as a proto-nationalist uprising directed at 'the British'. Inevitably, the reality was more complex. The Santals were an immigrant people, settled in Bengal for under forty years. The Bengalis, a railway engineer's Santal servant explained, had 'always looked upon us as intruders'.[43] Paradoxically Santals called Bengalis—almost all Hindus—'Dikkus' ('outsiders' or 'foreigners') and generally despised them, a feeling the Bengalis returned, though tinged with fear. A correspondent in the *Englishman*, blaming the 'cowardly, grasping Bengalies' for their failure to resist Santal incursions, claimed that 'a Sonthal had only to come to a village and say "The fouj is coming" and every Bengalee would run'.[44] The Santals' relations with other ethnic groups, and especially Hindu Bengalis and hill peoples ('Paharias'), became part of the Hul.

The Paharias, the original warlike inhabitants of the Rajmahal Hills, had been 'pacified' by Augustus Cleveland in the 1780s, who through power of personality induced them to accept the Company's rule and cease raiding Hindu communities on the adjoining plains, partly by forming a corps of Hill Rangers, for a time a formidable force. Though killed with his work left unfinished—assassinated by a Paharia—Cleveland's example was often invoked by the Company's directors as an example to its servants facing similar challenges. A plaque testifying to his virtues stood outside the imposing Georgian cutcherry at Bhaugulpore, a standing reproach to his vacillating successor, George Brown.[45] The Paharias remained in villages in the higher ridges of the hills, unwilling to clear and cultivate the jungle-covered valleys, as were the Santals, protected from the impositions of both the law and mahajans by Cleveland's paternal regime. The first Santals arrived in the hills after his death.

In 1855 civil officials exploited traditional enmities between the Santals and their neighbours, the Paharias, recruiting the latter as scouts or even fighters. When Major Charles Bruere of the 13th sallied out from Rajmahal with a strong force comprising 160 of the 7th and 190 of the 13th, Robert Richardson had recruited 200 'Hill Men … inveterate Enemies of the Sonthals' to accompany them.[46] Planters formed companies of 'Hill men' who, evicted from their village by Santals, had a reason to use their axes, bows and arrows. But could these men be trusted? Early in November Lieutenant William Hawes's detachment went in pursuit of a body of armed Santals near a village in western Beerbhoom, but just as he was about to seize the 'Rebel Manjee Thooloo', a party of Paharia burkendazes appeared. The leader of the burkendazes, Ali Baksh, interposed his men between the sepoys and the Santals, explaining that Thooloo had a perwannah issued near Jamtarra granting him amnesty, but could not explain which civil official had endorsed it. Ali Baksh reluctantly produced a perwunnah in 'Bengallee characters', but not until Hawes was able to puzzle out a Persian translation did he realise that they had tried to mislead him 'to aid the manjee's escape'. He prudently arrested both men. The incident suggested that Paharias could not necessarily be trusted, and that they might be in league with rebels.[47]

Other non-Santals also joined the Hul. Company records refer to rebels who were manifestly not Santals. Santal metal tools and weapons, for example, were made by Bengali smiths living in their villages, and the records contain references to Hindu cattle-herders and oil-men who often lived among their Santal neighbours, and who became swept up in the turbulence of the Hul. A list of prisoners awaiting trial at Raneegunge included non-Santals—Dangars, a Kroomar and a Paharia. Investigators at Sooree found two Bengali burkendazes who claimed that they had been coerced into fighting with the Santals—they carried copies of Halliday's proclamation as proof of their innocence.

Narahari Kaviraj saw the Hul had been a proto-proletarian uprising, a 'revolt of the lower orders', though relatively few non-Santals joined or supported the insurgents.[48] But the authorities feared that they might: officials seemed to regard 'rebellion' itself as a sort of communicable disease, rather than the product of discernable causes, in the Santals' case of economic oppression. The concern explains the efforts made to patrol the line of the Grand Trunk Road. Officials feared that a successful Santal insurrection would spread the idea of rebellion far beyond, and not just to other Santals in Chota Nagpore, but to non-Santals in Bengal itself. Sergeant Joseph Cheers repeated a widespread rumour, that the Kols 'who gave our government so much trouble in 29 and 30' had made common cause with the Santals.[49] When James Ward learned that low-caste Bengalis were joining the Hul, he observed that 'revolt is contagious'.[50] That added one further reason why this insurrection needed to be stopped.

That the Hul was an economic protest as well as a cultural reaction to change and oppression may explain the involvement of non-Santals—the 'outsiders' including what Digambar Chakraborti and Kaviraj identified as 'Hadees, Doms, Bhuias, Bagdees etc.' (that is, lower caste Hindus) and elsewhere minor artisan or service castes including milk-men, oil men, iron-workers, potters and even palanquin-bearers.[51] Early in December, for instance, Captain James Phillips apprehended 20 metal-workers and their families. They claimed to be merely shifting in search of work, but he believed that they had been making weapons for Santal bands and had been forced to abandon their employers because of the harassment of Company forces.[52] These non-Santals, evidently exempt from the Santals' antipathy, George Brown thought, could 'supply them with intelligence, beat their drums [to] direct their proceedings and act as spies'—they clearly would benefit as much as the Santals from the removal of oppressive mahajans.[53] Vincent Jervis also thought that 'several of the very low castes of the Hindus' joined the rebels, though it has to be said that little in the civil officers' reports suggests their involvement was of any significance in fomenting a more general rising.[54]

Nor did non-Santals necessarily join out of commitment to the Santal cause. The Hul threw up opportunists seeking to benefit from the conflict. Ashley Eden reported that around Aurungabad, which had not been attacked but was swollen with refugees, he found 'many bad characters (not Santals) who are taking advantage of the Panic to plunder villages'.[55] Ata Mallick cited an 1856 letter from Robert Richardson that revealed that Santal women minding their husbands' plunder were attacked and robbed by other Santal bands.[56] Newspapers also carried accounts of Bengali peasants turning on peaceful Santal neighbours. In July, Moorad Biswas had led a couple of hundred Bengalis against Santals, who, their men alerted by women beating drums, drove off Biswas and his neighbours, and then in turn burned down his village.[57] Elsewhere, a band of Santals attacked a Bengali village—the men drove the opportunistic villagers off and the women looted—but then the villagers rallied and drove the Santals off.[58] Likewise, in the Rajmahal Hills Paharias ('always at feud with the Santhals') took the chance to attack their neighbours.[59] Though taking no part in the Hul directly, the Paharias' predatory heritage re-surfaced, and Paharia bands followed Santal parties, 'seizing opportunities for loot' from vulnerable villagers—depredations perhaps attributed to Santal raiders.[60] That the Santal country seemed to be breaking into communal strife is suggested by a private letter published in Britain, whose author observed how around Rampore Haut 'large bodies of Bengallees' followed detachments of troops, 'destroying every Santhal village that came in sight and driving away all the cattle they could lay their hands on'.[61] Bengalis began appealing to James Pontet to allow them to take over the plots of Santals who had abandoned them to join the rebellion or been driven off their land. He may have done so. Despite his long association with the Santals he seems to have not expressed any great sympathy with their plight—Octavius Toogood was outraged that Pontet may have had Santals flogged who came in to Rajmahal looking to buy salt. Pontet denounced the allegation as a 'gross falsehood', saying that he only flogged prisoners, which hardly helped his defence.[62] The writer of the letter from Rampore Haut thought that 'when all is cleaned up' Pontet would have 'much to answer for'.

In this the Hul resembled a civil war. It exacerbated conflict between Santals and other ethnic groups, producing tension between communities, a phenomenon familiar from other insurgencies, in which groups become 'caught between two armies', as Alpa Shah described it in reflecting on her time with Naxalite guerrillas in Jharkhand in the early twenty-first century.[63] As the anonymous woman arrested buying comforts for her relatives or fellow villages found, it was hard for any Santal to keep clear of a conflict occurring in their own villages and fields. As civilians have found in many other conflicts before and since, staying out of the fight seemed safest, though that was not always possible. Company officials discovered that they could not necessarily rely on the support of zamindars, either for supplies or for intelligence, and that even when offering rewards for notice of Santals 'not a soul will venture near': evidently neither peasants nor zamindars were confident of Company victory, sure of British protection or free of the possibility of Santal retribution.[64] Bengali villagers and especially zamindars' uncertainty is understandable. A subaltern of the 40th, having seen devastated villages across northern Bhaugulpore, judged that rebellious Santals had been 'possessed by the devil; the cruelty and barbarity that they have shown to their helpless neighbours is terrible in the extreme', and few villagers could count on the troops' protection.[65]

Civil authorities, unable to send detachments to all villages threatened by raiders, apparently tried to induce them to defend themselves. When representatives of the people of Narainpore, near Rampore Haut, begged for aid they were 'startled and disappointed', so Kooshan wrote, to learn that they would only be protected by sepoys if they could raise a force of 500 armed men, and this the zamindar, Pertaub Chunder Singh, could not do. He had lost his house and his lands had been despoiled, but the implicit bargain that Bengalis had struck with the Company was that because it would protect them, they need not bear arms. Now the Company's officials were reneging on that understanding.[66]

Perhaps the clearest sign that the Hul expressed conflict between Indians rather than with their (as it turned out, temporary) rulers, the Company, was the way that Santals directed their aggression toward the zamindars and rajahs who most directly oppressed them. Zamindars living beyond the immediate protection of sepoy detachments could be forgiven for having a foot in both camps. With the Santals able to arrive, loot and leave much more swiftly than sluggish Company forces could move to defend them, zamindars had to decide how they should act. Some resolved to protect their property as best they could by arming retainers; others to risk abandoning their houses and fleeing as refugees; still others, perhaps, to just hope for the best. But other zamindars seem to have attempted to find an accommodation with the Santals who might threaten them; sometimes including manjees and their people who had formerly been employed by or even indentured to them. Civil officials came to suspect that some rajahs, including the ruler of Moheshpore (whose property Walter Birch had secured in July) had been 'playing us false'. The rulers of Moheshpore and of nearby Lulhampore, William Money suspected, were calling for troops in 'pretended emergencies … with the aim of covering … his own plundering parties', employing his own Santal retainers—for who could tell whence Santal raiders came?[67] Zamindars certainly enjoyed seemingly untrammeled economic power within domains secured by the Company's Permanent Settlement, but during the Hul, isolated on their estates and protected only by tenants or retainers armed with sticks or swords, their anxiety was understandable.

The complexity of allegiances and interests led to unexpected alliances. Captain James Phillips found that the rajah of Kurrown appeared to be in league with the Santals. Phillips's sepoys fought off an attack by about 600 Santals directed against his camp on 16 October. In the encounter they killed 60 Santals ('I am happy to say') and wounded more. But he noticed that 'the inhabitants of the village, which was not attacked, 'did not appear in the least alarmed'—Bengali villagers usually fled in terror. This left him 'more convinced than ever that the Rajah is siding with the enemy'—presumably under threat of his house and village being torched. James Ward called the rajah to Raneegunge to answer charges that he had colluded with the Santals, even if under duress.[68] Alongside the conflict between Santals and sepoys documented in detail in the Military Consultations, a more shadowy conflict continued between zamindar and tenant and Santal and Dikkus, barely noticed in Company sources.

As the conflict moved around the region it left in its wake thousands of displaced villagers, their homes destroyed, as refugees facing destitution—James Mangles at Govindpore felt 'overwhelmed' with appeals for food.[69] Some officials provided food to Bengali and Santal refugees—Sita Ram reflected on the oddity that 'in one part of the jungle we were firing at them, while in another the Sirkar [the government] was providing them with cart-loads of rice'. It was, he thought, 'a curious war'.[70] As the country became more settled, Bengali villagers returned, but now unable to sow crops, becoming dependent upon sepoy detachments. Crowds of dislocated villagers followed each military column, looting Santal camps, huts and villages just as they themselves had been looted. Sometimes they merely herded recovered cattle and other animals, but in the confusion, many must have replenished their livestock by helping themselves. Bengali villagers displaced by the fighting and needing employment followed, hoping to work as labourers, while units also employed Santals who cleared jungle campsites and scavenged what they could, and commandeered villagers as baggage carriers, demands which zamindars resented. In total, then, every sepoy in the column could have been outnumbered by five peasants surviving by laboring, carrying recovered goods or driving cattle taken from Santal villages.

Newspaper correspondents and leader writers had speculated for months about what had caused the Santals to break into such a prolonged and ferocious rebellion. Not until mid-September, however, did Frederick Halliday ask two of his senior officials, James Ward and the Special Commissioner Alfred Bidwell, to investigate why the Santals had risen. Ward had spoken to many Santal prisoners and he too ascribed the outbreak to 'fanaticism'; to the Santals believing the Thakur's 'message from heaven that the time had come when they were to become the rulers and sole possessors of the country'.[71] He deprecated the explanations that they had been driven to revolt by oppression, even though many of the men he had questioned spoke of the mahajans as 'a burden ... the cause of much of their misery and poverty'. Indeed, he thought that the Santals spoke of their oppression 'with less fear and loathing than most *ryots* (peasants) of Bengal usually do of their zemindars'. While sympathetic to Beerbhoom Santals having been 'more or less pressed into rebellion' by compatriots from Bhaugulpore, Bidwell blamed the entire insurrection on 'ignorance and superstition ... worked into a religious frenzy'.

Writers to newspapers often blamed the outbreak on railway employees preying on Santal women. Even before news of the outbreak became general, a correspondent to the *Bengal Hurkaru* claimed that a railway 'agent'—a European or Eurasian—had 'walked off' with a Santal woman—the railway people were 'most oppressive, taking anything they please'.[72] While this did occur—Sidhu himself confirmed that a 'Compass Sahib' (as Santals called surveyors) had abducted two women near Rajmahal—it was not a major cause, and resentment over sexual predation aggravated rather than provoked Santal anger.[73] Railway construction itself had little impact on Santal communities by 1855.

'Fear of the soldiers': sepoys and Santals

Native infantry regiments were accustomed to being split up into detachments. They were forever marching off as companies or smaller sub-units on escorts or guards or being separated into 'wings' located at neighbouring cantonments. The Hul, however, upset familiar routines and practices, and for long periods exposed sepoys to living in unfamiliar and uncomfortable conditions. Sent off in response to emergencies, companies became mixed up—in Beerbhoom in September, Bird was frustrated by having companies of three different regiments posted together, while the disorganisation of companies led to mix-ups by pay havildars, a problem several regiments reported. The records suggest that sepoys' religious sensibilities, always a delicate matter in the Bengal Army, were compromised, in rations and especially in cooking arrangements. Sepoys were reluctant to live in huts built by strangers, possibly men of inferior caste—regiments composed often of devout high-caste Hindus were always wary of contamination. All this, Bird complained to Atkinson, obstructed what contemporaries called the regiments' interior economy.[74]

Awaiting Lloyd's offensive left sepoys bored and fractious. A subaltern writing to the newspapers compared his sepoys to the Baltic Fleet (then watching the Russian fleet in St Petersburg) 'endeavouring to make ourselves comfortable [and] happy under the circumstances'.[75] But sepoys seem not to have been especially happy, restive in their temporary *bustees* (huts) separated from their families, whom they had to support living in the stations from which their regiments had been posted, or with their extended families in distant Oudh. The crowded and increasingly insanitary conditions in which sepoys lived led to friction—sepoys usually lived in cantonments deliberately distant from towns. At Rajmahal, for example, a stallholder, Mootee Shaw, complained to civil officials that sepoys had evicted him so they could erect larger quarters. They had not harassed his women, he said, but they had impounded his cattle and charged him 8 annas for their release.[76] Campaigning brought greater opportunities for sepoys to rob Santals and perhaps others. While dours were hard, they also brought loot: Santal plunder was, an observer said cynically 're-robbed by the troops and natives'.[77] When they learned they would be denied the proceeds of their dours, troops were disappointed.

The fundamental relationship defining the Hul was between sepoys and Santals. With virtually no direct evidence from either it is difficult to decide on relations between them, though reading between the lines of British officers' reports permits tentative conclusions. Troops certainly took rather than bought food in villages; rice, vegetables, milk, or sometimes fowls to eke out their rations.[78] Among the hardships of dours were that sepoys could not prepare food according to their often exacting caste rules. Accounts of their monsoon marches describe them often being unable to cook rations for several days— the 31st once not for five days.[79] Often sepoys subsisted on cold chupattis and stale dhal, and sometimes by munching on parched grain. Sepoys naturally felt apprehensive in the unfamiliar country amid an elusive and often unseen enemy. On the 7th Native Infantry's long march from Aurungabad through north-eastern Beerbhoom in July, Octavius Toogood described how armed Santals 'follow us on all sides and watch us from village to village and hill to hill'. Birch's sepoys refused to venture more than a hundred yards from their camps: understandably in the pitch black of a night in the jungle, when the moon was then in its first quarter.[80]

How did sepoys treat Santals? Neither Hindu sepoys nor Muslim sowars felt any compunction at killing Santals. But Vincent Jervis claimed that 'there was not a Sepoy in the war who did not feel ashamed of himself', by which Jervis meant for having to kill Santals who courageously persisted in assaults in the face of the troops' superior firepower.[81] How did they respond to Santals beyond the few, frantic clashes most sepoys experienced? Santal memories emphasise the brutality of the Company's forces. Durga Tudu's account is surely representative of the Hul as a whole and not just of its final phase:

> The British soldiers became very angry. They advanced setting fire to people's house [sic]. And whoever the British soldiers found on their way, they cut off their heads.[82]

'British' here means sepoys under British officers. So few Santal words were recorded that when an exchange survives it demands to be heard and considered. A Raneegunge correspondent recorded what had passed between a sepoy and a captured 'rebel'. The sepoy asked the man what he would do if he were released. 'Let me go!', the Santal said, 'You are afraid to do that, as if you unloosen me *you will be a dead man, the next moment!*' The observer admiringly commented that 'this will show you what sort of people they are'.[83] Indeed, a number of British witnesses and other writers commented favourably upon Santal courage. A civilian who had fought off an attack while he fled northern Bhaugulpore heading across the Ganges ('I shot 3 … I suppose we knocked over some 10 or a dozen') praised his assailants: 'the fellows never dodged but stood for one to have an open shot'.[84] A writer in the *Church Missionary Papers*, drawing on newspaper accounts of fights, told a story—possibly apocryphal—of a Santal band firing as its members fell back before the 'file-firing' of the sepoys. It claimed that one man was seen 'particularly fearless and persevering' running with a child. He repeatedly placed the child on the ground and loosed off an arrow, then picked up the child and ran on. The officer naturally 'wished to spare him', but at last felt compelled to order his men to shoot him. Evangelical readers might have been glad to learn that the officer himself rescued the child and placed him in the care of the Church Missionary Society school in Calcutta.[85]

Did sepoys harass or molest Santal women? When Jugia Haram's band was captured, somewhere in the south-west of Beerbhoom probably in October, 'the captain' threatened to kill the men. The captives replied, 'who will look after our girls and women?' 'We will look after them', the captain said, a phrase that to a modern sensibility suggests not chivalry but the possibility of rape. Did sepoys assault Santal women sexually? There is no evidence, but evidence of sexual assaults by soldiers in wartime often go undocumented in the absence of allegations, investigation or prosecution, and no Santal had recourse to any agency of justice. It is possible that sepoys regarded Santal women as they did their fowls and took what they wanted, their officers ignorant, apathetic or compliant. But the same sepoys in 1857 were accused of outraging British women when mutiny erupted, and extensive investigations disclosed no instances of rape, because Bengal sepoys were mostly Hindus, often high caste, and sex with outsiders would have meant defilement.[86] While individuals or even groups may have disregarded or risked such a religious offence, it is likely that the sepoys 'merely' mistreated and killed Santals. The judge Frederick Shore revealed that ordinarily sepoys were known to inflict 'the most gross outrages and wanton attacks on harmless villagers … hushed up with a mock inquiry': what would restrain them in suppressing rebellion?[87]

Chotrae Desmanjhi's reminiscence of the Hul is detailed and credible, even if his experiences cannot be precisely located on a European map, though he seemed to have been in northern Beerbhoom, in the fighting in August and after. Desmanjhi described how he joined in looting villages and zamindars' houses, and witnessed random killings, all to the sound of drums. He described in detail how he was one of a party led by Sham Souba, trying to break into a pucca house—a substantial dwelling—when Santals shot at and killed with arrows a Bengali trying to shelter from the attackers by hiding under some floating weed in a tank. Sham Souba seemed to become 'possessed', rushing about, brandishing a sword. 'A soldier'—possibly a sepoy, but perhaps a burkendaze or an armed retainer—shot Sham Souba from one of the building's windows. This broke the Santals' resolve: 'as soon as he fell we all fled for our lives stumbling and falling over ourselves from fear'. With that, he said, 'we gave up looting for good'.[88] Here, one fragment of an anecdote has to stand for thousands of unrecorded encounters. But Chotrae Desmanjhi did not go home, but like tens of thousands of Santals, remained at large, seeking safety in the forests. They 'hid in the lairs of tigers. From fear of the soldiers', he wrote, 'we lost our fear of tigers and bears'.[89]

Their fear is understandable. Officers' reports disclose sepoys' growing confidence. Early in October, hearing that 2000 Santals were 'burning and killing', and were said to be heading towards him, Hugh Pester marched his detachment towards the smoke on the horizon, but in the growing heat his men were 'getting knocked up'. While most sepoys rested under a large tree, a small party—sixteen men under a havildar—moved ahead to reconnoitre. Watching Santals, seeing how few men the havildar had, rushed down upon them. The sepoys reacted calmly, retiring steadily, firing as they fell back and killing ten or twelve rebels, who could not get close. As other officers were to find later in the campaign, these Santals stood the fire for up to ten minutes before they 'bolted into the jungle'. The rest of Pester's men probably joined in, because he estimated that some thirty Santals had been wounded. One of Pester's lieutenants pursued the Santals into the jungle—another change: troops had been reluctant to enter the jungle. They returned reporting having found blood trails and even pieces of bone, but lost the fugitives in the dense bush.[90] Sepoys no longer regarded the jungle with trepidation; they even became accustomed to moving through the jungle, and at night. Officers' reports increasingly mention beginning approach marches in the dark, surprising Santal encampments at dawn, hoping to catch them unawares but also avoiding the handicap of their red coats being seen at a distance.

While sepoys were less frightened of the jungle, they still needed to take care in it, as the fate of a man of the 63rd disclosed. As havildars mustered their men at Jamtarra around 21 October, they realised that a man was missing, and assumed that he must have become separated from his comrades on a recent dour. Captain Pester conjectured that he had got lost while his detachment returned from an expedition towards Nala. The jungle was especially thick, he recalled; indeed, he had elephants precede his men to bash a path.[91] A week later his comrades picked up the man's accoutrements on another dour and soon a passer-by told Pester that Santals had taken him. A further week on, James Ward's investigation revealed the grim fact that he had been captured in the jungle and taken to the village of Kantepoor, the home village of a notably aggressive manjee. The Santals had fed him and took him before their soubah. 'After some religious ceremonies' the poor man was sacrificed, decapitated 'in the most cold blooded manner'. Ward had, presumably with authority, offered Rs 1000 as a reward for the soubah's apprehension.[92]

Several months' experience of facing Santal bands now reinforced the boasts heard at the beginning of the rebellion. Accounts of clashes in October, admittedly mainly by junior military officers, confirm how native infantry regiments, trained to fight in line in actions like Chillianwallah, were adapting to the conditions of the rebellion. A letter described an action near Kurrown on 21 October when a detachment of 270 men of the 13th advanced against a Santal force of 10,000, believed to have been led by Kanhu himself, 'so rapidly … that they were aware of our approach [only] when we were on top of them'. Still, 'somehow', the Santals got away, though leaving 80 killed and wounded. Lieutenant Robert Aitken, in command, believed that he saw Kanhu, mounted on a bay mare (presumably captured) move fearlessly across the front of the companies pursuing his men, passing so close to Aitken that he fired on him.

Aitken's men shook out into skirmish order and pursued them across the plain, the Santals 'running fast as deer', the sepoys panting along constrained by knapsacks, cartridge boxes and uniform jackets. 'It was a pretty sight', the writer conceded, but of course the Santals escaped: this time the infantry had no sowars able to cut off or pursue the fugitives. But captured Santals confirmed what was becoming the accepted explanation for the rebellion: 'the wretched rack rent and the hopeless corruption of the police as well as the expense and delay in the dispensation of justice'.[93] Delays in decisions over justice concerned senior officials in Calcutta too.

'Cat and dog': wrangling over martial law

With practically all reports from both civil and military officers laboriously (and mostly legibly) copied for distribution to every senior official in Fort William, they knew what was happening in the districts, even if the detail may have overwhelmed them and reports arrived a fortnight after the event. With the insurgency far from over, Robert Richardson, beginning a diary in Sooree, still felt restive at the lack of reliable intelligence emanating from Santal-controlled country. 'Had I a few Mounted Irregulars', he mused, 'I would visit [the disputed tract] ... and by personal observation satisfy myself of what is really going on'.[94] Frederick Halliday remained concerned about how it was to be ended, with the question of whether and under what circumstances martial law was to be declared, still unresolved three months into the Hul. The season was at last turning. It was becoming dryer and while the rains had at last eased, George Lloyd still did not begin the offensive he had proposed.

An important reason for the delay was that the legal basis for Lloyd's renewed operations remained unresolved. Senior Company officials agreed that the rebellion was approaching a critical point, and many considered that the time for declaring martial law had long been reached. The newspapers overwhelmingly agreed. In analysing the difficulty of prosecuting rebels in its absence, James Ward put several arguments, from the legal—that under civil law guilty rebels would escape punishment—to the pragmatic, that 'however great the number of Santals who must be shot down, it will not be more than double that of victims of their savage brutality'. Martial law, Ward declared 'alone appeared to me sufficient'.[95]

While the Consultations dutifully copied and transmitted to Leadenhall Street revealed that the Supreme Council and the Bengal government differed over points of principle or high policy, in early October the London *Morning Herald*'s 'own correspondent' spilled the beans about the 'petty proceedings' in official Calcutta. This was hardly novel: a Company director admitted to a Parliamentary committee that 'the animus of the papers against the Government is often very great.[96] But 'the differences between the Lieutenant-Governor of Bengal and the Supreme Council still continue', he told the *Herald*'s readers—which was common knowledge in leaky official Calcutta.[97] It was partly personal: the council maintained a 'disinclination to accede to any measure proposed by Mr Halliday'; and Dorin, Peacock and Low formed a recalcitrant 'Bengal clique'. The 'leader of the assailants' against the Bengal clique was John Peter Grant.[98] Dalhousie knew that 'Halliday and the Council are cat and dog', as he wrote to his old friend and mentor, Sir George Couper.[99] He accepted the council's inertia because proclaiming martial law would, as the *Herald*'s correspondent explained, 'diminish the *éclat* with which he had hoped to close his pro-consulship'—Dalhousie admitted to Couper that the insurrection 'vexes me very much just at the close of my career'. But he did nothing to resolve the dispute. Late in October Dalhousie began a leisurely progress from Ootacamund via Bangalore, Madras and Rangoon 'bowed down and crippled by an exhausting disease', and would eventually return to Calcutta just as Lloyd's campaign ended.[100]

Key figures—Bidwell, Loch, Bird and Lloyd—and all the Calcutta newspapers, urged martial law. They all agreed that the Company force would soon go over onto what later generations would call the counter-offensive. But on what legal basis should those operations be conducted? Council members affirmed that martial law would be 'indispensable', as Grant advocated, but they stubbornly wanted Frederick Halliday to request its imposition.[101] Halliday, with characteristic obstinacy, refrained from asking for it to be declared. Ironically, Company forces stagnated, even as they moved faster than ever, physically.

'Our Indian miracle': steamers, trains and the telegraph

No study of relations between Indians and Britons in the mid-nineteenth century can ignore the impact of the introduction to India of western technology. The Hul occurred during (though not because of) technological change. In the year before its outbreak the Public Works Department responsible for building roads, canals and bridges had been established; postage stamps and a new post office organisation were introduced, and a new policy on English education was accepted and would lead to the establishment of universities in Calcutta, Madras and Bombay. Although much of the Santal country remained untouched by roads, three transport and communications innovations operated on its margins, in river steamers, the railway and the electric telegraph. The *Friend of India*, speaking for and to the portion of Britain's middle class with a strong interest in India, pronounced in a self-congratulatory editorial that 'it was worthwhile to have conquered India to give the natives the benefit of the rail and the electric telegraph'.[102] In 1855, however, those benefits accrued more to the Company than to its insurgent subjects.

Steamboats had operated on the Ganges for two decades, usually towing barges called 'flats', carrying European passengers in what were effectively floating hotels, troops on much less comfortable 'troop flats', and cargo. Steamers operated on schedules from Calcutta as far up-stream as Allahabad, though heavily dependent on the depth of the river which was deeper in summer but often dangerously torrential during the monsoon and equally hazardously low during autumn and winter. Whereas formerly fleets of 'country boats' could take weeks or months to laboriously toil upstream, often pulled along from the banks by gangs of coolies, steamers could reach Berhampore from Calcutta in two or three days, usually mooring at night for fear of striking hazards such as sandbanks or floating logs, and making Patna in ten days. The availability of steamers gave Company forces what later generations would call strategic mobility.

Visionaries had long espoused the military and economic value of railways in India, but the potential cost of laying lines over vast distances through challenging terrain in a harsh climate had deterred private investment. At last, in the early 1850s the Government of India agreed to underwrite the cost of construction and operation, and the first line in Bengal began construction. The East India Railway's first stage, from Howrah, across the Hooghly from Calcutta, to Raneegunge, a line built to exploit the region's coal reserves, allowed transport parallel to the Grand Trunk Road to what became the southern base of Company operations in the Hul. In mid-1855 work was well underway to extend the railways north and west, with teams of surveyors, engineers and large numbers of coolies, including Santals, laboring to build lines to Rajmahal and to Patna and beyond.[103]

What a Raneegunge correspondent to the Calcutta *Citizen* called 'our Indian miracle' began in February 1855.[104] The ceremony was effusively described by *Allen's Indian Mail* as the 'best arranged, the most perfect and the most completely successful public ceremony' Calcutta had ever seen. The superlatives were marred only by the absence of Lord Dalhousie from all but the blessing of the enterprise by the Bishop of Calcutta. Trains began running from Howrah to Raneegunge twice daily.[105] Though seemingly consecrated as a Christian undertaking, the new line attracted passengers of all faiths—by the year's end over 200,000 passengers, 93 per cent of them 'natives' travelling on third-class tickets.[106] The railway saved troops ten days of marching up the Grand Trunk Road to Raneegunge, 'the first instance in which the rail has been used for the conveyance of troops' in India.[107] The line represented a colossal undertaking. One 26-mile stretch in northern Beerbhoom, the responsibility of the contractors, Nelson, Smith, consumed prodigious quantities of materials and a huge labour force—650 tons of rails, 26,000 sleepers; 43 million cubic feet of embankments excavated and erected—tragically, some of the necessary ballast crushed from the stones of Rajmahal's ancient ruins.[108]

Both steamers and the railway accelerated communication between Calcutta and the mofussil. Rooboocaries which formerly could have taken weeks to arrive and be answered could reach Fort William and up-country cutcherries within a few days, a change which diminished the independence and initiative of men on the spot. Even more rapid communication followed the introduction in 1851 of the electric telegraph. By 1853 lines connected Calcutta as far as Peshawar, with the line following the Grand Trunk Road. The government's Electric

Telegraph Department, run by the extraordinary Irish scientific poly-math William O'Shaughnessy and staffed mainly by Indians and Eurasians with some serving and former European soldiers, planned further extensions. The telegraph was to provide a further techno-logical advantage to Company officers during the Hul.

Another manifestation of the British domination of India was the achievement of the Great Trigonometrical Survey of India. Supplemented by the work of revenue surveyors such as Walter Sherwill, it produced maps which Company officers were able to use to plot Santal locations and likely movements, a counter-weight to the Santals' intimate knowledge of their hills and jungle. While it would become critical in the suppression of the Hul, and indeed in time would transform Indian life, the new western technology that British officials and entrepreneurs were introducing to India made virtually no impact on the Santal country.

'Put to flight our enemies': Santal strategy and tactics[109]

Company officials hoped that military posts and increasing patrols in western Beerbhoom would induce the Santals to move away north-wards—treating Santals as so many droplets of water, channelled by the erection of dams. Santal bands did not of course simply react to these barriers. Their movements reflected decisions made by perhaps dozens of manjees, often after debate, in which groups obeyed the directions of their leaders and any superiors that they recognised. As with so much about the Hul, little direct evidence exists of actions and decisions within Santal camps. Company officials rightly antici-pated that blocking Santal movement into unplundered areas and forcing them back into areas already despoiled would place pressure upon their food supplies. While Santals had seized vast quantities of rice they must have found it hard both to transport and preserve it while on the move in the monsoon. The privation this brought would, officials thought, itself provoke 'fierce incursions' as Santal bands' leaders decided to break out of the Company's cordon. It is perhaps curious that they did not move further west, into Behar, but Santals there would have been conspicuous and unwelcome strangers. To meet such a move, the commissioner of Chota Nagpore asked for regular troops to garrison Hazaribagh, and the Supreme Council agreed to the 2nd Irregular Cavalry being stationed to block any movement westward.[110]

Santal performance and potential impressed some British officials: 'we must not despise our enemy however weak he is in military appliances', Bird wrote to George Atkinson, though the line seems like an aide-memoire to himself.[111] Even over the course of a few months, it is clear that some Santal leaders developed a flair for tactics. When Henry Nicholl's force drove off a large band, capturing its supplies on 18 October, not only did the Santals conduct what Native Infantry officers would have recognised as a fighting withdrawal, but for the first time they reported the possibility of being deliberately outflanked 'which they several times attempted to do'.[112] An account of this clash, 9 miles north-west of Jamtarra, recorded that the Santals 'stood well' and 'fought for every yard of ground and gave back very slowly', for about an hour, shooting arrows all the way. One Santal ran out and fired five arrows aiming at an officer, possibly Lieutenant Henry Mathias of the 50th's light company. Sepoys wounded the man, who fell over 'dead to all appearances', but then stood up, salaamed to the sepoys and calmly walked back into the jungle. Actions like these aroused the admiration of men to whom courage in battle was a particular virtue.[113] Vincent Jervis recalled that the Santals he faced in eastern Beerbhoom were 'brave to infatuation'; he was awestruck by their brand of reckless courage.[114] Mathias then led his light company in open order into the jungle in pursuit, but the Santals, unusually, did not sound their drums, enabling them to get away: both sepoys and Santals were learning new ways to fight in this conflict. After two miles the sepoys found the Santals drawn up before a village. They fired on the sepoys using matchlocks but by this time Nicholl's troop of cavalry had come up and they charged, cutting down about eighteen of the defenders. The Santals lost about a hundred casualties against several sepoys wounded: they had no defence against cavalry in open country.

If some Santals placed their faith in ritual incantations—one pleaded with the 'Mother Jaher Era' bonga to 'Put to flight our enemies before they enter our village'—others devised alternative ways to respond to the war they were fighting.[115] Company reports disclose how the Santals learned over the course of a few months, suggesting that individual manjees, newly applying themselves to war, attempted new expedients. At Koomerabad and Bowsee they had attacked openly, if unsuccessfully, while other bands attempted new tactics. A Santal band under Hoobrah Manjee tried to ambush Phillips's sepoys at Bewa, near Jamtarra on 21 September, a ploy that failed and cost the manjee his life and that of eight of his men. While at Moheshpore they had charged toward sepoys, believing that sorcery had turned their musket balls to water, they observed a sepoy firing drill and later devised tactics to minimise its effect. Perhaps the most striking illustration of how Santals adapted to the unfamiliar world of warfare was that in September, probably near Kurrown, as Captain Thomas Wilson's sepoys raised their muskets ready to fire, Santals on their manjees' command threw themselves flat on the ground.[116] Even though, as Frederick Middleton foresaw as he left the 7th Native Infantry to return to his regiment in August, 'the shooting and killing would become rather one-sided', Santals were able to respond to Company troops.[117] By the autumn, however, it is clear in retrospect that however bravely or cleverly individual Santal leaders were able to respond to the sepoys' tactics, the rebellion was being lost.

'The raiders are upon us': declining Santal morale

The dearth of direct evidence from the Santal side of the hill obliges inference from what Company officials recorded. Crucial indications exist. First, instances of Santal approaches—through what officials often called 'Sonthal spies' but what they really meant were envoys or messengers, albeit arriving covertly to forestall retribution by more resolute manjees. Second, examples of continuing resistance suggest that even if some manjees and the communities they led gave up on the cause, Santal resolution continued. One manjee, Ram—probably not the same man as the 'gossain' captured in August—was captured precisely because of his courage. When Lieutenant Frederick Dunbar's sepoys fired upon his followers they ran off, leaving him facing the sepoys alone. Dunbar returned with 'a man of some consequence ... the terror of that part of the District' as his prisoner, and received Bird's thanks.[118] Compared to the earlier months of the Hul, however, it became clear during October that the Santal cause was failing. The question remained: how would the rebellion end?

Some particularly active officers set out to seize Santal leaders. Among the most notable was Lieutenant Henry Norman of the 31st. Already a marked man of talent, he had been singled out by Sir Charles James Napier after he heroically rescued a sepoy under the Commander-in-Chief's eye in the Kohat Pass in 1851, Norman was among the officers recalled to his regiment from a staff position. Even in charge of an outpost on the western slopes of the Rajmahal Hills, he applied his very considerable analytical mind to the problem facing the Company's force. Concluding that figuratively decapitating the Santal leaders might end the rebellion, Norman arranged what James Pontet praised as a 'well contrived and successful capture' of Darvie Manjee, not only a soubah but a man who had attempted to assume the mantle of the Thakur. The affair, Pontet reported, was 'very judiciously managed—the surprise complete … effected without resistance'.[119] Darvie Manjee may have been merely a pretender, but equally, he may also have put new heart into the Santal cause in the Damin. Either way, his capture ensured that his appeal was never tested. A few days later Norman again led an expedition intending to capture Kanhu, and had been 'nearly successful'.[120]

Other officers reported capturing Santal leaders, or at least they made attempts to. Walter Birch tried to catch Khama Manjee near Amrapara, using his family as hostage. Their captives included Kowleah Manjee, taken by the 13th Native Infantry, who had been famed as a leader of the dacoits of 1854, if civil officers could be sure of his identity, a perennial problem in prosecuting men unknown to their accusers and who could conceal their names and histories if they chose.[121] Santals, reputed to be truthful, often admitted their identities and actions on being interrogated: they had merely defended their homes and livelihoods—what should they have been ashamed of? Increasingly, though, reports in the Military Consultations describe Santal manjees giving up the struggle. In one dispatch Hugh Pester mentioned that 'the Manjees of Singarpore, Kadhieu, Selanka and Talahee have all offered to give themselves up', along with about 500 of their followers.[122] Early in November, even the Soubah of Kantepore, who had commanded the death of the unnamed lost sepoy of the 63rd, came in to Operbandah to give himself up.

Santals who were able to move towards the huge encampments in the jungle of western Beerbhoom felt safe for a time. Chotrae Desmanjhi, part of a large group seeking refuge in the hills, found 'large crowds of people with their children and cattle', which left them 'greatly cheered'. But within a week 'the soldiers came … on horseback and on elephants'. Someone knocked a sowar off his horse with an arrow and a bugle sounded. 'The soldiers started firing wildly at anyone they saw' and Desmanjhi was among those captured. An officer addressed them: 'why are you doing this killing?' he asked. 'We are not killing any one', the captives replied, 'we have run away to save our lives'. This did not satisfy 'the captain'. He said, 'All you men including the boys, come to one side. We will kill you all'. But the sepoys did not. Instead, 'the captain ordered the soldiers to loot us' and they took all their weapons, cattle and everything they had. The captain threatened them with death if they returned to the forest. 'We then said, "We will return [home]", and after that, the soldiers left us'.[123] Although sepoys in the outposts could still hear what Captain Phillips called 'a great deal of TomToming' the tone of the drumming had changed.[124] A fortnight later, Phillips claimed that the Santals he encountered were 'most anxious for peace' and 'in great dread of being punished'. Sadly for them, they would suffer further until peace would return.[125]

A significant blow to the Santal cause came with Sidhu's capture in mid-August, treacherously turned over by rival manjees. A Raneegunge man who saw him on a steamer and sketched him found him 'very old, and much reduced from fatigue'.[126] He was questioned and confessed his 'evil deeds … his determination to kill certain of the Europeans'—notably James Pontet—but 'the idea that he has done wrong seems not to have entered his mind'. Soon, versions of Sidhu's 'confession' appeared in the newspapers. It certainly confirmed the rebellion's millenarian inspiration—a commentator remarked on the 'hazy, dreamy idea of divine intervention'—but it also confirmed how 'the tyranny of the mahajuns and vexation at the long continued refusal of redress' had provoked the Santals into rising up'; and these, and not religious fanaticism, were 'apparently the only causes'. The *Friend of India* commented that his testimony did not excuse the revolt, but affirmed that 'the rebellion had a cause beyond a mere savage thirst for blood, plunder and excitement'. Another observer admired his 'frank courage'.[127] Sidhu's testimony seems to have helped to change European public opinion from condemnation of the Santal cause to sympathy toward their exploitation, a change of understanding to have profound consequences in the rebellion's wake.

Whatever sympathy or admiration his testimony aroused, however, the testimony also gave the magistrates sufficient evidence to bring Sidhu to trial. He and his confederates were arraigned to be tried in Bhaugulpore at the end of October, mostly charged with 'rebellion, attended with murder, plunder and arson'. Ashley Eden had 'not the slightest doubt of obtaining a conviction' against Sidhu and eleven other leaders or their lieutenants.[128] In due course, as expected, Sidhu Manjee was executed—hanged—at Burhyte.[129]

'The very roads of Kendal': debating the Hul

Those advocating a robust military response satirised more moderate commentators. 'Nix' sent a sarcastic letter to the *Englishman*, claiming that magistrates had been instructed to 'use no kind of unnecessary violence', to conceal troops from the rebels 'for fear of irritating their feelings' and that while sepoys 'march slowly at the goose step towards the rebels' they were not allowed to 'poke the hinder parts of a rebel'.[130] 'Nix' suggested that these bogus instructions be sent to 'Exeter Hall', the symbolic London home of liberal and often Christian causes from Anti-Slavery to the YMCA, including the Peace Society. An article on the Santals later in 1855 claimed that many Europeans in Bengal, particularly those living in isolated stations, evidently believed that the Santals had 'received too much consideration from the government' and that misguided (but unspecified) partiality had somehow encouraged the outbreak.[131]

The *Morning Chronicle*'s opposition to the collective punishment of the Santals by forced deportation revealed its liberal credentials. It alone expressed sympathy for a people whom missionaries praised as brave, independent and industrious, comparing them with other 'Aborigines' of America, Australia and New Zealand. Why, its editor asked, should they obey a 'mysterious law' that obliged them to 'give way before the white man'. The Santals had done no more than many indigo planters in Bengal—that is, taken the law into their own hands.

'Yet who shall say that all their fears are unreasonable?' The *Morning Chronicle* called for 'conciliation and redress'.[132] The rebellion, a missionary magazine acknowledged, had acted to 'force us to think of these people', that is, the Santals, 'one of the most harmless, truthful, gentle people ... suddenly changed into cruel and bloodthirsty depredators': and why? The *Church Missionary Papers*'s author, having digested reports from Calcutta newspapers published in Britain, had a ready answer: 'the sufferings they endured at the hands of unprincipled money-lenders ... more and more hampered with debt until they could no longer bear it'.[133] As well as the outrage expressed over Santal atrocities in the rebellion's first months, a growing mood recognised the justice of the Santal cause: 'there is a limit to human endurance', the *Morning Chronicle* wrote; the beginnings of the sympathy for the Santals that grew through the rebellion.[134] So far did European attitudes change that by the time writers began reflecting on the Hul after its suppression, that the anonymous author of an article in the prestigious *Calcutta Review* considered that the murdered darogah Mohesh Dutta, 'merited his end'.[135]

As the controversy over the collective punishment of the Santals had suggested, European popular opinion was perhaps more divided than might be supposed. Newspaper correspondents reflected European residents' conversations on steamers, in railway waiting rooms, at clubs and in station assembly rooms. Some denounced 'squeamishness' in failing to introduce martial law.[136] Aware of the leaked minutes from Fort William, they blamed Frederick Halliday and Joseph Dorin, sarcastically asking what the Santals would respect if not military force. A Sooree correspondent mockingly pictured George Loch issuing 'roobacaries [writs] ... with no end of huzors [salutations] ... despatched to the enemy's camp by a well badged chuprassie'.[137]

Pugnacious newspaper editors derided this kind of 'milk-and-water person' who spoke in favour of the Santals, no doubt 'a member of the Peace Society'.[138] The *Citizen*'s editor fulminated against 'a point at which clemency fades into imbecility'. He asked his readers to consider the rebellion in British terms:

Imagine the dalesmen of Cumberland and Westmoreland suddenly take up arms ... Let them murder and mutilate every country gentleman, slay every merchant, burn every village … Let the very roads of Kendal and Windermere, of Grasmere and Appleby be heaped with corpses …

What, critics asked, would the response be in Britain? It would not, he suggested, be 'ill-timed forbearance'.[139] The *Englishman* especially continued to denounce 'milk and honey proclamations', blaming Barnes Peacock for being a lawyer ignorant of India.[140] As newspaper readers realised what the Hul's suppression entailed, more expressed doubt at the rigorous methods used. A reader of the *Friend of India* wrote that while 'the whole tribe must be punished', nevertheless affirmed that 'to slay whole bands even of marauding savages in cold blood, is not an act in accordance with English instincts or with modern civilization'.[141] It was a moral dilemma to be resolved by magnanimity, but only after the rebellion had been suppressed.

One of the pressing issues that Frederick Halliday and his officials considered was whether the Santals should be disarmed. Newspaper writers begged that they be deprived of weapons. Mr Nelson's delegation insisted that for the protection of his employees, 'battle axes', 'swords' and bows be confiscated. James Ward also discussed the idea of disarming the Santals. It could be done, if only to 'show the Santals how completely they are in our power', but recognised that to deny them arms with which to hunt would be 'almost cruel'.[142] Frederick Halliday accepted that attempting to deprive Santals of their arms would itself provoke resistance. In the event, though quantities of arms were confiscated, the Santals were allowed to use their traditional weapons to hunt, perhaps one of the concessions which helped to persuade the Santals that at least some Company officials understood their culture.

Just as newspapers carried news of the rebellion from India to Britain, so copies of British newspapers eventually brought word of the reaction at home. The *Morning Chronicle*, surveying the bundles of newspapers arriving in Calcutta thought that the Santal rebellion had 'excited much interest' in Britain, but in truth, while many British newspapers had re-published the paragraphs that they had lifted from Indian newspapers, the rebellion was regarded as a minor matter.[143] Bengal military officers anticipated that there would be 'a grand row in England' when Parliamentarians learned of 'the usurpation of the

Military command by the Civil arm' in Bengal, but their interest in the rebellion's implications for the theory of military-civil relations proved to be limited.[144]

There were proliferating reports on the rebellion in the newspapers and these included accounts that were not only mistaken, based on rumour, error or exaggeration, but seem to have been actually been invented as part of the continuing rivalry between newspapers. In August newspapers published a report that Santals had swarmed aboard the steamer *Jumna*. This was 'a simple invention', the *Hurkaru* asserted: 'our astute contemporary the *Englishman* has been strangely hoaxed'.[145] Other false reports appeared, including all those describing Santals 'throwing up entrenchments' or building 'stockades'; or that the Santals were minting silver coins bearing Sidhu's likeness, as well as the persistent rumours that Santals held hostage a European woman and that the Hul had been inspired by outside agencies. Was the engraving of 'Seedho Mangee' distributed in the *Citizen* drawn from life, or was it a facsimile of one of a 'Cole' chief dating from 1832, or was casting doubt on the attribution a ploy by the *Citizen*'s rival, the *Hurkaru*? 'You must receive with caution the fabulous inventions of certain correspondents in the Presidency journals', a Raneegunge correspondent warned, which remains salutary advice.[146]

'Rebels dying fast': the collapse of Santal resistance

It is widely accepted that about 10,000 Santals died in the course of the Hul, and there is no need to doubt or contest that figure, even if it cannot be substantiated.[147] It is clear that when Santals came within musket range of sepoys, as Jugia Haram remembered, 'the Santals were shot down in heaps'.[148] Where the common understanding needs to be qualified, however, is in the composition of that figure. Company officers were prepared, even eager, to kill Santals, and their reports often either give the numbers of Santal bodies they counted, or their estimates of the numbers killed and wounded in clashes with sepoys. But adding those estimates and reports amounts to about a thousand Santals killed in actual combat. I cannot claim to have read all reports of clashes, or recorded all estimates of Santal casualties, and after some notable actions none were recorded. In Henry Raikes's fight at Nagore his eighty sepoys ran out of ammunition, so some Santals must have been hit and died, but Robert Richardson's account of the action gave no actual figure, while in the scrambling, scattered fights that occurred during the final drive in November–December 1855, it may have been difficult to count or record Santals who died in thick jungle or out of sight of the British officers writing reports. Other estimates were clearly exaggerated, such as a claim by a detachment of the 56th whose officer reported that in 'a bloody week' his men had killed 'about 1,000' Santals, which would have been impossible given the weapons and ammunition they carried.[149] Company officers felt intensely frustrated that Santals so often eluded their musket fire, so we cannot be sure that all of those claimed probably represent actual casualties. It is also likely that Santal fatal losses in battle must have included a large proportion of those recorded as wounded. The effects of musket balls striking bone or flesh made death likely, from blood loss, shattered bone and infection. Santal wounded, it was said, 'crept into the jungle to hide and die'.[150] Despite these difficulties, and even if adding a number of unknown deaths inflicted in summary killings in the course of dours, it is clear that the number of Santal casualties in combat totaled perhaps 2,500–3,000, but could not have amounted to 10,000.

There is also the question of the losses that Santal bands inflicted upon Bengalis and other groups. A correspondent writing from Rajmahal claimed that in August that not twenty villages still stood within 60 miles of Bhaugulpore, and that 'at least 100,000 people must have been murdered' by Santal bands.[151] Even conceding that Santals perpetrated massacres, this seems far too many. While even an estimate seems risky, it must have been somewhere between the 1,000 Santals probably killed in battle and the 7,000 Santals who died in the Hul from other causes. No one knows how many people died in the six months of the Hul, but it could have been up to 20,000—Santals, Bengalis, but no more than ten Europeans.

What caused the deaths of the great majority of Santals who died during the Hul? The short answer is: malnutrition, starvation and the diseases that followed. The beginning of the Hul had coincided with the arduous process of planting the rice crop on which Santals depended. Men and beasts had to plough rice fields no fewer than three times, with seedlings then planted by women, by hand one after another. The Hul drew away the men and women who would have been tending the crop. The season that followed now saw the thousands of Santals at large in the jungle enduring increasing privation. The darogah who heard Santals near Rajmahal express their determination not to submit also observed that they were living only on Indian corn and 'suffering much hardship'.[152] Paradoxically, while they had migrated to the Damin within living memory, the conventions and traditions of Santal life depended upon a settled existence. The essential rice beer, for instance, took five days to brew, and then had to be stored and often transported in heavy clay jars: how could it be brewed on the move, and how could it be carried without transport? Every Santal household owned rice grinding stones, and rice itself was heavy and bulky; moving about the country made their accustomed life impossible. Other reports confirmed and corroborated that the effects of living in large groups in the jungle either as marauders or, increasingly, as fugitives, disrupted their way of life, imposing the hardship and destitution that arguably came to undermine the entire insurrection. A military officer writing to 'My dear Delane'—John Thadeus Delane, the long-serving editor of *The Times*—passed on the views of a subaltern who had told him that

> the rebels are dying by hundreds in the jungles; they have been driven with wives and families from their villages into the most pestiferous parts, and being without shelter and constantly exposed to the deadly effects of miasms, till many of them leave their bones where even the wild animals could not now exist.[153]

It seems that living in large temporary camps—in much larger concentrations than Santal villages—brought malnutrition, communicable diseases among populations formerly not exposed to them and the pollution of water supplies by water-borne diseases such as dysentery or cholera.

Reports from the Santal country, from witnesses, prisoners and visits to abandoned villages, increasingly pointed to widespread illness among homeless Santals. In the villages that William Gott passed through on patrol near Koomerabad, deaths from cholera had been 'a daily occurrence' in mid-September.[154] Another officer of the 50th simply wrote from around Koomerabad, 'Rebels dying fast'.[155]

Officers often noted the devastated condition of the country: Joseph Hampton passed '40 to 50 villages, many of them fine large ones, all destroyed by fire … the crops on the ground completely ruined and trodden down by cattle'.[156] Frederick Halliday was later told that Sidhu and Kanhu had ordered Santals not to grow crops; a sign of incipient megalomania, perhaps.[157] By November, officers were reporting the outbreaks of epidemic diseases such as what they called 'cholera', a disease which 'proceeds with violence … and … may quickly terminate in death'.[158] The Santal willingness to eat practically anything—including rats, frogs, tortoises, lizards and snakes as well as roots—enabled them to survive in the jungle, but the Hul severely disrupted their rice-based diet.

Rumours had surfaced early in the Hul that it dislocated traditional patterns of production and trade. Those who understood the country knew that in the cold weather the jungle gave up less food than during the monsoon, and then Santals living deep in the jungle came in to Bengali villages to trade, selling firewood, animal skins and labour and buying salt. In September James Ward had learned that a Santal party had planned to raid Mohamed Bazar, not for plunder as it had been assumed, but for salt, the lack of which was causing the Santals' health to suffer. By the autumn, months of living away from their villages and familiar country began to take a toll and would soon bring so much privation and hardship that it would effectively end the rebellion. That conclusion reflects a western scientific sensibility. Santals believed that spiritual disturbance caused defeat, starvation and disease. They implored their guardian spirits 'do not allow disease and pestilence to enter our village, keep a sharp eye on our enemies': that their prayers went unanswered made the failure seem their own.[159]

PART IV

RABAN (WINTER)

6

AGHAN (NOVEMBER) AND *PUS* (DECEMBER)

In November Bengal's 'cold' season began. 'The 'weather is clear and settled and ... temperate': in the first week of November, as expected, a copious dew induced a shiver.[1] The cooler weather—and in the hills winters were uncomfortably chilly—took a toll on both sides, who were either sleeping outdoors or were exposed more than they were used to. Military officers hopefully indented for warm clothing— woollen pantaloons—and bedding for their sepoys: Santals shivered in their jungle camps. It seems that practically all the Santals who had not returned to their homes in the villages, many of which had also been burned, lived in crude huts made of leaves, much less comfortable, or healthy, than the neat thatched mud huts in which they lived in better times. In the winter daytime, though, the weather was 'delightful'; ideal for George Lloyd's long-anticipated campaign.[2]

'Timely and secret': preparing for the final campaign

By mid-October, surveying reports as William Grey forwarded them, Frederick Halliday detected a hiatus. The Santals held the southern purgunnahs of Bhaugulpore and the western and northern portions of Beerbhoom, but for the past fortnight they had seemed 'perfectly quiet ... either satiated with plunder or because the districts in their power have been entirely devastated'.[3] Halliday foreshadowed what turned out to be one of the key explanations for the Hul's collapse—the despoliation of Santal food supplies—and the relative quiet of the month saw the initiative swing decisively from the Santals to the Company's forces.

While clashes in the disputed country west of Bird's north-south chain of posts accounted for most of the attention in October and into November, the troops in Joseph Hampton's force on the Grand Trunk Road made dours northwards from the road, though Hampton pursued a much less enterprising policy than his younger officers. Mounted troops kept a watch as a screen some miles out from the road. So many troops now guarded the road that Hampton was happy to release the Governor-General's Bodyguard to return to Calcutta where they would prepare to bid farewell to Dalhousie and welcome his successor. Hampton's patrols suggested that the large forces that Pester, Phillips, Nicholl and others had confronted were breaking up and this was confirmed when he took a strong dour out himself, Hampton thought that they actually had 'dispersed'—the officers' favourite word for months—into parties of from fifty to a hundred. While other reports did claim larger numbers (for instance Phillips encountered a band of about 400 but 'they had no desire to fight'), it seemed that by November the Company's policy of block-ing the Santals' freedom of movement had begun to work, up to a point.[4] Despite the chain of posts and frequent patrols, however, the road remained permeable. Alfred Bidwell's 'spies' told him that large Santal parties were still crossing in late October. 'I can scarcely believe this possible', he admitted, supposing that they did so in small parties.[5]

George Lloyd had about 9000 troops under his command, and planned that virtually all of them would be used in the coming offen-sive. But what would they actually do? James Ward understood that troops would be 'marching across the country', but what then? 'I am at a loss to understand how this force is to act', he complained to Grey (but not Lloyd). John Low, meeting Lloyd, probably aboard a steamer at Rajmahal, summarised his plan in characteristically Anglo-Indian terms: 'the whole of the Damin-i-koh will be swept in a line after Shikar principles'—that is, with the infantry acting as both beat-ers and shooters.[6] Ward thought it probable that when the Santals saw 'troops in line against them they will really wish to submit' but he did not trust military officers to obtain Santal surrender or submission. He had seen military officers inclined to shoot rather than treat with rebels, but Ward now knew that many Santals were looking for a way to stop fighting. 'Is every Sonthal to be shot down?' he asked, 'It would be murder'. And given that martial law had still not been proclaimed, the troops would be operating under the need to collect evidence admissible in court—'every naik [corporal]' should be instructed how to gather evidence.[7]

Knowing that as the country dried out troops would be able to move, officials began to wonder what their role might be. Lloyd's plans now needed civil officials to support them rather than direct military operations. As Halliday repeatedly reminded him, Lloyd needed the aid of Bengal officials. Some eagerly anticipated the coming offensive. The ambitious Robert Richardson had hoped to benefit from the opportunities the rebellion had opened—he had volunteered to help Walter Birch 'in search of a body of insurgents' near Moheshpore.[8] He had been so importunate, that he had been admonished for his presumption, and in October he was told by Halliday 'to discontinue any connection with the Santal Insurrection': a clear case of his superiors cutting off nose to spite face.[9] But as soon as he learned that George Loch had a sick certificate, Richardson solicited the appointment, impudently pointing out how he had been 'actively employed' throughout the Hul in doing his own work and, he was in no way abashed to mention, Mr Loch's office work as well.[10] He did not obtain Loch's job, but certainly did not want to be lumbered with the routine work of a commissariat officer, which he knew to be 'laborious in the extreme'.[11] He wanted 'special duty'; a part in both the suppression of the Hul and in the reconstruction of the Company's administration. As early as mid-October the Bengal government had begun alerting its civil officials to procure supplies and carriage (now not just elephants) in readiness for the coming drive. It was necessary to store supplies in advance not just because sepoys from the upper provinces could not live off the country in an unfamiliar land, but also because over large areas of the disturbed districts crops had not been grown for months. Officers in Sooree, which had barely seen a hostile Santal for a month, were already paying inflated prices for fowls and kids—troops, they conceded, acted 'like locusts'.[12] Peasants and refugees alike faced starvation.

Lloyd's staff officers calculated that the advancing columns would need to carry with them twenty days' supplies, most on elephants—as virtually no roads existed in the country through which they would pass, especially when the Santals were expected to seek refuge in the hills. Later they increased the duration of supplies to a month, and anticipated that they would have to provide for 2800 fighting men and 1200 'followers' (a ratio of nearly 3:2) as well as forage for at least 330 horses as most European officers and officials had several.[13] The broad plans Lloyd sketched out gave his few and overworked commissariat officers and the all-important civil officials a great deal of work. Where should provisions best be obtained? How should they be sent to the columns' various starting points? Could hackeries be used in the Santal country? Would they need escorts? Above all, how many elephants would be needed, and how could they be had? Aware of the porous nature of Indian cantonments where nothing was confidential, officers emphasised that arrangements should be kept 'timely and secret', especially from the merchants from whom the provisions would be bought. This was not so much for security—later they would be printed in newspapers—but because notice of the troops' requirements would inevitably bring higher prices and collusion between merchants.[14] The final offensive began just in time: supplies were becoming scarce and expensive—Richardson described paying 'famine prices'—and lacking proper storage much was spoiled.[15]

Although in October practically all the Company's military action occurred in Beerbhoom, Lloyd remained in Bhaugulpore, because it was from the northern district that his force would advance. His grand plan, devised in essence in late July when he assumed command, remained what he described as 'the Simultaneous March Southwards'. This would end with his troops 'debouching upon the line of the Grand Trunk Road when the whole of the insurgents shall have been captured or destroyed, and the intervening country cleared of them'.[16] It is easy to see why Lloyd commanded the respect and confidence of the civil officials who depended upon him for the rebellion's suppression.

When would Lloyd's march begin? He was firm, following Sherwill's advice, that 'the jungle cannot be marched through with impunity until the middle of November'. As the date for the opening of active operations approached, so scrutiny of them increased. Both the Governor-General and the Supreme Council asked for regular reports in addition to seeing routine Military and Judicial Consultations. This desire seems to have coincided with the receipt of the first unfavourable responses from Britain and especially from the Company's Directors.

Further signs appeared that the Hul was dying. In the weeks before the opening of what would prove to be the rebellion's final act, military officers from across the disturbed districts reported incidents in which Santals either tried to submit or claimed they had, or who avoided Company forces even more actively. Near Kurrown, Captain James Phillips reported that the Santals had stopped 'their former practice of beating the Tom Tom but now come up in as quiet a way as possible'. The inhabitants of a dozen villages where Phillips's detachment had been operating came in to beg him to allow them to remain 'quietly in their respective villages', while the local rajah, who seems to have persuaded civil officials of his loyalty, was now proving it by collecting arms from the Santals who lived on his estates.[17] In other villages, manjees were tendering perwunnahs testifying to their peaceable intentions. The certificates did not always relate to the manjees proffering them. Captain William Halliday, one of Frederick's relations, suspected that a manjee he questioned had borrowed his certificate from a neighbouring village; Halliday could read Bengali at least as well as the manjee could read English.[18] After one of his ensigns returned from a dour on which he gathered arms and drums given up from a village near Operbandah, the scene of so much skirmishing, Captain Anthony Lister reported that increasingly 'the Sonthals were peaceably inclined to us'.[19]

But could Santal professions of submission be trusted? Vincent Jervis heard a similar story while patrolling near Jamtarra a week later. A Sultanpore manjee presented him with a perwunnah, explaining that he and his people had submitted, had surrendered their arms and were now 'peaceably inclined'. Jervis suspected the man and had his sepoys search the village. They turned up 'quantities' of bows and arrows, axes, tulwars and drums; the submission was a ruse.[20] Jervis's experience demonstrates why so many Company officers did not believe the sudden apparent collapse of Santal resistance, but in fact by November Santal bands had become almost entirely passive, responding to Company movements but making no aggressive moves of their own.

'We heard their drums beating': Santal tactics

The end of Santal offensive movements by November permits an assessment of the Santals' conduct of what was effectively their first and only armed conflict until the emergence of Naxalite guerrillas from the 1960s. Observers accustomed to the traditional, formal warfare, of the kind experienced or idealised by many Europeans in Bengal, had much to deprecate in the small, brief 'affairs' character-istic of the Santal Hul. A Raneegunge correspondent argued that it was 'surely high time to treat with contempt, the report of two hours hard fighting which has resulted in the wounding of [only] five men by unpoisoned arrows', even if that occurred during 'a collision … between 150 sepoys and 4,000 Santhals'.[21] It is true that the rebel-lion's unnamed and inconclusive encounters were hardly comparable with the battles whose names appeared on the colours of the native infantry regiments—Bhurtpoor, Ghuznee, Chillianwallah. More sepoys of the 56th Native Infantry alone were named on the memorial to the dead of the one-day battles of the Gwalior campaign, dedicated on Calcutta's river-side esplanade in 1847, than died among the Sonthal Field Force during the entire Hul. And yet, on both sides, fighting the rebellion demanded a great range of tactical innovation and adaptation. Just as the rebellion was hardly known or studied at the time (in fact no officer published anything about the experience of fighting it) so as an armed conflict it has been utterly neglected in the 170-odd years since.

The Santals' military responses are most interesting, because although they used shields in 'mock battles' in ceremonies, they had no experience of actual war at all.[22] At the beginning of the rebellion few Santals had even seen a soldier and were 'ignorant of our method of fighting', as William Money observed.[23] Finding patterns of Santal actions is complicated both by the need to rely on Company and newspaper reports, and by the absence of anything like a Santal war-like tradition. The Santals had no customary way of fighting, nor any firearms but those few they picked up from burkendazes and, more rarely, sepoys. Nor did they use all of the advantages available, a restraint that Edward Man called a 'rude kind of chivalry'.[24]

At first, Europeans deprecated and denigrated Santal military capacity. A correspondent to the *Englishman* was only one of several who asserted that 'one company of any regiment of sepoys ought to thrash a body of five thousand' Santals.[25] Soon, however, observers began generalising from the reports they heard or read. A Berhampore writer was surprised to learn that Santals 'have not that wholesome dread of attacking armed sepoys which was expected'.[26] It is clear from reports by Company officers that Santal bands acted and reacted differently at various stages of the Hul. Unused to facing volleys of muskets, at first Santal bands often simply broke and fled, or approached too close and were shot; quite possibly some had not seen a musket fire before the one that killed them. But in later encounters, Santals not only faced sustained musket fire, even if they came on 'gingerly', but adopted—improvised—what can only be described as battle tactics.[27] Vincent Jervis, on whose recollections William Hunter drew, recalled that one of his lieutenants—probably John Delamain—had once felt compelled to 'shoot down seventy-five men before their drums ceased' and the Santals fell back before the sepoys' muskets.[28]

Accounts of several dozen encounters between sepoys and Santals demonstrate that while the rebels gained in military experience, they were unlikely to make up the deficit, especially when almost every situation was different, and few individual Santal leaders had many encounters from which to learn from as mistakes usually meant death, wounds or capture. Digambar Chakraborti reflected on the expertise of Gocho, the Santal leader who had led dacoits against mahajans in 1854. He was leading a party near Moheshpore, prob-ably early in August when he found that a detachment of sepoys, possibly Hunter Smalpage's, had got between two Santal bodies, but Gocho did not take advantage of his position in the troops' rear. 'Had Gocho a little military tact', Chakraborti concluded, 'he would have attacked the soldiers from behind when they were facing a vast number of Santals'. Instead, 'The Captain' (Chakraborti often named Santal leaders but hardly ever Company officers) allowed Gocho's party to join the larger Santal force, and then used the sepoys' fire-power to kill 'a vast number of Santals'. Gocho, he recorded, 'barely escaped with his life'.[29]

For the most part Santal tactics were defensive though, as several detachments discovered, Santals were sometimes willing to charge sepoys. Santals usually had a choice over whether to stand, and often either fled or decided not to challenge the sepoys in one of their crucial military advantages: firepower. As the Hul developed it became clear that the Santals made the most of one of their critical advantages: mobility in the jungle, obliging Company officers to devise ways to counter it. Some British observers credited Santal leaders with great cunning: 'I fear their playing at hide and seek in the jungle … drawing the troops from the place they intend to loot'.[30]

In a few encounters the Santals took the initiative and attacked sepoy forces. In Bhaugulpore late in July, 'a very large body' of Santals attacked the camp of 80 men of the 40th Native Infantry, pressing their attacks so strongly that Major Henry Shuckburgh esti-mated that his men killed a hundred Santals, including their leader, who had been carried about in a palki, perhaps because of his age. The sepoys' musketry, firing volleys to order, seems to have kept the attackers at a distance greater than arrow range, because Shuckburgh reported that no sepoys had even been wounded.[31] Other Santal bands in the area also showed 'considerable determination', as Lloyd was surprised to read. Another detachment of the 40th had been 'attacked in an open plain' by 600 Santals who only desisted after facing two volleys.[32] Later in the rebellion, near Kurrown on 16 October, James Phillips's sepoys of the 63rd faced attacks by 'a large body with more courage than prudence', which then stood their ground for more than half an hour, discharging their arrows without wounding any sepoys, again suggesting that they, too, were held at a distance.[33] Santal bands understandably preferred enclosed country, the jungle in which they lived. 'The Sonthals will not face a maydan', James Ward affirmed—meaning a 'maidan', the open parade and exercise grounds adjoining many Indian cantonments.[34] It was another argument he used to condemn George Burney's supine attitude in garrisoning Sooree, which stood on a slight ridge with open ground for miles around.

Henry Raikes of the 56th also faced a Santal attack west of Sooree. 'After some sharp fighting', he reported, 'they were driven back into the jungle', having lost seven dead and as many wounded, but with a sepoy killed and three wounded the Santals seem to have pressed their attacks to within arrow range.[35] It was reported that Santals boldly called to sepoys, taunting them, slapping their 'b_tt_ms' and calling 'come over and fight', though from the security of an opposite river bank, beyond musket range.[36]

This response suggests that one of the Santals' weapons deserves particular attention. Just as officials such as Loch and Elliott sought to exploit Santal misgivings of the likely success of their cause, so Santals in turn played upon the minds of their opponents. If the Santals lacked experience in war and weapons that were able to hurt their enemies at more than fifty yards, they possessed other advantages—as we have seen: the ability to move rapidly, even if that usually meant evading approaching troops, and a greater knowledge of the country, especially the jungle. They also possessed, and appeared to use, another advantage, the sound of what Company officers called their 'war drums'. Given the Santals' complete lack of warlike demeanour, they were actually ordinary drums, possibly beaten by non-Santals, though Durga Tudu, the narrator of *The Story of the Santal Rebellion* was asked by a manjee, Buka Pargana, to be a drummer. Songs and dances were an important part of Santal culture, and they used drums of various sizes and timbres, usually made of clay or wood with bullock- or monkey-hide or goatskin tightly stretched across. The drums, civil officers told their uniformed counterparts, were generally called 'doogdoogees', and practically ubiquitous in Santal ceremony, though anthropologists later investigating Santal culture recorded no such instrument. The ubiquitous drums were probably 'dhaks': large, long wooden tubes carried by two men on a bamboo pole. 'It is the reverberations of this drum which can be heard throughout the surrounding countryside', wrote W.J. Culshaw, an Anglican missionary who lived among Santals in the nineteen thirties and forties.[37] When later in the rebellion sepoys began recovering weapons abandoned by fleeing

Santals, troops often swept up doogdoogees as well, treating them as weapons of war, as the Santals used them.

The sound of drums, their enemies observed, gave heart to the Santals in battle. In the decade after the rebellion Vincent Jervis explained their importance. He told William Hunter that 'as long as their national drums beat, the whole party would stand and allow themselves to be shot down … we had to fire on them as long as they stood'. It was the results of the Santals' willingness to withstand sustained musket fire that so sickened Vincent Jervis.[38] Troops at Raneegunge, the southern force's headquarters, could hear Santal drums beating at night in mid-August and, as at Koomerabad, this unnerved the sepoys facing the huge force besieging the post. It is possible that the Santals used drums to communicate between what Company officers sometimes called their 'divisions', signalling intentions, or at least presence and perhaps the timing of movements. We have no idea of whether they did, or how, or what messages they sent, but the doogdoogees' reverberations remained for those who lived through or served in the rebellion, its characteristic sound.

'Public elephants': the Company's supply crisis

Besides functional command, steam-powered communication and fire-power, the Company's strategic advantages included a supply system which faltered but did not fail. As the campaign spread across Lower Bengal, from Bhaugulpore, into the Rajmahal Hills, through eastern Beerbhoom around Sooree and Rampore Haut and into the west of that district, calls upon supply elephants grew. More troops arrived and more posts had to be supplied. Stationary detachments needed fewer beasts, but no one was reported as giving up spare animals. By early October, when Lloyd's Bhaugulpore front had become quieter, Bird's force was covering from Sooree in the east to Parasnath in the west. Lack of elephants limited his detachments' mobility, Bird complained: 'detachments are confined to their immediate neighbourhood whereas had they elephants they could follow up the enemy taking supplies with them and keeping out as long as [needed]'.[39] He asked if Lloyd's northern force could spare elephants, though even if they could it would take many days to move them from, say, Rajmahal and Jungeypore south to Sooree. Elephants could not be moved by steamer, and they could not walk there directly because Santal bands still roamed the country in between.

While officials struggled to meet units' many needs across a huge area, they knew that animals were being withheld, unused, by other government agencies. The Governor-General's retinue 'needed' 140 animals—even though Dalhousie was away in Madras and the animals were idle in Calcutta. But Frederick Halliday's establishment also held forty beasts, none of which he had given up. Headquarters further up-country could, the Commissary General, Major James Ramsay, helpfully suggested, use camels or bullocks instead. Ramsay pointed out that during the campaign in Pegu three years before, the dearth of elephants had obliged the Governor-General's establishment to lend animals: why not again? Ramsay was also at pains to explain that the Commissary General's elephant sheds were denuded because he had had to lend animals to other agencies—nine to the Survey department in Calcutta, ten to the executive engineer in Dacca, three to railway parties in Benares.[40] So desperate did Bird become to supply his widely scattered detachments that when he encountered forty 'public elephants' ambling down the Grand Trunk Road, reported by his road sowars, he took the unusual step (unusual in Bengal's bureaucracy) of detaining them at Raneegunge to carry supplies from the railhead and effectively defied his superiors to order him to release them.[41] Extraordinarily, it took just four days for George Atkinson to secure approval for Bird high-handedly commandeering the animals, word he sent by telegraph.[42] As the river levels eased more elephants could be transported across them, and animals arrived at Raneegunge from Malda and Dacca, at last giving Bird what he needed.

But by this time some elephants had been working continuously for four months, and the demands to which they had been subjected began to tell. Elephants were becoming sicker and weaker. Because detachments needed to 'borrow' and return them, to be used again immediately, the animals were rarely able to get the rest they needed. Among various instances, of the animals acquired in Purneah, two had died, one called Bucktowar Guj, while crossing a river and the other, Rullun Wallah, of sickness. Each cost the government a thousand rupees in compensation, but neither, Alfred Bidwell admonished, should have been accepted at all.[43] It was a sign of the Company's forces' need. For months after the Hul, elephant owners were claiming and being paid compensation for animals who had sickened or died in official service.

'Speedy and effectual suppression': martial law proclaimed

At last, after months of waiting and planning, Lloyd was finally able to fix dates to his force's movement 'for the information of Government'. What he called 'the Northern Division' would begin its move on 11 November, moving in seven columns, detailed in Dean Shute's movement orders. Lloyd would march with the troops from Bowsee, starting on the 12th and he planned to reach Nya Dumka, in the north of Belputteh purgunnah, on the River Mor, by the 20th: taking eight days to march a notional fifty miles. The methodical advance was carefully plotted on the Surveyor General's and Walter Sherwill's maps. Because the columns' starting points varied, so did their starting dates. The 40th, still at Colgong, marched off first and had furthest to go. Other columns left on five successive days, and the last on the 18th, with two columns arranged to wait at intermediate halts in case orders changed. It was a complex march table, an expression of the Bengal Army's, or at least Shute's, fundamental professionalism. The detachments had to maintain an even pace, and they would surely face some Santal resistance on the way, in order to arrive at Dumka, as it was called, on schedule. The march would be only the first stage of the advance. What came next would largely depend on the success of its first stage, and Lloyd was too canny to leave hostages to fortune by giving Halliday and the Supreme Council an unduly optimistic programme.[44] But before he could issue final orders the long-awaited proclamation had to be issued.

'The time has now come for proclaiming martial law', the Supreme Council's secretary at last wrote to Frederick Halliday on 8 November.[45] After debating for months whether martial law should be declared, the Government of Bengal finally issued a proclamation on 10 November—literally the day before the first of Lloyd's troops were to step off. Cecil Beadon, Dalhousie's 'Home' secretary—that is, responsible for 'regulation' provinces—had warned that the proclamation needed to be made public 'before systematic military operations commence'. Given the time taken to get the text to Bhaugulpore—at least two days, even going by telegraph as far as Berhampore—the government only met the deadline technically. After Halliday wanting it but not actually asking for it, and the Supreme Council thinking it desirable but being unwilling to act without Halliday's request, at last the proclamation was approved without much of the quibbling pedantry and pusillanimity which had marked their protracted deliberations. It would seem that William Grey, and possibly George Atkinson, the two officials most familiar with the arguments, and perhaps the most frustrated at their sterility and repetition, had essentially drafted a text. Grey presented this to his superior, perhaps with the firm advice that the time for parsing philosophical points had long passed. Even then, Dorin could not resist making qualifications and comments, which Grey naturally accepted with the good grace he had learned after seventeen years in the Company's bureaucracy.

Under William Grey's signature but authorised by the lieutenant-governor under Regulation X of 1804 with the assent of the President in Council, the proclamation opened portentously:

> Whereas certain persons of the tribe of Sontals and others, inhabitants of the Rajmahal Hills, of the Damin-i-Koh, and of certain Pergunnahs in the Districts of Bhaugulpore, Moorshedabad, and Beerbhoom … are and for some time past have been, in open Rebellion against the authority of the Government …'

While the government had offered clemency, it had 'become necessary for the speedy and effectual suppression of this Rebellion that advantage should be taken of the season to commence systematic Military operations against the Rebels'. To that end, it was 'expedient that Martial Law should be declared and that the functions of the ordinary Criminal Courts of Judicature should be partially suspended in the said districts'.[46] Two hundred copies of the proclamation were printed in Bengali to begin with—'Hindee and Oordoo' were to follow—and the text appeared in the English language newspapers, and possibly their vernacular counterparts, on 12 November. A thousand copies were distributed to magistrates in the disturbed districts. Barely a single Santal, the subject of the document, could read a word of it, in any language, nor did any see it or even hear it proclaimed.

Even this legal instrument did not give George Lloyd complete freedom. Recognising Frederick Halliday's sensitivity about his authority over military officers—or rather, its limits—Dorin made sure to explain that the lieutenant-governor was to 'exercise entire political control over the Major General commanding the Troops': it was Lloyd's force's task to suppress the Hul, not to govern the districts now under martial law. It was a subtle point, but one that Halliday, whose authority was so closely trammelled by the Supreme Council, cared about deeply. The proclamation of martial law ended Alfred Bidwell's term as 'special commissioner', though he certainly benefitted from his service in the Hul, even if not as much as he might have liked. Bidwell became commissioner in Bhaugulpore, taking the disgraced George Brown's former position, on the day martial law was proclaimed.

The Supreme Council had emphasised that the point of martial law was not to 'exterminate or destroy unnecessarily these ignorant savages', but was to 'reduce them to complete submission with as little bloodshed as possible'.[47] Newspaper editors, at last granted the severity for which they had pressed, rejoiced that 'rooboocaries and other Mofussil law ... will have to give way to the rope and the bayonet'.[48] On that basis, George Lloyd's troops set out to suppress the Hul. On the same day as the proclamation appeared, the Calcutta newspapers carried the news that the Crimean war had finally ended, at a cost to Britain of about 40,000 lives and £120,000,000. The Santal rebellion had become Britain's only active conflict.

'Soliciting orders': the advance delayed

Despite all of the planning over the weeks before the opening of Lloyd's advance, matters changed almost immediately. A week before the first column was due to leave, Lloyd advised George Atkinson that rather than the month's provisions Lloyd's staff officers had planned to accumulate, the supply columns would only be able to carry twelve days' worth. This was only just enough to provide for most, and if the columns were denied re-supply (and in the hills), would entail 'considerable delay', possibly even the cancellation of the entire operation. This advice seems to have unsettled the Supreme Council, already nervous at the unfavourable reaction the insurrection had evoked in London. Four days after his first contingent should have left, Lloyd was outwardly politely still 'soliciting orders'. Atkinson could do nothing but forward Lloyd's request to Grey, reassuring him that he was pressing him to get Halliday to approve starting the advance.[49] Lloyd, keeping his temper with difficulty, pointed out that postponement meant an even greater delay—the troops were now eating rations they should have consumed thirty miles south—and urged his commissariat officers to obtain more supplies, from further afield and presumably at greater cost. They also needed to obtain larger quantities. Lloyd's northern force now numbered 4450 sepoys, twice the original estimate, with correspondingly more followers.[50]

Lloyd, presumably realising that martial law actually gave him the freedom to act without Halliday's consent in purely military matters, perhaps gambling that a successful outcome would obviate any complication, decided that he could delay no longer and told Atkinson that he would be ordering his troops to start on the 15th regardless. To demonstrate his resolve, he himself then started for Bowsee. He still hoped to receive 'final and decisive orders' from Halliday, but left Atkinson in no doubt that he was serious.[51] Lloyd's act was perhaps the boldest and most decisive in his career.

What explains the Supreme Council's cold feet after deliberating for so long and over a rebellion that they had clearly wanted to see suppressed? No official seemed willing to acknowledge the delay, still less allot responsibility for it, but despite arguing about and advocating martial law for so long, by the time Lloyd's long-anticipated drive was ready, Halliday and his officials had still not prepared the necessary papers for the Supreme Council's approval. British Bengal's official tendency to prevarication cost Lloyd a further week.

Postponing the offensive must have concerned the force's medical officers especially. Company leaders calculated their opportunity to defeat the rebels against an invisible biological time-table. Walter Sherwill, the Company's expert on the Santal country, had warned that 'from the day the west wind sets in, the Hills and the Damin-i-koh become instantly and invariably fatal to all but the natives of the place'.[52] This, Sherwill had affirmed with unsettling confidence, would come in February or March, leaving the Company just three months to end an insurgency that had already continued for that length of time. Sherwill's authority comprised all the expertise they had to work with; James Pontet was no help—it was alleged that even after twenty years in the Damin he could not speak Santali.[53] Over the past season, medical officers had charted the gradual rise and fall of sickness cases, which recalling the detachments in to headquarters and large posts had been intended to forestall. In fact, bringing men together to occupy thatched sheds in damp weather had arguably helped to spread communicable diseases. The Bengal Army's characteristic parsimony did not help. For some reason sweepers were not allowed in standing camps, but only in permanent cantonments. When units occupied lines for any length of time (in this case two months or more), 'rubbish and filth' began to accumulate. Bird's doctors warned him that his troops' temporary shelters, though they had been 'particularly healthy' might become 'quite the reverse'.[54] Now the sepoys were obliged to wait another week. Typically, Bird had to apply to the lieutenant-governor himself to obtain sanction for a cart, a pair of bullocks and a couple of sweepers to clean up the sepoys' lines at Raneegunge, and that trifling expense had to be forwarded to the Governor-General's approval.

The delay in its commencement had one beneficial effect for the Company, in that it further weakened Santal resolve. James Phillips, whose reports are among the most detailed and perceptive, was reporting that Santal parties were beginning to negotiate with officers, now as often a military officer as a civil official. Some tried to bargain amnesty by surrendering their arms—or at least some of them; others by offering to turn in their leaders or the leaders of other bands; or professed their desire to submit, asking for a certificate proving their loyalty. Still others, it seems, simply gave up the fight and started walking towards what had been home. Santal bands still in the field sought to avoid conflict, and officers' reports again describe how seldom they turned to fight.

The units preparing for the offensive included the Bhaugulpore Hill Rangers, now under new officers. Frederick Burroughs faced a closed court of enquiry investigating his conduct and that of his corps at Peer Pointee in July: 'the charge is cowardice'.[55] India being India, the proceedings of the 'closed' court leaked almost immediately, published in the *Delhi Gazette* and then across Bengal, in a highly sympathetic account. The Hill Rangers, though 'not regular troops', had been 'called to account for not doing what never should ... have been expected from them'. 'We think', the *Delhi Gazette*'s editor opined, 'a great deal too much has been made of ... seventy men of a provincial corps not standing before an enemy the first time they ever encountered one'.[56] The Rangers survived and remained loyal to the Company in 1857, but the disaster at Peer Pointee spoiled more than Frederick Burroughs's Christmas. Though he retired as a major-general in 1868 he seems never to have exercised command again.

'Through a whole jungle': Santal bands in limbo

As Lloyd had foreseen, the more the Santals plundered the more they would become burdened. Grain was heavy and bulky, and Santal saggers moved no faster than those of the troops, even if the country was beginning to dry out—the hills made movement difficult, but large numbers of saggers stood in the passes and valleys. Cattle, which the Santal commandeered in vast numbers, moved equally slowly, and larger herds became unwieldy in the jungle, particularly as Santals sought refuge in the hills. Durga Tudu's reminiscence gives a sense of the dislocation the Hul wrought:

> ... they [Santal bands] occupied the country [moving] hither and thither, to the four points of the compass. Some moved forward to the east, some to the west, some to the north and some to the south. As they became leaders—each one on their own account—they began to plunder ...[57]

Among the large parties of Santals that Company patrols and local 'spies' reported late in September and into October, were many which were not 'war bands' in any sense. Sepoys of the 50th under George Fooks, patrolling in dense jungle in western Beerbhoom came across 'great numbers' of women and children. Troops reported seeing huge temporary settlements—an account by a subaltern of the 63rd describes his men advancing through the jungle and finding 'an immense encampment'. These were not the small, neat, permanent Santal villages with which troops had become familiar earlier in the rebellion, but vast collections of leaf 'wigwams'. These improvised encampments were the opposite of the 'regularly organized community' that Kaviraj described in his *Santal Village Community*.[58] They covered valley floors, inevitably fouling water supplies. These Santals were refugees, 'escaping for their lives'. But from whom were they fleeing? The immense numbers showed how profoundly the people of the disturbed districts had been dislocated by the rebellion. These people were not growing food, were eating only what they could carry and were moving where they could. When he moved on Fooks met more such parties.[59] Their unpreparedness arguably explains the rebellion's collapse.

The drives which the native infantry made into the hills in Hendweh and Belputteh bore little resemblance to the clashes of the early months of the Hul. Here the sepoys were practicing what a subaltern called 'a little light infantry work through the jungle'. Their men pushed into the jungle, 'Jacks' climbing trees to try to 'twig' where Santals were, engaging them as 'they stood at bay on the edge of the jungle', and pursuing them up and over hills, 'blazing into them at close quarters … jungle or no jungle'. Sometimes 'the crafty soors' (that is, 'pigs') crept back 'to get a quiet pot at us', but were always driven back. While Santals often offered resistance, as the subaltern put it, 'they were … fairly boned'.[60] Even the thick jungle provided little aid—musket balls could crash through bamboo when arrows could not. Many died, though no one counted the bodies, many surrendered and some were executed on the spot but most fled, often leaving behind all their possessions, including their 'plunder', that is, their food supplies and the cattle they valued so highly. Behind each detachment came a party of bildars, often quick in grabbing loot, but usefully driving off captured cattle.

Civil officials accompanying the detachments again proved their worth by providing intelligence; on one occasion alerting troops that the band before them was led by Baichoo Rao, one of Kanhu's most senior soubahs. A civilian—it is not certain if he was an official—went ahead of the sepoys, riding into an encampment with a party of sowars and seized him. Finding 'ample proof of his guilt' Baichoo Roa was tried by court martial at Rampore Haut and executed on 20 November, one of 'the first to suffer by martial law'.[61]

Again, vigorous young leaders stood out, such as Lieutenant Henry Finch of the 31st, who led the green-clad rifle companies of the 31st and 42nd, the only two regiments of the force with these specialist sub-units. Adventurous civil officials again accompanied the leading troops. Ashley Eden seems to have actually commanded parties of the 42nd Light Infantry. He described how a Santal band stood, daring the troops to come on, the skirmishers firing into the dense bush and driving them up a hill. Eden described how he 'formed a portion of my men in line and took them up to where the Insurgents were the most cockey', holding their fire until the Santals were only 20 yards away, then firing and rushing at them. Eden claimed to have counted at least fifty Santal dead.[62] Eden was acknowledged to have been 'one of the officers who have "come on" in the insurrection', largely because of his energy ... and a disposition to rely solely on himself'.[63]

'Neither honour nor glory': the final advance

By 25 November Lloyd had actually arrived in Dumka, five days behind schedule but with his columns approximately in the order and on the routes Dean Shute had specified. Merely reaching his initial objective was, however, the relatively easy part of the campaign. The explanation for choosing Dumka as his intermediate point now became clear. It was at this time merely a large village, but it, and the string of places his detachments had reached, lay 'more or less approaching the boundary of Purgunnah Belputtah'. This was the southernmost purgunnah of Bhaugulpore, the heart of what remained of the rebellion. Its country was jungle-clad, with green rolling uplands occasionally punctuated by low ranges of hills—the Mal, Ural, Luckimpore and Subchulla Hills; outcrops and continuations of the chain that formed the Rajmahal Hills. Lloyd's headquarters, escorted by a detachment of the 40th, a couple of light guns, some sowars of the 2nd Irregular Cavalry, 25 elephants and 300 bullocks, reached Koomerabad on 27 November, on the south-western end of the cordon—the ring was closing.[64]

From the north, after a brief rest, Lloyd's columns were to push on, now advised by Santal informers who recognised that their cause was lost. They advanced against the most recalcitrant of the Santals, encountering bands which more often demonstrated not only 'a hostile disposition', but marked aggression—Santals attacked the rear-guard of the 31st Native Infantry as it advanced from Aurungabad and Skreekond.[65] Anthony Lister recorded that the Santals his men met had 'displayed much spirit and strenuously resisted the troops'.[66]

From late November, they would not be advancing into a void, but would be implementing the second part of Lloyd's plan, with Bird's force acting as the anvil to Lloyd's hammer. To the south, Bird's detachments now occupied a crescent of tiny villages, all carefully marked on Walter Sherwill's revenue survey map—Gopalpore, Goomroo, Jamjorie, Baboopore and Boomkoolee: between one and seven miles from the boundary of Belputteh.[67] Detachments would be 'so placed', the *Bengal Hurkaru* explained, 'that as the General moves down, the Sonthals will be driven upon them and cannot well escape, turn as they will'.[68] The first part of the offensive, in Bhaugulpore, had largely passed through country in which few Santal bands remained active, and the only substantial action was on the Brahmini river at Jhilmillee, which Walter Sherwill had described in 1851 as 'a fine Sonthal village'.[69] Here the 40th Native Infantry emerged from the Damin where 'a few were shot' and other Santals captured. They indeed seemed to have been driven south by the co-ordinated, slow-moving columns. When troops converged on Dumka, scouts watched as Santals fled across the river and into the jungle of the Luckinpore Hills.

Lloyd's columns' advance into Belputteh and Hendweh purgun-nahs is actually poorly documented in the Military Consultations, possibly because his headquarters was literally in the saddle for the month it took to advance from Bhaugulpore into Beerbhoom. The gap is filled by the many detailed letters submitted to Calcutta newspapers either by military officers themselves or by their friends, which almost uniformly took a jocular but triumphant tone in describing the operations which seemed to bring the rebellion to its end.

The sepoys made prodigious marches—13 miles before even reaching the hills in which the Santals sheltered; a day's march of 30 miles, much of it through jungle and across creeks, now lower than in the monsoon but often against the grain of the country and always wary of Santals appearing. Officers' accounts reveal how much they and their sepoys had learned. They repeatedly describe how sepoys now plunged into thick jungle, advancing in small detachments under subalterns, native officers and even havildars. While earlier in the Hul detachments operated at strengths of a company or a half-company, that is 100 or 50 men, usually under at least a British ensign, in the final operations detachment commanders sent off smaller groups to pursue, outflank and block the Santals they sought. Santals now were very obviously 'closely pursued', as an officer described the 63rd's movements near Golpore.[70] Some bands made the 'stand' so often predicted, loosing arrows, but invariably gave way. The officers sensed that the end approached: 'we only want a few energetic dours', another subaltern wrote, 'to ... end this unfortunate and stupid insurrection'.[71] The contempt which European officers had formerly expressed had been supplanted by a frank admiration. 'They showed some pluck', the subaltern conceded.[72]

In these final operations, figures for casualties, on both sides, became even more vague, with the publication of anonymous letters evidently describing the same operations adding to the confusion. The numbers recorded, however—150 'shot down', 50 killed—suggest that perhaps 500 Santals died directly in this phase of the campaign, but it can only be a guess. Santal losses in killed and wounded were certainly agreed to be 'very severe'.[73] Direct contact with the most desperate or committed Santals for weeks together, led to higher casualties among sepoys than had been seen since July and August. Many sepoy detachments seem to have suffered a few wounded, most lightly, though eight of Lieutenant William Hawes's detachment were reported to have been wounded, an unusually heavy toll. The relative casualty rate was maintained, however: in the same clash the 63rd reported killing 150 rebels.[74] The soundness of delaying the offensive until a healthier season seemed to be justified—by the end of the campaign the 56th had up to fifty men in hospital; presumably a proportion which would surely have been greater in the monsoon, with losses among British officers—Captain William Gott fell 'dangerously ill ... as bad as could well be'.[75]

Newspaper editors realised that the sepoys were fighting a quite different kind of war to the recent wars in the Punjab or the Crimean war that had filled their columns over the previous two years. The *Englishman*'s 'Editorial Commentary' observed that 'the little war which is being waged here affords neither honour nor glory'.[76] Santal accounts of these months are, understandably, effectively non-existent, at least in describing the experience of specific groups in particular places. Across the range of the songs collected and translated in the century after 1855, however, the impact of the Hul, and especially its final, traumatic months, seems to emerge. Images which seem to describe this period, 'the hunt on the big mountain', recur in the songs, even when their subject seems not to relate to 1855 itself:

> 'Get up, father ... the cobra is approaching'
> 'You have no wife/ I have no husband'
> 'The vultures circle in the sky'
> 'My lover went there, and never returned'
> 'The smoke rises, to the mouth of the dead'
> 'O my love the land is dark'

Santal poetry offers glimpses of the horror of the Hul's end: death, dislocation, separation, grief. As another lament put it: 'The land has gone dim/ the raiders are upon us'.[77]

'The Thakur's Perwannah': the Hul explained

Having been in the field for several months, officers became increasingly familiar with the country in which they operated. Captain Anthony Lister, who served around Operbandah for most of November, realised that the nearby Golepore Hills were 'one of the Insurgents strong holds'. He 'most respectfully' suggested to Bird to be allowed to lead an expedition into the hills. He had been in the area twice, once reconnoitering so close that Santals wounded one of his sepoys with an arrow, and felt 'pretty well acquainted with the country'. Lister thought that a force of five companies and a couple of howitzers would enable him to break up one of the most notorious known bands in western Beerbhoom.[78]

As it happened, Bird did not need to approve Lister's plans. In the final days of November, a party of ghatwals, the hill auxiliaries employed by civil officers to watch the tracks through the hills, came upon a Santal party of a dozen unarmed men in a rice field. They had been trying to reach a village near Parasnath, fifty miles to the south-west, where some had relatives. The ghatwals suspected they were actually rebels and detained them. They were right. Not only had they apprehended a party of manjees, they had taken the fabled Kanhu and his surviving brothers, Bhairab and Chand. Lister, denied his howitzer-supported assault, arranged for the prisoners to be taken to Raneegunge. Lloyd, informed immediately by an express carried by sowars via Koomerabad, was naturally jubilant. 'This important capture will I have no doubt bring the insurrection to a close', he exulted, 'their prestiges will be gone ... we shall find no further resistance offered'.[79] This was a further coup for Company forces. By the opening of Lloyd's offensive all the key Santal leaders, or at least the only ones known to their enemy, had been captured.

Curious officers looked Kanhu over. A by-stander had caught a glimpse of him at Raneegunge. He seemed 'a better looking fellow than most of the Sonthals', with 'a bold and independent manner'. Another observer found him a 'small limbed man', but taller than most Santals at 5'6", aged about 35 and with 'nothing in his appearance to denote hero or assassin'. A third found him 'a repulsive looking man', but admired how he spoke out 'very freely' explaining and justifying his resort to arms. Having been found wearing Tom Toulmin's waist-belt clasp on his arm and carrying Toulmin's purse would seem to implicate him beyond hope.[80] By 8 December Kanhu had been bought to Barrackpore. He seemed to anticipate and accept his fate: when told that his brother Sidhu had been hanged and that he probably would be too 'he appeared quite indifferent'.[81] Having been treated poorly by every European or Bengali figure of authority he had known, why would he expect anything better? But Kanhu, one of the Hul's major Santal leaders, was now able to speak to his antagonists for himself.[82]

Kanhu made a succinct statement of his cause, reiterating that the Santals' enemies were zamindars and mahajans, and that they had wished to 'lay their sorrows before the Governor General'.[83] A letter published in the *Hurkaru* quoted him professing that 'they had none of them any intention to harm any European'.[84] He explained why he had led his people in rebellion. The order in which he described events suggested that the vision of the Thakur acted as the mechanism for mobilising Santal opposition to economic oppression and it was not merely a 'religious frenzy'. Kanhu's words exposed the needlessness of the Hul, if only Company officials had noticed, heeded or acted upon Santal concerns. His first statement was that he had complained to James Pontet and to the darogah Mohesh Dutta 'that the mahajuns oppressed us'—for example, that they charged 500 per cent interest—but 'they did not listen to my complaints'. He repeated that the Thakur had appeared to him from heaven, saying 'Kill Pontet and the darogah, and the Mahajuns and then you will have justice': it was a political manifesto, not merely a spiritual vision. He expressed the visitation in mystical terms, and explained the mechanism—neither Kanhu nor Sidhu could read, but Chand, his brother, and another man, named Lehira, claimed to be able to read the message that Sidhu had received. 'The Thakoor has written to you', they explained, 'to fight the Mahajuns and then you will have justice'. Kanhu's testimony at last clarified what Europeans had speculated about for months: why and how the Santals had risen.

Accepting the Thakur's mantle, Kanhu and Sidhu had sent out sal branches, the traditional means of communication, calling manjees to Bhugnadihee. Because the branches were carried by messengers, they surely explained the meaning of the symbol. Sidhu also dictated letters sent to nearby rajahs, bluntly demanding that they 'settle our matter with the mahajans, or else we will fight you'. Naturally, 'the rajahs abused us', replying derisively 'who are the Sonthals that they should be able to fight with us'? Mohesh Dutta had done what James Pontet did not (he was not due to return to Burhyte until later in the year) and visited the district. Kanhu confronted Dutta: 'I have been complaining for 5 years against the mahajuns and up till now no investigation has been made'. Dutta abused Kanhu for his temerity, 'like a coolie', his brother Sidhu had added) 'I then killed Mohesh Dutt with a sword with my own hand', Kanhu said, 'by the order of God'. Kanhu did not dissemble. His account has a tragic simplicity about it. It was a confession that would not only illuminate Santal motives and events in a remote village in the Damin on a hot day in 1855: but would would ensure his execution, something he surely knew. Sidhu had also claimed to have killed Dutta 'on the spot': both presided over the confrontation; both faced their inevitable deaths with equanimity.[85]

Kanhu's testimony revealed in passing that he had no notion that by seeking justice from the mahajans and rajahs would be drawing upon his people the might of the Company's army. At Moheshpore, virtually the first clash between Santals and sepoys, Kanhu described how he advanced toward the sepoys, not to slay them, but 'to make my salaam and tell them that I was not fighting with the Govt but with the zamindars'. Nothing else exposes the Santals' lack of understanding of the enemy they created by their actions. Hundreds of Santals had died never understanding that they faced the Company. Ironically, in defending their traditional rights by attacking the manifestations of the Company's new regime, that is exploitative mahajans and landlords, the Santals had drawn on themselves the power of the Company.

Inevitably, and like his brother Sidhu two months before, Kanhu was hanged. 'It fell to my disagreeable lot', a Scots official wrote home, to take him to Bhugnadihee from Sooree, a week's journey, carried on a 'stretcher'—an open palanquin or dhoolie—in irons, with a strong escort of sepoys and sowars. For all but the last day's march, Kanhu seemed indifferent to his fate, 'if anything ... rather proud of being taken so much trouble with'. As the party approached the valley of Burhyte where the Hul had begun he grew uneasy, asking for 'a great feast'—a leg of mutton, a fowl, rice and peas, and a quantity of rice spirit. At Burhyte, less than a couple of miles from the gallows, he drank more rice spirits and ate sweetmeats, now laughing hysterically. Only at the foot of the gallows did he seem suddenly sober, and behaved calmly—'he did not seem to fear'. 'Mr T'—presumably Octavius Toogood, who had done as much as anyone to suppress the rebellion—explained that he had no desire to see him executed. Kanhu displayed a compelling dignity. 'Ah, well,' he said, 'I suppose you must do what you're ordered'. At Bhugnidihee early in the afternoon of 23 February 1856, on the spot on which he and Sidhu professed to have seen the Thakur, and here he performed obeisance, pouring libations on the ground, 'for he kept up his pretension of divine inspiration to the last'. He made a speech, predicting that the Santals should not rise again for six years, but then he would return to lead them. At last, he climbed a ladder with the noose around his neck and two low caste by-standers were induced to pull it away at Toogood's order. He was left hanging for half an hour before being cremated.[86]

HUL! HUL!

'A combined movement': the final campaign

In proclaiming martial law, Joseph Dorin had emphasised that it was not only conceived to enable the government to suppress the rebellion, but also for 'the protection of the Military from the operation of the Civil Law' while they were doing so.[87] That is, theoretically, martial law allowed the troops to get away with murder, literally. But did they? How did the troops of Lloyd's columns actually behave once they reached the 'fastnesses' which the recalcitrant Santals defended? Officers' accounts, including letters published in the press, describe sepoys firing on and killing Santals as much as ever, while some Santals resisted as doggedly as ever. An officer of a rifle detachment described how they pursued Santals trying to get their supplies to safety, when 'a few of the enemy stood by their carts and fought with some determination', wounding sowars and horses with axes in close fighting. They were 'soon cut down or dispersed', but even after being forced into the surrounding hills the Santals 'showered down arrows'.[88]

While Lloyd's columns were advancing south, Bird's detachments were not merely awaiting orders to meet them, but acted as a flank guard to deter Santal bands from breaking out to the west and exerting pressure by advancing from the south. They continued patrols from their outposts, harrying Santal bands and the 'gangs' into which they were increasingly fragmenting. These small detachments, often included ten or a dozen sowars and were usually commanded by lieutenants and even ensigns, all now experienced leaders. 'The whole jungle was alive', Lieutenant William Hawes of the 63rd reported of the hills near Gopalpore but the Santals he faced were disorganised, rarely making a stand, abandoning weapons, including drums, stores of grain and hundreds of animals. Dozens of Santals surrendered.[89] These dours seemed to find Santals more often than Company troops had earlier in the rebellion, suggesting greater collaboration from Bengali and even Santal informers, and they seemed to be able to attack them, as well as merely driving them off. Almost every report listed impounded loot—grain, cattle, sheep and goats. Crowds of villagers following the columns carried or drove off the booty, though the sepoys often seem to have expected or been given a share of the profits when it was sold. Sepoys, burkendazes and chowkidars counted about 40,000 impounded cattle, many sold off by officials: the rebellion became the vector for the redistribution of wealth in the disturbed districts.[90]

While the Field Force's columns had made great progress in the previous fortnight, not everyone shared the prevailing optimism. The *Citizen*'s 'military newswriter' thought that the Hul would continue through the cold weather and even 'gain in vigor' in the hot season of 1856.[91] George Lloyd, receiving reports from his ten regiments, did not entertain that view. With his troops rested and in place around the Santals' final refuges in hills in Beerbhoom and the Belputteh and Hendweh purgunnahs of Bhaugulpore, on 4 December Lloyd distributed orders for a 'combined movement' to begin on 10 December, the final Company operations of the campaign.[92] The orders, even more detailed than those Lloyd had issued a month before, had columns again starting at daybreak and marching into the hills. In Confidential Circular Orders to regimental commanders, Lloyd emphasised that 'no party should allow itself to be stopped by jungle or Hills', but should advance steadily, in concert with the parties on either side. 'All armed parties of Sonthals' were to be attacked, and plunder recovered.

With victory literally within sight, accounts adopted a jaunty tone. 'If you have any sporting gents still in Calcutta', the *Citizen* offered, 'tell them to come up here and try their luck and aim'.[93] Reports from Europeans in the field described Lloyd's drive as 'shikar'— sport; one described how he 'put up a covey of Sonthals', for example.[94] Accustomed now to dealing harshly with Bengalis and Santals, officers advancing near Nagore freely described capturing rebels whom they 'soon induced to point out the position of a large body of Sonthals', jocularly acknowledging them as 'our forced guides'. Lloyd certainly took advantage of the procedural liberty which martial law afforded. His officers openly described him 'hanging a few' rebels.[95]

At last, in the middle of December, Lloyd's troops advancing from the north met Bird's force in the south. On the crest of an unnamed ridge 'to the great delight of the sepoys', an officer of one of Lloyd's units met his brother in one of Bird's—probably the Campbells, John of the 42nd and Robert of the 63rd.[96] Further west, men of the 37th met parties of the 2nd Grenadiers: the ring was closing. With units of the two field forces now in contact, the remaining Santals were to be harried from all sides.

Company officers evidently discussed how they might meet Santal parties in the hills. Several officers' accounts describe them separating their detachments into two or three groups, each under a subaltern, one advancing frontally, the others trying to work around the flanks—the hill country was often too rugged for mounted troops. The sepoys were now all veterans and displayed a toughness bred by long exposure in the field. One of their officers praised his men (and himself), boasting that after a long day marching and fighting they were 'ready for the same amount of work today' with sixty rounds in their cartridge boxes.[97] European officers of native infantry had long been criticised for their alienation from their men—even twenty years before Frederick Shore had been appalled at their use of 'the most disgusting terms of abuse' at their men—but these younger officers shared their men's hardships and appreciated their endurance.[98]

The most striking discovery came when sepoys under Lieutenant Henry Campbell of the 63rd found a European woman's torn white dress and what they took to be the slipper belonging to the abducted European lady, discoveries reported and speculated about in all the Calcutta papers. This, officers, editors and doubtless readers, all assumed was evidence of the mysterious deaths of Mrs Thomas and Miss Pell. The rumours about Miss Pell re-surfaced. She had been carried about respectfully in a palanquin; she had married a Santal, she was *enceinte*: pregnant. Other rumours were probably whispered rather than published. Some took the discovery of the dress as proof Miss Pell had been abducted and carried about as a trophy or worse; one newspaper even reported that Lloyd had actually 'rescued a Missy baba', the term for a female European child.[99] Other newspapers were adamant: the two ladies had been murdered and not abducted. Curiously, no official investigation appears to have been held, but the discovery encouraged officers to 'scour every foot' of the hills.[100]

It became clear that the Santals were now disorganised, their once powerful bands diminished in size and strength. Many included large numbers of women and children, who had been on the move for months, and lately, under the pressure of military parties, fleeing, abandoning food and possessions. Women, as Professor Ata Mallick, the premier scholar of their part in the rebellion, affirms, were its 'worst sufferers'.[101] Often separated from their men, either by the disruption of war or by death, they bore the brunt of their communities' suffering and survival. They had to endure the ordeal of living in the jungle, increasingly as fugitives, risking being denounced as witches or abducted by predatory manjees. If captured, they invariably succumbed to illness because of the conditions in crowded and insanitary jails. Enduring terrible suffering, anonymous and voiceless in history, they became the rebellion's most numerous but least visible victims.

Nevertheless, the troops encountered resistance: 'more ... than I was led to believe', 'Our Friend in Beerbhoom' admitted.[102] The detachment under Lieutenant William Hawes of the 63rd came up against 'numerous' rebel groups which fired arrows at his men, 'seemingly controlled by the beat of their doogdoogees' sounding in the thickets beyond sight. But then the Santal fighters all fled, 'leaving many dead on the ground'.[103] Among the traumatic consequences of the rebellion was that last rites for the Santal dead could not be fittingly observed by the community. Santals believed that 'until the final funeral rites are offered, the soul of the individual hovers' without rest.[104] The Hul left many unquiet Santal spirits.

Early in December officers began predicting 'that the Sonthal campaign will be all over by the 25th'.[105] And it was: the campaign against the Santal rebels was one of the few wars that really was over by Christmas. On Christmas Day, which happened to be his birthday, Frederick Halliday wrote from his home to Lloyd to thank him for the 'well directed and energetic exertions' of his force. While grateful, Halliday had never liked having to share his province with a general, and he bluntly told Lloyd that he saw 'no further occasion for keeping that force together'. He was already suggesting to the Governor-General that it be 'broken up'.[106] On 18 December the *Citizen* was able to report that 'it is believed that offensive operations have ceased'.[107] Some 20,000 Santals were said to have submitted.[108] The Hul was effectively over 'The fire is now put out', the *Church Missionary Papers* was able to declare with assurance.[109] But had the rebellion been directly suppressed by military force, or did it wither from other, less obvious causes?

'Died a natural death': did the Santals collapse?

The most recent account of the Hul, a valuable edited collection of Santal accounts, presents the end of the Hul as a military defeat for the Santals:

> At the end of the rainy season in 1855 about twelve to fourteen thousand Company soldiers fought the insurgents and crushed the rebellion.[110]

However, the Company force involved was only about a third to a half of that figure, and the Company's claim to achieving military victory is at best suspect, but of long standing. George Lloyd's report to the Bengal government described how his troops 'beat' from the Ganges to the Mor, likening the campaign to a hunting expedition, in which his troops had 'pushed their way over the hills and through jungle'; and the Santals had 'fled in amazement and consternation' from them.[111] Notwithstanding the understandably self-congratulatory tone of much of the accounts of Lloyd's final drive, which contemporaries accepted had snuffed out Santal resistance, it did not by itself suppress the rebellion. Rather, it is much more probable that the Hul was dying by November 1855, collapsing from within. Civil and military reports for months had noted waning Santal morale and commitment, and more recent accounts made clear that Santal communities were suffering from the extreme dislocation the rebellion had brought. Lloyd himself, while boasting that 'these ignorant and misguided savages' had been 'scared by the appearance of so many troops', also acknowledged that they had been 'straitened by want of food'.[112] Lloyd's offensive, as Charles Buckland's laudatory account of Halliday's term as lieutenant-governor claimed, 'speedily subjugated all those who had not been broken by the ravages of hunger and disease'. Buckland thought that this was because 'the line of troops had been drawn around them', but the Santals imported nothing. They suffered want not because the rebellion had prevented them obtaining food from beyond their country, but because they had abandoned their plots, depriving themselves of sustenance and had been unable to live off grain taken from the region's Bengalis.[113]

There is a great deal of evidence to suggest that the rebellion essentially collapsed. From the Subchulla Hills Lieutenant Henry Campbell described how the 'effluva from dead bodies of all kinds between the hills is such as to render them nearly impossible' to remain in.[114] These corpses could not have been the result of sepoy muskets. Of course, it is possible that troops killed more than they recorded, diminishing or concealing the numbers. But the proclamation of martial law indemnified sepoys and their officers from legal penalty, and both they and the newspapers' readers saw nothing reprehensible in killing armed rebels. The 'dead bodies' that Lieutenant Campbell saw and smelled had overwhelmingly died of disease: the Santal rebellion was finally ending because the Santals themselves were literally dying, and in huge numbers. Other accounts confirmed Campbell's; his fellow subaltern William Hawes also described seeing many dead bodies—'families decimated by disease and exposure ... fugitives ... in great distress'.[115]

The rebellion disturbed not only the rhythm of planting and harvest, but also the ceremonies and festivals part of the Santal year—its outbreak corresponded with the Erok and Hariars festivals of planting and growth. In September, Santals celebrated the harvest of the millet, accompanied by sacrifices in village groves, and then Janthar, performed in a village's own fields, and lastly Sohrae, a celebration of harvest marked by drinking and feasting. None of these ceremonies could be properly performed in 1855, either because there was no planting or harvest, or because Santal villagers were far from their familiar groves and the bongas that dwelt in them. Bongas that ordinarily 'by their active intervention sustain welfare and morale' were in 1855 absent, deserted, powerless, resentful of neglect; spiteful or malign.[116] Tending the rice crop ordinarily entailed 'days ... full of anxiety', as Bradley-Birt explained; not only back-breaking labour, but also because bongas needed 'constant propitiation'.[117] Narahari Kaviraj explained the Hul as 'a desperate effort to defend the Santal way of life'.[118] Santal culture had propelled them into rebellion, and its disruption drained their commitment and made victory impossible.

'The Santhal rebellion', a correspondent wrote to the Calcutta *Citizen* in March 1856, 'has died a natural death'.[119] George Lloyd naturally accepted praise for the military operations which seemingly resulted in the rebellion's suppression. As we have seen, the movements he ordered had sent columns into the Santal country, which fought bands of armed Santals, killing those who resisted and capturing or 'dispersing' the survivors. Within six weeks this seemingly ended the rebellion. But Stephen Fuchs's judgment, made in the course of considering the rebellion as a messianic movement, seems apposite: 'deprived of their leaders, decimated and starved by Government troops, and finally tired of their own violence and opposition, the Santals gave themselves up and sued for peace'.[120]

'Sorrow, misery, suffering and scarcity': aftermath

On 3 January, William Grey promulgated another order, suspending the operation of martial law. 'Open rebellion against the authority of the Government of Bengal', it announced, 'no longer exists'.[121] Some expressed scepticism: 'what measures have been devised to prevent a recurrence?' asked the *Citizen*: should not troops remain in 'the infected places' for at least a further year?

Edward Man, a district officer who spoke to Santals in the years after the rebellion, described how the new year found the Santals 'houseless and wretched', with 'a great portion of their tribe annihilated' and with villages and crops destroyed. On the other hand, as Santals defiantly pointed out to Man, 'they had cut to pieces every mahajun they could get hold of'. The Santals had 'to a certain extent … temporarily gained their end, but at a fearful cost'.[122] The *Sheffield Daily Telegraph* quoted at length a military officer who had served in the rebellion. Evidently well informed about the Santals and the situation in Bengal, he argued that 'could the Santals half comprehend the substantial and lasting good which they have effected … they would doubtless again undergo these and even worse evils' to gain such 'grand results'.[123]

But if open resistance ended, suffering continued. Even as the rebellion died more Santals became prisoners. A report early in 1856 disclosed that Bengal's district prisons were almost all over-crowded, but that in Beerbhoom and Bhaugulpore they were unhealthy and over-crowded mostly with Santals.[124] The capacity of Sooree's prison was 48 but it held 193, Bhaugulpore's 233 but held 356.[125] Augustus Rivers Thompson, another official seconded to serve in the disturbed districts, complained that prisoners escaped while on work details loading supply elephants and even when allowed to defecate in fields. He complained not only of 'a want of discipline' among the burken-dazes, but also 'a strong sympathy' between them and the prisoners.[126] Even identifying prisoners was almost impossible, still less tying them to actual offences. William Halliday believed that Dargoo Manjee, who had tendered what he thought was a fraudulent perwannah, was in fact the leader of the band that had killed Tom Toulmin.[127] The only way to check was to summon Robert Richardson, who had issued the perwunnah. But not every case justified an officer travelling across the district for days, and many manjees suspected of acts of violence must have evaded retribution. Many trials of accused Santals may have been 'farces' (as Narahari Kaviraj alleged), but many more trials simply did not occur.

Many prisoners were held not in jails but in open sheds, leading to many more escapes. Early in 1856 124 prisoners escaped from one such shed, though guards soon recaptured 44 of them. Their sickness and mortality were explained when it was reported that some were reduced to eating leaves. Sceptical officials were directed that Santals' destitution should be 'relieved if it actually exists'.[128] Deaths among Santal prisoners helped to build sympathy among Bengal's European inhabitants. A letter to Buckinghamshire from Calcutta in 1857 praised Santals as justifiably 'condemned for the rebellion, but they are otherwise not a bad race'. Reports of Santal prisoners absconding from work camps afflicted by cholera in the Hooghly delta only to ask to be admitted to the healthier Alipore jail 'excited strong sympathy'.[129]

Relatively small numbers of Santals were tried and convicted, very few sentenced to death, but some to imprisonment in irons often with hard labour. An analysis of two groups totaling 42 prisoners documented by Rivers Thompson gives a portrait of the Santals captured and tried at the rebellion's end. All but three of the first group, numbering 22, received sentences of five years in irons, mostly for 'illegally and riotously assembling'. All but three were men from

Beerbhoom, with an average age of 37—the oldest was 56: these were mainly respected leaders. But three were under 18—one was only 15—but they too claimed the title 'manjee'. One was a Paharia, substantiating claims that some non-Santals joined the Hul. The second group of twenty were also Santals from Beerbhoom, sentenced similarly, though with greater variation, between one and six years in irons. But as well as including three men under 20, this group averaged over 41 years old, though only eight claimed the title of 'manjee'. The rebellion arguably diminished the presence of older manjees; the youths were perhaps leaders because of the losses among their seniors: only one of the profound changes the Hul would entail for the Santals.[130]

They continued to suffer that cost in the months and years after the end of martial law. Those Santals who gave up the cause and returned home found that they had nothing. Chotrae Desmanjhi, who arrived home to Benegaria west of Rampore Haut, probably sometime in November, found the village 'burnt to ashes'. 'Overwhelmed with grief' his surviving family wondered where they could live. The village manjee, who had returned shortly before, which would seem to suggest that the entire village had gone to war, explained their predicament: 'We have no buffalo or bullock so how can we drag out wood? We cannot make our houses in our own village ...' But they hauled timber from the forest by hand and built a new village, surviving though 'reduced to great sorrow, misery, suffering and scarcity'.[131] Desmanjhi's family was only able to recover its modest living because he was able to obtain a pair of bullocks that had been taken and sold, recovered thanks to a ruling, attributed by grateful villagers to Halliday, that livestock could be claimed, even by former rebels. The Hul must have introduced changes at every level, impoverishing many, possibly benefitting some like Desmanjhi's family. In that it killed many village leaders, new manjees must have emerged. A fragment of Desmanjhi's memoir conveys a Santal perspective:

> ... we Santals came on sorrow and misfortune through the rebellion; many died, many were widowed, many children were orphaned ... a great curse fell upon us.[132]

PART V

AFTER THE HUL

7

AFTERMATH AND INTERPRETATION

'Tardy and uncertain action': verdict on the Hul

To Dalhousie's lasting irritation, the Santal rebellion had disturbed the even tenor of the final months of his term, detracting from his record of technical progress, imperial victories in the Punjab and Burmah and portentous policy in India. He grudgingly gave it a paragraph in the lauded 'Farewell Minute' he composed in February while steaming home. But the Hul had been 'repressed'—'local outbreaks will from time to time occur', he wrote smoothly—and 'measures of precaution' had been taken.[1] The Hul's outbreak arguably extended Dalhousie's time in India and led him to urge that more European troops be sent to Bengal, both matters had a bearing upon the outbreak of the great mutiny-rebellion in 1857.[2]

It was only after the rebellion ended that most Britons, besides those taking *Allen's Indian Mail* for family or occupational reasons, realised that Bengal had been convulsed by insurrection. Over the following six months two dozen further articles appeared in the metropolitan or provincial press, albeit shorter and assuring readers that an insurrection had ended. Perhaps the most visible press coverage came in articles in the *Illustrated London News*, which in February, August and October 1856 published engravings vividly depicting incidents and images of the Hul.[3] These were based on drawings by

Walter Sherwill, who had arrived in Britain on sick leave late in 1855 and, perhaps invigorated by the voyage home, produced a dozen drawings to be engraved, probably by William Linton. Sherwill, who had accompanied the 7th and 40th Native Infantry on dours in Bhaugulpore in July and August, depicted sepoys in action against Santals at Bissohuwa, especially in a large drawing strikingly framed from the Santals' perspective which showed them vainly but heroically facing the sepoys' volleys. Just before his departure in October, Sherwill had drawn Sidhu, virtually on the eve of his execution, giving British readers a physical and a written portrayal of the man who had led the Hul. Either Sherwill or his engraver depicted Sidhu as seeming penitent, whereas he seems to have been apathetic toward his fate and defiant in regarding his cause as just. Other engravings, published in August 1856, showed railwaymen attacking Santals and sepoys bringing in prisoners, and in October pictures of railway peons being drilled as auxiliaries, and forlorn Santal prisoners. But most Britons only became aware of the rebellion after its end, and probably most never knew of it, at the time or since.

The Company's staff and shareholders, however, had followed its progress through the proceedings arriving with every mail. They also charted its financial cost: the Company's accountants soon computed it to have been £28,320 in addition to quotidian expenses.[4] The Court of Directors delivered its verdict on the suppression of the insurrection early in 1856.[5] Its members and their London officials had noted successive Special Narratives and the Military Consultations and Judicial Proceedings detailing the progress of what it was also happy to call the 'repression' of the uprising, considering it 'one almost unmitigated series of plundering and burning villages, and murdering men, women and children', which had seen 'every aggravation of outrage and cruelty'. But the measures ordered by the Supreme Council and by the Government of Bengal, it judged as 'from first to last inadequate to the emergency'. The insurrection had 'demanded the employment of a greater number of troops' than the Board considered necessary, unhappy that it had required the proclamation of martial law. Few officials were commended. George Brown of course had 'given way to unnecessary alarm', but William Elliott had also been unduly apprehensive, and the Court deprecated Alfred Bidwell's futile 'conciliating measures', and Frederick Halliday's 'unnatural hesitation' in delaying asking for martial law to be declared. In general, the Directors 'noted'—and implicitly criticised—the 'tardy and uncertain action of all the superior authorities' of matters 'imperatively demanding promptitude and decision'. Military officers (except the unfortunate Frederick Burroughs) individually escaped direct censure, partly because the use of military measures was exactly what the Directors expected, but they still expressed 'our regret that they were not much earlier adopted'. Even Dalhousie was effectively admonished because although he was at Ootacamund he was 'within reach of consultation and ought to have interfered and put an end to the discreditable divisions and disputes which were the cause of the delay in proclaiming martial law'. '*I* had nothing to do with the whole business', he defensively wrote to Sir George Couper.[6] That this judgment came, in the traditional phrase, from 'your affectionate friends' did not soften the blow.[7] The Company's investigation summed up the Santals' predicament. They were:

> industrious and hard working, frank and manly, peaceable and inoffensive, a simple and unlettered people, who can appreciate none but the simplest mode of adjusting a disputed demand and are utterly unable to contend for their rights, with any hope of success, under a complicated legal system like that of our Regulation code.[8]

This the Hul transformed by precipitating a decisive political change in the way the Company was to govern the Santal. It would end the worst abuses of the Santals' relationship with oppressive mahajans and an inflexible legal system, and introduce a more suitable, if paternal, administrative system. But did that make the Hul worthwhile? Was it a conflict that needed to happen? Did it justify the enormous cost in the sufferings of the Santal people and the Bengali inhabitants of the disturbed districts who became its victims?

In 1853, as part of the debate over what turned out to be the final renewal of the East India Company's Charter Act, John William Kaye, a Bengal Artillery officer turned gentleman author, had published his account of *The Administration of the East India Company*, his intent disclosed by its subtitle: 'A History of Indian Progress'. Kaye described the origins and evolution of Britain's dominion over India, concentrating on its benefits in the construction of public works such as the Jumna and Ganges canals, in the suppression of Suttee, Thuggee and Dacoity and the promotion of justice, education and trade. On his opening page, Kaye adopted as the essential test of Company rule the question posed by the great orientalist Sir William Jones who, when asked to comment on a draft of George Barlow's minute outlining the new Bengal Regulations of 1793, the legal foundation of the Company's rule, suggested that 'surely the principal object of every Government is the happiness of the governed', a sentiment which Kaye endorsed.[9] On that basis, the Company had comprehensively and catastrophically failed the Santals.

'A fresh outbreak': continuing resistance

Early in the new year, Frederick Halliday travelled to Raneegunge by train and visited Sooree and Koomerabad, the scene of one of the rebellion's most dramatic episodes. The *Citizen*, no admirer of Halliday, sarcastically described Halliday's 'Big Fiddle'—his considerable entourage—and the alleged cost of the excursion: '*two lacs of rupees*' [that is, Rs 200,000].[10] By this time as many officers as could get away had taken leave, leading to a sudden shortage of dawk gharries at Raneegunge.

Lloyd was as eager to return to the uneventful life of a divisional commander at Dinapore as Halliday was to see the back of him. Almost immediately, his staff arranged for most of the regiments of the Sonthal Field Force to move to the stations they were to occupy under the Bengal Army's 'General Relief' for 1856 while the cold weather allowed them to march. The force broke up with precipitate haste. The 31st, 50th and 56th returned to Barrackpore, the 7th to Berhampore, along with the 11th Irregular Cavalry; the 40th returned to Dinapore and the 13th went up-river to Lucknow. For the time being, the 2nd, the 42nd and 63rd would garrison the Santal country, along with the 2nd Irregular Cavalry, its task of watching the south-western border ended. Berhampore would be 'reattached' to the Presidency Division. Bird commanded the force as it shrank. For a time, Sooree, its headquarters, looked like 'a regular Military Station', with bazaars, elephant sheds and bungalows being built.[11]

But before he boarded the steamer to Dinapore, Lloyd had one final, pleasant duty, to praise his force through the traditional valedictory order. He asked Dalhousie to express the government's approbation of the 'energy, endurance, courage and good conduct' which his regiments had displayed. He acknowledged that they had faced 'much difficulty and deprivation ... the insalubrity of the climate, the dearness of provisions and the nature of the country', even though they had faced 'no very considerable foe'. While praising the sepoys generally he especially thanked both regimental officers (European and native) and Brigadier Bird and the force's staff and senior officers for their 'admirable foresight, energy and judgment'.[12] All this Dalhousie was glad to endorse, and his General Order appeared accordingly on New Year's Eve. If the rebellion had begun with the murder of Mohesh Dutta on 7 July, it ended almost exactly six months later, the East India Company's final uprising before the great mutiny-rebellion which would destroy it.

With the restoration of peace, refugees, zamindars and rajahs returned—those who had not been murdered. The Ranee Khema Sundaree Debi, zamindar of Pakaur, eventually returned to her palace. Despite being looted, it still stood, and her retainers had managed to keep her portable wealth safe. Likewise, the Ranee Janki Kumari of Moheshpore, who had sought refuge at Jungeypore, returned to her palace, not least because it was the centre of the estates from which she drew her wealth, which, after an interval returned to production under the impulse of a further monsoon. Both landlords, officials reported, continued to accept as tenants non-Santals, leading to further friction between Santals and Bengalis.[13] Bengali peasants were reportedly not ploughing during the 1856 monsoon, fearing that their crops would only be taken again.[14]

Despite Dalhousie's triumphal General Order, resistance in the Santal country did not end so neatly. Officers noticed that the district was full of parties of Santals, some refugees making their way home, others fugitive, wandering without purpose, others not ready to give in. The Indigo Planters' Association, representing members living in isolated factories, lobbied the Bengal government, in 'great alarm' over 'a fresh outbreak'. To support their campaign, the planters tendered copies of 'notices' supposedly served by recalcitrant Santals. Purporting to come from a 'Subah' and threatening the destruction of their factories, the documents were patently a hoax.[15] It became clear that while 'a few marauding parties' were still 'wandering about plundering', they were evading patrolling troops and no threat to the province's stability.[16] William Hawes, commanding a 63rd detachment in western Beerbhoom met 'unarmed Sonthals calling themselves fugitives' and wondered what to do about them.[17]

After Christmas, Captain George Sinclair at Operbandah also found unarmed Santal families peaceably moving south-west towards Singbhoom. One of Sinclair's mahouts told him that he had seen a body a thousand strong. In fact, the entire disturbed districts were full of Santals, individually and in groups, trying to find a place to live, and Bengali refugees also trying to pick up lives disrupted by conflict. These streams of dislocated people included Santals who either refused to accept defeat or who found dacoity more lucrative or congenial than working as a tenant farmer or as a labourer on an indigo plantation. Among the refugees passing Sinclair's post were men forming 'a small renegade group', though he had yet to learn of any acts of violence being committed.[18] One unduly alarmed young magistrate took to arresting Santals 'more or less at random'; hardly an action calculated to reassure them.[19]

The East India Railway's engineers and supervisors, although they had returned to work, also remained apprehensive. At Pakaur, Nelson, the railway contractors, built on a ridge over-looking the cutchery a 30-feet-high masonry, loop-holed, 'Martello tower' to enable watchers to see Santal bands approaching and to provide a bastion to withstand attack. The tower is still there, in the negligent custody of the Archaeological Survey of India, strictly speaking not actually a relic of the 1855 rebellion, because it was erected in 1856. In 1857 railway officials and military officers took shelter in it when a party of mutineers passed through Pakaur.[20]

A month after the supposed end of hostilities, Bird reported that the area between Deogurh and Operbandah, the most contested country the previous autumn, was again disturbed. The 50th, though expecting to leave, was sent to re-occupy several posts, while the 63rd and 56th also sent parties out. Bird 'strongly objected' to Eden 'ordering small parties from my detachments'—the rebellion had given some civil officials a taste for command. He was happy to provide parties on request, but reserved the right to decide on their strength. As well as isolated bands of marauders, Bird realised that now the cordon on the Grand Trunk Road had been dismantled, Santals were again trying to pass in numbers: a duffadar of the 2nd Irregular Cavalry saw up to 5000 of them heading towards Chota Nagpore. Bird sent the cavalry, which had expected to go to Berhampore, to patrol the road and the Bhaugulpore-Beerbhoom border. He also sought Halliday's advice, asking what policy the Bengal government wanted to adopt towards these 'armed bands'? Bird suggested that 'timely active operations against these marauders might check the evil', remembering that no declaration of martial law protected his men.[21]

One of the clashes between troops and recalcitrant Santals in 1856 was described—uniquely—by Naib-Rissaldar Gooman Singh of the 2nd Irregular Cavalry. Singh, a veteran of Arracan in 1824–25, the second Anglo-Sikh war and the Kohat campaign of 1851, received the Indian Order of Merit for capturing a large party of recalcitrant Santals in January 1856. He told his officer how he led a party of sowars against Santals, attacking Kuknee, a village about 14 miles north-west of Noni Haut. Singh's words, recorded and forwarded by his European officer, comprises the only account of action against the Santals by an Indian soldier:

> I was on duty at Kuknee with twenty-five sowars … The Sonthals came to loot some villages. The villagers came to complain … I took a Dafadar and ten sowars and … found the Sonthals in the act of looting a village, they were all armed … I surrounded them and called upon them to give up their arms and said I have got a number of sowars, if you don't do so I will kill you all. They gave up their arms and after securing the prisoners I gave back the stolen property to the villagers and marched the prisoners off to Kuknee. I reported the circumstance, among the prisoners were six *sardars*. For this service I was thanked by Government.[22]

Gooman Singh's words are prosaic, almost purely descriptive, but they suggest the professionalism of the troops employed against the Santals, in his decisive action in surrounding a large group of Santals with a few sowars, and his calculated use of violence: Singh threatened to kill them if they did not comply. In a longer statement of his service, he described how in Kohat he had decapitated 'Hill men' on orders without compunction. Gooman Singh's unique statement explains the Company's military competence in the Hul.

These 'renegades' justified the continuation of what was called in January 1856 the 'Sooree Field Force' under George Burney—surprising, given his pusillanimous command in August, but perhaps Halliday was happy to have an officer prepared to accept civil officials' presumptions. Did this wave of unrest suggest that the impulse to rebellion was not quite exhausted? In late January, a band of about 200 Santals burned an indigo factory at Sangrampore; they were 'dispersed' by a party of the Bhaugulpore Hill Rangers, now under new British officers. In the fight eleven Rangers were wounded by arrows and they killed 31 Santals, fulfilling the confidence of those who had argued that the corps should remain.[23] Though they remained loyal to the Company in 1857, the Rangers were disbanded in 1858, subsumed into a new police force. A senior official attributed the arson to 'evil disposed persons' using Santal refugees to cover a crime. Further isolated incidents convinced officials that they did not herald a renewed outbreak, but that Santals were 'evincing a manifest disposition to settle down ... seeking employment of the Roads and other Public Works', including the railway, now being finished.[24]

Officers continued to report 'outrages', repeating the dours they had undertaken during the rebellion, stalking and pursuing parties, 'dispersing' them, collecting weapons and plunder and counting bodies. But when returning from such an encounter Lieutenant Henry Gordon of the 63rd also noticed that the Santal villages through which his men passed 'had all the appearance of having quietly settled down' and dismissed the fears of alarmed Bengali neighbours, understandable in the circumstances, as 'very much exaggerated'.[25] Occasional incidents by 'destitute' Santal 'marauders' did not affect the trend towards peace. By January 1857 local officials reported 'no intelligence of outrages committed by Sonthals since the month of June last'. Frederick Halliday could rightly conclude that 'the pacification of the lately disturbed districts may now be considered complete'.[26]

'Yule's rules': George Yule and the creation of the Santal Parganas

There remained the question of how the districts affected by the Hul should now be governed. The most far-reaching of its results was the

17. The Marquess of Dalhousie, Governor-General of British India 1849–56. Though formally responsible for the suppression of the Hul, he was convalescent in the Nilgiri Hills throughout it, claiming '*I* had nothing to do with the whole business'. (Colesworthy Grant, *An Anglo-Indian Domestic Sketch*)

18. Sir Frederick Halliday, Lieutenant-Governor of Bengal, whose officials directed the civil side of the suppression of the Hul. Halliday at first dismissed the Hul as a local rising and then resisted calls for the imposition of martial law. (Charles Buckland, *Bengal Under the Lieutenant-Governors*)

19. Three Santal prisoners under the guard of a chuprassie (right), based on an engraving by Walter Sherwill. These men were likely to suffer months of hardship in crowded and unhealthy makeshift jails. (*Illustrated London News*, 28 February 1856)

20. Railway employees drilling, possibly to serve as 'bildars', also depicted by Walter Sherwill. While these men worked for railway construction contractors, the auxiliaries led by Serjeant Gillon would have appeared similarly. (*Illustrated London News*, 28 February 1856)

21. Sepoys, members of a regiment of Bengal Native Infantry, drawn by an engineer officer who plainly admired them. Though depicted in their tight and uncomfortable dress uniforms, from day-to-day sepoys would usually wear sandals, donning their heavy leather shakos as little as possible. (*Illustrated London News,* 4 April 1846)

22. Each regiment's officers and men employed dozens of private and public 'followers', including 'bhisties' such as this man, who carried water in a goat-skin 'mussick'. (John Capper, *The Three Presidencies of India*)

23. A clash between sepoys of the 40th Native Infantry and Santals, probably depicting the fight at Bissohuwa on 1 August, which Sherwill witnessed. He or the engraver gave the Santals a distinctively heroic cast. (*Illustrated London News*, 28 February 1856)

24. An assistant magistrate's bungalow in Lower Bengal, the focus of the Company's power locally, depicted by Colesworthy Grant, an itinerant artist who recorded *Rural Life in Bengal*. Most of the junior civil officials in the 'disturbed districts' lived and worked in bungalows like these.

25. The steamer *Mirzapore*, from Colesworthy Grant's *Rural Life in Bengal*. River steamers like this enabled Company forces to move men, supplies and messages swiftly on the navigable rivers Ganges and Bhagirutty on the Hul's northern and eastern periphery.

26. Elephant transport, from Michael Rafter's *Our Indian Army*, a scene suggesting the bustle in a native infantry camp as sepoys, followers, coolies and hangers-on prepared to march. The Company's forces used hundreds of elephants. Had the Santals attacked the Field Force's supply columns they could have prolonged their resistance.

27. A 'sagger'—one of the ramshackle bullock carts that Santals impressed to carry food and plunder—from Capper's *Three Presidencies*. Company troops seized hundreds in 'drives' in the Hul's final months. The distinctive roofs of the houses in the background can still be seen in the Santal country.

28. An advertisement in the Calcutta *Citizen* in 1855 announcing the scheduled services on the East Indian railway between Howrah and Raneegunge, a reminder of the advantage that steam-powered transport gave to Company forces.

29. Sidhu Manji depicted by Walter Sherwill after his capture. Sherwill, or the engraver who prepared the image for publication, gave Sidhu a curiously penitent expression, though his assertive demeanour when interrogated was anything but submissive. (*Illustrated London News*, 28 February 1856)

30. Singra, the alleged murderer of Miss Pell, depicted as a defiant prisoner. (*Illustrated London News*, 28 February 1856)

31. The 'martello tower' at Pakur, Jharkhand, today. It is located in a memorial park, now fallen into disrepair, named in honour of Sido and Kanhu. (Peter Stanley)

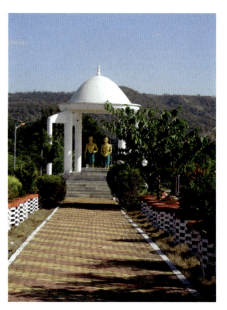

32. The major memorial to the Hul at Bhagnadihi, Jharkhand, the most extensive of dozens of village memorials to the heroes of the Hul located throughout the Rajmahal Hills. It is practically on the site of the 'Thackoor' which sustained the Hul, at the house of the four brothers of Bhugnadihee. (Peter Stanley)

creation of what was called the Santal Parganas, a new district carved out of Bhaugulpore and Beerbhoom, covering essentially the area of the Damin and the purgunnahs which Santal die-hards had held in December 1855. Halliday's officials, anticipating the rebellion's end, prepared legislation to enact the new province, which came into existence a fortnight after martial law ended.

An investigation by the Judicial Department at East India House in 1856 revealed profound deficiencies in the way the Santals had been governed. James Pontet came under censure as 'wanting in the capacity and energy needed to meet and overcome the difficulties of his position'. He lost the temporary promotion he had gained during the insurrection and received 'more limited duties'. Conveniently, perhaps, the man largely blamed for allowing the oppression of the Santals to continue for so long was George Brown, the disgraced commissioner of Bhaugulpore. He had been the 'controlling authority' in the district for nearly twenty years and should, so the London officials considered, have noticed and rectified the mahajans' abuse, and especially heeded the Santal's grievances. Had he done so, 'it seems very probable that the insurrection would never have occurred'; except that the deeper effects of Companys' rule, especially the impositions of landlords and money-lenders, would have persisted.[27]

One of the key conclusions of the Company's 1856 investigation was that the nature of Santal culture or rather what its authors thought of as the Santals' inherent character, made them unfitted to survive in Bengal's 'Regulation system' and that they required a regime 'more in accordance with the habits and notions of a simple people'.[28] This justified an idea already advanced in Calcutta, that the Santals required a particular mode of government. The crucial difference between the region's civil administration before and after the insurrection was that the Santal Parganas was to be a 'non-regulation province'. The essence of the new arrangement was that Santals would no longer be subject to the complex 'regulation' Bengal judicial code, only simple rules, suitable for such a supposedly unsophisticated people. An unknown hand annotated the Board's copy of this minute, ironically deploring the tendency to 'reduce every thing ... to the European standard'.

Like so much in the Company's conduct in suppressing Santal unrest, the creation of a non-regulation province echoed the response to the Kol rebellion of 1832. That rebellion had led to the creation of a new administrative sub-division—the South-Western Frontier Agency—and officials saw in it a model for governing the Santal country. 'Our system of administration in the old Bengal districts', Halliday belatedly acknowledged, was 'totally unsuited to the character and habits' of the Santals. He professed to remaining uncertain of exactly what had provoked the insurrection, despite much advice and speculation, but from the testimony of captive Santals he believed that 'the whole disturbance was ultimately owing to the want of some immediate … paternal means of conciliation between the Santals and Mahajuns'.[29]

Central to the new system was the idea of direct, personal rule. The *Friend of India*, whose editor seems to have swung from demanding the deportation of all Santals to advocating a regime avoiding the excesses that had provoked rebellion, called for 'a new Cleveland'. Meredith Townsend advocated a man who could 'unite to soldierly activity and nerve, great calmness of judgment and immoveable tenacity of purpose'.[30] Robert Carstairs, one of several officials who fell in love with the Santals, concisely explained that the difference between Regulation and non-Regulation provinces was that in one 'machine dominates; in non-Regulation, man'.[31] In the Santal Parganas that man was George Yule, the eldest of three brothers who served British India. His *Rules for Civil Procedure in the Sonthal Parganas* famously numbered only 33, covering just seven pages of foolscap in print, an extraordinary achievement in an administrative culture comfortable with voluminous and detailed regulation. Their essence was that the new commissioner and his assistants would forge a personal relationship with the people in their divisions, removing the corrupt court functionaries and repudiating the complex, expensive and inflexible processes that had contributed to the Santals' oppression. The 'Sonthal Police Rules' that Yule proclaimed late in 1856 were even simpler, just 19, making clear that 'the Assistant Commissioner will visit every village sooner or later' and stressed that the village chowkidar was 'a village not a zemindar servant'.[32] 'Yule's Rules' were actually drafted by Ashley Eden, but he soon left on sick leave and Yule implemented and refined them. Yule's rules gradually became diluted by the adoption of provincial laws (for example, the

Indian Penal Code in 1862) but for the following several decades the spirit of the new regime prevailed, perpetuated by officials who for years administered in the direct and personal manner that the founders of the Santal Parganas had deemed necessary.

A commissioner and four deputies, with another four assistants, constituted the 'hakims'—givers of orders, running the new province from cutcherries in Dumka (the head station), Godda, Rajmahal and Deoghur. Under the new system Santal prisoners awaiting trial were swiftly dealt with. Augustus Rivers Thompson, Eden's successor, kept them under guard in large enclosures rather than in unhealthy cells, and he tried them robustly, releasing all but the most clearly guilty. The 'hakims', Robert Carstairs explained, largely 'did their work without written rules': 'Justice was informal. There was no distinction between civil and criminal Courts ... no lawyers, clerks or process-servers; no fees'—the oppression that had provoked rebellion diminished.[33] The key figure in the new relationship became not so much the European administrator but the village manjee— paradoxically, the leaders who had been instrumental in leading Santals to rebellion. Yule saw the wisdom of strengthening rather than destroying traditional village authority, and manjees became the agents of local administration—revenue—and justice rather than the victims or enemies of it. Yule was soon drafted away from the Santal Parganas, becoming chief commissioner in Oudh, the centre of civil rebellion in 1857, but his system essentially survived, maintained by successors who imperfectly resisted the encroachment of the paperwork inescapable in Indian administration.

No one thought that regular troops were the best way to deal with Santal resistance after 1855. The Bengal government's answer was to raise an effective police force.[34] Santal bands that continued to prey upon both Santal and Bengali communities were, it seems, not motivated by Santal identity or any devotion to the vision vouchsafed by the Thakur to Sidhu and Kanhu, but shaded into everyday dacoity. As the observant William Gordon noted, Santal marauders were now 'obliged to plunder to live'.[35] The old Mofussil Police darogahs who by their apathy, greed and oppression, had helped to provoke the rebellion could not remain. John Peter Grant denounced them as 'absolutely useless ... notoriously a set of cowardly rogues', and while individual darogahs had behaved well, the local police had clearly failed.[36] A few notable darogahs received rewards: Jeehoo Manjhee, for example, received a sword 'for services on several occasions during the insurrection', but the old force was disbanded in May 1858.[37]

William Elliott urged that its successor be recruited from 'up country men', located in large detachments and moved about the region to preclude fostering either enmity, which was likely to exacerbate oppression, or friendship, which could lead to corruption.[38] Early in 1856 Thomas Rattray, who had commanded the Ramghur Horse on the Grand Trunk Road, was already enrolling a force of 'foreigners'—Sikhs from the Punjab, many former soldiers of the defeated Sikh Khalsa.[39] In a typical case of official confusion, Rattray recruited the wrong number of Punjabi sowars on mistaken pay scales, an error requiring the intervention of the new Governor-General, Lord Canning.[40] By 1861 over a thousand military police were stationed across the Santal Parganas.[41] Replacing the oppressive darogahs and burkendazes in the villages also entailed empowering village manjees as local officials. 'Bringing the village Manjee ... into immediate contact with the European officer' became one of the corner-stones of the non-regulation system.[42] Though new, the Santal Parganas survived the disruption that shook British Bengal in 1857.

'Given to the missionaries': changes after 1856

Even while the insurrection continued, officials considered how to prevent a recurrence. Frederick Halliday wanted roads built, and by enforced Santal labour. Under this plan, Santals would 'work out their own subjugation ... the consequence of their present offence ... rendered long and painfully memorable'.[43] William Elliott, as well as conscripting Santal labourers, essayed some primitive propaganda, showing Santals 'two very spirited engravings' depicting the advantages of roads as the route to prosperity and peace.[44]

In the aftermath of the rebellion the Annual Military Statements, the Bengal Army's budget, included a sum for 'opening up roads through the Suntal Country'.[45] Hungerford Boddam, who had struggled to transport his rockets over the execrable tracks from Sooree, was given the job of making them into roads. In modest investments in public works, the Bengal government also constructed grain stores, contributed Rs 1500 to plant crops while by the end of 1857 the railway reached Rajmahal, directly employing Santals and bringing development to the region. Railway contractors sought compensation from the Bengal government for damage inflicted on the unfinished line, but the Company refused to meet the cost of 'private losses', on a line on which its investors were guaranteed a profit anyway. The collieries at Raneegunge also continued to attract Santals seeking a cash income.

The insurrection also brought changes which worsened the condition of some Santals, such as in the permanent alienation of land to zamindars, who appropriated farms apparently abandoned by Santals, refusing to give them up after their owners returned, a stance accepted by Alfred Bidwell, now commissioner in Bhaugulpore.[46] Indeed, petitions received by the commissioner of the newly established Santal Parganas late in 1856 might have suggested that little had changed. Petitions from 'certain Sonthals' complained of 'oppressive treatment by the zamindars' and appealed for relief from the exactions of revenue. A deputy commissioner ruled that the petitioner had 'no reasonable ground of complaint', secure in the conviction that rejection would not provoke rebellion among a chastened and exhausted people.[47]

The *Bucks Herald*, describing events in India for the newspaper readers of Aylesbury, explained just before the insurrection was eclipsed by more momentous events that the Santals, lately so rebellious, were now to be 'given to the missionaries'. The Santals had 'excited strong sympathy' among evangelicals in Britain, and Christian fervor allied with the Bengal government's desire for a tractable population, gave missionaries a much greater role in the new Santal Parganas.[48] The evangelical *Church Missionary Papers* admitted that beyond the desirability of saving Santal souls for Christ, there was 'the necessity of permanently tranquilizing the Santhals'.[49] Evangelical needs coincided with the Company's desire for tractability.

Though still preyed upon by absentee landlords and money lenders, under a more benign administrative and legal regime, with greater autonomy over village affairs, able to work on the railways, in the collieries of Raneegunge or in tea gardens, Santals arguably had an easier time after 1855. While it is hardly true, as Bradley-Birt claimed in 1905, that they were 'blissfully content', and still less that they lived in 'the manner of life that has passed changeless through the centuries', the Santals of the Santal Parganas at least enjoyed better lives than fifty years before.[50] But in his memoir, Chotrae Desmanjhi emphasised the irony of the change in the Santals' economic situation: 'for hunger, we Santals who set out to rule ourselves, [then] attached ourselves by the hundreds to the Deko for our living'.[51]

Between 1859 and 1862 Bengal's indigo industry was wracked by conflict between indigo planters and those growing the crop, often under duress, some of whom were Santals. Remarkably, despite the destruction of factories in the rebellion, neither the Santals nor the rebellion figured in the Bengal government's investigation, though missionaries, who supported the oppressed indigo cultivators, thought that the Hul had fostered 'independent habits' among the peasants.[52] Even so, and perhaps understandably given the devastation of 1855, they 'remained a suspicious people, with constant under-current of unrest', coming close to further threatened outbreaks: in 1861–62; in the 'Santal Excitement' of 1871–72; in 1881 and 1891; and periodically into the twentieth century. No further Hul occurred, but the Company's raj ended following mutinies among the sepoys who had suppressed it.

'One great powder magazine': 1857

When Lord Canning arrived in Calcutta on 29 February 1856, men of the 2nd Grenadiers and the 31st, as well as the Governor-General's Bodyguard, formed the 'streets of Troops' leading from Chandpal Ghat to Government House.[53] Though Canning had famously warned that in India trouble could appear as a cloud smaller than a man's hand, he surely little suspected that the great challenge of his life would come from some of these men. In the Hul the sepoys had done well—an officer, probably Anthony Lister of the 63rd, described his men as 'covered with muck and glory'.[54] An admiring civilian praised them for the 'alacrity with which they obey[ed] their officers … their steadiness and patience after long and harassing [dours]'.[55] Not so some of their elderly European officers. Newspapers delicately alluded to the 'incapacity and indecision' of a major commanding a regiment in the southern force.[56] This, it seems, was John Nembhard of the 56th, who died at Bowsee in March 1856, and who had probably been terminally ill during the campaign. But the native infantry performed well in the last active campaign the old Bengal Army fought before it destroyed itself in the mutiny-rebellion of 1857. In his valedictory address, distributed from his camp at Ferozepore, in the Punjab on New Year's Eve, Sir William Gomm, in his customarily colourless way, praised the 'efficient manner which the native troops of the presidency engaged in the suppression of the late Sonthal revolt'.[57] He was replaced by another elderly Queen's officer, Major-General George Anson, whom Kendal Coghill soon decried as 'Old Bitters'.[58] A 'slow coach' who disliked sepoys (the bulk of his army), his fussy and indecisive ways would be exposed in May 1857, but he died within days of the outbreak of the great mutiny.

'Punjabee', who had denounced the Bengal government's conduct of the Hul in the *Friend of India*, warned in November 1855 how the Santal rebellion provided a portent; that 'British India is, as it were, one great powder magazine, to be ignited by one spark of successful treason'.[59] In 1857 that spark brought a conflagration dwarfing the Santal Hul. While most of the native corps of the Bengal Army broke into mutiny and precipitated widespread civil insurrection in the Ganges valley and Central India, the Santal Parganas remained largely undisturbed except for the mutiny of the 32nd Native Infantry at Deoghur and the 5th Irregular Cavalry at Rohini. Calcutta correspondents, afflicted by panic, inevitably heard rumours that in Beerbhoom, 'the Santals have been committing great depredations'.[60] In fact, the Santal Parganas and neighbouring Santal districts remained quiet. The historian of Jharkhand in 1857 found that in contrast to the Ganges valley, where mutiny sparked civil rebellion, in the Santal Parganas 'the violence and plundering ... of the insurgents alienated the civil population'.[61] Apart from isolated incidents, in which local landholders incited Santals to violence, the area affected by the 1855 Hul remained largely unaffected. Indeed, George Yule called for the formation of a 'Regiment of Santhals', vouching for their 'fidelity, honesty and many good qualities'; and this less than two years after the insurrection.[62] Five hundred Santal auxiliaries were enlisted.[63]

Although the *Friend of India* had asserted that 'the Sonthal will not be speedily forgotten in England', the magnitude of 1857 ensured that that was exactly what happened.[64] The mutiny-rebellion of 1857 was so vast it pushed the Santal rebellion out of memory. Had the 1857 mutiny-rebellion not occurred, the Santal insurrection might have been the most significant insurrection under Company rule.

Most of the sepoys who had suppressed the Hul joined and died in the mutiny, but it is worth noticing that while only eight of the Bengal line's 74 infantry regiments did not break into mutiny, of these eight which remained loyal to the Company, no fewer than four (the 13th, 31st, 42nd and 63rd) had served against the Santals. At Lucknow, sepoys of the 13th 'greatly lamented' the death of Major Charles Bruere, who had commanded them throughout the Hul.[65] In the siege of Lucknow, men of the 13th who helped to defend Lucknow were awarded 109 stars of the Indian Order of Merit, all veterans of the Santal rebellion. Their loyalty perhaps stemmed from fellow feeling fostered in the jungle of Bhaugulpore.[66] The 31st was now commanded by William Hampton, who had not only served with it in the Kol and Santal rebellions, but was married to a Hindu; did his long service with the regiment and familiarity with Indians deter mutiny? At Berhampore, though the 63rd under the command of James Phillips, with Hugh Pester one of two other captains on duty, was disarmed, it was retained and re-numbered in the reorganisation of the Bengal Army, becoming the 9th Bengal Infantry.[67] Even at Dinapore, where the 7th Native Infantry mutinied, a hundred of its sepoys remained loyal to the Company. (Tragically, most were bayonetted by enraged British troops after the first attempt to relieve the besieged station of Arrah failed with heavy British losses.[68])

Sowars of the 2nd Irregular Cavalry, the Ramghur Irregular Cavalry and of course the Governor-General's Bodyguard also remained faithful to the Company, though not the 11th Irregular Cavalry, which had also served in the insurrection. It was disarmed and unhorsed at Berhampore and not re-formed after the mutiny. But that nearly half of the Field Force's infantry and two-thirds of its cavalry did not mutiny, suggests that the shared bonds of arduous campaigning recently may have helped to dissuade their men from taking drastic action. It is possible that the experience of sharing the hardships of the Santal campaign helped to diminish the alienation that brought the great majority of the Bengal Army's regular infantry regiments to repudiate their oaths and even kill their officers.

But most of the sepoys involved in the suppression of the Santal insurrection mutinied and joined the rebels in 1857. Of the ten regiments that served in the Hul, men of the 2nd, 7th, 40th, 42nd, 50th, and 56th joined the mutiny. It was a sepoy of the 2nd Grenadiers at Barrackpore who famously (if apocryphally) expressed horror at a coolie telling him that because of the introduction of unclean greased cartridges he would lose his caste. The 56th, at Cawnpore, mutinied in June and besieged Hugh Wheeler's entrenchment, taking part in the massacre at the Satchi Chowra Ghat and killing their own officers and their families.[69] But even the regiments which mutinied largely maintained their discipline. Two of the three regiments of the Dinapore Brigade that mutinied in July 1857, the 7th and 40th, had served in Lloyd's force. A European described them as fighting as a disciplined body, at Lucknow and then again around Shahabad, withdrawing in 'good order' and giving 'much trouble' to the no fewer than nine British columns that chased them around Behar until the survivors dispersed to flee to their homes.[70] Perhaps the most startling evidence comes in the lithograph based on the descriptions of the relieved garrison of Arrah, which depicts the sepoys besieging the building in full uniform, lined up in company columns, with their colours, as if on parade.[71] All but 50 of the 42nd mutinied at Saugor but it was nevertheless reconstituted. Oddly, only part of the 50th also mutinied at Nagode and though they spared their officers and 250 remained loyal, it was still disbanded.[72]

1857 saw both acts of great courage but also startling incompetence by Company officers. Ironically, in the light of his success in 1855, one of greatest casualties in reputation in 1857 was George Lloyd. Sir William Gomm had commended Lloyd in 1855 in his farewell general order, mentioning Lloyd with 'special pleasure'. His entry in the Service Army List recorded the 'ability and energy he has shown' and his 'great skill and intelligence'.[73] In 1857, Lloyd was again at Dinapore commanding the station and his division. He could not believe that the three Native Infantry regiments there, including the 7th and the 40th, would mutiny, and both failed to disarm them and acted so incompetently that he attracted derision at the time and since. In fulminating on 'Military Blundering in India', *The Times* damned his 'age, incapacity and gouty legs' and approved of his dismissal.[74] George Malleson's short *History of the Indian Mutiny* excoriated Lloyd, portraying him as having 'completely lost his head', giving way to 'panic'.[75] Lloyd was widely reviled. John Blackett, a young railway engineer who had spent much of 1857 sheltering in the fort at Agra wrote to his family decrying the lamentable lack of initiative and energy that 'the old colonels' had displayed during the mutiny/ rebellion. They were 'just old fools who had lived among the Niggers and been bamboozled by them'. Chief among these was Lloyd: 'he was … warned but all to no purpose'.[76] How do we reconcile Lloyd's energy and success in 1855 with his apathy and failure in 1857, just 18 months later? How and why did this happen? Perhaps Lloyd did not devise the plan for the suppression of the Hul. The reasons for the mutiny of the native army of Bengal is one of the central questions in the military history of British India and indeed, given the significance of the rebellion it precipitated, one of the great questions in the wider history of India. The causes of the outbreaks that flared across the Ganges valley and into the Punjab in the summer of 1857 were the subject of speculation at the time, and have been investigated by historians seeking answers ever since. The conduct of both sepoys and their European officers in 1855 and its consequences forms a small part of that perennial problem in British India's history.

'The extraordinary hold': remembering the Hul

The story of the Hul, the missionary W.J. Culshaw, who spent years in the Santal Parganas, acknowledged that the rebellion remained 'part and parcel of the consciousness of Santals everywhere', who remembered the Hul of 1855 through their rich oral and song culture.[77] William Archer, one of the anthropologists who did much to document their changing culture in the early twentieth century, recorded a number of 'Santal Rebellion Songs', notably:

> Sidhu, why are you bathed in blood?
> Kanhu, why do you cry Hul, Hul?

For our people we have bathed in blood
For the trader thieves
Have robbed our land.[78]

Robert Carstairs's 1935 novel, *Harma's Village*, was translated into Santali (now with a script) within a decade and was read avidly; 'its popularity testifies to the extraordinary hold which the Hul still has on the Santal mind', as W.J. Culshaw observed.[79]

Santals who remembered the Hul did not necessarily endorse it. Two of the Santal witnesses whose memoirs were recorded explicitly condemned Sidhu and Kanhu for the devastation that the Hul brought to the Santals. Durga Tudu, probably speaking in the 1890s, made the most strident criticism:

> They only caused others' lives to be destroyed. That is not right ... Not even for one day were they kings, or not even for one year did they collect rents. They only caused the lives of other people to be lost ...[80]

While Jugia Haram also reviled Sidhu and Kanhu's 'mad plans' and condemned the 'cruel and deceitful boastings' which had brought the Santal people to ruin, in the twentieth century, as part of the growth of the 'Freedom movement', they acquired the status of folk heroes. Even in defeat, Santal insurgents, Ranjan Gupta, the authority on Beerbhoom's economic history, declared, 'left behind a glorious record of heroism and militancy'.[81] The brothers were appropriated by the nationalist movement as pioneering heroes of the freedom struggle. As much as it was noticed by nationalist historians, the Santal rebellion was conscripted into the epic of the freedom struggle, though without paying much attention to the details. Arun Chowdhury, who translated and published Chakraborti's *History of the Santal Hool* in English, wrote that 'the revolt of the Santals were such an awe-inspiring look as to thrush the British rulers into a quagmire' [sic].[82] Today, statues of the brothers of Bhugnadihee adorn the entrances or main squares of many towns and villages in Jharkhand: appropriated afresh as symbols of Santal identity.

'History of the Santal Hool': the history of the history

Paradoxically, the overwhelming neglect of the Hul in Indian history cannot be ascribed to a lack of published accounts. The first substantive analysis of the rebellion came within weeks of its end. The influential *Calcutta Review*, established by John Kaye in 1844, had become the premier organ of a community notably devoted to debating the issues of the day in British India by publishing lengthy, not to say portentous, articles by anonymous authors, each prompted by a recent publication. The occasion for Article VII in the March 1856 issue were articles on the rebellion published in the *Friend of India* in 1855, and Walter Sherwill's report of his tour of the Damin in 1851.[83] These pieces formed merely the springboard for the author to express opinions he had formed over the previous nine months. In the manner of *Review* articles, the article opened sententiously, with a ten-page disquisition on 'the dreadful state of society and morals in the Roman world' before the empire's adoption of Christianity. At length, the author reached the Santals, through comparisons with Spartan helots, Sicilian slaves, Norman serfs via the Highland clans of Scotland and 'predatory tribes' of Central India. He paraphrased and quoted Sherwill's 1851 report, offering a potted history of the Santals since their migration to the Damin. The *Calcutta Review* article established the canonical version of the rebellion.

Edward Man, another of the district officers entranced by the Santals, met many survivors of the Hul in the decade after, and in 1867 published *Sonthalia and the Sonthals*, a work of amateur ethnography (he speculated that the Santals had descended variously from the ancient Egyptians, Greeks or Israelites) but who at least listened to Santals who had survived the rebellion. On the origins of the rebellion, he gave 'the opinion of the Sonthals on it ... inferred from their chance expressions and desultory conversation', sometimes when they were drunk—their circumspection a result of their fear of repercussions, perhaps.[84] The resulting 'scraps' he 'jotted down ... after a hard day's work in Cutcherry' included their reminiscences of it, even if he got its years wrong. Though patronising and often fundamentally wrong, Man at least listened to individual Santals (and Bengalis), but essentially confirmed the *Calcutta Review*'s analysis of an unsophisticated people goaded by landlords' and mahajans' oppression into revolt and defeated by force, though now protected by the benevolent regime devised by Ashley Eden (Man's particular hero) and codified by George Yule.

A year later, a second substantial account of the Santal rebellion appeared, in William Hunter's *The Annals of Rural Bengal*. Hunter, a protégé of Cecil Beadon, had become interested in the history of Bengal's peasants, and specifically its Santal population, while serving as an assistant magistrate in Beerbhoom from 1862. The epitome of an antiquarian researcher, he drew on 'worm-eaten manuscripts' in English, Bengal and Persian in repositories in Sooree, Calcutta and London, and on his observations as a working district official. Hunter offered observations on Santal culture, religion and language and his book included a 20-page account of the Hul, based on, but also elaborating on *Calcutta Review*'s anonymous article, in which he quoted Vincent Jervis's recollections which presented the rebellion's suppression as 'not war', but 'execution', a view confirmed by Lewis O'Malley's volume on the Santal Parganas in the *Imperial Gazetteer*.

All of these accounts understandably concentrated on the Santals. It has to be said that the Bengal Army, traumatised and virtually destroyed by the 1857 mutinies, did not much remember the Santal campaign. Few of the regiments that survived 1857 published histories: the 31st's successor, the 2nd Queen's Own Rajput Light Infantry, devoted just two short paragraphs to the rebellion in its brief, 20-odd page history, published in 1872. The disbandment of most regiments after 1857 and the absence of British troops in 1855 ensured its victors made little effort to document the conflict.

Among Santals, stories of the Hul seem to have been told through their vigorous song culture, though little of it has survived in English. In Bengali, one account of the Hul was collected, though not published, by Digambar Chakraborti. Born in Pakur in 1849, he had little personal memory of 1855 but 'remembered vividly ... hearing the story numberless times'. A distant kinsman of the Pakaur Raj, educated at Krishanath College, Berhampore, he became a teacher at his old school, the Pakur Raj High School, and then a lawyer, one of the first in the Santal Parganas. In the mid-1890s, possibly at the suggestion of Robert Carstairs, Chakraborti collected memories of the rebellion and wrote in Bengali a history which, though used by Kali Kinkar Datta in 1940, for nearly a century remained in manuscript and untranslated. The significance of Chakraborti's history cannot be over-stated, because it remains the only account based on the memories of the insurrection's Bengali victims, with the author's connections (as both a lawyer and a relative of the rajah) giving him access to memories of the insurrection's effects on Bengalis, and during its crucial opening weeks.[85]

By the time Chakraborti had finished his history, the first stirrings of what became a 'freedom movement' could be detected in British India. In the great march to nationhood a failed 'tribal' uprising was largely neglected. When it was discussed, the Hul tended to be shaped to fit a nationalist narrative. In 1959, in introducing his name-sake's compilation of Santal folk tales, Pranab Chandra Roy Chaudhury praised the Santals of 1855 as 'pioneers in the struggle for India's freedom'.[86] Fifty years later, Bipan Chandra's 2009 *History of Modern India* was still representing the Hul as having 'revealed the potentialities of a popular uprising', supposedly.[87] Ramkrishna Mukherjee, for example, an orthodox Indian Marxist, attributed the Hul to 'the people's anger at colonial bondage'.[88] Tarapada Ray dedicated his *Santal Rebellion Documents* to 'immortal Sidhu [and] Kanu & all compatriots in the fight against imperialist and feudal oppression'. The tendency to associate the Hul with the struggle of India's peasants and workers found its apotheosis in Narahari Kaviraj's *Santal Village Community and the Santal Rebellion of 1855*. Kaviraj, a doctrinaire veteran of the Communist Party of India, at the age of 84 connected the Santal 'village community' to 'low-caste' popular resistance to imperialism. Jagdish Jha, in his pioneering study of the Kol rebellion, had already pointed to the problem that presenting tribal rebellions largely directed against Indian but non-tribal antagonists (as in the Kol and Santal rebellions) 'as part of the general freedom struggle against the British', had the effect of producing 'a lop-sided view'.[89] Like Datta, Kaviraj consulted only Judicial Proceedings, not military records, but his careful use of Company sources enabled him to enter into the life of Santal insurgents, using prisoners' 'confessions' to especially good effect. Kaviraj presented the Santals as under much greater unified command and 'government' than any other historian (indeed more than the evidence supports).

If the primary sources are abundant and the ethnographic literature on Santal culture also rich, the historical literature devoted to analysing the events of 1855 in detail is by contrast curiously thin. The current conventional view of the Santal rebellion is still based largely upon Kali Kinkar Datta's partial 1940 book. As recently as 1993 Sugata Bose, in his volume of the New Cambridge History of India, placed the Santal resistance in the context of 'solidarity of tribal social structures ... in the face of the economic incursions by outsiders'. He saw the Hul as 'a complex convergence or mingling of tribalism, religious communitarianism and class consciousness'.[90] Mainly Indian scholars have in recent decades investigated aspects of the rebellion, on women or sorcery in the rebellion, the power of the idea of a 'Thakur', virtually all published as scholarly articles.[91] The Indian studies invariably rely on Hunter or Datta or, at best, some of the Judicial Consultations available in the West Bengal State Archives. While all contributing to understanding, often opening up aspects on which this book in turn builds, none of them have used the full range of primary and archival sources available, and none of them deal centrally with the rebellion as an armed conflict. They perpetuate an understanding of the rebellion which this study revises, a new interpretation based on engagement with unused primary sources. For example, Atis Dasgupta's 2013 article argues that the rebellion was 'subdued by the cruel repression unleashed by the English rulers', a conclusion based on just four published sources, including Roy's *Santal Rebellion Documents*, Datta's 1940 book and Chakraborti's *History of the Santal Hool*. Saptarshi Sengupta and Pramila Lochan's 2013 article is based on a wider range of published sources, but virtually no primary sources, and it too accepts that the rebellion was 'ended by the British'.[92] Narahari Kaviraj's *Santal Village Community*, however skewed it may be by its Marxist assumptions, its valorisation of an imaginary Santal 'government' and its undue reliance on civil records, seems to not have been noticed as it deserves. A new study of the rebellion is both necessary and possible, offering revisionist interpretations: for example, contesting the idea that it was 'suppressed' militarily.

No formal history of the Hul using primary sources appeared until the mid-twentieth century.[93] The Berhampore-educated scholar Kali Kinkar Datta (1905–82) published in 1940 a book of about a hundred pages, *The Santal Insurrection of 1855–57*.[94] It drew largely on civil records in what became the West Bengal State Archives, but also on correspondence in the Records Rooms of district offices in Bhagalpur and Dumka, and Bengali documents, including Chakraborti's *History of the Santal Hool*. Datta's book—the first published book dedicated to the rebellion, though appearing 85 years after it—provided a valuable account of both the Hul's origins and spread, and of the British response, especially as it was reported by civil officials. Datta's account was firmly empirical: a biographical note in an online encyclopedia notes that he 'relied more on concrete evidences than abstract theorisation'.[95] While he drew on records now either lost or impossible to trace (including some Bengali sources, unobtainable for this study), Datta actually only dealt with events in northern Bhaugulpore district—he ignored events in Beerbhoom altogether. He almost exclusively used 'judicial', district records, and did not consult military records, perhaps unavailable to a Bengal-based researcher, nor the higher records of the Bengal and Indian governments and only a few newspapers. While his book seems to offer a history of the Hul it actually only deals with 'civil' aspects of it in part of one district. Sadly, Datta's imperfect account has seriously skewed the understanding of the Hul for 75 years.

The only two other books referring substantively to the insurrection took exactly the opposite approach to Datta. In *Elementary Aspects of Peasant Insurgency in Colonial India*, Ranajit Guha, the pioneer of the school of Subaltern Studies, included the Santal Hul in his study (actually more complex than elementary) of relations between rulers and ruled in nineteenth-century India. More directed at substantiating a Gramscian interpretation of Indian history than documenting the Hul as such, his *Elementary Aspects* is neither empirical nor indeed intelligible to non-believers in 'subalternity'. Guha also drew upon the civil records held in the West Bengal State Archives, but he also did not use any of the Military Consultations. While he sensibly cautioned his successors against simply accepting the words and prejudices of colonial officials, sadly, he remained what he described as 'a prisoner of empty abstractions'.[96]

Likewise, the author of the only other substantive book touching on the insurgency, Daniel Rycroft, who in 2006 published his *Representing Rebellion*, a book based on his University of Sussex PhD.[97] Rycroft concentrated on interpreting contemporary depictions of the

Hul, especially those published in the *Illustrated London News* in 1856, and, in severe contrast to Datta, did so unhelpfully in terms of post-modernist theory. His concentration was 'subaltern insurgency and its visual representation'. While useful in understanding how British readers saw the Hul through images, he unfortunately relied unduly on Datta's inadequate account (and the limited judicial records he quoted), and Guha's esoteric theorising. Rycroft's book is of limited value in interpreting the events of 1855. He was concerned not so much with the course, experience, consequences or memory of the Hul, but with the conditions under which various 'representations' had been created, disseminated and received, expressed in unfortunately opaque theoretical terms.

However, Rycroft's interest became part of a welcome engagement by historians with Santal communities, resulting in a series of meetings, conferences and films exploring Santal popular memory of the Hul and the ways in which it helped to preserve Santal culture, assailed as it was by both proselyting by Christian missions and the inroads made by the dominant Indian society in which Santals lived. Films such as *Hul Sangal: the Spirit of the Santal Revolution*, produced to mark the Hul's 150th anniversary, reveal how Santals revere Sidhu and Kanhu but without actually knowing much of what actually happened, with Adivasi activists understandably using the rebellion as a focus for contemporary politics.[98] This movement also produced academic articles mentioned above, including Atis Dasgupta's 'Some aspects of the Santal Rebellion of 1855–56' and Saptarshi Sengupta and Pramila Lochan's 2015 article, 'Santhal Rebellion—A Counter Insurgency against "Outsiders" as Ordained by a "Thakur"'.[99] Again, though, neither article drew fully upon the available contemporary military records.

A detailed understanding of the Hul remains elusive. Ferdinand Mount, who devoted several pages of his recent 640-page family saga, *The Tears of the Rajas*, to 'Robert [Low] and the Santals', which draws upon the Low and Dalhousie papers and the involvement of a subaltern of the Governor-General's Bodyguard in the suppression of the Hul.[100] Mount drew on the inadequate existing literature to endorse Vincent Jervis's judgment that 'it was not war …' 'No explanation for this curious change in behaviour appears in the official accounts', he concluded, though he, like every other author writing about the Hul, did not actually consult all the official records. The most recent scholarly investigation of Santal material culture, Anshul Avijit's 'Visual Culture of the Santals and their Image', acknowledges the centrality of the Hul but understandably decided that 'its details are not significant' to the thesis.[101] Positive signs of future scholarship are emerging, however. A two-day webinar hosted at Jadavpur University in Kolkata in June 2020, 'Revisiting Hul—The Santal Rebellion, 1855', saw younger scholars, including Santal researchers, focus on hitherto neglected Santal sources in remembering the Hul.[102]

Beyond the literature specifically on the Santals, the insurgency has been treated surprisingly neglectfully. Despite its massive death toll, the Hul has been either ignored or mentioned cursorily. It was accorded no entry in the 895-page *Encyclopedia of Nineteenth-Century Land Warfare*, by Byron Farwell (a specialist in British imperial war in India), nor mentioned in Saul David's recent *Victoria's Wars*, nor in Dierk Walter's recent synoptic (and otherwise insightful) *Colonial Violence*. Jeremy Black's 'global history' of *Insurgency and Counterinsurgency* does not mention it, or indeed any Indian rebellion besides 1857. The Hul continues to be neglected. Richard Gott's *Britain's Empire*, a study of 'resistance, repression and revolt' does devote several pages to an account of the rebellion, necessarily based on secondary sources often 75 years old and more (and offers inter-pretations revised by this book): at least he noticed it. Clearly, there is both a need and an opportunity for those interested in the nature of resistance to British imperialism in India to reconsider the Hul and especially to ask, as a question at the 2020 Jadavpur webinar put it, whether the Hul was unique and how it compared to other rebellions against Company and British colonial rule.

'Bush-fighting tactics': the Hul and counter-insurgency history

Many of the reports published in British newspapers in 1855 repro-duced a commentary from Bombay which, summarised developments to the middle of August and, foreseeing that the Santals would oblige Company forces to 'seek him out in his deadly and almost impenetra-ble jungle', anticipated that the Santals would 'adopt bush-fighting tactics'.[103] As this study makes clear, that is exactly what many Santals did, if inconsistently and ultimately unsuccessfully.[104]

The sources documenting the suppression of the Santal Hul also show that Company forces learned and applied lessons in what today would be called counter-insurgency warfare. Reports from Company officials in the field read like nuggets of hard-won experience in military manuals:

> A company may hold a village successfully but it cannot destroy the rebels ... The moment a body of them has emerged from the shade of the jungle, its retreat should be cut off, and not one rebel left alive ... This, however, cannot be effected without Cavalry.[105]

The Bengal Army's experience in 'bush-fighting' against the Santal insurgency would in fact not become a part of the history of counter-insurgency. To list books that do *not* mention the Santal rebellion would constitute virtually a bibliography of the global history of counter-insurgency. Military historians of India have likewise simply not noticed that the Bengal Army fought against Santal insurgents. It may have been thought, perhaps, that such a brief campaign revealed little either about how the Company's army responded to challenges to its rule, or about the development of counter-insurgency as it was seen in the mid-nineteenth century. Such a view would perpetuate European condescension toward the Santals as a 'savage' people, even though the Hul's British protagonists developed a growing respect for the Santals' qualities as fighters. This neglect unwittingly precluded serious examination of what the Hul might disclose.

As this study shows, not only did Santals invent and adapt their insurgency as they went along, but their opponents also devised strategies and tactics which anticipated many of the classic methods of colonial counter-insurgency warfare. Whatever lessons the Santal rebellion may have taught, they were not offered or picked up. Colonel Charles Callwell's *Small Wars: Their Principles and Practice* first appeared in 1896, by which time the Hul was beyond the recall of all but the oldest retired officer of the Bengal Army, which Field Marshal Frederick Roberts had in fact abolished the year before. Though replete with historical examples from conflicts in the Americas, Africa, Central Asia and New Zealand, as well as expeditions and risings on India's frontiers (north-east as well as north-west), neither

Moheshpore nor Koomerabad, and still less Nagore nor Peer Pointee figured in the clashes with which he illustrated his principles; not least because none of the rebellion's military participants had published a word about their experiences.

'The "learning of lessons"', Jeremy Black observed in introducing his 'global history' of insurgency and counterinsurgency, 'is very much part of the story'.[106] But it was not to be a part of the story of the Hul. The decisions and experience of Company officers remained unshared—they did not offer, and no one asked, and within two years mutiny had washed away their army. But that does not nullify their experience. The officers of the Sonthal Field Force evidently reflected on the tactical and practical problems they confronted in trying to suppress the Hul. They devised and tested expedients which would be familiar to officers facing insurgencies elsewhere, in Morocco, South Africa, Kenya, Indo-China, Malaya and many other places. They formed columns to engage Santal bands, tried to destroy their enemies' subsistence, learned to enter, live and fight in the Santals' jungle, formed lines of posts or patrols to direct or confine their adversaries' movements, gained mobility by using elephants and cavalry, used lightly-equipped auxiliaries, and tried to eliminate resistance by making 'drives' into Santal refuges. Not all of these tactics worked—the agile Santals could easily elude slow-moving infantry columns, and the 'drive' in late 1855 arguably succeeded only because Santal resistance had been sapped by starvation, disease and demoralisation. But the officers of the Bengal Army, who were widely believed to have been shown by the mutiny of their sepoys in 1857 to have been unprofessional and ineffective, arguably demonstrated in their final campaign that they were capable of responding flexibly and intelligently to taxing operational problems.

EPILOGUE

'A LITTLE WAR'

This book opens with an account of Walter Sherwill's visit to the valley of Burhyte in January 1850. In the first days of 2020 I too travelled to the valley, as part of a five-day circuit of places connected with the Hul. On a warm winter's afternoon I looked down from the same pass from which both Sherwill in 1850 and Walter Birch in 1855 had seen the valley. At what is now Bugnadee, visiting the Sidho-Kano memorial park (though it was locked), I met Mr Bajal Hansda, a teacher in what is now called Berhet and whose forebears included the brothers of Bhugnadihee. When I told him why I was visiting his village, he kissed my hand. The memory of the Hul lives.

As I had learned in exploring battlefields in other conflicts from other centuries and in other continents, paradoxically, little of the Hul could still be found. I was able to stand within a few hundred metres of where the brothers listened to the message of the Thakur, to visit the impressive hill-top cutcherry where George Brown made his misjudgments, and to identify the 'large tank' where Santals and elephant-borne sepoys of the 7th Native Infantry first confronted each other at Moheshpore. But at Peer Pointee and Nalhati I was unable to find where the Rangers were routed, or where Vincent Jervis besieged the Santals in the mud-brick house: the area of the fighting at Koomerabad has been lost—largely submerged with the construction of the Massenjore Dam on the Mor in the mid-1950s.

But visiting the Santal country became a vital part of the creation of this book. The Hul had been fought for a few months in many small, scattered places, by forces dressed in and using perishable organic materials (wood, cotton, wool, monkey-skin or leather; even iron corrodes)—any discarded material rotted in Bengal's soil long ago. Perhaps thousands of lead musket balls remain in the soil; for a time, to be discovered by Indian detectorists. Though India is rightly revered for the antiquity of its human story, the Hul involved people who were essentially new to the country over which the Hul was fought and who made little physical impact on it—both sepoys and Santals lived in huts made of mud, bamboo and grass, which dissolved with the monsoon. While they had made the country and its bongas their own, the Santals themselves had been settled in what were briefly the 'disturbed districts' for a few decades. The native infantry, both officers and men, were strangers to this country, sojourners for a few months, who disliked it, and within a couple of years most were dead. Even literate British officers, truly birds of passage, wrote almost nothing about their experience after 1855. Santal oral traditions preserved memories, but only for other Santals, and even they diminished over time. Today, the only human reminders of the Hul are the unexplained 'martello tower' in Pakur and statues of the brothers of Bhugnadihee erected in many villages in Jharkhand, though not in West Bengal or Bihar, states which do not value 'tribal' heritage as highly.

One of the most striking realisations the briefest visit imposes is just how much the country has changed; utterly, in almost every way. Intensive human settlement,including the overwhelming presence of non-Santals, the clearing of jungle, the planting of crops, the massive enlargement of towns and cities and pollution, notably the despolia-tion of plastic waste, has effaced pristine jungle, which human settle-ment almost everywhere except in the more remote stretches of the hills. The very roads which now permit the penetration of the Santal country barely existed 170 years ago: the country *sounds* different to the way it had; roads are rarely free of car horns and the calls of wild animals have almost entirely disappeared. But on quiet stretches of road in the Rajmahal Hills it is still just possible to stand and look at rice fields backed by jungle-clad hills to capture something of the feeling of the Santals who still live there, still distinctive in dress, architecture and physiognomy, toward the land for which they gave so much.

Visiting the places where the Hul happened powerfully informed the understanding on which this book is founded. Seeing the Santal country makes clear that it was not one environment but several. The flat plain of Bhaugulpore helps to explain why insurgents stayed away from George Brown's station after a few weeks of inchoate rage, while the equally flat fields and groves around Rampore Haut reveal how the Santals could always see the slow-moving, red-coated sepoys first. The hills of Pirpanti and the Rajmahal Hills themselves, some of which remain covered with the jungle in which the Santals made their homes, make explicable the Santals' ability to elude their pursuers. Reflecting on the events of 1855 in the Santals' country led to many useful insights, many of which became part of the manuscript on the spot. (I am writing this paragraph in the 'Abir Tee Stall' a few kilometres south of Nalhati, in country in which sepoys and Santals certainly faced each other during *Japut* in 1855.)

* * *

If tangible reminders of the Hul hardly exist, its intangible consequences are durable and discernable. The Hul ameliorated the system under which Santals were governed, though it did nothing to change British dominion over the sub-continent. Even though Santals continued to be oppressed and exploited individually, and indeed endured a further 90 years under colonial rule, the grosser abuses which had prompted the rising eased after 1855. How individual Santals fared in the aftermath of revolt remains to be assessed; that must be the subject of further work, perhaps by Santal authors. It seems from those who know the community much better than I ever will, that the Hul continues to permeate Santal consciousness and identity. I hope that this book will enable the events of 1855 to be understood in greater detail among that community especially, despite the handicap of its unavoidably Anglophone perspective, however balanced or inclusive I have tried to be.

If the Hul's impact on and meaning for Santals remains unclear to me, I can trace the fates of its European protagonists more readily.

Of the senior Company officials, Joseph Dorin left India soon after the 1857 rebellion, as did John Low, both by then enfeebled and reportedly, practically senile. As the former military member of the Supreme Council, Low especially faced criticism for his 'vacillation and pusillanimity' during the mutiny.[1] Sir Frederick Halliday gave up the position of lieutenant-governor in 1859, having earned no friends in Bengal, native or European. The *Hindoo Patriot* denounced his term as dominated by his 'selfishness, … intense meanness … insolent blunders, systematic insincerity and a number of hasty doings which it will take a quarter of a century to undo'.[2] The forceful John Peter Grant followed as lieutenant-governor and then became governor of Jamaica. William Grey, knighted, in turn became lieutenant governor in Bengal and also governor of Jamaica. Ashley Eden proved to be one of the rebellion's long-term winners. Though he had to take sick leave from his lucrative post as deputy commissioner in the Santal Parganas after only a few weeks, he returned to Bengal and rose steadily to become in 1877 lieutenant-governor.[3] A sycophantic biographer claimed that 'the speedy suppression of the [1855] rebellion was entirely due to Mr Eden's untiring efforts'.[4] The former indigo man-ager Edward Braddon, who became one of Yule's devoted assistant commissioners in the Santal Parganas, retired to Tasmania, where he became Premier and in time one of the progenitors of the Australian Commonwealth and the only civilian participant to write about the insurrection.[5] Frederick Middleton, a Queen's officer, published a ten-page memoir about Birch and Toogood's march to Burhyte, but only in 1893. The only Company military officer to write about it was Henry Norman, but his biographer devoted only two pages to Norman's recollections of the Hul, amounting to a few hundred words, regarding it as an unimportant episode in a distinguished career.[6] Few other district officers achieved the eminence of Ashley Eden, though as the nephew of a former governor-general he perhaps enjoyed an edge. Several retired as judges: George Loch, Octavius Toogood and Robert Richardson. But none, not even officials who did well during the Hul such as Alfred Bidwell or James Ward, appeared in Charles Buckland's *Dictionary of Indian Biography*. For a few, notably George Brown, the Hul ended their careers. James Pontet died two years after the Hul, 'brokenhearted'.[7]

The military officers who served against the Santals became caught up in the maelstrom of the sepoy mutinies and the rebellion that consumed the Bengal Army and north India. In the ensuing massacres, sieges and battles more than twenty officers of ten former Sonthal Field Force regiments died. They included three who died at Delhi, four at Lucknow and no fewer than nine killed at Cawnpore, including the gunner Burnett Ashburner, in the siege of General Wheeler's entrenchment or the massacre at the Satchi Chowra Ghat. The officers of the 56th suffered especially severely, with nine dying with their families, mainly at Cawnpore. A few won renown in 1857. Three out of the 25 Company officers awarded the Victoria Cross had served against the Santals: Robert Aitken and William Cubitt, both of the 13th and William Cafe of the 56th. Henry Norman who had distinguished himself in the Damin, served as a staff officer in 1857, becoming military secretary at the India Office and eventually governor of Queensland. Many of the survivors remained in the reconstructed Bengal Army and many retired as generals. *The Times* and other British newspapers recorded former officers' deaths, sometimes noting the curiosity that they had served in the Santal rebellion (and in the case of Major-General Bernard Cracroft, that he had been 'slightly wounded', though not mentioning in the buttocks).[8] Seemingly the last obituary was that of Major-General Archibald Campbell, formerly of the 31st, who died at 87 in 1921, almost certainly out-living all of the Santals who survived the rebellion and its aftermath. Walter Sherwill, after becoming professor of surveying, training Indians in surveying their own land, retired aged 46 in 1861, dying in Scotland in 1890.

Others fared poorly, including the two military officers who contributed most to the suppression of the Hul. Extraordinarily, George Atkinson, who had handled virtually every military communication relating to the rebellion was at the time of his death in Paris in 1859, on sick leave, worn out, still only third-from-the-bottom of the Bengal Engineers' list of captains. In the meantime, he had produced another two books of engravings, published posthumously, *The Campaign in India*, depicting events in the mutiny-rebellion, and *Indian Spices for English Tables*, a witty satire on the travails of a griffish 'Special Correspondent' arriving in India to report on the 1857 rebellion.[9] George Lloyd, disgraced after his ineffectual command at Dinapore, died in Darjeeling, the hill station he had founded, in 1865. As a whole, their sepoys, of course, suffered even more severely. With six of the ten regiments that had formed the Sonthal Field Force breaking into mutiny, virtually all of their members were either killed in battle or executed if captured, with the survivors living as fugitives, fearful of exposure.

The 1857 mutiny-rebellion overshadowed the Hul, and it was soon unfairly condemned in the words of one of its victors, Vincent Jervis: 'not war … execution'. First quoted by William Hunter in 1868 (with Jervis named in Lewis O'Malley's *Bengal District Gazetteer* account)—his epitaph has for over a century misled those seeking to understand the Santal rebellion. For all his sympathy towards those he had felt impelled to kill, Jervis did the Santals an unwitting disservice. Hundreds of Santals died directly by sepoys' muskets and bayonets, but they died to free their people from exploitation. And they did so by fighting 'a little war', but a war nevertheless. As this book shows, by chronicling and analysing the Hul in unprecedented detail using previously unused military sources, it is clear that the Santals had not merely been the victims of Company troops' retribution. They resorted to armed force deliberately, at the instigation of leaders who recognised the causes of their oppression and who acted to change their situation. They formulated aims and devised strategies and tactics, adapting to the terrifying and utterly new challenges of waging a guerrilla war. Certainly they failed, and arguably because the manner of insurgency they adopted could not sustain a people in revolt, but throughout the Hul they manifested agency, not passivity. The Hul did at times see execution, but it was also certainly a war, and deserves to be remembered as one.

Though lasting only six months, the Hul remained British India's largest armed rebellion besides the 1857 mutiny-rebellion. But, as Ranajit Guha and others have shown, it was only one of dozens of instances of resistance, on a spectrum ranging from refusal to pay taxes and general 'agrarian unrest' through persistent armed outbreaks, such as among the 'Moplahs' of the Malabar coast or the 'Kol' rebellion which provided a model for the suppression of the Santals. This study suggests the potential value of revisiting these and other insurgencies using the neglected sources which have informed it. As this book seeks to have shown, while indigenous sources offer vital perspectives, all the more valuable for their scarcity, the records of the colonial authorities offer complementary insights into the nature both of subaltern resistance and of suppression of it by colonial authorities. It would be premature to comment on how a detailed examination of the Santal Hul might revise the understanding of resistance across the sub-continent and across more than a century, but not to suggest the potential value of a series of such studies. I hope that *Hul! Hul!* might suggest a programme of such studies.

APPENDIX 1

GLOSSARY

Adjutant	usually a lieutenant, responsible to the commanding officer for the efficiency and discipline of a regiment; in the field, effectively its 'operations officer'
Amlah	an inferior functionary of a judicial court
Anna	a sixteenth part of a rupee
Bildar	an auxiliary soldier
Bonga	Santal deity
Brigade-major	the chief staff officer of a brigade; confusingly, usually a captain
Brigadier	in 1855 an appointment rather than a rank, and usually held by a colonel
Burkendaze	an armed constable under the command of a darogah
Bustee	slum, typically of crowded, temporary dwellings
Cantonment	a station housing troops, usually comprising both military and civil 'lines'
Captain	an officer usually in his thirties with perhaps a dozen years' military service, supposedly commanding a company, though in the Bengal Army sometimes a regiment
Chowkidar	a watchman

Chuprassie	a watchman or care-taker; identified by a 'chuprass' or badge
Collector	the most senior revenue-collecting civil official
Colonel	The most senior regimental rank, attained by seniority and often enabling the appointment as brigadier
Commissioner	a senior civil official, responsible for the judicial and civil rule of a district; sometimes applied to a senior official appointed to a particular role, such as when Alfred Bidwell was appointed 'Special Commissioner for the Suppression of the Sonthal Insurrection'
Company	a sub-unit of up to a hundred sepoys, nominally commanded by a captain
Coolie	a labourer; also 'cooley', etc.
Cutcherry	a magistrate's office or by extension any official administrative building; anything from a thatched bungalow to (in the case of Bhaugulpore) an imposing classical building
Dacoit	a bandit or robber, often a professional criminal
Darogah	a police constable, appointed to a 'thannah'
Dawk	also dak; the postal service; also an arrangement of guest bungalows for travellers
Dikkus	Santal term for 'foreigner' or 'outsider'; usually applied to Bengalis; also Dekus, etc.
Diwan	chancellor or steward to a ruler
Dour	literally a run; a military patrol, drive, foray or expedition
Duffadar	a native cavalry sergeant
Ensign	the most junior European commissioned rank; typically young men in their late teens new to India and to military service
Fauj	army

Ghatwal	a civilian watchman, especially over a 'ghat' or pass
Go-down	warehouse
Gossain	Supposedly a Santal 'priest'
Haut	a bazaar or market, as in Noni Haut, Rampore Haut, etc.
Havildar	a sergeant
Jemadar	the more junior of the two ranks of 'native officer' in regiments of Bengal native infantry; notionally twenty in each regiment
Lieutenant	the second-most junior European commissioned rank; typically young men in their twenties, often commanding a company or acting as adjutant of a regiment
Lieutenant-Colonel	the commander of a regiment; typically a man in his late 50s with upwards of thirty years of service
Magistrate	an official specifically exercising judicial responsibility in a district
Mahajan	a merchant or money-lender; often rendered 'mahajun'
Mahout	an elephant driver
Major	the second-in-command of an infantry regiment; typically a man in his forties
Major-General	the commander of a division
Manjee	in Santal culture, the usually hereditary leader of a village; co-opted from 1856 as an official of local administration
Mofussil	'up-country'; the provinces, as opposed to 'the Presidency' (Calcutta, for instance)
Moonsiff	the lowest grade of judicial officer, held by uncovenanted officers
Naik	a corporal
Ojha guru	literally a medicine man; a Santal healer
Palki	a litter, usually borne by four men, shortened from 'palankeen', formerly used for long journeys and supplanted by the horse-drawn 'palki-gharry'; also 'palkee'

Peon	variously an orderly or servant, or an armed guard
Purgannait	in Santal culture, the usually hereditary leader of a group of several villages
Perwannah	an official document; a certificate or a message
Purgannah	a sub-division of a district, also called a zillah
Rissaldar	a junior native officer of cavalry
Rooboocary	an official statement of legal proceedings, and by extension any report, summons or official document
Seer	a unit of weight of about 1.25 kilograms or 2.75 pounds
Shikar	hunting
Sickman	a sepoy sent to hospital
Soubah	a senior 'native' official; in 1855 referring to Santal leaders
Subadar	the senior 'native officer' in the native infantry, usually an older soldier; but still junior to all European officers
Syce	a servant responsible for caring for riding horses
Thannah	a police station
Zamindar	a landlord, under any of a range of complex arrangements, ranging from a kind of share-cropping or rental to revenue farming or outright land ownership, and ranging in scale from a superior peasant to a wealthy landholder richer than some rajahs; also 'zemindar'

APPENDIX 2

FIGHTS

This is the first list compiled of armed clashes in the Santal rebellion, mainly based on reports in the Military Consultations. It cannot be definitive, and many locations remain unknown. Figures for Santal casualties are approximate. Abbreviations: k. = killed; w. = wounded; NI= Native Infantry; nr = near; N, S, etc. = north, south; BHR = Bhaugulpore Hil Rangers. The list is keyed to the numbers on Map 2.

Date	Place	Unit(s)/ commanders	Comments
1. 13 July	Kuddamshaw	Maseyk & civilians	unknown losses
2. 15 July	Moheshpore	7NI, Birch	100–200 Santals k.
3. 16 July	Peer Pointee	BHR, Burroughs	25 sepoys k.
4. 20 July	Nungolea	56NI, Delamain?	200 Santals k. + w.
5. 21 Jul	Nagore	56NI, Raikes	7 Santals k.+ w.?
6. 22 Jul	Nagore	56NI, Raikes	'large number' of Santals k. + w.?
7. 22 Jul	Nungolea	56NI, Delamain	50 Santals k. + w.?
8. 24 July	Pealpore	BHR/40, Burroughs	250 Santals k. + w.

9. 24 Jul	Raghunathpore	7NI, Birch	unknown
10. 24 Jul	Beerbhoom?	56NI, Toulmin	20 sepoys k. + w.?
11. 26 Jul	nr Burhyte	7NI, Birch	4 k.
12. 26 Jul	Nalhati	56NI, Jervis	siege of house; 30 Santals k.
13. 29 Jul	Derrypoor	40NI, Cahill	unknown
14. Late Jul	Rampore Haut	56NI, Rose	unknown
15. 1 Aug	Bissohuwa	40NI, Burn	6 Santals k.; 15 w.; depicted by Sherwill
16. 3 Aug	Bowsee	40NI, Misser	Santal attack; 'at least' 2 Santals k.; more w.
17. 3 Aug	nr Moorshedabad	31NI, Sitwell	unknown
18. Early Aug	nr Rampore Haut	56NI, Chalmers	15 Santals k.; more w.
19. 5 Aug	nr Moheshpore	31NI, Smalpage	8 Santals k.; 'many more' w.
20. 13–18 Aug	Koomerabad	50NI, Fooks	siege; 'some scores were left dead on the plain'
21. Mid-Aug	S of Bowsee	13NI, Francis	8–15 Santals k. + w.?
22. c. 17 Aug	nr Koomerabad	37NI, Dunbar	12 Santals k. + w.?
23. 31 Aug	Noni Haut	42LI, Liptrap	11 Santals k. + w.?
24. c. 14 Sep	Jamtarra	63NI, Phillips	50–60 Santals k. + w.?
25. 21 Sep	Bewa, nr Jamtarra	63NI, Phillips	8 Santals k. + w.?
26. 22–24 Sep	nr Jamtarra	63NI, Phillips	c. 30 Santals k. + w.?
27. Late Sep	nr Jamtarra	Gillon's irregulars	200 Santals k.? + w.?
28. c. 10 Oct	nr Jamtarra	63NI, Pester/ Boddam	13 Santals k.
29. 15 Oct	Kurrown	63NI, Phillips	63 Santals k. + w.

30. 17–19 Oct	W. Beerbhoom	50NI, Nicholl	210 Santals k. + w.
31. 21 Oct	Kurrown	37NI, Aitken	80 Santal k. & w.
32. Late Nov	Sthn Bhaugulpore	several regiments	unknown
33. late Nov	Jhilmillee	40NI	unknown
34. Late Nov	Hendweh	several regiments	unknown
35. Dec	Belputteh	several regiments	unknown

Exact locations unknown

25 Jul	N. Bhaugulpore	40NI, Shuckburgh	100 Santals k. + w.?
c. 25 Jul	Salbudra	Burkendazes	Police defended house—losses unknown
27 July	Bundlebund	50NI, Fooks v 200 S	12 Santals k.; Ens Craycroft & 1 sepoy w.
27 Jul	Banskole	56NI, Raikes/ Toulmin	Toulmin & 20 sepoys k.; 200 Santals k.?
28 Jul	Gaupore	56NI, Goad	5 Santals k.
Late Jul	Nunkole	56NI, Delamain	60 Santals k. & w.
1 Aug	Chunakuthi	13NI, Francis	unknown
4 Aug	N. Bhaugulpore	13NI, Francis	'more or less severe'
c. 20 Aug	Mor River	56NI, irregulars	20 Santals k. + w.?
10 Oct	Sarbe Barra	63NI, Pester	25 Santals k. + w.?
18 Oct	Namenpore	50NI, Mathias	80 Santal k. & w.?

While all Santal casualty figures are approximate, this list suggests a minimum of about 2000 Santals killed in battle, with more dying of their wounds. And there were undoubtedly more encounters than this list records—Captain William Halliday, for example, recorded that his detachment of the 56th had seen 'a good many skirmishes', in unnamed places, none of which appear in this list. Likewise, Lieutenant Robert Francis's clash on 4 August was regarded (from the detachment's ammunition state) as involving 'more or less severe' Santal losses, but he submitted no formal report. Santal sources record a fight at Danuspuja, west of Pakur, with which no Company report corresponds. From mid-November operations became so general, and so geographically uncertain, that it is difficult to establish exactly when and where actions occurred, as discussed in Part IV. In summary, perhaps 3,000 Santals died in combat while Company forces lost about 50 sepoys killed in action, most at Peer Pointee and Nagore.

APPENDIX 3

PEOPLE

Most European protagonists whose surnames appear in footnotes are listed here, with their positions at the outbreak of the rebellion and their season of appointment. Details vary, because of course men changed positions and gained promotions in the course of the year.

Civil officials

Robert Abercrombie (1840) Officiating Collector, Moorshedabad; served India 1840–75

William Allen (1829) Commissioner, Chota Nagpore Agency

Cecil Beadon (1836) Secretary of the Home Department of the Government of India; served in India 1836–67; d. 1880

Alfred Bidwell (1829) Special Commissioner for the Suppression of the Santhal Rebellion; served in India 1830–57

George Brown (1820) Commissioner for Revenue and Circuit, Nuddea; served in India 1821–58

Lord Canning Governor-General of India, 1856–62

Charles Chapman	(1852) Assistant to the Magistrate and Collector, Bhaugulpore
Marquis of Dalhousie	Governor-General of India, 1848–56
Joseph Dorin	(1820) 1st Ordinary Member, Supreme Council of India, appointed 1853; served in India 1821–58
Ashley Eden, Hon.	(1852) Assistant Magistrate, Rajeshye, later Aurangabad; Lt-Gov of Bengal 1878–82
William Elliott	(1829) Chief Magistrate, Calcutta; served in India 1830–65
John Peter Grant	(1826) 3rd Ordinary Member, Supreme Council of India, appointed 1854; served in India 1827–62; Lt-Gov Bengal 1860–62
William Grey	(1840) Secretary to the Government of Bengal; served in India 1840–74; Lt-Gov Bengal 1871–74
Frederick Halliday	(1824) Lt-Gov of Bengal, 1854–59; served in India 1825–59
Richard Heywood	(1845) Magistrate, Bhaugulpore; served in India 1845–62
George Loch	(1833) Officiating Collector, Purneah; served in India 1834–73
James Mangles	(1851) Assistant to Magistrate and Collector, Gobindpore
William Money	(1853) Assistant to Magistrate and Collector, Monghyr; served in India 1853–79
Barnes Peacock	4th Ordinary Member, Supreme Council of India, appointed 1852
James Pontet	(c. 1835) Superintendent of the Damin-i-koh (Uncovenanted)

Robert Richardson (1844) Collector, Beerbhoom; served in India 1844–79

Henry Rose (1847) Assistant to Magistrate and Collector, Pubna; served in India 1847–63

Alexander Russell (1847) Under-Secretary to the Government of Bengal; served in India 1847–68

Edward Samuells (1830) Commissioner, Cuttack; served 1832–60

Augustus Rivers Thompson (1850) Assistant to Commissioner, Chota Nagpore; detached to Lower Bengal, 1855

Octavius Toogood (1845) Magistrate, Jessore; later Moorshedabad; served in India 1845–71

William Tucker (1845) Magistrate, Monghyr; served in India 1845–73

James Ward (1833) Collector, East Burdwan

George Yule (1830) Collector, Dinagepore; served in India 1832–68

Military officers

Lt Robert Aitken (1847) 13th Bengal Native Infantry

1st Lt Burnett Ashburner (1848) 4th Company, 5th Battalion, Bengal Artillery

Lt George Atkinson (1842) Bengal Engineers, Officiating Secretary of the Government of India, Military Department

Capt. Walter Birch (1837) 7th Bengal Native Infantry

Lt-Col Louis Bird (1807) 13th Bengal Native Infantry, later commanding Beerbhoom and Bancoorah Field Force

1st Lt Hungerford Boddam	(1843) 3rd Company, 2nd Battalion, Bengal Artillery
Capt. Charles Bruere	(1828) 13th Bengal Native Infantry
Lt James Burn	(1845) 40th Bengal Native Infantry
Col George Burney	(1819) 32nd; 56th Bengal Native Infantry
Maj Frederick Burroughs	(1824) 17th Bengal Native Infantry; Bhaugulpore Hill Rangers
Ens. Archibald Campbell	(1851) 31st Bengal Native Infantry
Lt Henry Campbell	(1849) 63rd Bengal Native Infantry
Lt John Campbell	(1853) 42nd Light Infantry
Lt Robert Campbell	(1850) 63rd Bengal Native Infantry
Ens. William Cubitt	(1853) 13th Bengal Native Infantry
Capt. Thomas Dalyell	(1821) 42nd Light Infantry
Lt John Delamain	(1845) 56th Bengal Native Infantry
Ens. Thomas Dennehy	(1851) 2nd Grenadiers
Lt Frederick Dunbar	(1848) 37th Bengal Native Infantry
Col James Eckford	(1804) 56th Bengal Native Infantry; Commanding Presidency Division as Major-General
Lt Henry Finch	(1840) 31st Bengal Native Infantry
Lt George Fooks	(1840) 50th Bengal Native Infantry
Lt Robert Francis	(1840) 13th Bengal Native Infantry
Maj David Gaussen	(1827) 42nd Light Infantry
Ens. Charles Goad	(1852) 56th Bengal Native Infantry
Lt Henry Gordon	(1854) 63rd Bengal Native Infantry
Lt William Gordon	(1824) 68th Bengal Native Infantry; Adjutant, Bhaugulpore Hill Rangers

Capt. William Gott	(1849) 56th Bengal Native Infantry
Maj. Joseph Hampton	(1822) 50th Bengal Native Infantry
Capt. William Hampton	(1827) 31st Bengal Native Infantry
Lt William Hawes	(1846) 63rd Bengal Native Infantry
Lt Charles Hawtrey	(1845) 50th Bengal Native Infantry
Lt-Col Richard Houghton	(1819) 63rd Bengal Native Infantry
Capt. Vincent Jervis	(1842) 56th Bengal Native Infantry
Lt George Kempland	(1847) 56th Bengal Native Infantry
Lt Hans Leslie	(1842) 37th Bengal Native Infantry
Maj John Liptrap	(1817) 42nd Light Infantry
Capt. Anthony Lister	(1841) 2nd Grenadiers
Maj-Gen. George Lloyd	(1804) 28th Bengal Native Infantry; Commanding Dinapore Division and Sonthal Field Force
Maj-Gen. John Low	(1804) Madras Army; Ordinary Member, Supreme Council of India, appointed 1853
Cornet Robert Low	(1854) Governor-General's Body-Guard
Lt Henry Mathias	(1849) 50th Bengal Native Infantry
Lt-Col William Mitchell	(1825) 13th Bengal Native Infantry; later commanding 42nd Light Infantry
Maj. John Nembhard	(1840) 56th Bengal Native Infantry
Capt. Henry Nicholl	(1835) 50th Bengal Native Infantry
Lt Henry Norman	(1844) 31st Bengal Native Infantry
Capt. Benjamin Parrott	(1840) 37th Bengal Native Infantry; later brigade-major, Sonthal Field Force

Lt Gilbert Pasley	(1850) 7th Bengal Native Infantry
Capt. Hugh Pester	(1840) 63rd Bengal Native Infantry
Lt James Phillips	(1842) 63rd Bengal Native Infantry
Lt Henry Raikes	(1850) 56th Bengal Native Infantry
Capt. Walter Sherwill	(1832) 66th Bengal Native Infantry; Quarter-Master General, Sonthal Field Force
Maj. Henry Shuckburgh	(1824) 40th Bengal Native Infantry
Capt. Dean Shute	(1837) 19th Bengal Native Infantry; Deputy Assistant Quarter-Master General, Sonthal Field Force
Capt. George Sinclair	(1844) 63rd Bengal Native Infantry
Ens. Francis Sitwell	(1851) 31st Bengal Native Infantry
Lt Hunter Smalpage	(1839) 31st Bengal Native Infantry
Lt-Col Henry Templer	(1813) 7th Bengal Native Infantry
Lt Thomas Toulmin	(1847) 56th Bengal Native Infantry
Lt-Col Stephen Wheeler	(1818) 37th Bengal Native Infantry
Capt. Thomas Wilson	(1838) 13th Bengal Native Infantry

Santals

While it is impossible to compile a similarly detailed list for Santal protagonists, still less to trace their involvement in the Hul, the names of the following manjees, parganaits or soubahs, the counterparts and antagonists of the Bengal Army officers, may at least be recorded:

Alhar	Hareedas	Nemay
Anta	Hingoo Chowdry	Nuffer
Bagud	Hoobra	Parash
Baichoo Rao	Jugoo	Pertoo

Ballorom
Beersing
Bhagna
Bhuro
Bijul
Binod Manjhi
Bir Singh
Bishoo
Bobadar
Brahma
Bugna
Bursha
Bursha
Bychand
Chandra
Chand Ray
Chundry
Churoo
Darvie
Denoo
Dhona
Dhrum
Dhunae
Dolel
Doman
Domum
Doolubn
Durga
Ghuttoo Sing
Gocho
Gopal
Gora

Gujoo Sing
Jutha
Jutoo Rae
Kaloo
Kamoo
Kanchan
Kanleh
Kanhu
Kaoleh Paramanik
Khama
Kisto
Koondan
Kowleah
Kurn
Lall
Lehra
Luckun
Lulkin
Manick
Mani Pargana
Megh Roy
Megre
Mochua
Moochea
Moohea
Morarea
Mota
Motha
Mungle
Mungus
Murria

Muttah
Nemai
Poosa
Quttor
Rabaan/Raboo
Raj
Ram
Raman
Ranjeet
Rumbasa
Ruroo
Salkho
Sallor
Sam Suba
Seero
Seetul
Sham
Sham Mal
Sham Soubah
Shekhar
Shyam
Sidhu
Singray
Singroy
Sona
Sooree
Soorjee
Sora
Thooloo
Tribuhan

These men are not, of course, all the Santals who led their people in the Hul, only some of those whose names were recorded in Company records, in the reports and correspondence of their antagonists or lists of prisoners: hence the idiosyncratic spelling by negligent or ignorant European or non-Santal clerks.

APPENDIX 4

PLACES: CONCORDANCE

Since the 1850s the names of most of the places associated with the rebellion have changed, either in spelling or in their entirety. Berhet today was in 1855 rendered Burhyte, Barheit, Barhyte, Barhet and possibly Burhuttee; Kadamsha was rendered Cuddam Shaw, Cudumshar, Kadamsar, Kudumshar, Kuddamshaw etc.. This book uses the names commonly found in English-language sources in 1855. This appendix provides a concordance between contemporary and modern names. Abbreviations: BD = Bangladesh; BR = Bihar; JH = Jharkhand; WB = West Bengal.

Afzulpore	Afzalpur, JH
Amrapara	Amrapara, JH
Aurungabad	Aurangabad, WB
Bancoorah	Bankura, WB
Benagaria	Benagaria, WB
Bissohuwa	Possibly 4 m. E of Dighi, JH
Burhyte	Berhet, JH
Berhampore	Berhampur, WB
Bhaugulpore	Bagalpur, BH
Bhugnadihee	Bugnadee, JH
Boree Bottan	Barabathan, JH
Bowsee	Bausi, BR

Burdwan	Bardaman, WB
Colgong	Kahalgaon, BR
Dautiapore	unknown
Derrypoor	Dariyapur, JH
Deoghur	Deoghar, JH
Dighe	Dighi, JH
Dinapore	Dinapur, BR
Dinagepore	Dinajpur, BD
Godda	Godda, JH
Govindpore	Gobindpur, JH
Heerampore	Hiranpur, JH
Ilam Bazar	Ilambazar, JH
Jamtarra	Jamtara, JH
Jhilmillee	Jhilimili, JH
Jungeypore	Jangipur, WB
Kantepore	unknown
Koomerabad	Kumrabad, JH
Kuddumshaw	Kadamsha, WB
Kundahit	Kundahit, JH
Kurrown	Karon, JH
Kusma	Kusma Bazar, JH
Litipara	Litipara, JH
Malda	Malda, WB
Mohamed Bazar	Mohamed Bazar, WB
Moheshpore	Mahespur, JH
Monghyr	Munger, JH
Moorshedabad	Murshidabad, WB
Nagore	Rajnagar, WB
Nala	Nala, JH
Nalhati	Nalhati, WB
Narainpore	Narayanpur, WB
Noni Haut	Nonihat, JH
Nungolea	Nuncole, WB
Nya Dumka	Dumka, JH
Operbandah	Uperbanda, JH
Pakaur	Pakur, JH
Palgunge	Palganj, JH

Parasnath	Parasnath, JH
Pealpore	Pealapur, JH
Peer Pointee	Pirpainte, JH
Pubna	Pubna, BD
Pulsa	Palsa, WB
Purneah	Purnia, BR
Rajmahal	Rajmahal, WB
Raksandangal	10m N of Uperbanda, JH
Rampore Haut	Rampurhat, WB
Raneebehal	Ranebhal, JH
Raneegunge	Raniganj, WB
Sabunpore	Sabanpur, JH
Sangrampore	Sangrampur, BR
Sarbe Barra	unknown
Saruth	Sarath, JH
Skreekond	near Kankjole, WB
Sooree	Suri, WB
Subhunpore	Sobanpur, JH
Sultanpore	Sultanpur, WB
Taldanga	Taldangal, JH
Telaboonee	6 or 11 m W of Suri, WB
Topchaunce	Topchanchi, JH
Umurpoor	Amarpur, JH

NOTES

PROLOGUE

1. [Map] No. 23 Rajmuhal Hills or Damin-i-koh, 1848–50, 3 b.43, BL.
2. Sherwill, *Geographical and Statistical Report of the District of Bhaugulpoor*, pp. 46–48.
3. Sherwill, *Geographical and Statistical Report of the District of Beerbhoom*, p. 8; Sherwill, 'Notes upon a tour through the Rajmahal Hills', *Journal of the Asiatic Society of Bengal*, 1851, pp. 574–80.
4. O'Malley, *Bengal District Gazetteers Santal Parganas*, p. 21.

INTRODUCTION

1. Hunter, *The Annals of Rural Bengal*.
2. Macphail, *The Story of the Santal*; Carstairs, *Harma's Village: a Novel of Santal Life*, and Sanjay Bahadur, *Hul—Cry Rebel!* In Bengali: Tarasankar Bandopadhyay's *Aranya Banhi* and Satish Chandra Mukhopadhyay's *Santal Bidroher*.
3. Culshaw & Archer, 'The Santal Rebellion', *Man in India*, Vol. XXV, No. 4, Dec 1945, pp. 218–39.
4. Hunter, *The Annals of Rural Bengal*, p. 248.
5. Chttopadhyay, *Redefining Tribal Identity*, p. 57.
6. 'The Santals', *Household Words*, Vol. XXXV, p. 107.
7. *Caledonian Mercury* (Edinburgh), 3 December 1855.
8. O'Malley, *Bengal District Gazetteers: Santal Parganas*, p. 99.
9. Datta-Majumdar, *The Santal: a Study in Culture Change*, p. 66.
10. *Citizen*, 3 January 1856.
11. *Friend of India*, 2 August 1855.
12. *Friend of India*, 9 August 1855.
13. Culshaw & Archer, 'The Santal Rebellion', *Man in India*, December 1945, though they spell his surname in three different ways, an early sign of the problems of variable spelling that bedevilled the entire project.

14. 'The Story of the Santal Rebellion', in Anderson and others, *From Fire Rain to Rebellion*, pp. 173–87.

15. Guha, *Elementary Aspects of Peasant Insurgencies in Colonial India*, pp. 14–15.

16. Wagner, *The Great Fear of 1857*, p. 25.

17. One attempt to counter the dominance of the English sources has been to structure this book according to Santal seasons and months, ordering it according to the rhythm of the year in Bengal and the names given by the great majority of those affected by the Hul—the Santals. The Santal lunar calendar corresponds closely enough with the Gregorian calendar used by Europeans to make the gesture feasible.

1. PROTAGONISTS AND CONTEXTS

1. Biswas, *Santals of the Santal Parganas*, p. 51; O'Malley, *Bengal District Gazetteers: Santal Parganas*, p. 90; Man, *Sonthalia and the Sonthals*, p. 62.

2. Carstairs, *The Little World of an Indian District Official*, pp. 219–20.

3. O'Malley, *Bengal District Gazetteers: Santal Parganas*, p. 102.

4. Archer, 'Santal Transplantation Songs', *Man in India*, 1946.

5. Archer, *The Hill of Flutes*, p. 27.

6. Hunter, *The Annals of Rural Bengal*, p. 224. Extraordinarily, in 1832 Company officials had marked the boundary of the Damin with a ring of masonry pillars.

7. Loch to Brown, 18 September 1850, Choudhury, *1857 in Bihar*, pp. 4–8. Pontet's appointment as Superintendent is given in various sources in every year between 1832 and 1838; not that it really matters.

8. Despatches to India & Bengal, Jan-Feb 1856, E/834, BL.

9. O'Malley, *Bengal District Gazetteers: Santal Parganas*, p. 45.

10. Judicial Department minute 'Sonthal Insurrection', 1 October 1856, E/4/839, BL.

11. *Friend of India*, 11 October 1855.

12. *Citizen*, 19 July 1855.

13. Judicial Department minute 'Sonthal Insurrection', 1 October 1856, E/4/839, BL.

14. Archer, *The Hill of Flutes*, p. 39.

15. Sen, *The Santals of Jungle Mahals*, p. 126.

16. 'Unaccustomed to calculate consequences', as a senior civil official patronisingly put it: Samuells to Grey, 1 October 1855, Judicial Proceedings, P/145/23, BL. Narahari Kaviraj claimed that Santals deliberately chose to rebel at the beginning of the monsoon, which would make movement by troops difficult: Kaviraj, *Santal Village Community*, p. 175, fn 25.

17. Kaye, *The Administration of the East India Company*, p. 101.

18. Atkinson, *Curry and Rice (on Forty Plates)*. Simon Riches gives a useful biography of Atkinson as an introduction to the Royal Armouries 2009 facsimile edition of *The Campaign in India* but he does not mention his time in the Military Department.

19. *Friend of India*, 26 July 1855.

20. Maclagan, *'Clemency' Canning*, p. 32.

21. Kaye, *The Administration of the East India Company*, p. 99.

22. *Friend of India*, 6 December 1855.

23. Kaye, *The Administration of the East India Company*, p. 421. It may have been fixed, but was fixed at a generous rate: *Allen's Indian Mail* conceded that the Company's civil servants were part of 'the best paid service in the world': 2 April 1855.

24. Clarke, *The Regulations of the Government of Fort William in Bengal*, p. iii.

25. Kaye, *The Administration of the East India Company*, p. 431.

26. Shore, *Notes on Indian Affairs*, Vol. I, p. 10.

27. O'Malley, *The Indian Civil Service*, pp. 67–70; 75; Campbell, *Modern India*, pp. 273–77.

28. Appendix 3 gives biographical details of the most significant civil officials involved in the suppression of the Hul.

29. Lee-Warner, *The Life of the Marquis of Dalhousie*, Vol. I, p. 111. Scholars may echo his plaint.

30. Braddon, *Life in India*, pp. 204–05.

31. Kaye, *The Administration of the East India Company*, pp. 351–52.

32. *Friend of India*, 1 November 1855.

33. *Citizen*, 28 August 1855.

34. Rafter, *Our Indian Army*, p. 1.

35. *Colburn's United Service Magazine*, 1855, Part 1, p. 144.

36. Maunder, *The Scientific and Literary Treasury*, p. 685.

37. Shore, *Notes on Indian Affairs*, Vol. II, p. 416.

38. Stanley, *White Mutiny*, p. 17.

39. Eyre, *The Military Operations at Cabul*, p. 36.

40. Narrative by Sergeant-Major Lissant, 37th Native Infantry, 1842, 9007–76, NAM.

41. Malleson, *The Decisive Battles of India*, p. 377.

42. *Standing Orders of the Bengal Native Infantry*, p. 61.

43. *Ibid.*, pp. 9–10.

44. Liptrap to Mayhew, 29 July 1855, P/46/4, BL.

45. *Citizen*, 21 November 1855.

46. Braddon, *Life in India*, p. 157.

47. *Citizen*, 17 August 1855.

48. Kaviraj, *A Peasant Uprising in Bengal 1783*.

49. Samuells to Grey, 1 October 1855, Judicial Proceedings, P/145/23, BL. Samuells was Commissioner of Cuttack.

50. Kaye, *A History of the Sepoy War in India, 1857–1858*, Vol. III, p. 61.

51. Guha, *Elementary Aspects of Peasant Insurgency in Colonial India*, p. 1.

52. Bose, *Peasant Labour and Colonial Capital*, pp. 143–50; Datta, *Anti-British Plots and Movements before 1857*, Chapters 4 and 5.

53. Jha, *The Kol Insurrection*, p. 1. The name 'Kol' was a term of abuse, akin to 'Kaffir',

but no other name appears to be available, and 'Coles' was what Company officers and officials used; Jha, *The Kol Insurrection*, p. 23.

54. *Hindoo Patriot*, 19 July 1855.

55. Sherwill, *Geographical and Statistical Report of the District of Bhaugulpore*, p. 26.

56. Bose, *Peasant Labour and Colonial Capital*, p. 72.

57. Gupta, *The Economic Life of a Bengal District: Birbhum 1770–1857*, p. 271.

58. Bodding, *Santal Folk Tales*, Vol. I, p. 33n.

59. Guha, 'The Prose of Counter-Insurgency', in Guha & Spivak, *Selected Subaltern Studies*, p. 44.

60. Guha, *Elementary Aspects of Peasant Insurgency in Colonial India*, p. 99.

61. Datta, *Anti-British Plots and Movements before 1857*, pp. 52–54.

62. Judicial Department minute 'Sonthal Insurrection', 1 October 1856, E/4/839, BL.

63. *Ibid.*

64. Minute, Halliday, 19 October 1855, Judicial Proceedings, P/145/21, BL.

65. Jugia Haram in Culshaw & Archer, 'The Santal Rebellion', *Man in India*, December 1945, p. 230.

66. Judicial Department minute 'Sonthal Insurrection', 1 October 1856, E/4/839, BL.

67. Anderson, *From Fire Rain to Rebellion*, p. 175.

68. Chotrae Desmanjhi in Culshaw & Archer, 'The Santal Rebellion', *Man in India*, December 1945, pp. 220; 230; 233.

2. *SAN* (JULY)

1. *Bengal Directory and Annual Register*, 1855, p. 4.

2. *Citizen*, 14 July 1855.

3. Fuchs, *Rebellious Prophets*, p. 1. While some of Fuchs's criteria do not fit the Santals, those that do confirm that notwithstanding the simplistic contemporary dismissal of the Hul as being based on 'religious frenzy' considering it as a religious expression of social and economic stress is highly productive.

4. Eden to Grey, 9 July 1855, Military Consultations, P/46/1, BL.

5. Translation by Toogood; Toogood to Grey, 11 August 1855, Judicial Proceedings, P/145/17, BL.

6. Durga Tudu in Anderson and others, *From Fire Rain to Rebellion*, p. 185.

7. Datta-Majumder, *The Santal: a Study in Culture Change*, p. 29.

8. Gupta, *The Economic Life of a Bengal District*, p. 299.

9. Chakraborti, *History of the Santal Hool*, p. 26.

10. Jugia Haram in Culshaw & Archer, 'The Santal Rebellion', *Man in India*, December 1945, p. 231.

11. The story of Dutta's death appears in various versions, including an imaginative reconstruction by James McPhail in his *The Story of the Santal*. Datta's *The Santal*

Rebellion wrongly gives the number killed as 19: Kaviraj, *Santal Village Community*, p. 166, fn 6.

12. Brown to Grey, 10 July 1855, Military Consultations, P/46/7, BL.
13. Brown to Grey, 9 July 1855, Military Consultations, P/46/1, BL.
14. Francis Bradley-Birt described Pontet confronting Santals early in the Hul, attempting to persuade them to desist and being virtually kidnapped by respectful older manjees, fearful that he would be killed by vengeful younger men, and taken to a place of safety: *The Story of an Indian Upland*, p. 192. The episode hints at the generational tensions later apparent within the Hul.
15. Minute, Halliday, 12 July 1855, Military Consultations, P/46/1, BL.
16. Chakraborti, *History of the Santal Hool*, pp. 26–27.
17. Ballad by Babu Dhanakrishna Ruj, quoted by Datta, 'Original Records about the Santhal Insurrection of 1855', *Bengal Past & Present*, 1934, p. 34.
18. *Citizen*, 19 July 1855.
19. Jugia Haram in Culshaw & Archer, 'The Santal Rebellion', *Man in India*, December 1945, p. 233.
20. Toogood to Elliott, 23 July 1855, Military Consultations, P/46/3, BL.
21. Datta-Majumder, *The Santal: a Study in Culture Change*, p. 29.
22. William Hunter, who consulted official papers in the 1860s, 'never discovered one of these curious missives', but he did not doubt that they had been sent (*The Annals of Rural Bengal*, p. 238). But in what form or language were they written? Is it possible that a junior functionary—perhaps one of the amlahs who stood between Santals and European Company officials—simply discarded them?
23. Chakraborti, *History of the Santal Hool*, p. 33.
24. Ballad by Ray Krishnadas, Ratan Library, Birbhum, MS No. 2096, quoted by Datta, 'Original Records about the Santhal Insurrection of 1855', *Bengal Past & Present*, 1934, p. 34. My attempt to consult these sources was unavailing.
25. Chakraborti, *History of the Santal Hool*, pp. 35–36; 40.
26. Kaviraj, *Santal Village Community*, p. 28.
27. Chakraborti, *History of the Santal Hool*, pp. 37–39. Roy's executioner was allegedly one Jagarnath Sikdar, but his name appears nowhere else in the records, one of many Santals who emerge from obscurity and then disappear.
28. O'Malley, *Bengal District Gazetteers: Santal Parganas*, p. 52.
29. 'The Sonthal Pergunnahs', *Calcutta Review*, 1 December 1860, p. 512.
30. Grey to Atkinson, 13 July 1855, Military Consultations, P/46/1, BL; *Friend of India*, 19 July 1855, quoted in *Allen's Indian Mail*, 19 September 1855.
31. *Morning Chronicle* (Calcutta), 14 July 1855.
32. Anon, *The Experiences of a Landholder and Indigo Planter in Eastern Bengal*, p. 3.
33. Kling, *The Blue Mutiny*.
34. Braddon, *Thirty Years of Shikar*, p. 80; though Lewis Carroll's poem 'Jabberwocky' appeared only in 1871.
35. *The Times*, 5 October 1855. Mudge wrote to his father in Bristol on 3 August, and

Mr Mudge forwarded his son's letter to it. It was re-published in several provincial newspapers.

36. 'Delta', *Indigo and Its Enemies*, p. 20.

37. *Morning Chronicle* (Calcutta), 20 July 1855.

38. Birch to Ross, 15 July 1855, Military Consultations, P/46/2, BL.

39. Richardson to Grey, 24 July 1855, Military Consultations, P/46/3, BL.

40. *Morning Chronicle* (Calcutta), 3 August 1855.

41. O'Malley, *Bengal District Gazetteers: Santal Parganas*, p. 50.

42. *Friend of India*, 9 August 1855.

43. Lloyd to Atkinson, 10 August 1855, Military Consultations, P/46/5, BL.

44. Bidwell to Grey, 18 August 1855, Judicial Proceedings, P/145/17, BL.

45. *Citizen*, 28 August 1855.

46. Scott Bennett, 'Sir Edward Nicholas Coventry Braddon (1829–1904)', *Australian Dictionary of Biography*.

47. *Citizen*, 30 July 1855.

48. *Citizen*, 2 August 1855.

49. *Morning Chronicle* (Calcutta), 23 July 1855. Edward Man heard, perhaps from a Santal, that the Henshawes' attackers 'split their skulls' with axes: *Sonthalia and the Sonthals*, p. 123. Because their bodies were never recovered, they do not appear in the extensive records of 'Bengal Burials' in the India Office Records.

50. *Morning Chronicle* (Calcutta), 3 August 1855.

51. *Citizen*, 28 July 1855.

52. *Morning Chronicle* (Calcutta), 31 July 1855; *Friend of India*, 30 August 1855.

53. *Morning Chronicle* (Calcutta), 31 August 1855.

54. *Citizen*, 25 July 1855.

55. 'The Savage and the Maiden', *Punch*, 23 February 1856, p. 73.

56. *Allen's Indian Mail*, 19 September 1855.

57. Grey to Atkinson, 21 July 1855, Military Consultations, P/46/2, BL.

58. Bidwell to Grey, 10 September 1855, Judicial Proceedings, P/145/19, BL.

59. Brown to Grey, 9 July 1855, Military Consultations, P/46/1, BL.

60. Hobsbawm, *Social Bandits and Primitive Rebels*, introduction. In his later *Bandits*, Hobsbawm connected dacoity with 'rebellion rather than mere law-breaking' (p. 86), but did not discuss the Santal case. Hobsbawm's *Captain Swing* discusses agricultural protest in southern England in the 1830s which contested challenges to traditional life—a similar motivation to the Santals, and in regions from which many Company officers hailed.

61. *Hindoo Patriot*, 19 July 1855. Asoka Kumar Sen's study of *Popular Uprisings and the Intelligentsia* examines educated 'native' opinion toward the Hul, using mainly vernacular newspapers, essentially finding that Bengali intellectuals disdained the 'uncivilized' and 'savage' Santals; chapter 2; p. 30.

62. Pontet, letter, 26 July 1855, Military Consultations, P/46/3, BL.

63. Russell to Judge at Bhaugulpore, 2 November 1855, Judicial Proceedings, P/145/22, BL.

64. Judicial Department minute 'Sonthal Insurrection', 1 October 1856, E/4/839, BL.
65. *Friend of India*, 11 October 1855.
66. Samuells to Grey, 1 October 1855, Judicial Proceedings, P/145/23, BL.
67. Dhagamwar, *Role and Image of Law in India*, p. 158.
68. 'Thackoors Perwunnah', Richardson to Grey, 24 July 1855, Military Consultations, P/46/3, BL.
69. Kaviraj, *Santal Village Community*, p. 20.
70. *Citizen*, 19 July 1855.
71. *Morning Chronicle* (Calcutta), 31 July 1855.
72. *Morning Chronicle* (Calcutta), 1 August 1855.
73. *Friend of India*, 26 July 1855.
74. Eden to Grey, 9 July 1855, Military Consultations, P/46/1, BL.
75. *The Times*, quoted *Morning Chronicle (Calcutta)*, 20 October 1855, though the original *Times* story cannot be found.
76. *Hindoo Patriot*, 2 August 1855; *Citizen*, 3 August 1855.
77. *Citizen*, 1 August 1855.
78. *Friend of India*, 23 August 1855; *Cheshire Observer*, 27 October 1855.
79. Brown to Grey, 20 August 1855, Judicial Proceedings, P/145/17, BL.
80. *Friend of India*, 20 December 1855.
81. Chotrae Desmanjhi in Culshaw & Archer, 'The Santal Rebellion', *Man in India*, December 1945, pp. 219–220.
82. Kaviraj, *Santal Village Community*, p. 134; his section 'The Rebel Government at Work' (pp. 138–42) is unconvincing.
83. *Englishman*, 22 December 1855.
84. *Citizen*, 24 July 1855.
85. *Morning Chronicle* (Calcutta), 18 July 1855.
86. Anon, *Nizam's Memorial of 1860*; Majumdar, *The Musnud of Murshidabad 1704–1904*, p. 53.
87. *Morning Chronicle* (Calcutta), 25 July 1855.
88. Money to Bidwell, 6 September 1855, Military Consultations, P/46/9, BL.
89. Bose, *Peasant Labour and Colonial Capital*, p. 152.
90. Eden to Toogood, nd [c. 15 July 1855], Military Consultations, P/46/1, BL.
91. *Citizen*, 3 August 1855.
92. Richardson, Diary, 20 September 1855, Judicial Proceedings, P/145/20, BL.
93. Man, *Sonthalia and the Sonthals*, p. 119.
94. *Citizen*, 19 July 1855.
95. Grey to Templer, 12 July 1855, Military Consultations, P/46/1, BL.
96. *Citizen*, 3 August 1855.
97. Brown to Grey, 10 August 1855, Judicial Proceedings, P/145/17, BL.
98. Brown to Grey, 21 July 1855, Military Consultations, P/46/3, BL.
99. Minute, Grant, 15 September 1855, P/206/54, BL.
100. Minute, Halliday, 10 November 1855, Judicial Proceedings, P/145/23, BL.

101. *The Indian News and Chronicle of Eastern Affairs*, 16 January 1858.

102. The unfamiliar term 'South-West Frontier' needs explaining. The Company-ruled Presidency of Bengal extended up the Ganges, but to its south and west lay 'native' states and dependencies, formerly the South-West Frontier Agency, from 1854 the Chota Nagpore Agency.

103. Grey to Atkinson, 21 July 1855, Military Consultations, P/46/2, BL.

104. Minute, Halliday, 19 October 1855, Judicial Proceedings, P/145/22, BL.

105. Allen to Russell, 15 October 1855, Judicial Proceedings, P/145/23, BL.

106. *Morning Chronicle* (Calcutta), 20 October 1855, quoting *The Times*. *The Times* edition in which the article appeared has not, it seems, been digitised, but the *Nottinghamshire Guardian* also copied the article, on 6 September 1855.

107. *Caledonian Mercury*, 17 December 1855.

108. The *Hurkaru*'s suggestion was derided in the *Citizen* of 20 August 1855.

109. *Citizen*, 9 August 1855.

110. *Morning Chronicle* (Calcutta), 25 July 1855.

111. *Citizen*, 19 July 1855; 23 July 1855.

112. *Morning Chronicle* (Calcutta), 31 July 1855.

113. *Citizen*, 28 July 1855.

114. Grey to Atkinson, 21 July 1855, Military Consultations, P/46/2, BL.

115. Letters to Grey, 28 July 1855, Military Consultations, P/46/3, BL.

116. *Citizen*, 25 July 1855.

117. *Citizen*, 7 August 1855.

118. *Morning Chronicle* (Calcutta), 4 August 1855.

119. *Citizen*, 3 August 1855. Robert Carstairs explained that they were 'Bhunyas by race—aborigines who had become Hindoos … bound to turn out for military or Police service': *The Little World of an Indian District Officer*, p. 216.

120. *Citizen*, 30 July 1855.

121. Saunders to Lloyd, 16 July, 1855, Military Consultations, P/46/2, BL.

122. *Friend of India*, 6 December 1855.

123. Minute, Dorin, 14 July 1855, Military Consultations, P/46/1, BL.

124. Atkinson to Grey, 14 July 1866, Military Consultations, P/46/1, BL.

125. 'Present state of the Troops at Barrackpore', 19 July 1855, Military Consultations, P/46/1, BL. Detachments hastily recalled and men returning from furlough boosted their strength.

126. Grey to Atkinson, 21 July 1855, Military Consultations, P/46/2, BL.

127. Elliott to Grey, 19 October 1855, Judicial Proceedings, P/145/23, BL; Shore, *Notes on Indian Affairs*, Vol. II, p. 435. The Native Militia was not a regular regiment and did little but mount guards around the capital. In back-handed praise, an enquiry in 1851 had found its discipline 'satisfactory': India and Bengal Despatches, E/4/811, BL.

128. Middleton, 'A Reminiscence of the Santhal Rebellion', *United Service Magazine*, 1893, p. 1063.

129. *Morning Chronicle* (Calcutta), 31 July 1855.

130. 'The Maroon War', *Colburn's United Service Magazine*, 1830, Part I, pp. 137–44; 'Conquests and encroachments of the Dutch in the Indian Archipelago', *Colburn's United Service Magazine*, 1849, Part I, p. 19–30; 229–36.

131. 'Our Little War', *Colburn's United Service Magazine*, 1852, Part I, p. 144.

132. Minute, Dorin, 22 July 1855, Military Consultations, P/46/2, BL.

133. Guha, *Elementary Aspects of Peasant Insurgency in Colonial India*, p. 2.

134. Elliott to Grey, ND [c. 15 July 1855], Military Consultations, P/46/1, BL; emphasis in original.

135. In his article 'A Sad Episode of the Kol Insurrection (1832)', *Proceedings of the Indian History Congress*, Vol. 42, 1981, pp. 413–18, Jagdish Chandra Jha discussed a case in which men of the 50th Native Infantry decapitated a minor raja in the Kol insurrection.

136. Minute, Halliday, 19 October 1855, Judicial Proceedings, P/145/22, BL.

137. Middleton, 'A Reminiscence of the Santhal Rebellion', *United Service Magazine*, 1893, p. 1067; *Citizen*, 20 July 1855.

138. This account of the fighting at Moheshpore is based on Toogood to Grey, 15 July, Military Consultations, P/46/1, BL, Toogood's letter of 15 July published in several Calcutta newspapers, including the *Citizen* of 20 July 1855 and John Mudge's account published in *The Times*, 5 October 1855. Birch had expected a Santal force of up to 30,000: he had 400 sepoys. Within weeks of the Hul's outbreak, William Elliott had proposed mounting sepoys on elephants and sending them 'straight across country'. I visited what I believe to be the site of the action in January 2020.

139. Middleton, 'A Reminiscence of the Santhal Rebellion', *United Service Magazine*, 1893, p. 1068.

140. Chakraborti claimed that 'the wily captain' had ordered his men to fire blanks, in order to trick the Santals into thinking that the musket balls were turned to water and to entice the Santals to approach more closely, but there is no mention of this ploy in the Company sources, and no indication that at this time British officers knew of the Santal belief; *History of the Santal Hool*, pp. 41–42.

141. Sidhu testimony, Bidwell to Grey, c. 17 September 1855, Judicial Proceedings, P/145/22, BL.

142. *Friend of India*, 11 October 1855.

143. *Morning Chronicle* (Calcutta), 25 July 1855.

144. Chakraborti, *History of the Santal Hool*, p. 41. Chakraborti rarely mentions place names, but his account of an action (though he places 'Mr Jarvis' in command), probably refers to Moheshpore because he describes one of the brothers being wounded in the arm.

145. *The Times*, 5 October 1855.

146. Ram, *From Sepoy to Subedar*, p. 160. The reliability of Sita Ram's memoir, transcribed, edited and published as *From Sepoy to Subedar*, has been disputed. Kim Wagner (in *The Great Fear of 1857*) describes the memoir as 'at best heavily edited and, at worst, a complete fabrication'; p. 16. That Sita Ram supposedly served in every significant campaign from 1815 to 1857 (as no single native infantry regiment

did) undermines the case for its authenticity, but I have relied on it because it seemed perversely purits to ignore such a source. Without endorsing all of his claims, it seems at least credible that Sita Ram had been in the 56th Native Infantry, since it travelled to Raneegunge by rail, served at Sooree, and spent the hot weather of 1856 on the Grand Trunk Road, as the memoir relates.

147. Birch to Ross, 15 and 18 July 1855, Military Consultations, P/46/1, BL.

148. His Bengal counterparts thought that Middleton was of the 29th. In fact, he was a member of the 70th Foot: like many Queen's officers he had transferred units to make the most of promotion opportunities: *The Army List*, 1855; *Hart's Army List*, 1855.

149. Toogood to Bidwell, 25 July 1855, Military Consultations, P/46/4, BL. This despatch was reprinted in the newspapers verbatim by 7 August. Middleton's reminiscences confirm the difficulty of the march.

150. Birch to Mayhew, 24 and 30 July 1855, Military Consultations, P/46/3, BL. They carried 82,000 rounds of ammunition including 4,000 rounds condemned as unserviceable (probably soaked in the rain) but which under the Bengal Army's exacting audit regulations could not simply have been dumped.

151. *Citizen*, 15 August 1855.

152. Ibid.

153. Parrett & Chhina, *Indian Order of Merit*, p. 182, quoting *Bengal General Orders* 1058/1857.

154. Toogood to Bidwell, in Grey to Atkinson, 3 August 1855, Military Consultations, P/46/4, BL.

155. *Morning Chronicle* (Calcutta), 23 July 1855.

156. Brown to Elliott, 18 July 1855, Military Consultations, P/46/3, BL.

157. Brown to Grey, 21 July 1855, Military Consultations, P/46/3, BL.

158. Burroughs to Becher, 21 August 1855, Military Consultations, P/46/12, BL.

159. *Morning Chronicle* (Calcutta), 3 August 1855; *Delhi Gazette*, 23 August 1855.

160. Burroughs to Becher, 21 August 1855, Military Consultations, P/46/12, BL.

161. *Citizen*, 3 August 1855.

162. Sherwill, 'Notes upon a tour through the Rajmahal Hills', *Journal of the Asiatic Society of Bengal*, p. 548.

163. *Citizen*, 3 August 1855.

164. *Morning Chronicle* (Calcutta), 3 August 1855. Chapman threatened his accuser with a libel suit but withdrew it when it seemed likely he would lose.

165. Brown to Grey, 21 July 1855, Military Consultations, P/46/3, BL.

166. Ibid.

167. *Bengal Hurkaru*, 27 July 1855.

168. *Delhi Gazette*, 23 August 1855.

169. Lloyd to Mayhew, 22 July 1855, Military Consultations, P/46/3, BL.

170. Atkinson to Lloyd, 26 July 1855, Military Consultations, P/46/2, BL.

171. *Allen's Indian Mail*, 19 September 1855.

172. Money to Bidwell, 6 September 1855, Military Consultations, P/46/9, BL.

173. Ram, *From Sepoy to Subedar*, p. 160.

174. *Citizen*, 7 August 1855.

175. O'Malley, *Bengal District Gazetteers: Birbhum*, p. 26. O'Malley implies that he had consulted an account written by Jervis, but if so, it seems to have disappeared. Jervis seems to have *spoken* to Hunter.

176. Richardson to Grey, 23 July 1855, Military Consultations, P/46/3, BL. Richardson conceded that his was 'a rambling unconnected letter', but explained that he was 'perfectly worn out'.

177. *Morning Chronicle* (Calcutta), 16 August 1855.

178. Service Army List Bengal, 1855, 407 Nembhard, L/MIL/10/60, BL.

179. *Citizen*, 31 August 1855.

180. *Citizen*, 7 August 1855.

181. Report by Nembhard in Mayhew to Atkinson, 31 July 1855, Military Consultations, P/46/3, BL.

182. Nembhard to AAG Presidency Division, 24 July 1855, Military Consultations, P/46/3, BL.

183. *Morning Chronicle* (Calcutta), 3 August 1855.

184. Service Army List Bengal, 1855, 557 Toulmin, L/MIL/10/60, BL.

185. *Morning Chronicle* (Calcutta), 3 August 1855.

186. *Morning Chronicle* (Calcutta), 13 August 1855.

187. Wilson, *List of Inscriptions on Tombs or Monuments in Bengal*, p. 150.

188. Minute, Dorin, 22 July 1855, Military Consultations, P/46/2, BL.

189. Atkinson to Lloyd, 23 July 1855, Military Consultations, P/46/2, BL.

190. Atkinson to Lloyd, 24 July 1855, Military Consultations, P/46/2, BL.

191. It is possible that Eckford was denied command of the Sonthal Field Force because he had recently blotted his copybook by approving a court martial contrary to the Company's Directors' wishes: Service Army List Bengal 1855, 46 Eckford, L/MIL/10/60, BL.

192. Becher to Offg AG Army, 7 August 1855, Military Consultations, P/46/6, BL.

193. Eckford to Atkinson, 26 July 1855, Military Consultations, P/46/3, BL.

194. Bird to Atkinson, 30 July 1855, Military Consultations, P/46/3, BL.

195. Both Atkinson and Grey signed their correspondence as emanating from Fort William, and wrote to each other often, more than once a day. Did they also meet to discuss business? There are no references to them having done so, however close their offices may have been, though they also surely met socially at the Bengal Club or at functions in Calcutta.

3. *BHADER* (AUGUST)

1. *Friend of India*, 9 August 1855.

2. *Friend of India*, 2 August 1855.

3. *Morning Chronicle* (Calcutta), 27 July 1855.

4. Minute, Goldie, 11 December 1855, Military Consultations, P/46/26, BL. The rule-bound Andrew Goldie did not intend this as a compliment.

5. Atkinson to OC Allahabad, 31 July 1855, Military Consultations, P/46/3, BL.

6. *Morning Chronicle* (Calcutta), 27 July 1855.

7. Minute, Grant, 31 July 1855, Military Consultations, P/46/3, BL.

8. *Ibid*.

9. Minute, Low, 31 July 1855, Military Consultations, P/46/3, BL.

10. Grey to Atkinson, 4 August 1855, Military Consultations, P/46/4, BL.

11. Tucker to Atkinson, 4 August 1855, Military Consultations, P/46/4, BL.

12. *Citizen*, 28 August 1855. Dalhousie was already planning to annexe the Muslim kingdom of Oudh, unsettling sepoys hailing from the Ganges valley.

13. *Delhi Gazette*, 25 August 1855.

14. Minute, Halliday, 2 August 1855, Military Consultations, P/46/4, BL.

15. Minute, Halliday, 10 November 1855, Judicial Proceedings, P/145/23, BL.

16. India and Bengal Despatches, Jan-Mar 1855, E/4/829, BL.

17. Bidwell to Grey, 14 August 1855, Judicial Proceedings, P/145/17, BL.

18. Minute, Halliday, 'Sonthal Rising', 26 July 1855, Military Consultations, P/46/3, BL.

19. The disparity in salaries aggravated tensions between the two. Covenanted officials at least were paid handsomely, rather more than their military counterparts. While Bidwell's assistants received Rs 500 per month (a sum immediately known through the newspapers), military officers received much less. Even with field allowances, lieutenants (the most numerous rank) made only Rs 254 monthly, and even captains only Rs 411.

20. Atkinson to Grey, 28 July 1855, Military Consultations, P/46/3, BL.

21. Minute, 'Sonthal Rising', Halliday, 28 July 1855, Military Consultations, P/46/3, BL.

22. Grey to Atkinson, 28 July 1855, Military Consultations, P/46/3, BL.

23. Loch to Grey, 27 July 1855, Military Consultations, P/46/3, BL.

24. Minute, 'Sonthal Rising', Halliday, 28 July 1855, Military Consultations, P/46/3, BL.

25. *Citizen*, 28 August 1855. Skipwith Tayler (not Taylor), the assistant magistrate at Burdwan, figures nowhere else in the Hul.

26. Grey to Richardson, 17 September 1855, Ray, Santal Rebellion Documents, p. 20.

27. *Citizen*, 28 August 1855.

28. *Citizen*, 15 September 1855.

29. O'Malley, *The Indian Civil Service*, p. 51.

30. Lloyd to Atkinson, 2 August 1855, Military Consultations, P/46/4, BL.

31. Lloyd to Atkinson, 6 August 1855, Military Consultations, P/46/4, BL.

32. Bidwell to Grey, 14 August 1855, Judicial Proceedings, P/145/17, BL.

33. Lloyd to Mayhew, 22 July 1855, Military Consultations, P/46/3, BL. Such large guns would have been useless against the Santals, but they did not, it seems, even reach Bhaulgulpore.

34. Lloyd to Atkinson, 10 August 1855, Military Consultations, P/46/5, BL.

35. Lloyd to Becher, 13 August 1855, Military Consultations, P/46/5, BL.

36. Lloyd to Becher, 12 August 1855, Military Consultations, P/46/5, BL.

37. *Citizen*, 24 August 1855.

38. Cahill to Lieutenant J. Brown, 29 July 1855, Military Consultations, P/46/4, BL.

39. Lloyd to Atkinson, 2 August 1855, Military Consultations, P/46/4, BL.

40. *Englishman*, 23 August 1855. The author of an article sympathetic to Santals in the *Church Missionary Papers* in 1856 clearly adapted the *Englishman*'s account of this clash.

41. *Englishman*, 23 August 1855.

42. Lloyd to Tucker, 14 August 1855, Military Consultations, P/46/10, BL.

43. Lloyd to Atkinson, 14 August 1855, Military Consultations, P/46/5, BL.

44. Lloyd to Atkinson, 19 August 1855, Military Consultations, P/46/6, BL.

45. Francis to Mayhew, 9 August 1855, Military Consultations, P/46/5, BL. 'Lall Soubah' might not be his name, but might refer to the red clothing that Santal leaders sometimes adopted.

46. Lloyd to Atkinson, 10 August 1855, Military Consultations, P/46/5, BL.

47. Lloyd to Tucker, 14 August 1855, Military Consultations, P/46/10, BL.

48. *Citizen*, 15 August 1855.

49. Lloyd to Atkinson, 19 August 1855, Military Consultations, P/46/6, BL.

50. Lloyd to Atkinson, 15 October 1855, Judicial Proceedings, P/145/23, BL.

51. Lloyd to Atkinson, 19 August 1855, Military Consultations, P/46/6, BL.

52. Lloyd to Atkinson, 3 August 1855, Military Consultations, P/46/4, BL.

53. Bidwell to Grey, 18 August 1855, Judicial Proceedings, P/145/17, BL.

54. *Ibid.*

55. Money to Bidwell, 16 August 1855, Judicial Proceedings, P/145/17, BL.

56. *Ibid.*

57. *Friend of India*, 3 January 1856.

58. *Citizen*, 30 July 1855.

59. Petition of Gungaram, 17 September 1855, Judicial Proceedings, P/145/20, BL.

60. Chakraborti, *History of the Santal Hool*, p. 34.

61. *Bengal Hurkaru*, 30 August 1855. Europeans often referred to 'hunting' Santals. A letter in the *Morning Chronicle* (27 July) wanted to 'hunt down the scoundrels like wild beasts' and described the Santals as 'game'.

62. *Citizen*, 6 August 1855.

63. *Friend of India*, 9 August 1855.

64. Lee-Warner, *Memoirs of Field Marshal Sir Henry Wylie Norman*, p. 44. He learned, among other things, how deeply sepoys from Oudh resented Dalhousie's annexation of their king's domain.

65. Bird to Atkinson, 31 July 1855, Military Consultations, P/46/3, BL.

66. *Hindoo Patriot*, 13 September 1855.

67. *Hindoo Patriot*, 26 July 1855.

68. *Citizen*, 16 August 1855.

69. Hunter, *The Annals of Rural Bengal*, p. 248.

70. Kaviraj, *Santal Village Community*, p. 52, quoting McPhail, *The Story of the Santal*, p. 61. In Hindoostanee '*katl*' means 'murder' and '*kare*' 'let us do this': idiomatically, therefore, 'kill him/her'.

71. *Hindoo Patriot*, 4 October 1855.

72. Braddon, *Thirty Years of Shikar*, p. 79.

73. *Citizen*, 8 August 1855.

74. *Morning Chronicle* (Calcutta), 29 August 1855.

75. Barat, *The Bengal Native Infantry*, p. 171, quoting the Report of the Sanitary Commission in India, p. 63.

76. Bidwell to Atkinson, 8 August 1855, Military Consultations, P/46/4, BL.

77. Loch to Grey, 20 August 1855, Judicial Proceedings, P/145/17, BL.

78. *Hindoo Patriot*, 4 October 1855.

79. *Citizen*, 13 August 1855.

80. The saga occupies about twenty folios of Military Consultations, P/46/11, BL.

81. Lloyd to Atkinson, 30 August 1855, Military Consultations, P/46/7, BL.

82. Muller to Grey, 7 September 1855, Judicial Proceedings, P/145/20, BL.

83. Bidwell to Grey, 28 July 1855, Military Consultations, P/46/4, BL.

84. Pontet, letter, 26 July 1855, Military Consultations, P/46/3/BL.

85. Bidwell to Grey, 26 July 1855, Military Consultations, P/46/3, BL.

86. Lloyd to Atkinson, 17 August 1855, Military Consultations, P/46/5, BL.

87. Sitwell report, 8 August 1855, Military Consultations, P/46/6, BL.

88. *Citizen*, 4 August 1855.

89. Birch report enclosed in Brey to Mayhew, 10 August 1855, Military Consultations, P/46/4, BL.

90. *Hindoo Patriot*, 9 August 1855.

91. *Englishman*, 23 August 1855.

92. *Friend of India*, 18 October 1855.

93. *Citizen*, 20 August 1855.

94. Minute, Halliday, 19 October 1855, Judicial Proceedings, P/145/22, BL.

95. *Hindoo Patriot*, 6 September 1855.

96. *Caledonian Mercury*, 15 January 1856.

97. *Morning Chronicle* (Calcutta), 31 August 1855.

98. *Ibid.*, 31 July 1855; Elliott to Grey, 9 August 1855, Military Consultations, P/46/4, BL.

99. *Citizen*, 19 July 1855.

100. *Citizen*, 23 July 1855.

101. *Morning Chronicle* (Calcutta), 14 August 1855.

102. *Cheshire Observer*, 27 October 1855.

103. Kaviraj, *Santal Village Community*, p. 130.

104. Choudhury, *1857 in Bihar*, p. 20.

105. Chotrae Desmanjhi in Culshaw & Archer, 'The Santal Rebellion', *Man in India*, December 1945, p. 237. Narahari Kaviraj claims that 'there was not a single case of rape' by Santals (*Santal Village Community*, p. 132), but there is a great differ-

ence between rapes not committed and not reported. The idea that Bengali village women would report rapes to Company officials is highly implausible.

106. *Morning Chronicle* (Calcutta), 31 July 1855.

107. Money to Bidwell, 16 August 1855, Judicial Proceedings, P/145/17, BL.

108. Bird to Atkinson, 30 July 1855, Military Consultations, P/46/3, BL.

109. Bird to Atkinson, 6 August 1855, Military Consultations, P/46/4, BL.

110. Elliott to Bird, 2 August 1855, Military Consultations, P/46/4, BL.

111. Rose to Eckford, 16 July 1855, Military Consultations, P/46/1, BL.

112. De Bourbel, 22–26 July 1855, Military Consultations, P/46/3, BL.

113. *Citizen*, 25 July; 24 July 1855.

114. *Englishman*, 6 August 1855.

115. *Citizen*, 18 August; 24 August 1855.

116. Grey to Atkinson, 28 July 1855, Military Consultations, P/46/3, BL.

117. Loch to Grey, 30 July 1855, Military Consultations, P/46/3, BL.

118. Minute, Halliday, 19 October 855, Judicial Proceedings, P/145/22, BL.

119. *Friend of India*, 9 August 1855.

120. Grey to Atkinson, 21 July 1855, Military Consultations, P/46/2, BL.

121. Bidwell to Grey, 26 July 1855, Military Consultations, P/46/3, BL.

122. *Morning Chronicle* (Calcutta), 16 August 1855.

123. Money to Bidwell, 16 August 1855, Judicial Proceedings, P/145/17, BL.

124. *Morning Chronicle* (Calcutta), 8 August 1855.

125. Lee-Warner, *Memoirs of Field Marshal Sir Henry Wylie Norman*, p. 45.

126. Richardson to Bidwell, 12 August 1855, Judicial Proceedings, P/145/17, BL.

127. Most recently, in Richard Gott's *Britain's Empire*, p. 438.

128. Jervis to Delamain, 27 July 1855, Military Consultations, P/46/4, BL.

129. Hunter, *The Annals of Rural Bengal*, p. 247. The phrase is repeated in many accounts drawing on Hunter's *Annals*.

130. Kaviraj, *Santal Village Community*, p. 7. Because he entirely neglected evidence of armed conflict, Kaviraj had no real explanation for the Hul's failure.

131. Jugia Haram in Culshaw & Archer, 'The Santal Rebellion', *Man in India*, December 1945, p. 232.

132. Chotrae Desmanjhi in Culshaw & Archer, 'The Santal Rebellion', *Man in India*, December 1945, p. 235.

133. Durga Tudu in Anderson and others, *From Fire Rain to Rebellion*, p. 181.

134. *Citizen*, 28 August 1855.

135. *Citizen*, 16 August 1855.

136. Elliott to Grey, 26 July 1855, Military Consultations, P/46/3, BL.

137. *Ibid.*

138. Bidwell to Grey, 14 August 1855, Judicial Proceedings, P/145/17, BL.

139. *Calcutta Literary Gazette*, 5 April 1856.

140. Atkinson to Lloyd, 17 August 1855, Military Consultations, P/46/4, BL.

141. Chapman to Bidwell, 22 October 1855, Judicial Proceedings, P/145/22, BL.

142. Shore, *Notes on Indian Affairs*, Vol. I, p. 16.

143. 'Delta', *Indigo and Its Enemies*, p. 20.

144. Bidwell to Grey, 14 August 1855, Judicial Proceedings, P/145/17, BL.

145. *Citizen*, 28 August 1855.

146. *Morning Chronicle* (Calcutta), 30 October 1855.

147. Bidwell to Grey, 14 August 1855, Judicial Proceedings, P/145/17, BL; Grey to Loch, 30 July 1855, Military Consultations, P/46/3, BL.

148. Lloyd to Atkinson, 10 August 1855, Military Consultations, P/46/4, BL.

149. Delamain to Gott, ND [September 1855], Military Consultations, P/46/9, BL.

150. According to the *Bengal Register*, officers of the Sonthal Field Force were variously proficient in Arabic, Assamese, Burmese, Hindee, Ordoo, Persian, and Punjaubee, but none in Bengali or Santali.

151. Shore, *Notes on Indian Affairs*, Vol. II, p. 25.

152. Fooks to Bird, 14, 17 and 18 August; Military Consultations, P/46/5, BL.

153. Pester to Parrott, c. 1 November 1855, Military Consultations, P/46/13, BL. William Halliday of the 56th also employed his own 'spies'.

154. Elliott to Grey, 9 August 1855, Military Consultations, P/46/4, BL.

155. *Ibid.*

156. *Ibid.* Halliday approved of Elliott's initiative.

157. Hampton to Parrott, 16 September 1855, Military Consultations, P/46/9, BL.

158. Burroughs to Becher, 21 August 1855, Military Consultations, P/46/12, BL.

159. Loch to Grey, 20 August 1855, Judicial Proceedings, P/145/17, BL.

160. Sherwill, *Geographical and Statistical Report of the District of Beerbhoom*, p. 1.

161. Loch to Grey, 11 August 1855, Military Consultations, P/46/4, BL.

162. Loch to Hampton, 16 August 1855, Military Consultations, P/46/4, BL.

163. Minute, Halliday, 20 August 1855, Military Consultations, P/46/5, BL.

164. Loch to Grey, 11 August 1855, Military Consultations, P/46/4, BL.

165. Bird to Becher, 16 August 1855, Military Consultations, P/46/5, BL. Significantly, the 42nd operated as part of Lloyd's field force, though the move did not eventuate.

166. Fooks to Bird, 16, 17 August 1855, Military Consultations, P/46/5, BL.

167. Service Army List Bengal, 407, Fooks, L/MIL/10/60, BL.

168. Durga Tudu, in Anderson and others, *From Fire Rain to Rebellion*, p. 183.

169. Fooks to Parrott, 25 August 1855, Military Consultations, P/46/6, BL.

170. Bird to Atkinson, 9 September 1855, Military Consultations, P/46/7, BL.

171. Lloyd to Atkinson, 15 October 1855, Military Consultations, P/46/12, BL.

172. Bird to Atkinson, 17 August 1855, Military Consultations, P/46/5, BL.

173. Bird to Atkinson, 20 August 1855, Military Consultations, P/46/5, BL.

174. Sherwill, *Geographical and Statistical Report of the District of Beerbhoom*, p. 4.

175. Joseph, *New and Improved Map of the Grand Trunk Road*.

176. Culshaw, *Tribal Culture*, p. 46.

177. Sherwill, *Geographical and Statistical Report of the District of Bhaugulpoor*, p. 3.

178. Sherwill, 'Notes on a tour through the Rajmahal Hills', *Journal of the Asiatic Society of Bengal*, p. 562.

179. Bernstein, *Steamboats on the Ganges*, p. 85.

180. T.E. Rogers to Halliday, 13 September 1855, Judicial Proceedings, P/145/20, BL.

181. Bird to Atkinson, 31 July 1855, Military Consultations, P/46/3, BL.

182. Bidwell to Grey, 18 August 1855, Judicial Proceedings, P/145/17, BL.

183. Chakraborti claimed that the Santals were 'proverbially afraid of deep waters'; that is, swollen rivers, but that Sidhu and his brothers professed to be able to lower the water level at fords by 'uttering magical formulas'; *History of the Santal Hool*, p. 41.

184. Minute, Halliday, 19 October 1855, Judicial Proceedings, P/145/22, BL.

185. Moncrieff to Loch, August 1855, Judicial Proceedings, P/145/20, BL.

186. 'Rolling Stock for transport of a whole Regiment at once, not considered desirable …'; Index to Military Consultations, 25 May 1855, Z/P/1648, BL.

187. Loch to Grey, 29 July 1855, Military Consultations, P/46/4, BL.

188. Bird to Templer, in Lloyd to Atkinson, 26 July 1855, Military Consultations, P/46/4, BL.

189. In his popular history of elephants, Charles Holder claimed that elephants had been 'rarely used' in revolts in India since the 1830s: again, the Santal rebellion was unknown (*The Ivory King*, p. 265).

190. Later in the rebellion experienced regiments could move with only three elephants for each company, including officers' baggage, surely the lightest the Bengal Army had ever marched: *Citizen*, 20 October 1855.

191. Atkinson to Lloyd, 4 August 1855, Military Consultations, P/46/4, BL; Grey to Atkinson, 13 August 1855, Military Consultations, P/46/4, BL.

192. Ravenshaw to Grey, 13 August 1855, Judicial Proceedings, P/145/17, BL.

193. *Morning Chronicle*, 17 September 1855.

194. Kaye, *The Administration of the East India Company*, p. 307.

195. Elliott, quoted in Atkinson to Tucker, 29 September 1855, Military Consultations, P/46/10, BL.

196. Atkinson to Deputy Commissary General and related papers, 4 August 1855, Military Consultations, P/46/4, BL.

197. Orders, Lloyd, 18 August 1855, Military Consultations, P/46/6, BL.

198. Lloyd to Mayhew, 22 July 1855, Military Consultations, P/46/3, BL.

199. *Morning Chronicle* (Calcutta), 18 August 1855.

200. Kaviraj claimed that the Santals maintained their own dawk system, but provided no evidence. (*Santal Village Community*, p. 134.)

201. *Englishman*, 22 December 1855.

202. Connor, *The Australian Frontier Wars*, pp. 93–100. Governor George Arthur's line used over 2000 soldiers and civilians in an operation lasting five weeks and costing £30,000; almost the same as the direct cost of the suppression of the Santal rebellion. It resulted in the capture of just two Tasmanian Aborigines.

203. *Bengal Hurkaru*, 6 December 1855.

204. Grey to Bidwell, 6 August 1855, Ray, *Santal Rebellion Documents*, p. 19.

205. Jha, *The Kol Insurrection*, pp. 103–16.

206. Bidwell to Grey, 20 August 1855, Judicial Proceedings, P/145/17, BL.

207. Money to Bidwell, 10 September 1855, Military Consultations, P/46/9, BL.

208. Money to Bidwell, 10 September 1855, Judicial Proceedings, P/145/20, BL.

209. Mangles to Hampton, 27 August 1855, Military Consultations, P/46/6, BL.

210. *Sheffield Daily Telegraph*, 22 October 1855.

211. Grey to Atkinson, 30 August; Atkinson to Bird, 31 August, Military Consultations, P/46/6, BL.

212. *Morning Chronicle* (Calcutta), 1 October 1855.

213. *Morning Chronicle* (Calcutta) 27 September 1855.

214. *Citizen*, 21 August 1855.

215. *Citizen*, 1 September 1855.

216. *Friend of India*, 16 August 1855.

217. Minute, Peacock, 30 September 1855, Military Consultations, P/46/10, BL.

218. *Citizen*, 26 September 1855.

219. Rose to Elliott, 24 September 1855, Military Consultations, P/46/10, BL.

220. Minute, Dorin, 2 October 1855, Military Consultations, P/46/10, BL.

221. Minute, Low, 3 October 1855, Military Consultations, P/46/10, BL.

4. *DESAE* (SEPTEMBER)

1. Bidwell to Grey, 26 September 1855, Judicial Proceedings, P/145/22, BL.

2. Sherwill, *Geographical and Statistical Report of the District of Bhaugulpoor*, p. 2. He left Lloyd's headquarters on 11 September.

3. India Military Letters Received 1855, 7 August 1855, L/MIL/3/69, BL.

4. *Glasgow Herald*, 29 August 1855.

5. *Daily News*, 8 September 1855.

6. *Daily News*, 13 September 1855.

7. *Sherborne Mercury*, 25 September 1855.

8. *Caledonian Mercury* (Edinburgh), 5 November 1855. The same brief line comprised the only mention in half-a-dozen other papers; about half the total coverage for November.

9. Wolley, *A Lecture on 'The War'*, p. 11.

10. Minute, Halliday, 19 October 1855, Judicial Proceedings, P/145/22, BL.

11. Grey to Atkinson, 31 August 1855, Military Consultations, P/46/7, BL.

12. *Citizen*, 3 September 1855.

13. *Citizen*, 15 August 1855.

14. Minute, Dorin, 3 October 1855, Military Consultations, P/46/10, BL.

15. Loch to Grey, 18 August 1855, Judicial Proceedings, P/145/17, BL.

16. *Citizen*, 3 August 1855; *Morning Chronicle* (Calcutta), 31 July 1855. Others, however, in the same issue described the pensioners as 'decrepid old men'.

17. Halliday, Minute, 30 July 1855, Military Consultations, P/46/3/BL.

18. Letter from 'Mr Atkinson', 25 July 1855 in Halliday, Minute, 30 July 1855, Military Consultations, P/46/3, BL.

19. *Friend of India*, 6 September 1855.

20. Elliott to Grey, 13 September 1855, Judicial Proceedings, P/145/20, BL.

21. Bird to Atkinson, 21 September 1855, Military Consultations, P/46/10, BL.

22. Minute, Grant, 11 October 1855, Military Consultations, P/46/10, BL.

23. Long Descriptive Roll, Town Major's List, 1854–55, L/MIL/10/175.

24. Atkinson to Bird, 18 October 1855, Military Consultations, P/46/11, BL.

25. Bird to Atkinson, 16 October 1855, Military Consultations, P/46/11, BL.

26. Lloyd to Atkinson, 10 October 1855, Military Consultations, P/46/11, BL.

27. Diary, Richardson, 1 October 1855, Judicial Proceedings, P/145/20, BL.

28. Chapman to Bidwell, 22 October 1855, Judicial Proceedings, P/145/22, BL.

29. Ward to Grey, 30 September 1855, Military Consultations, P/46/10, BL.

30. *Englishman*, 3 October 1855.

31. Boddam to Parrott, 11 October 1855, Military Consultations, P/46/11, BL.

32. *Englishman*, quoted in *Allen's Indian Mail*, 1 July 1856.

33. Liptrap to Ross, 11 September 1855, Military Consultations, P/46/9, BL.

34. *Englishman*, 13 September 1855.

35. *Hindoo Patriot*, 13 September 1855.

36. *Englishman*, 4 September 1855.

37. Bidwell to Grey, 5 September 1855, Military Consultations, P/46/8, BL.

38. C.J. Turner [?] to Nelson, 7 September 1855, Military Consultations, P/46/8, BL.

39. Diary, Richardson, 30 September 1855, Judicial Proceedings, P/145/20, BL.

40. Ward to Grey, 30 September 1855, Judicial Proceedings, P/145/20, BL.

41. Diary, Richardson, 1–3 October 1855, Judicial Proceedings, P/145/22, BL. Walter Sherwill described seeing such symbols in 1851—'prohibitory' marks 'strictly observed by all parties': 'Notes upon a tour through the Rajmahal Hills', *Journal of the Asiatic Society of Bengal*, p. 568.

42. Report of the Select Committee on East India (Railways), PP 1857–58, Vol. XIV, pp vi; 42.

43. Minute, 'Sonthal rising', Halliday, 17 September 1855, Military Consultations, P/46/8, BL.

44. Minute, Dorin, 2 October 1855, Military Consultations, P/46/10, BL.

45. Ward to Grey, 26 September 1855, Military Consultations, P/46/10, BL.

46. Lloyd to Atkinson, 15 September 1855, Military Consultations, P/46/9, BL.

47. 'The Thakoor's Perwannah', in Bidwell to Grey, 13 September 1855, Judicial Proceedings, P/145/20, BL.

48. Narahari Kaviraj explained that as Santal agriculture left plots fallow (and therefore unproductive), assessing rent according to land was less fair than assessments based on ploughs or animals: *Santal Village Community*, p. 193, fn 30.

49. Minute, Grant, 31 July 1855, Military Consultations, P/46/3, BL.

50. Cadell letter, 31 August 1855, Kendal Coghill papers, Box 1, Cambridge Centre for South Asian Studies.

51. *Citizen*, 3 August 1855.

52. 'History of the Services of the 3rd Bengal European Regiment', RSR.Ms 2–2, West Sussex Record Office.

53. Bird to Atkinson, 31 July 1855, Military Consultations, P/46/3, BL.

54. AG of Army [Mayhew] to Atkinson, 11 August 1855, Military Consultations, P/46/8, BL. Of 47 officers nominally on its strength, no fewer than 30 were absent.

55. Bird to Ross of the Army, 15 September 1855, Military Consultations, P/46/8, BL.

56. For example, Dutta-Majumder, *The Santal: a Study in Culture Change*, p. 29, but many other examples could be cited.

57. Lee-Warner, *Memoirs of Field Marshal Sir Henry Wylie Norman*, p. 44.

58. Braddon, *Thirty Years of Shikar*, pp. 85–86.

59. Hodson index, NAM; *Allen's Indian Mail*, 15 January 1856. On release he was cashiered after assaulting his wife.

60. Briggs to Atkinson, 22 August; Atkinson to Briggs, 11 September, Military Consultations, P/46/7, BL.

61. It was said that a Santal had hidden under Kempland's bed in a foiled attempt to murder him: if so it represented the Santals' only attempt to strike at Company leadership—*Morning Chronicle* (Calcutta), 30 October 1855.

62. *Morning Chronicle* (Calcutta), 13 August 1855.

63. Tucker to Atkinson, 11 August 1855, Military Consultations, P/46/4, BL. It was, however, made by telegraph, imparting a hint of urgency to the idea.

64. *Bengal Hurkaru*, 26 November 1855.

65. Tucker to Atkinson, 11 August; Mowatt to Atkinson, 17 August 1855, Military Consultations, P/46/5.

66. Inspector-General of Ordnance to Atkinson, 28 August 1855, Military Consultations, P/46/6, BL.

67. Diary, 12 August 1855, Dalhousie Papers, GD45/6/545, National Records of Scotland.

68. Inspector of Ordnance to Atkinson, 8 August 1855, Military Consultations, P/46/4, BL.

69. Mayhew to Atkinson, 16 August 1855, Military Consultations, P/46/5, BL.

70. Atkinson to Lloyd, 4 August 1855, Military Consultations, P/46/4, BL.

71. Ward to Grey, 25 October 1855, Judicial Proceedings, P/145/22, BL.

72. Bird to Atkinson, 10 August 1855, Military Consultations, P/46/4, BL.

73. Nembhard to Parrott, 23 October 1855, Military Consultations, P/46/13, BL.

74. Loch to Grey, 18 August 1855, Judicial Proceedings, P/145/17, BL.

75. *Citizen*, 23 August 1855. The 200,000 figure, Sherwill's 'calculation', soon became accepted as fact, such was his authority, though other sources put the Santal population of the region at under 100,000. Vasudha Dhagamwar was sceptical of the higher estimate: *Role and Image of Law in India*, p. 184n.

76. Sherwill, *Geographical and Statistical Report of the District of Beerbhoom*, p. 7.

77. Ward to Grey, 15 September 1855, Military Consultations, P/46/8, BL.

78. Bird to Atkinson, 16 September 1855, Military Consultations, P/46/9, BL.

79. Richardson to Bird, 13 September 1855, Military Consultations, P/46/9, BL.

80. Rose to Elliott, 24 September 1855, Military Consultations, P/46/10, BL.

81. Rose to Elliott, 24 September 1855, Military Consultations, P/46/10, BL.

82. Hampton to Parrott, ND, c. 16–21 September, Military Consultations, P/46/9, BL.

83. Bird to Atkinson, 19 September 1855, Military Consultations, P/46/9, BL.

84. Ward to Grey, 26 September 1855, Judicial Proceedings, P/46/10, BL.

85. Ward to Grey, 23 September 1855, Military Consultations, P/46/10, BL.

86. Richardson to Burney, c. 20 September 1855, Military Consultations, P/46/10, BL.

87. Ward to Grey, 26 September 1855, Military Consultations, P/46/10, BL.

88. Elliott to Grey, 26 September 1855, Military Consultations, P/46/10, BL.

89. Ward to Grey, 26 September 1855, Military Consultations, P/46/10, BL. Vincent Jervis told William Hunter a similar story.

90. Ward to Grey, 13 October 1855, Judicial Proceedings, P/145/22, BL.

91. Ward to Grey, 26 September 1855, Military Consultations, P/46/10, BL.

92. *Citizen*, 6 October 1855.

93. *Morning Chronicle* (Calcutta), 20 August 1855.

94. Bird to Becher, 5 October 1855, Military Consultations, P/46/10, BL.

95. Bird to Atkinson, 6 October 1855, Military Consultations, P/46/10, BL.

96. Bidwell to Bird, 4 October 1855, Military Consultations, P/46/10, BL. Lloyd approved of the order when he returned.

97. Lloyd to Atkinson, 4 October 1855, Military Consultations, P/46/10, BL.

98. Culshaw, *Tribal Heritage*, p. 10.

99. Bose, *Peasant Labour and Colonial Capital*, p. 152.

100. Eden to Grey, 9 July 1855, Military Consultations, P/46/1, BL.

101. Kaviraj, *Santal Village Community*, pp. 21, 45–53.

102. *Morning Chronicle* (Calcutta), 27 July 1855.

103. *Hindoo Patriot*, 19 July 1855.

104. *Morning Chronicle* (Calcutta), 28 July 1855.

105. *Morning Chronicle* (Calcutta), 31 July 1855.

106. *Friend of India*, 3 January 1856.

107. Raghavaiah, *Tribal Revolts*, p. 152.

108. Chapman to Bidwell, 22 October 1855, Judicial Proceedings, P/145/22, BL; Reports by Lloyd, 11 & 17 August 1855, Military Consultations, P/46/5, BL.

109. Guha, *Elementary Aspects of Peasant Insurgency in Colonial India*, p. 96.

110. *Bengal Hurkaru*, 21 July 1855.

111. *Friend of India*, 3 January 1856.

112. Archer, *The Hill of Flutes*, p. 25; Datta-Majumder, *The Santal: a Study in Culture Change*, p. 39. These hunting parties could number up to 4,000 men—roughly the size of some Santal bands reported during the Hul: 'The Sonthal Parganas', *Calcutta Review*, 1 December 1860, p 528.

113. *Allen's Indian Mail*, 119 September 1855.

114. *Citizen*, 7 August 1855.

115. O'Malley, *Bengal District Gazetteers: Santal Parganas*, p. 49.

116. Chapman to Bidwell, 22 October 1855, Judicial Proceedings, P/145/22, BL.

117. Bidwell to Grey, 13 September 1855, Military Consultations, P/46/9, BL.

118. Money to Bidwell, 6 September 1855, P/36/9, BL.

119. Diary, Richardson, 1 October 1855, Judicial Proceedings, P/145/20, BL. Richardson did not record who Mr Kerr was or how he had acquired this knowledge. Kaviraj refers to another meeting, near Raksandangal, p. 46.

120. Ward to Grey, 29 September 1855, Judicial Proceedings, P/145/20, BL.

121. Minute, Halliday, 19 October 1855, Judicial Proceedings, P/145/22, BL.

122. Hampton to Parrott, 16 September 1855, Military Consultations, P/46/9, BL.

123. Mallick, 'Santal Women and the Rebellion of 1855 in Colonial India', *Indian Journal of Women and Social Change*, p. 13.

124. Richardson, Diary, 20 September 1855 and Ward to Grey, 21 September 1855, Judicial Proceedings, P/145/20, BL.

125. Burney to Parrott, 12 October 1855, Military Consultations, P/46/12, BL.

126. Money to Bidwell, 6 September 1855, Military Consultations, P/46/9, BL.

127. Bird to Atkinson, 30 September 1855, Military Consultations, P/46/10, BL.

128. *Morning Chronicle* (Calcutta), 20 July 1855.

129. Lloyd to Atkinson, 5 August 1855, Military Consultations, P/46/4, BL.

130. *Englishman*, 31 July 1855.

131. Ward to Richardson, 16 October 1855, Judicial Proceedings, P/145/22, BL.

132. Jugia Haram in Culshaw & Archer, 'The Santal Rebellion', *Man in India*, December 1945, p. 232.

133. Durga Tudu in Anderson and others, *From Fire Rain to Rebellion*, p. 185.

134. Lloyd to Atkinson, 19 August 1855, Military Consultations, P/46/6, BL. This was evidently a different Ram Manjee to the one taken by Frederick Dunbar's sepoys in October.

135. For example, Datta describes divisions between Tribuhan and Jagannath Sirdar (who killed the Henshawes) and Sidhu and Kanhu, who deprecated the murder of Europeans, after which Tribuhan operated independently: Datta, 'The Santhal Insurrection of 1855–56', *Bengal Past & Present*, 1935, p. 42.

136. Chakraborti, *History of the Santal Hool*, p. 43. This suggests that Chakraborti's informants must have included Santals, if not participants, then probably their sons or grandsons.

137. Culshaw & Archer, 'The Santal Rebellion', *Man in India*, December 1945, p. 221. Was the palki loot? Avijit acknowledges that 'the origin and nature of the palanquins used during the rebellion of 1855 remain uncertain', 'Visual Culture of the Santals and their Image', p. 144.

138. Jugia Haram in Culshaw & Archer, 'The Santal Rebellion', *Man in India*, December 1945, p. 232.

139. Money to Bidwell, 6 September 1855, Judicial Proceedings, P/145/20, BL.

140. Ward to Grey, 9 September 1855, Military Consultations, P/46/8, BL.

141. *Friend of India*, 20 September 1855.

142. *Citizen*, 14 September 1855. 'Kilkenny cats refers to a *Punch* cartoon by Richard

Doyle, referring to two Irish cats which, left 'alone' would 'fight to the bone/ And leave but their tails behind 'em'. *Punch*, 8 August 1846.

143. Jugia Haram in Culshaw & Archer, 'The Santal Rebellion', *Man in India*, December 1945, p. 232.

144. Minute, Grant, 14 July 1855, Military Consultations, P/46/1, BL.

145. Hunter, *The Annals of Rural Bengal*, pp. 250–51. The official record contains few angry messages, but the Military Consultations did not include 'private letters'.

146. Elliott to Grey, ND [15 July 1855], Military Consultations, P/46/1, BL.

147. *Friend of India*, 15 November 1855.

148. Campbell, *Modern India*, p. 276.

149. Grey to Atkinson, 21 July 1855, Military Consultations, P/46/2, BL.

150. Jha, *The Kol Insurrection*, p. 92.

151. Minute, Dorin, 22 July 1855, Military Consultations, P/46/2, BL.

152. Minutes by Low, Grant and Peacock, 22–23 July 1855, Military Consultations, P/46/2, BL. Low's 17-year-old son was an 'unattached cornet'—the most junior cavalry officer—but through Low's influence had been attached to serve with the Governor-General's Bodyguard.

153. *Morning Chronicle* (Calcutta), 14 August 1855.

154. Minute, Halliday, 19 October 1855, Judicial Proceedings, P/145/22, BL.

155. *Morning Chronicle* (Calcutta), 20 August 1855.

156. *Citizen*, 24 October 1855.

157. *Citizen*, 30 October 1855.

158. *Colburn's United Service Magazine*, July 1855, p. 446.

159. *Citizen*, 15 November 1855.

160. *Citizen*, 24 January 1856.

161. Kaye, *The Administration of the East India Company*, p. 306.

162. The Grand Trunk Road was so smooth here because it was actually brand new. Though mainly constructed under the Mughals, the new stretch of road patrolled by Company troops during the rebellion had been completed only in 1848 after the bridge over the Baraker had been built, a further demonstration of how the Company's policy of creating infrastructure changed India: Houlton, *Bihar: the Heart of India*, pp. 174–77.

163. Bird to Atkinson, 5 August 1855, Military Consultations, P/46/4, BL.

164. Bird to Atkinson, 15 August 1855, Military Consultations, P/46/5, BL.

165. Kaye, *The Administration of the East India Company*, p. 308.

166. Sherwill to Halliday, 8 August 1855, Military Consultations, P/46/5, BL.

167. It became clear that many, perhaps most Santals remained in or returned to their villages. An officer of the 50th affirmed that 'the whole Santhal population has *not* collected ready for migration': *Morning Chronicle* (Calcutta), 8 September 1855.

168. Bird to Hampton, 15 August 1855, Military Consultations, P/46/5, BL.

169. Hampton to Mayhew, 2 August 1855, Military Consultations, P/46/6, BL.

170. *Morning Chronicle* (Calcutta), 20 August 1855.

171. Needham to Hampton, 19 August 1855, Military Consultations, P/46/5, BL.

172. Report, Phillips, 23 September 1855, Military Consultations, P/46/10, BL.

173. Hampton to Parrott, 26 September 1855, Military Consultations, P/46/10, BL.

174. Phillips to Mangles, 16 September 1855, Military Consultations, P/46/10, BL.

175. *Citizen*, 2 October 1855.

176. Bird to Atkinson, 21 September 1855, Military Consultations, P/46/10, BL.

177. Ward to Grey, 26 September 1855, Military Consultations, P/46/10, BL.

178. Ward to Grey, 25 September 1855, Military Consultations, P/46/10, BL.

179. *Ibid.*

180. *Citizen*, 24 September 1855.

181. *Citizen*, 16 October 1855.

5. *KARTIK* (OCTOBER)

1. Bidwell to Grey, 26 September 1855, Judicial Proceedings, P/145/22, BL.

2. Ward to Grey, 25 September 1855, Military Consultations, P/46/10, BL.

3. Bird to Atkinson, 20 September 1855, Military Consultations, P/46/9, BL.

4. Ward to Grey, 30 September 1855, Judicial Proceedings, P/145/20, BL.

5. Service Army List Bengal, 1855, 408 Parrott, L/MIL/10/60, BL.

6. Bird to Atkinson, 7 October 1855, Military Consultations, P/46/10, BL.

7. Bird to Atkinson, 14 October 1855, Military Consultations, P/46/11, BL.

8. *Citizen*, 16 October 1855.

9. Boddam to Parrott, 11 October 1855, Military Consultations, P/46/11, BL. It seems that Phillips, the senior officer, was absent, and that Boddam acted on his own initiative.

10. Diary, 26 September 1855, Military Consultations, P/46/10, BL.

11. Bird to Atkinson, 7 October 1855, Military Consultations, P/46/10, BL.

12. Ward to Grey, 30 September 1855, Military Consultations, P/46/10, BL.

13. Minute, Grant, 11 October 1855, Military Consultations, P/46/10, BL.

14. *Morning Chronicle* (Calcutta), 30 October 1855.

15. Pester to Parrott, 5 October 1855, Military Consultations, P/46/10, BL.

16. Ward to Grey, 25 October 1855, Judicial Proceedings, P/145/22, BL; *Citizen*, 28 November 1855.

17. Grey to Beadon, 15 November 1855, Judicial Proceedings, P/145/23, BL.

18. Phillips to Parrott, 8 October 1855, Military Consultations, P/46/10, BL.

19. Nicholl report, 19 October, in Bird to Atkinson, 22 October, Military Consultations, P/46/12, BL. A newspaper report described the Santals use of matchlocks in this action as the first, but a few had used captured guns before, probably at Koomerabad in August.

20. Nicholl report, 20 October, in Bird to Atkinson, 23 October, Military Consultations, P/46/12, BL.

21. *Sambad Pravakar*, 3 August 1855, quoted in Gupta, *The Economic Life of a Bengal District*, p. 305.

22. *Morning Chronicle* (Calcutta), 27 July 1855.

23. *Morning Chronicle* (Calcutta), 31 July 1855.

24. Index entry, 16 August 1855, Z/P/237, BL.

25. *Morning Chronicle* (Calcutta), 26 July 1855.

26. Elliott to Grey, 18 June 1855, Judicial Proceedings, P/145/19, BL.

27. Richardson to Bidwell, 12 August 1855, P/145/17, BL.

28. *Ibid.*

29. *A Penal Code prepared by the Indian Law Commissioners*, p. 15.

30. *Friend of India*, 30 August 1855.

31. Ward to Grey, 21 September 1855, Judicial Proceedings, P/145/20, BL.

32. Mallick, 'Santal Women and the Rebellion of 1855 in Colonial India, *Indian Journal of Women and Social Change*, p. 13.

33. Kaviraj, *Santal Village Community*, p. 53.

34. Ward to Grey, 28 October 1855, Judicial Proceedings, P/145/23, BL.

35. Bidwell to Grey, 26 October 1855, Judicial Proceedings, P/145/22, BL, and subsequent folios, in exchanges continuing into November.

36. Bengal Criminal Proceedings, 1855, E/4/842, BL.

37. *Morning Chronicle* (Calcutta), 28 July 1855.

38. *Citizen*, 8 November 1855.

39. Mallick, 'Santal Women and the Rebellion of 1855 in Colonial India', *Indian Journal of Women and Social Change*, p. 16, quoting the Weekly Sanitary Report for 10 November 1855.

40. Bidwell to Toogood, 22 October 1855, Judicial Proceedings, P/145/23, BL.

41. India and Bengal Despatches, 4 February 1857, E/4/842, BL.

42. Ward to Grey, 13 October 1855, Judicial Proceedings, P/145/22, BL.

43. *Citizen*, 19 July 1855.

44. *Englishman*, quoted in *Allen's Indian Mail*, 1 July 1856.

45. Ironically, Cleveland's cutcherry became part of Bhagulpur University, later renamed Tilka Manji in honour of his assassin, re-fashioned as a precursor of the 'freedom movement'.

46. Lloyd to Atkinson, 3 August 1855, Military Consultations, P/46/4, BL.

47. Hawes to Parrot, 2 November 1855, Military Consultations, P/46/13, BL.

48. Kaviraj, *Santal Village Community*, Chapter 6, p. 123.

49. *Cheshire Observer*, 27 October 1855. The Kol insurrection actually occurred over the winter of 1831–32.

50. Ward to Grey, 13 October 1855, Judicial Proceedings, P/145/22, BL.

51. Chakraborti, *History of the Santal Hool*, p. 32; Kaviraj offers a similar list of castes captured among Santals; *Santal Village Community*, pp. 116–19.

52. Phillips to Parrott, 4 December 1855, Military Consultations, P/46/16, BL.

53. Gupta, *The Economic Life of a Bengal District*, p. 301, quoting a letter from Brown to Grey, 28 July 1855.

54. Hunter, *The Annals of Rural Bengal*, p. 250.

55. Lloyd to Atkinson, 5 August 1855, Military Consultations, P/46/4, BL.

56. Mallick, 'Santal Women and the Rebellion of 1855 in Colonial India, *Indian Journal of Women and Social Change*, p. 13, quoting Judicial Consultations, 27 March 1856.

57. *Morning Chronicle* (Calcutta), 23 July 1855.
58. *Morning Chronicle* (Calcutta), 4 August 1855.
59. *Morning Chronicle* (Calcutta), 24 July 1855.
60. Man, *Sonthalia and the Sonthals*, pp. 121–22.
61. *Leicester Journal*, 5 October 1855.
62. Bidwell to Grey, 13 September; Pontet to Bidwell, 13 September 1855, Judicial Proceedings, P/145/20, BL.
63. Shah, *Nightmarch*, p. 135.
64. Elliott to Grey, 26 July 1855, Military Consultations, P/46/3, BL.
65. *Englishman*, 23 August 1855.
66. *Citizen*, 18 August 1855.
67. Lloyd to Atkinson, 15 September 1855, Military Consultations, P/46/9, BL.
68. Bird to Atkinson, 17 October 1855, Military Consultations, P/46/12, BL.
69. *Citizen*, 4 October 1855.
70. Ram, *From Sepoy to Subedar*, p. 160.
71. Ward to Grey, 13 October 1855, Judicial Proceedings, P/145/22, BL.
72. *Bengal Hurkaru*, 15 July 1855.
73. Sidhu's testimony, in Bidwell to Grey, c. 17 September 1855, Judicial Proceedings, P/145/22, BL.
74. Bird to Atkinson, 14 September 1855, Military Consultations, P/46/8, BL.
75. *Englishman*, 22 September 1855.
76. Court of Inquiry, Rajmahal, 8 October 1855, Judicial Proceedings, P/145/22, BL.
77. *Citizen*, 24 August 1855. Narahari Kaviraj quoted Chand as claiming that sepoys of the 7th Native Infantry 'plundered' the money the brothers had stored at Bhugnadihee: *Santal Village Community*, p. 175, fn 39.
78. Braddon, *Thirty Years of Shikar*, p. 85.
79. *Morning Chronicle* (Calcutta), 28 July 1855.
80. Toogood to Elliott, Chief Magistrate, Calcutta, 23 July 1855, Military Consultations, P/46/3, BL.
81. Hunter, *The Annals of Rural Bengal*, p. 248.
82. Durga Tudu, in Anderson and others, *From Fire Rain to Rebellion*, p. 181.
83. *Citizen*, 30 July 1855.
84. *Citizen*, 3 August 1855.
85. *Church Missionary Papers*, No. CLXV, Lady Day, 1857. The article implies that this officer was Lieutenant James Burn of the 40th Native Infantry.
86. A pamphleteer, a missionary at Benares, one of many seeking to explain the mutiny of the native army, claimed that the 37th when it mutinied at Benares included 400 or even 600 Brahmins; Kennedy, *The Great Indian Mutiny of 1857*, p. 52. In assessing whether European women had been 'given up to the sensual licence of the sepoys', Edward Leckey concluded that 'it seems doubtful that … a sepoy would have polluted himself with their touch': *Fictions connected with the Indian Outbreak of 1857 Exposed*, p. 109.
87. Shore, *Notes on Indian Affairs*, Vol. I, p. 419.

334

88. Jugia Haram in Culshaw & Archer, 'The Santal Rebellion', *Man in India*, December 1945, p. 232.

89. *Ibid.*, p. 234.

90. Bird to Atkinson, 7 October 1855, Military Consultations, P/46/10, BL.

91. Pester to Parrott, 22 October 1855, Military Consultations, P/46/13, BL.

92. Bird to Atkinson, 6 November 1855, Military Consultations, P/46/13, BL. Human sacrifice was hardly known among the Santals, and then only because of sorcery: O'Malley, *Bengal District Gazetteers: Santal Parganas*, pp. 122–23.

93. *Citizen*, 31 October 1855.

94. Diary, Richardson, 26 September 1855, Military Consultations, P/46/10, BL.

95. Ward to Grey, 13 October 1855, Judicial Proceedings, P/145/22, BL.

96. J.P. Willoughby before the Select Committee on Indian Territories, 28 May 1852, PP 1852, Vol. X, p. 153.

97. Halliday and members of the Council also differed over many matters unrelated to the Hul, such as over land tenure and the admission of uncovenanted officials to lucrative positions: see W. Theobald, *Indian Tracts No. 1* and 'H.R.', *A Very Few Words Respecting the Constitution of the Covenanted and Uncovenanted Services of India*.

98. *Standard* (London), 15 November 1855.

99. Dalhousie to Couper, 22 August 1855, Baird, Private Letters, p, 354.

100. Trotter, *Life of The Marquis of Dalhousie*, pp. 62–63.

101. Minute, Grant, 11 October 1855, Military Consultations, P/46/10, BL.

102. *Friend of India*, 10 May 1855, quoted in *Allen's Indian Mail*, 3 July 1855.

103. As Sidhu called surveyors when questioned by Ashley Eden after his capture; Judicial Proceedings, P/145/22, BL.

104. *Citizen*, 30 July 1855.

105. *Allen's Indian Mail*, 21 March 1855.

106. *Friend of India*, 3 January 1856.

107. *Friend of India*, 26 July 1855.

108. *Friend of India*, 20 September 1855.

109. Culshaw, *Tribal Heritage*, p. 47.

110. Allen to Grey, 29 September 1855, Military Consultations, P/46/10, BL; Lloyd to Atkinson, 1855, Military Consultations, P/46/12, BL.

111. Bird to Atkinson, 30 September 1855, Military Consultations, P/46/10, BL.

112. Nicholl report, 19 October, in Bird to Atkinson, 22 October, Military Consultations, P/46/12, BL.

113. *Citizen*, 26 October 1855.

114. Hunter, *The Annals of Rural Bengal*, p. 248.

115. Mahapatra, *Bakhen*, p. 39.

116. Lloyd to Atkinson, 4 October 1855, Military Consultations, P/46/10, BL.

117. Middleton, 'A Reminiscence of the Santhal Rebellion', *United Service Magazine*, 1893, p. 1075.

118. Dunbar to Bird, 17 October 1855, Military Consultations, P/46/12, BL; Anderson, *Ubique*, p. 200.

119. Lloyd to Atkinson, 19 October 1855, Military Consultations, P/46/12, BL.

120. Bidwell to Grey, 26 October 1855, Judicial Proceedings, P/145/22, BL.

121. Lloyd to Atkinson, 19 October 1855, Military Consultations, P/46/12, BL.

122. Pester to Parrott, 20 October 1855, Military Consultations, P/46/12, BL.

123. Chotrae Desmanjhi in Culshaw & Archer, 'The Santal Rebellion', *Man in India*, December 1945, p. 236.

124. Phillips to Parrott, 14 October 1855, Military Consultations, P/46/12, BL.

125. Phillips to Parrott, 30 October 1855, Military Consultations, P/46/13, BL.

126. *Citizen*, 19 October 1855.

127. *Friend of India*, 11 October 1855.

128. Eden to Bidwell, 24 October 1855, Judicial Proceedings, P/145/22, BL.

129. Bradley-Birt added that Sidhu was hanged by Pontet, and 'in the presence of a vast concourse of Santals, who watched the proceedings with the apathy born of defeat'; *The Story of an Indian Upland*, p. 206.

130. *Morning Chronicle* (Calcutta), 18 July 1855.

131. 'The Santals', *Household Words*, Vol. XXXV, p. 111.

132. *Morning Chronicle* (Calcutta), 31 August 1855.

133. *Church Missionary Papers*, No. CLXV, Lady Day 1857.

134. *Morning Chronicle* (Calcutta), 31 July 1855.

135. 'The Sonthal Pergunnahs', *Calcutta Review*, 1 December 1860, p. 511.

136. *Englishman*, 2 August 1855.

137. *Morning Chronicle* (Calcutta), 3 August 1855.

138. *Allen's Indian Mail*, 19 September 1855.

139. *Citizen*, 1 September 1855.

140. *Citizen*, 27 September 1855. Though subtitled the *Military Chronicle*, the *Englishman* apparently did not appeal to military officersas much as the *Citizen*. The *Citizen* claimed that its rival published 'more scandal and abuse', though all Calcutta papers seem to have vied on that score: *Citizen*, 28 November 1855.

141. *Friend of India*, 15 November 1855.

142. Ward to Grey, 13 October 1855, Judicial Proceedings, P/145/22, BL.

143. *Morning Chronicle* (Calcutta), 19 October 1855.

144. *Citizen*, 24 January 1856.

145. *Bengal Hurkaru*, 25 August 1855.

146. *Citizen*, 31 August 1855; *Friend of India*, 29 November 1855; *Citizen*, 9 October 1855.

147. For example, McPhail, *The Santal Mission*, p. 11; Ghurye, *The Scheduled Tribes*, p. 40; Gupta, *The Economic Life of a Bengal District*, p. 305. Anderson and others in *From Fire Rain to Rebellion* gives 12,000 Santal deaths.

148. Jugia Haram in Culshaw & Archer, 'The Santal Rebellion', *Man in India*, December 1945, p. 231.

149. *Allen's Indian Mail*, 19 September 1855.

150. *Citizen*, 16 August 1855.

151. *Friend of India*, 23 August 1855.

152. *Morning Chronicle*, 1 October 1855.

153. *Morning Chronicle*, 1 September 1855.

154. Hampton to Parrott, 16 September 1855, Military Consultations, P/46/9, BL; *Citizen*, 14 September 1855.

155. *Morning Chronicle* (Calcutta), 10 September 1855.

156. Hampton to Parrott, 31 October 1855, Military Consultations, P/46/13, BL.

157. Kaviraj, *Santal Village Community*, p. 92, quoting a minute dated 25 January 1856 in the Judicial Proceedings.

158. Maunder, *The Scientific and Literary Treasury*, p. 135.

159. Mahapatra, *Bakhen*, p. 33.

6. *AGHAN* (NOVEMBER) AND *PUS* (DECEMBER)

1. *Bengal Annual Register and Directory*, 1855, p. 5.

2. *Citizen*, 20 November 1855.

3. Minute, Halliday, 19 October 1855, Judicial Proceedings, P/145/22, BL.

4. Phillips to Parrott, 30 October 1855, Military Consultations, P/46/13, BL.

5. Bidwell to Grey, 26 October 1855, Judicial Proceedings, P/145/22, BL.

6. *Morning Chronicle* (Calcutta), 8 September 1855.

7. Ward to Grey, 30 October 1855, Judicial Proceedings, P/145/23, BL.

8. Bidwell to Grey, 18 August 1855, Judicial Proceedings, P/145/17, BL.

9. Richardson to Burney, 12 October 1855, Ray, *Santal Rebellion Documents*, p. 28.

10. Richardson to Grey, 1 September 1855, Judicial Proceedings, P/145/17, BL.

11. Richardson to Ward, c. 8 October 1855, Military Consultations, P/46/11, BL.

12. *Citizen*, 15 November 1855.

13. Lloyd to Atkinson, 30 October 1855, Military Consultations, P/46/13, BL.

14. *Ibid.*

15. Richardson to Grey, 31 December 1855, Roy, *Santal Rebellion Documents*, pp. 52–53.

16. Lloyd to Atkinson, 15 October 1855, Military Consultations, P/46/11, BL.

17. Phillips to Parrott, c. 28 October 1855, Military Consultations, P/46/13, BL.

18. Halliday to Bird, 19 November 1855, Military Consultations, P/46/16, BL.

19. Lister to Parrott, 21 November 1855, Military Consultations, P/46/14, BL.

20. Jervis report in Bird to Parrott, 27 November 1855, Military Consultations, P/46/16, BL.

21. *Morning Chronicle* (Calcutta), 27 July 1855.

22. Avijit's thesis on Santal material culture documents shields of bamboo, wood and metal, and Sherwill's drawings, published in the *Illustrated London News* in 1856, depict Santals with them; 'Visual Culture of the Santals and their Image', pp. 155–57.

23. Money to Bidwell, 16 August 1855, Judicial Proceedings, P/145/17, BL.

24. Man, *Sonthalia and the Sonthals*, p. 121.

25. *Englishman*, 20 July 1855.

26. *Citizen*, 23 July 1855.
27. *Englishman*, 13 September 1855.
28. Hunter, *The Annals of Rural Bengal*, pp. 248–49.
29. Chakraborti, *History of the Santal Hool*, p. 46.
30. *Citizen*, 19 July 1855.
31. Lloyd to Atkinson, 28 July 1855, Military Consultations, P/46/3, BL.
32. Lloyd to Atkinson, 6 August 1855, Military Consultations, P/46/4, BL.
33. *Morning Chronicle* (Calcutta), 22 October 1855.
34. Ward to Grey, 29 September 1855, Judicial Proceedings, P/145/20, BL.
35. Nembhard to Assistant Adjutant-General, Presidency Division, 24 July 1855, Military Consultations, P/46/3, BL.
36. *Morning Chronicle* (Calcutta), 29 August 1855.
37. Culshaw, *Tribal Culture*, pp. 43–44.
38. Hunter, *The Annals of Rural Bengal*, p. 248.
39. Bird to Atkinson, 14 October 1855, Military Consultations, P/46/11, BL.
40. Ramsay to Atkinson, 23 August 1855, Military Consultations, P/46/11, BL.
41. Bird to Atkinson, 14 October 1855, Military Consultations, P/46/11, BL.
42. Atkinson to Bird, 18 October 1855, Military Consultations, P/46/11, BL.
43. Bidwell to Grey, 25 October 1855, Judicial Proceedings, P/145/22, BL.
44. The southward advance would involve four full regiments (the 13th, 31st, 40th and 42nd) with some irregular cavalry and the Rangers, along with a small artillery detachment marching with Lloyd.
45. Beadon to Grey, 8 November 1855, Judicial Proceedings, P/145/23, BL.
46. The text of the proclamation was recorded in all newspapers and of course in the Military Consultations and Judicial Consultations.
47. Beadon to Grey, 8 November 1855, Military Consultations, P/46/13, BL.
48. *Citizen*, 12 November 1855.
49. Atkinson to Lloyd; Atkinson to Grey, 15 November 1855, Military Consultations, P/46/14, BL.
50. Monthly return of the Troops under the Command of Major-General G.W. Lloyd, 1 November 1855, Military Consultations, P/46/16, BL.
51. Lloyd to Atkinson, 8 November 1855, Military Consultations, P/46/14, BL.
52. Minute, Halliday, 19 October 1855, Judicial Proceedings, P/145/22, BL. The wind in March, he predicted, was 'a messenger of death': 'Notes upon a tour through the Rajmahal Hills', *Journal of the Asiatic Society of Bengal*, 1851, p. 549.
53. *Sheffield Daily Telegraph*, 25 March 1856.
54. Bird to Grey, 6 December 1855, Military Consultations, P/46/16, BL.
55. *Citizen*, 1 December 1855.
56. *Citizen*, 1 January 1856.
57. Durga Tudu, in Anderson and others, *From Fire Rain to Rebellion*, p. 185.
58. Kaviraj, *Santal Village Community*, p. 59.
59. Bird to Atkinson, 30 September 1855, Military Consultations, P/46/10, BL.
60. *Bengal Hurkaru*, 5 December 1855.

61. *Bengal Hurkaru*, 6 December 1855.
62. *Ibid.*
63. *Allen's Indian Mail*, 4 March 1856.
64. *Bengal Hurkaru*, 3 December 1855.
65. *Bengal Hurkaru*, 30 November 1855.
66. *Bengal Hurkaru*, 5 December 1855.
67. Bird to Shute 25 November 1855, Military Consultations, P/46/16, BL.
68. *Bengal Hurkaru*, 5 December 1855.
69. Sherwill, 'Notes upon a tour through the Rajmahal Hills', *Journal of the Asiatic Society of Bengal*, p. 564.
70. *Englishman*, 22 December 1855. Presumably a copying error for 'Gopalpore'.
71. *Bengal Hurkaru*, 6 December 1855.
72. *Ibid.*, 1855.
73. *Bengal Hurkaru*, 18 December 1855.
74. *Bengal Hurkaru*, 21 December 1855.
75. *Bengal Hurkaru*, 6 & 21 December 1855.
76. *Englishman*, 22 December 1855.
77. Santal songs, culled from the many compiled in Archer, *The Hill of Flutes*.
78. Lister to Parrott, 27 November 1855, Military Consultations, P/46/16, BL.
79. Lloyd to Atkinson, 4 December 1855, Military Consultations, P/46/16, BL.
80. *Friend of India*, 13 December 1855.
81. *Citizen*, 6 December 1855.
82. Bidwell to Grey, 17 September 1855, Judicial Proceedings, P/145/22, BL.
83. *Englishman*, 22 December 1855.
84. *Bengal Hurkaru*, 10 December 1855.
85. *Friend of India*, 11 October 1855.
86. *Sheffield Daily Telegraph*, 2 May 1856; copied from Edinburgh's *Evening Courant*, nd; Kaviraj, *Santal Village Community*, p. 99. Chand and Bhairab were transported, probably to Burmah, dying far from their native land.
87. Beadon to Grey, 8 November 1855, Military Consultations, P/46/13, BL.
88. *Bengal Hurkaru*, 6 December 1855.
89. Report by Hawes, 27 November 1855, Military Consultations, P/46/16, BL.
90. Dalhousie to Couper, 15 December 1855, Baird, *Private Letters*, p. 362.
91. *Citizen*, 12 December 1855.
92. Bird to Grey, 5 December 1855, Military Consultations, P/46/16, BL.
93. *Citizen*, 13 December 1855.
94. *Bengal Hurkaru*, 15 December 1855.
95. *Englishman*, 22 December 1855.
96. *Ibid.*
97. *Ibid.*
98. Shore, *Notes on Indian Affairs*, Vol. I, p. 13.
99. *Bengal Hurkaru*, 12 December 1855.
100. *Englishman*, 19 December 1855.

101. Mallick, 'Santal Women and the Rebellion of 1855 in Colonial India', *Indian Journal of Women and Social Change*, p. 19.

102. *Citizen*, 22 December 1855.

103. Hawes, report, 11 December 1855, Military Consultations, P/46/16, BL.

104. Mahapatra, *Bakhen*, p. 27.

105. *Bengal Hurkaru*, 10 December 1855.

106. Halliday to Lloyd, 25 December 1855, Military Consultations, P/46/26, BL.

107. *Citizen*, 18 December 1855.

108. *Citizen*, 26 December 1855.

109. *Church Missionary Papers*, No. CLXV, Lady Day, 1857.

110. Anderson and others, *From Fire Rain to Rebellion*, p. 15.

111. Lloyd to Grey, 13 December 1855, Military Consultations, P/46/17, BL.

112. *Ibid.*

113. Buckland, *Bengal Under the Lieutenant-Governors*, p. 15.

114. Campbell to Parrott, 14 December 1855, Military Consultations, P/46/16, BL.

115. Hawes, report, 14 December 1855, Military Consultations, P/46/16, BL.

116. Archer, *The Hill of Flutes*, pp. 27–31.

117. Bradley-Birt, *The Story of an Indian Upland*, pp. 279–80.

118. Kaviraj, *Santal Village Community*, p. 7.

119. *Citizen*, 22 March 1856.

120. Fuchs, *Rebellious Prophets*, p. 52.

121. *Citizen*, 7 January 1856.

122. Man, *Sonthalia and the Sonthals*, p. 120.

123. *Sheffield Daily Telegraph*, 25 March 1856.

124. Mouat, *Report on Jails Visited and Inspected in Bengal, Behar, and Arracan*, pp. 50–58; 134–8.

125. India and Bengal Despatches, 4 February 1857, E/4/842 NBI/174?.

126. Report, Thompson, 19 December 1855, Roy, *Santal Rebellion Documents*, pp. 49–51.

127. Halliday to Bird, 19 November 1855, Military Consultations, P/46/15, BL.

128. India Judicial Department, E/4/845, BL.

129. *Bucks Herald*, 23 May 1857.

130. 'Some court records relating to the Santal Rebellion, December 1855', Roy, *Santal Rebellion Documents*, pp. 54–67.

131. Chotrae Desmanjhi in Culshaw & Archer, 'The Santal Rebellion', *Man in India*, December 1945, p. 236.

132. *Ibid.*, p. 222.

7. AFTERMATH AND INTERPRETATION

1. *Copy of a Minute by the Marquis of Dalhousie … Reviewing his Administration in India*, p. 4. Nor did Edwin Arnold's sycophantic *The Marquis of Dalhousie's Administration of British India*, published in 1865, even mention the Hul.

2. Ghosh, 'Dalhousie and the Santal Insurrection of 1855', *Bengal Past and Present*, 1971, pp. 91–96.

3. *Illustrated London News*, 23 February, 9 August, 18 October 1856. On 6 October 1855 the pictorial newspaper had published a view of the Rajmahal Hills seen from the Ganges, presumably from a block on hand, but without any commentary.

4. Accounts of Revenues and Disbursements of the East India Company, 1856–57, PP 1857–58, Vol. XLII, p. 45 (and a further £3,528 in the following year).

5. Despatches to India & Bengal, Jan-Feb 1856, E/834, BL.

6. Dalhousie to Couper, 26 January 1856, Baird, *Private Letters*, p. 368.

7. Dalhousie's later biographer acknowledged that he often complained of the 'peremptory tone which his "friends" too frequently assumed': Lee-Warner, *The Life of the Marquis of Dalhousie*, Vol. I, p. 105.

8. Judicial Department minute 'Sonthal Insurrection', 1 October 1856, E/4/839, BL.

9. Kaye, *The Administration of the East India Company*, pp. 1–2.

10. *Citizen*, 7 January 1856.

11. *Citizen*, 18 April 1856.

12. Lloyd to Atkinson, 27 December 1855, Military Consultations, P/46/26, BL. George Atkinson, who had arguably done more for the campaign's success than any single person, went un-thanked, but at least he gained his permanent captaincy, on 19 November.

13. Raghavaiah, *Tribal Revolts*, p. 149.

14. *Allen's Indian Mail*, 31 July 1856.

15. *Citizen*, 5 February 1856.

16. *Allen's Indian Mail*, 16 August 1856.

17. Hawes to Parrott, 18 December 1855, Military Consultations, P/46/26, BL.

18. Sinclair to Bird, 27 December 1855, Military Consultations, P/46/26, BL.

19. Roy Chaudhury, *Old Hazaribagh Records*, p. 81.

20. O'Malley, *Bengal District Gazetteers: Santal Parganas*, p. 272. Similar towers were evidently built at other stations on the railway line, but they have disappeared.

21. Bird to Atkinson, 23 January 1856, Military Consultations, P/46/29, BL.

22. Parrett & Chhina, *The Indian Order of Merit*, p. 184.

23. *Citizen*, 2 February 1856.

24. Judicial Department minute 'Sonthal Insurrection', 1 October 1856, E/4/839, BL.

25. Report, Gordon, 18 January 1856, Military Consultations, P/46/29, BL.

26. India Judicial Department, Minute, 'Matters connected with the Sonthal Insurrection, E/4/841, BL.

27. Judicial Department minute 'Sonthal Insurrection', 1 October 1856, E/4/839, BL.

28. *Ibid*.

29. Minute, Halliday, 19 October 1855, Judicial Proceedings, P/145/22, BL.

30. *Friend of India*, 27 December 1855.

31. Carstairs, *The Little World of an Indian District Officer*, p. 223.

32. 'Sonthal Police Rules', papers of Sir George Yule, Mss.Eur F 357/25, BL.

33. Carstairs, *The Little World of an Indian District Officer*, p. 229.

34. Extraordinarily, Saroj Bhowmik's study of Bengal's rural police, *Rural Police Local Justice*, manages to offer a history of the force's reorganisation but without mentioning the Hul at all.

35. Report, Gordon, 18 January 1856, Military Consultations, P/46/29, BL.

36. Minute, Grant, 11 October 1855, Military Consultations, P/46/10, BL.

37. 'Bengal Extra Regulation Provinces', 1857, E/4/846, BL.

38. Elliott to Grey, 19 October 1855, Judicial Proceedings, P/145/23/, BL.

39. Judicial Department minute 'Sonthal Insurrection', 1 October 1856, E/4/839, BL.

40. India Judicial Department, Minute, 'Matters connected with the Sonthal Insurrection, E/4/841, BL.

41. Military Police posts were located at: Soory (300 men), Rampore Haut (100), Pakour (50), Rajmahal (60), Peerpointee (100), Bowsee (100), Godda (50), Deogurh (60), Dumka (60) and Raneegunge (200)—all centres of insurrection; Sen, *The Santals of Jungle Mahals*, p 155.

42. India Judicial Department Bengal Extra Regulation Provinces, 10 March 1858, E/4/850, BL.

43. Minute, Halliday, 19 October 1855, Judicial Proceedings, P/145/22, BL.

44. *Morning Chronicle* (Calcutta), 24 August 1855.

45. Bengal Annual Military Statement, 1855–56, L/MIL/8/63, BL.

46. India Revenue Department, Bengal Miscellaneous, 16 September 1857, E/4/847, BL.

47. India Judicial Department Bengal Extra Regulation Provinces, 10 March 1858, E/4/850, BL.

48. *Bucks Herald*, 23 May 1857.

49. *Church Missionary Papers*, No. CLXV, Lady Day, 1857.

50. Ghurye, *The Scheduled Tribes*, pp. 41–42.

51. Chotrae Desmanjhi in Culshaw & Archer, 'The Santal Rebellion', *Man in India*, December 1945, p. 222.

52. Papers relating to Indigo Cultivation in Bengal, Parliamentary Papers, House of Commons, 1861, Vol. XLV; Rao & Rao, *The Blue Devil*, p. 76.

53. *Citizen*, 29 February 1856.

54. *Bengal Hurkaru*, 3 December 1855.

55. *Englishman*, 22 December 1855.

56. *Citizen*, 7 January 1856.

57. *Citizen*, 17 January 1856.

58. Kendal Coghill, letter 6 April 1857, Coghill papers, Box 1, Cambridge Centre for South Asian Studies.

59. *Friend of India*, 15 November 1855.

60. *Daily Telegraph* (London), 2 October 1857.

61. L.N. Rana, 'The 1857 Uprising and Civil Rebellion in Jharkhand', in Battacharya, *Rethinking 1857*, p. 81.

62. Yule to Grey, 5 August 1857, in Choudhury, *1857 in Bihar*, p. 39.

63. Roy Chaudhury, *Hazaribagh Old Records*, p. 13.

64. *Friend of India*, 27 December 1855.

65. Leckey, *Fictions connected with the Indian Outbreak of 1857 Exposed*, p. 24.

66. Parrett & Chhina, *Indian Order of Merit*, pp. 835–36.

67. A.R. Allen, 'Disarmed but not dishonoured—the 63rd Bengal Native Infantry in 1857', *Journal of the Society for Army Historical Research*, Vol. 46 (1968), pp. 57–60.

68. Comments by the former Assistant-Surgeon Alfred Eteson, who annotated his copy of John Halls's *Arrah in 1857*; f. 68a, Mss Eur A10, BL.

69. Gimlette's *A Postscript to the Records of the Indian Mutiny* gives potted histories of the Bengal Native Infantry regiments' role in the mutiny.

70. Comments by the former Assistant-Surgeon Alfred Eteson, who annotated his copy of John Halls's *Arrah in 1857*; ff. 78a-79a, Mss Eur A10, BL.

71. Lithograph, 'Defence of Arrah House', 1858, P1021, BL.

72. Notes on a reminiscence by Lt-Col L.J. Mathias (father of Lt Henry Mathias), 1908, Papers of Lt-Col G.E. Fooks, 1999–03–143, NAM.

73. Service Army List Bengal 1855, 46 Lloyd, L/MIL/10/60, BL.

74. *The Times*, 5 June 1858.

75. Malleson, *The Indian Mutiny of 1857*, p. 221.

76. Blackett, letter, 4 November 1857, University of Durham Special Collections.

77. Culshaw, *Tribal Heritage*, p. 6.

78. Archer, 'Santal Rebellion Songs', *Man in India*, 1945.

79. Culshaw & Archer, 'The Santal Rebellion', *Man in India*, December 1945, p. 223.

80. Durga Tudu in Anderson and others, *From Fire Rain to Rebellion*, p. 187.

81. Gupta, *The Economic Life of a Bengal District*, p. 304.

82. Chakraborti, *History of the Santal Hool*, p. 5.

83. Anon., 'The Sonthal Rebellion', *Calcutta Review*, 1 Mar 1856, pp. 223–64.

84. Man, *Sonthalia and the Sonthals*, p. 2. Man also admired Ashley Eden, dedicating his book to him.

85. Chakraborti, *History of the Santal Hool of 1855*.

86. Chaudhury, *Folk Tales of the Santals*, p. 10.

87. Chandra, *History of Modern India*, p. 142.

88. Mukherjee, *The Rise and Fall of the East India Company*, p. 284n.

89. Jha, *The Kol Insurrection*, p. 4.

90. Bose, *Peasant Labour and Colonial Capital*, pp. 151–52.

91. The Bibliography includes more than a dozen citations of such articles.

92. Dasgupta, 'Some aspects of the Santal Rebellion of 1855–56', *Social Scientist*, 2013 and Sengupta & Lochan, 'Santhal Rebellion—A Counter Insurgency against 'Outsiders' as Ordained by a 'Thakur', *International Journal of Social Science and Humanities Research*, 2015.

93. Anon., 'The Sonthal Rebellion', *Calcutta Review*, 1856, pp. 223–64 and Anon., 'The Sonthal Pergunnas', *Calcutta Review*, 1860, pp. 510–31.

94. Kali Kinkar Datta, *The Santal Insurrection of 1855–57*. Datta simply reproduced

much of his 1940 text in his *Anti-British Plots and Movements Before 1857*, published in 1970.

95. *Banglapedia*, http://en.banglapedia.org/index.php?title=Datta,_Kalikinkar; consulted 11 December 2018.

96. Guha, 'The Prose of Counter-Insurgency', p. 84.

97. Daniel Rycroft, *Representing Rebellion: Visual Aspects of Counter-insurgency in Colonial India*.

98. Rycroft & Tudu, *Hul Sangal: the Spirit of the Santal Revolution*, 2005.

99. Atis Dasgupta, 'Some aspects of the Santal Rebellion of 1855–56', *Social Scientist*, Vol. 41, Nos 9–10, Sep-Oct 2013, pp. 69–74 and Saptarshi Sengupta & Pramila Lochan, 'Santhal Rebellion—A Counter Insurgency against 'Outsiders' as Ordained by a 'Thakur', *International Journal of Social Science and Humanities Research*, Vol. 3, Issue 4, Oct-Dec 2015, pp. 102–08.

100. Mount, *The Tears of the Rajas*, pp. 491–93.

101. Avijit, 'Visual Culture of the Santals and their Image', p. 48.

102. 'Revisiting Hul—The Santal Rebellion, 1855', available at https://www.youtube.com/watch?v=xdcV0yoEg8M.

103. *The Times*, 18 September 1855.

104. Though Kaviraj claimed that Karl Marx wrote that the Santals could have prolonged their resistance by resorting to 'guerrilla warfare', in fact in Marx's *Notes on Indian History* he only describes that the Santals ('a half-savage tribe') were 'put down after seven months guerrilla warfare'.

105. *Friend of India*, 4 October 1855.

106. Black, *Insurgency and Counterinsurgency: A Global History*, p. x.

EPILOGUE

1. Mount, *The Tears of the Rajas*, p. 603.

2. *Hindoo Patriot*, 5 May 1859; quoted in Kling, *The Blue Mutiny*, p. 64.

3. A March 1856 note in Dalhousie's papers (a briefing note for Canning) reads 'A very promising young Officer—distinguished in the Sonthal business and entitled to much consideration'—beside the names of other officials involved in 'the Sonthal business' are blanks: GD45/6/499, National Records of Scotland.

4. Anon, *Sketch of the Official Career of the Hon'ble Ashley Eden*, p. 5.

5. In Braddon's 1872 *Life in India*, he described the Hul on only three pages, but devoted ten to it in his 1895 *Thirty Years of Shikar*. Coincidentally, for nearly forty years I have lived next to the suburb in Canberra named after Braddon, unknowingly until now.

6. Lee-Warner, *Memoirs of Field Marshal Sir Henry Wylie Norman*, pp. 44–45.

7. Bradley-Birt, *The Story of an Indian Upland*, p. 210.

8. *The Times*, 21 December 1909.

9. The images in Atkinson's *The Campaign in India* are a staple of books on the conflict. His *Indian Spices* is little known, but reveals him as a man of sharp observation and gentle humour, perhaps satirizing *The Times*'s William Howard Russell and certainly his ilk.

BIBLIOGRAPHY

Archival Sources

Ames Library, University of Minnesota, Minneapolis

    James Wyld, India Shewing the Post Roads and Dawk Stations.
    John Walker, Military Map of India, c. 1850.
    Map of the Routes in India.

British Library (London)

    India Office Records

        East India Company, General Correspondence.
            E/1/303–04, Miscellaneous, Jul 1855—Jun 1856.
        Letters from the Company to the Board.
            E/2/2223 Aug–Nov 1855.
        Letters received from India-Bengal.
            E/4/248–54 May–Dec 1855.
        India & Bengal Despatches.
            E/4/811–850, 1851–57.
        India Military Consultations.
            P/46/1–17 Jul-Dec 1855.
        Bengal Military Board.
            P/49/36 Ordnance Reports.
        Bengal Judicial Proceedings.
            P/145/14–27 July–December 1855.
        Bengal Army records.
            L/MIL/3/69 India Military Letters Received 1855.
            L/MIL/3/570–91 Enclosures to Military Letters and Despatches from Bengal.
            L/MIL/8/62 Bengal Annual Military Statement, 1855.
            L/MIL/9/177 Cadet Papers.

BIBLIOGRAPHY

L/MIL/10/1 Index to Bengal military officers.
L/MIL/10/60–67 Officers' Records of Service.
L/MIL/10/122–24 Registers of European Soldiers.
L/MIL/10/176 Long Roll, Town Major's List, 1855.
L/MIL/17/2/304 Bengal, *General Orders*, 1855.
L/MIL/17/2/305 Bengal, *General Orders*, 1856.

Maps

3 b.43 No. 23 Rajmuhal Hills or Damin-i-koh, 1848–50.
X/352/4 Military map of India.
X/352/3 Revenue map of India.
X/789, Map of railway Howrah to Ranegunge, 1853.
X/1022/1, The New Bengal Atlas, 1841.
X/1023, Postal map of Bengal and Bihar, 1862.
X/1041/1 Map of the District of Bhaugulpoor, 1841.
X/1044, District of Bhagalpur, 1875.
I.5.49 The Bardwan Division, 1874.
I.5.59 District of Beerbhum, 1854.
Charles Joseph, *New and Improved Map of the Grand Trunk Road*, Calcutta, 1855.

European manuscripts

Mss.Eur F236/375, James Macphail, 'The Story of the Santals'.
Mss.Eur F357/25, Sir George Yule.
Mss.Eur A10, Assistant-Surgeon Alfred Eteson.

Centre for South Asian Studies, Cambridge

Kendal Coghill papers.

National Army Museum, London

1999–03–143, Papers of Lt-Col G.E. Fooks.
9007–76, Narrative by Sergeant-Major Lissant, 37th Native Infantry, 1842.
Hodson index cards to officers of the Indian Army.

National Library of Australia, Canberra

J.R. Burlton Bennett, *Post Office map of the Provinces of Bengal, Behar, Orissa and Arracan*, 1853.

National Records of Scotland, Edinburgh

GD/45/5–6 Dalhousie Papers.

Royal Scottish Geographical Society, Perth

Atlas of India, c. 1859/1895, sheets 112 & 113.

University of Durham Special Collection

Add.MSS 835/14 Letter, John Stephen Blackett.

BIBLIOGRAPHY

West Bengal State Archives, Kolkata

 Bengal, Judicial Proceedings, 19–25 July 1855.

West Sussex Record Office, Chichester

 RSR.2.2 3rd Bengal European Regiment.

Published Contemporary Sources

Charles Acland, *A Popular Account of the Manners and Customs of India*, John Murray, London, 1847.

T.C. Anderson, *'Ubique': War Services of all the Officers of H.M.'s Bengal Army*, privately published, Calcutta, 1863.

'An Ex-MP', *The War Unmasked: Its Causes, Its Facts, Its Consequences*, Richardson Brothers, London, 1855.

Anon., *Standing Orders for the Bengal Native Infantry*, Adjutant-General's Office, Calcutta, 1840.

————, *Railways in India: Their Present State and Prospects*, W.H. Allen, London, 1855.

————, 'The Sonthal Rebellion', *Calcutta Review*, 1 Mar 1856, pp. 223–64.

————, *The Experiences of a Landholder and Indigo Planter in Eastern Bengal*, John Smith, Aberdeen, 1859.

————, 'The Sonthal Pergunnas', *Calcutta Review*, 1 Dec 1860, pp. 510–31.

————, *Minutes of Evidence taken before the Indigo Commission in Calcutta*, [Calcutta?], [1860].

————, *Brahmins and Pariahs: An Appeal by the Indigo Manufacturers of Bengal … for Protection against the Lieut.-Governor of Bengal*, James Ridgway, London, 1861.

————, *Illustrated Hand-Book of the Eastern Bengal Railway*, [Calcutta?], 1862.

————, *History of the 2nd Regiment Native Light Infantry*, privately published, Julpigoree [?], 1872.

————, *The Nawab Nizam's Memorial of 1860, with a History of the Relations of the British Government with the Nizamut and its Funds*, Home Secretariat Press, Calcutta, 1872.

————, *Sketch of the Official Career of the Hon. Ashley Eden, CSI*, Prosong Dev, Calcutta, 1877.

————, *The Santal Mission, North India*, Church Missionary society, London, 1894.

Edwin Arnold, *The Marquis of Dalhousie's Administration of British India*, 2 vols, Saunders, Otley, & Co., London, 1865.

George Francklin Atkinson, *Curry and Rice (on Forty Plates) or "Our" Station in India*, Day & Son, London, 1859.

————, *The Campaign in India*, Day & Son, London, 1859.

————, *Indian Spices for English Tables, or a Rare Relish of Fun from the Far East*, Day & Son, London, 1859.

————, (ed. Simon Riches), *The Campaign in India*, Royal Armouries, Leeds, 2009.

J.G.A. Baird, (ed.), *Private Letters of the Marquess of Dalhousie*, William Blackwood, Edinburgh, 1910.

Edward Braddon, *Life in India*, Longmans, Green, & Co., London, 1872.

————, *Thirty Years of Shikar*, William Blackwood, London, 1895.

George Campbell, *Modern India: A Sketch of the System of Civil Government*, John Murray, London, 1853.

John Capper, *The Three Presidencies of India*, Ingram Cooke, London, 1853.

Richard Clarke, *The Regulations of the Government of Fort William in Bengal, in Force at the End of 1853*, East India Company, London, 1854.

Charles Northcote Cooke, *The Rise, Progress, and Present Condition of Banking in India*, P.M. Craneburgh, Calcutta, 1863.

[Marquis of Dalhousie], *Copy of a Minute by the Marquis of Dalhousie ... Reviewing his Administration in India*, East India Company, London, 1856.

'Delta', *Indigo and Its Enemies*, James Ridgway, London, 1861.

John Dickinson, *Reply to the Indigo Planters' Pamphlet*, P.S. King, London, 1861.

Vincent Eyre, *The Military Operations at Cabul*, John Murray, London, 1843.

Government of India, *A Penal Code prepared by the Indian Law Commissioners*, Pelham, Richardson, London, 1838.

Colesworthy Grant, *Rural Life in Bengal*, W. Thacker & Co., London, 1860.

————, *An Anglo-Indian Domestic Sketch*, Thacker, Spink, Calcutta, 1862.

Charles Frederick Holder, *The Ivory King: A Popular History of the Elephant and its Allies*, Charles Scribner's Sons, New York, 1886.

W.W.W. Humbley, *Journal of a Cavalry Officer*, Longman, Brown, Green and Longmans, London, 1854.

Robert Hunter, *The History of India, from the Earliest Ages*, T. Nelson & Sons, London, 1864.

John William Kaye, *Peregrine Pultuney, or Life in India*, John Mortimer, London, 1844.

————, *The Administration of the East India Company*, Richard Bentley, London, 1853.

————, *A History of the Sepoy War in India, 1857–1858*, 3 Vols, W.H. Allen, London, 1874–76.

James Kennedy, *The Great Indian Mutiny of 1857: Its Causes, Features and Results*, Ward & Co., London, 1858.

Edward Lecky, *Fictions connected with the Indian Outbreak of 1857 Exposed*, Chesson & Woodhall, Bombay, 1859.

Patrick Macdougall, *The Theory of War illustrated by Numerous Examples from Military History*, Longman, Brown, Green, Longmans & Roberts, London, 1858.

George Malleson, *The Decisive Battles of India*, W.H. Allen, London, 1883.

————, *The Indian Mutiny of 1857*, Seeley & Co., London, 1891.

————, (ed.), *Kaye and Malleson's History of the Indian Mutiny of 1857–58*, 6 vols, Longmans, Green & Co., London, 1898-99.

Edward Man, *Sonthalia and the Sonthals*, Geo Wyman, Calcutta, 1867.

Frederick Middleton, 'A Reminiscence of the Santhal Rebellion', *The United Service Magazine*, Vol. VII (NS), Apr-Sep 1893, pp. 1063–75.

Frederick Mouat, *Report on Jails Visited and Inspected in Bengal, Behar, and Arracan*, Military Orphan Press, Calcutta, 1856.

'H.R.', *A Very Few Words Respecting the Constitution of the Covenanted and Uncovenanted Services of India*, Smith, Elder & Co., London, 1860.

BIBLIOGRAPHY

Michael Rafter, *Our Indian Army: a Military History of the British Empire in the East*, David Bryce, London, 1855.

Sita Ram, (ed. James Lunt), *From Sepoy to Subedar*, Routledge & Kegan Paul, London, 1970.

Walter Sherwill, 'Notes upon a tour through the Rajmahal Hills', *Journal of the Asiatic Society of Bengal*, 1851, pp. 544–606.

————, *Geographical and Statistical Report of the District of Bhaugulpoor*, Calcutta Gazette, Calcutta, 1854.

————, *Geographical and Statistical Report of the District of Beerbhoom*, Calcutta Gazette, Calcutta, 1855.

Frederick Shore, *Notes on Indian Affairs*, 2 vols, John W. Parker, London, 1837.

S.C. Starkey, *The Standing Orders for the Bengal Native Infantry*, Adjutant-General's Department, Calcutta, 1846.

J.H. Stocqueler, *The British Officer: His Position, Duties, Emoluments, and Privileges*, Smith, Elder and Co., London, 1851.

————, *The Military Encyclopaedia*, William Allen & Co., London, 1853.

————, *The Hand-Book of British India*, William Allen & Co., London, 1854.

————, *Memoirs of a Journalist*, Times of India, Bombay, 1873.

J.M. Strachan, *A Letter to Captain Eastwick*, Seeley, Jackson, and Halliday, London, 1858.

Francis Stubbs, *History of the Organization, Equipment, and War Services of the Bengal Artillery*, W.H. Allen, London, 1895.

W. Theobald, *Indian Tracts No. 1, Parliamentary Papers*, W. Benning and Co., London, 1857.

George Otto Trevelyan, *Cawnpore*, Macmillan & Co., London, 1865.

'Two Sisters' [Madeline & Rosalind Dunlop], *The Timely Retreat; or a Year in Bengal*, Richard Bentley, London, 1858.

John Wolley, *A Lecture on 'The War'*, PP, 1856.

Parliamentary papers

1852, Vol. X, Report of the Select Committee on Indian Territories.

1852–53, Vol. LXIX Statistical Papers (India).

1857–58, Vol. XLIV, Papers relative to Mutinies in the East Indies.

1857–58, Vol. XIV, Report from the Select Committee on East India (Railways).

1857–58, Vol. XLII, Accounts of Revenues and Disbursements of the East India Company.

1861, Vol. XLV, Papers relating to Indigo Cultivation in Bengal.

1863, Vol. XL Return of Regiments in Native Bengal Army that Remained Faithful …

Contemporary serials

India

Bengal Directory and Annual Register
Bengal Hurkaru (Calcutta)
Bombay Times & Journal of Commerce

Calcutta Literary Gazette
Calcutta Review
Citizen (Calcutta)
Delhi Gazette
Englishman and Military Chronicle (Calcutta)
Friend of India (Serampore)
Hindoo Patriot (Calcutta)
Morning Chronicle (Calcutta)
Thacker's Bengal Directory

Britain

Allen's Indian Mail (London)
The Army List
Baptist Magazine (London)
Bath Chronicle and Weekly Gazette
Bucks Herald (Aylesbury)
Cheshire Observer (Chester)
Church Missionary Papers (London)
Cork Examiner
Daily Telegraph (London)
East India Register
Elgin Courier and Morayshire Advertiser
Exeter and Plymouth Gazette
Freeman's Journal (Dublin)
Glasgow Herald
Hart's Army List
Hereford Times
Household Words (London)
Indian News and Chronicle of Eastern Affairs
Illustrated London News
Inverness Courier
John Bull
Lady's Newspaper
Leeds Intelligencer
Leeds Times
Missionary Herald (London)
Morning Chronicle (London)
Morning Post (London)
Norfolk Chronicle (Norwich)
Nottinghamshire Guardian
Observer (London)
Preston Chronicle
Punch (London)

BIBLIOGRAPHY

Reading Mercury
Sheffield Daily Telegraph
Shields Daily Gazette
Standard (London)
The Times (London)
Trewman's Exeter Flying Post

Secondary Sources

Seema Alavi, *The Sepoys and the Company: Tradition and Transition in Northern India 1770–1830*, Oxford University Press, Delhi, 1995.

A.R. Allen, 'Disarmed but not dishonoured—the 63rd Bengal Native Infantry in 1857', *Journal of the Society for Army Historical Research*, Vol. 46 (1968), pp. 57–60.

Clare Anderson '"The wisdom of the barbarian": Rebellion, incarceration, and the Santal body politic', *South Asia: Journal of South Asian Studies*, 31:2, 2008, pp. 223–240.

Peter Anderson and others, (eds), *From Fire Rain to Rebellion: Reasserting Ethnic Identity through Narrative*, Manohar, New Delhi, 2011.

Anon., *A Short History of the Loyal House of Murshidabad*, Thacker, Spink, Calcutta, 1910.

W.G. Archer, 'Santal Rebellion Songs', *Man in India*, Vol. XXV, No. 4, Dec 1945.

———, 'Santal Transplantation Songs', *Man in India*, Vol. XXVI, 1946 pp 6–7.

———, *The Hill of Flutes: Life, Love and Poetry in Tribal India. A Portrait of the Santals*, George Allen & Unwin, London, 1974.

———, *Tribal Law and Justice: A Report on the Santal*, Concept Publishing Company, New Delhi, 1984.

Sanjay Bahadur, *Hul—Cry Rebel!*, Roli Books, New Delhi, 2013.

Prathama Banerjee, 'Historic Acts: Santal Rebellion and the Temporality of Practice', *Studies in History*, Vol. 15, No. 2 (New Series), 1999, pp. 209–46.

Amiya Barat, *The Bengal Native Infantry: its Organisation and Discipline 1796–1852*, Firma K.L. Mukhopadhyay, Calcutta, 1962.

Margarita Barns, *The Indian Press: A History of the Growth of Public Opinion in India*, George Allen & Unwin, London, 1940.

Scott Bennett, 'Sir Edward Nicholas Coventry Braddon (1829–1904)', *Australian Dictionary of Biography*, Vol. 2, Melbourne University Press, Melbourne, 1979.

Henry Bernstein, *Steamboats on the Ganges: an Exploration in the History of India's Modernization through Science and Technology*, Orient Longmans, Bombay, 1960.

Sabyasachi Bhattacharya, (ed.), *Rethinking 1857*, Orient Longman, Hyderabad, 2007.

Saroj Kumar Bhowmik, *Rural Police Local Justice in Bengal (1772–1870)*, Nalanda Publications, Calcutta, 1991.

P.C. Biswas, *Santals of the Santal Parganas*, Bharatiya Adimjati Sweak Sangh, Delhi, 1956.

Jeremy Black, *Insurgency and Counterinsurgency: a Global History*, Rowman & Littlefield, Lanham, 2016.

Paul Olaf Bodding, *Santal Folk Tales*, 3 vols, Instituttet for Sammenlegende Kultur-forskning, Oslo, 1924–29.

BIBLIOGRAPHY

————, *A Chapter of Santal Folklore*, Kristiana Etnografiske Museums, Kristiana, 1924.

————, *Santal Riddles … Witchcraft among the Santals*, Oslo Etnografiske Museums, Oslo, 1940.

Cecil Henry Bompas, *Folklore of the Santal Parganas*, Gyan Publishing House, New Delhi, 2001.

Sugata Bose, *Peasant Labour and Colonial Capital: Rural Bengal since 1770*, The New Cambridge History of India, III, 2, Cambridge University Press, Cambridge, 1993.

F.B. Bradley-Birt, *The Story of an Indian Upland*, Smith, Elder, & Co., London, 1905.

Charles Buckland, *Bengal Under the Lieutenant-Governors*, S.K. Lahiri, Calcutta, 1901.

Charles Callwell, *Small Wars: Their Principles and Practice*, HMSO, London, 1906.

Robert Carstairs, *The Little World of an Indian District Officer*, Macmillan & Co., London, 1912.

————, *Harma's Village*, Santal Mission Press, Manbhum, 1935.

Digambar Chakraborti (ed. Arun Chowhury), *History of the Santal Hool of 1855*, Rajnagar Lamps, Aligarh, 1989.

Bipan Chandra, *History of Modern India*, Orient Black Swan, Hyderabad, 2009.

Pradip Chattopadhyay, *The Changing Identity of the Santhals of West Bengal*, Primus Books, New Delhi, 2014.

Sashi Bhusan Chaudhuri, *Civil Rebellion in the Indian Mutinies*, The World Press, Calcutta, 1957.

Indu Roy Chaudhury, *Folk Tales of the Santals*, Sterling Publishers, New Delhi, 1973.

Pranab Chandra Roy Choudhury, *Hazaribagh Old Records*, Revenue Department, Patna, 1957.

——, *1857 in Bihar (Chotanagpur and Santhal Parganas)*, Revenue Department, Patna, 1959.

Church Missionary Society, *The Santal Mission*, *North India*, Church Missionary Society, London, 1894.

John Connor, *The Australian Frontier Wars 1788–1838*, UNSW Press, Sydney, 2002.

W.J. Culshaw & W.G. Archer, 'The Santal Rebellion', *Man in India*, Vol. XXV, No. 4, December 1945, pp. 218–39.

W.J. Culshaw, 'Early records concerning the Santals', *Man in India*, Vol. XXV, No. 3, September 1945, pp. 191–93.

————, *Tribal Heritage: A Study of the Santals*, Lutterworth Press, London, 1949.

Atis Dasgupta, 'Some aspects of the Santal Rebellion of 1855–56', *Social Scientist*, Vol. 41, Nos 9–10, Sep-Oct 2013, pp. 69–74.

Kali Kinkar Datta, 'Original Records about the Santhal Insurrection of 1855', *Bengal Past & Present*, Vol. XLVIII, No. 95, Jul-Sep 1934, pp. 32–37.

————, 'The Santhal Insurrection of 1855–56', *Bengal Past & Present*, Vol. L, Part 1, Jul-Sep 1935, pp. 30–43.

————, *The Santal Insurrection of 1855–57*, University of Calcutta, Calcutta, 1940.

————, *Anti-British Plots and Movements Before 1857*, Meenakshi Prakashan, Meerut, 1970.

BIBLIOGRAPHY

Nabendu Datta-Majumder, *The Santal: a Study in Culture-Change*, Government of India Press, New Delhi, 1956.

Saul David, *The Indian Mutiny 1857*, Penguin, 2002.

————, *Victoria's Wars: the Rise of Empire*, Penguin, 2007.

Frederick Davies and others, *Memorials of Old Haileybury College*, Archibald Constable & Co., London, 1894.

Vasuda Dhagamwar, *Role and Image of Law in India: the Tribal Experience*, Sage Publications, New Delhi, 2006.

R.R. Diwarkar, *Bihar Through the Ages*, Orient Longmans, Bombay, 1959.

John French, *Armies of the Nineteenth Century: the British in India 1825–59*, Foundry Books, Nottingham, 2006.

Ngaire Gardner, *Illustrated Pursuits: W.S. Sherwill in India 1834–1861*, Adivaani, Kolkata, 2016.

Suresh Chandra Ghosh, 'Dalhousie and the Santal Rebellion', *Bengal Past and Present*, Vol. XC, No. 169, Jan-Jun 1971, pp. 85–98.

G.H.D. Gimlette, *A Postscript to the Records of the Indian Mutiny: An Attempt to Trace the Subsequent Careers and Fate of the Rebel Bengal Regiments*, H.F. & G. Weatherby, London, 1927.

Richard Gott, *Britain's Empire: Resistance, Repression and Revolt*, Verso, London, 2011.

Ranajit Guha, *Elementary Aspects of Peasant Insurgency in Colonial India*, Oxford University Press, Delhi, 1983.

————, 'The Prose of Counter-Insurgency', in Ranajit Guha & Gayatri Chakravorty Spivak, *Selected Subaltern Studies*, Oxford University Press, New York, 1988, pp. 45–84.

G.S. Gurye, *The Scheduled Tribes*, G.R. Bhatkal, Bombay, 1963.

Ranjan Kumar Gupta, *The Economic Life of a Bengal District: Birbhum 1770–1857*, University of Burdwan, Burdwan, 1984.

Eric Hobsbawm, *Social Bandits and Primitive Rebels: Studies in Archaic Forms of Social Movement in the 19th and 20th Centuries*, The Free Press, Glencoe, 1959.

————, *Bandits*, Weidenfeld & Nicolson, London, 1969.

———— and George Rude, *Captain Swing*, Penguin, Harmondsworth, 1973.

V.C.P. Hodson, *List of the Officers of the Bengal Army 1758–1834*, Constable & Company, London, 1927.

John Houlton, *Bihar: the Heart of India*, Orient Longmans, Bombay, 1949.

W.W. Hunter, *The Annals of Rural Bengal*, Smith, Elder and Co., London, 1868.

————, *The Imperial Gazetteer of India*, Clarendon Press, Oxford, 1908.

Jagdish Chandra Jha, *The Kol Insurrection of Chota-Nagpur*, Thacker, Spink & Co., Calcutta, 1964.

————, 'A Sad Episode of the Kol Insurrection (1832)', *Proceedings of the Indian History Congress*, Vol. 42, 1981, pp. 413–18.

Narahari Kaviraj, *A Peasant Uprising in Bengal 1783: the First Formidable Peasant Uprising Against the Rule of East Indian Company*, People's Publishing House, New Delhi, 1972.

BIBLIOGRAPHY

———, *Santal Village Community and the Santal Rebellion of 1855*, Subarnarekha, Calcutta, 2001.

Blair Kling, *The Blue Mutiny: The Indigo Disturbances in Bengal 1859–1862*, University of Pennsylvania Press, Philadelphia, 1966.

John Kochuchira, *Political History of Santal Parganas from 1765 to 1872*, Inter-India Publications, New Delhi, 2000.

William Lee-Warner, *The Life of the Marquis of Dalhousie*, 2 vols, Macmillan & Co., New York, 1904.

———, *Memoirs of Field Marshal Sir Henry Wylie Norman*, Smith, Elder, & Co., London, 1908.

Ursula Low, (ed.), *Fifty Years with John Company: From the Letters of General Sir John Low of Clatto, Fife*, John Murray, London, 1936.

Michael Maclagan, *'Clemency' Canning: Charles John, 1st Earl Canning, Governor-General and Viceroy of India 1856–1862*, Macmillan & Co., London, 1962.

James Macphail, *The Story of the Santal, with an Account of the Santal Rebellion*, Thacker, Spink, Calcutta, 1922.

Sitakant Mahapatra, *Bakhen: Ritual Incantation Songs of a Primitive Community*, Prachi Prakashan, New Delhi, 1979.

Purna Majumdar, *The Musnud of Murshidabad 1704–1904*, Saroda Ray, Murshidabad, 1905.

Ata Mallick, 'Santal Women and the Rebellion of 1855 in Colonial India', *Indian Journal of Women and Social Change*, 2(1), pp. 11–25.

Daniel Marston & Chandar Sundaram, (eds), *A Military History of India and South Asia: From the East India Company to the Nuclear Era*, Praeger Security International, Westport, 2007.

Karl Marx, *Notes on Indian History*, Foreign Languages Publishing House, Moscow, nd.

Nita Mathur, *Santal Worldview*, Concept Publishing Company, New Delhi, 2001.

H.G. St M. McRae, *Regimental History of the 45th Rattray's Sikhs*, Vol. I 1856–1914, Robert Maclehose, Glasgow, 1933.

Ferdinand Mount, *The Tears of the Rajas: Mutiny, Money and Marriage in India 1805–1905*, Simon & Schuster, London, 2015.

Ramakrishna Mukherjee, *The Rise and Fall of the East India Company: A Sociological Appraisal*, Monthly Review Press, New York, 1974.

L.S.S. O'Malley, *Bengal District Gazetteers: Birbhum*, Bengal Secretariat Book Depot, Calcutta, 1910.

———, *Bengal District Gazetteers: Santal Parganas*, Bengal Secretariat Book Depot, Calcutta, 1910.

———, *The Indian Civil Service 1601–1930*, John Murray, London, 1931.

Cliff Parrett & Rana Chhina, *Indian Order of Merit: Historical Records*, Vol. I, 1837–1860, Tom Donovan Editions, Brighton, 2010.

Douglas Peers, *Between Mars and Mammon: Colonial Armies and the Garrison State in India 1819–1835*, I.B. Tauris, London, 1995.

R.H. Phillimore, *Historical Records of the Survey of India*, Vol. III, Surveyor General of India, Dehra Dun, 1954.

BIBLIOGRAPHY

V. Raghaviah, *Nomads*, Bharateeya Adimatjati Sevak Sangh, New Delhi, 1968.

————, *Tribal Revolts*, Andhra Rashtra Adimajati Sevak Sangh, Nellore, 1971.

Amiya Rao & B.G. Rao, *The Blue Devil: Indigo and Colonial Bengal*, Oxford University Press, Calcutta, 1992.

Tarapada Ray, (ed.), *Santal Rebellion Documents*, Subarnarekha, Calcutta, 1983.

Elizabeth Rottger-Hogan, 'Insurrection ... or ostracism: A Study of the Santal Rebellion of 1855', *Contributions to Indian Sociology*, Vol. 16, No. 1 (1982), pp. 79–96.

Kaushik Roy, *Frontiers, Insurgencies and Counter-Insurgencies in South Asia*, Routledge, New Delhi, 2015.

Daniel Rycroft, *Representing Rebellion: Visual Aspects of Counter-insurgency in Colonial India*, Oxford University Press, Oxford, 2006.

Asoka Kumar Sen, *The Popular Uprising and the Intelligentsia: Bengal Between 1855–1873*, Firma KLM, Calcutta, 1992.

Suchibrata Sen, *The Santals of Jungle Mahals (An Agrarian History) 1793–1861*, Ratna Prakashan, Calcutta, 1984.

Saptarshi Sengupta & Pramila Lochan, 'Santhal Rebellion—A Counter Insurgency against 'Outsiders' as Ordained by a 'Thakur', *International Journal of Social Science and Humanities Research*, Vol. 3, Issue 4, Oct-Dec 2015, pp. 102–08.

Alpa Shah, *Nightmarch: Among India's Revolutionary Guerrillas*, Hurst Publishing, London, 2018.

P.K. Shukla, 'Tenants' protests to British rule (1861) in Santal Parganas', *Proceedings of the Indian History Congress, 1989–90*, pp. 613–19.

George Somers, *The Dynamics of Santal Traditions in a Peasant Society*, Abinhar Publications, New Delhi, 1977.

Peter Stanley, *The Remote Garrison: the British Army in Australia 1788–1870*, Kangaroo Press, Dural, 1986.

————, *White Mutiny: British Military Culture in India, 1825–75*, Christopher Hurst, London, 1998.

Raman Sukumar, *The Asian Elephant: Ecology and Management*, Cambridge University Press, Cambridge, 1989.

J. Troisi, *The Santals: A Classified and Annotated Bibliography*, Manohar, Delhi, 1976.

L.I. Trotter, *Life of The Marquis of Dalhousie*, W.H. Allen, London, 1889.

C. Von Fürer-Haimendorf, *Tribal Populations and Cultures of the Indian Subcontinent*, E.J. Brill, Leiden, 1985.

Dierk Walter, *Colonial Violence: European Empires and the Use of Force*, Hurst & Company, London, 2017.

Andrew Waugh, *Historical Records of the Survey of India*, Vol. V, Surveyor General of India, Dehra Dun, 1968.

C.R. Wilson, *List of Inscriptions on Tombs or Monuments in Bengal possessing Historical or Archaeological Interest*, Superintendent of Government Printing, Calcutta, 1896.

Abha Xalxo, 'The Great Santal Insurrection (Hul) of 1855–56', *Proceedings of the Indian Historical Congress*, Vol. 69, (2008), pp. 732–955.

M. Yorke, 'History and Anthropology: A New Model with Examples from the Santal Parganas', *Indian Anthropologist*, Vol. 4, No. 2, December 1974, pp. 81–91.

BIBLIOGRAPHY

Theses

Anshul Avijit, 'Visual Culture of the Santals and their Image: Myth, Morals and Materiality', PhD, Cambridge University, 2018.

Niladri Chatterjee, 'The Uprising in the "Periphery": Bengal 1857–58', PhD, SOAS, 2015.

Film

Daniel Rycroft & Joy Raj Tudu, *Hul Sangal: the Spirit of the Santal Revolution*, University of Sussex, 2005.

Revisiting Hul—The Santal Rebellion.

Literally dozens of videos and films dealing with the Hul can be found on, say, YouTube.

INDEX

Numbers in **bold** indicate illustrations

INDEX

INDEX

INDEX

INDEX